THE LIES WE TELL
AND
THE CLUES WE MISS

Professional Papers

Bella DePaulo, Ph. D.

2009

CONTENTS

Lying in everyday life

Who lies?

Everyday lies in close and casual relationships

Truth and investment: Lies are told to those who care

Nonverbal behavior and self-presentation

Cues to deception

Preface

In the decades I've spent studying the lies that we tell and the clues that we miss, I've published many papers in the professional journals. There are some in particular, though, that scholars, journalists, and smart, savvy readers and thinkers come back to over and over again. The articles in this collection are the ones that seem to have generated the most interest. Some were originally published years ago, yet I still get inquiries about them every week – sometimes every day.

When I first started looking into the psychology of lying and detecting lies, I was stunned to find that the most basic questions about the place of lying in our lives had never been answered in a systematic way. How often do we lie? Who lies most often? To whom do we tell our lies? Eventually, my colleagues and I did some studies to address those kinds of questions. College students, as well as a much more diverse group of people from the community, kept track of all of their social interactions and all of the lies that they told during those interactions every day for a week. When we typed up all of their hand-written descriptions, we had a pack of more than 1,500 lies. Read all about them in the first three papers in this book.

The fourth paper is a report of a perverse study in which participants entered the lab room that we had transformed into an art gallery, picked out a painting that they hated, and wrote down what they despised about it. Only then did a new person enter the room – an artist. What would each participant say when the artist pointed to the disliked painting and said something like, "That's one of my own. I painted it. What do you think of it?"

Next in the collection is "Nonverbal behavior and self-presentation." It is a review paper and a thought piece. I spent months with articles spread across my living room floor, trying to figure out what our nonverbal behaviors say about what we think of ourselves and what we try to get other people to think of us. Can we control our own nonverbal behaviors to convey particular impressions of ourselves to others? Do we?

Finally, the past paper addresses the question I am asked most often by people who first learn that I study lying: What are the cues to deception? The article is the result of a huge undertaking. My colleagues and I scoured the journals for every instance we could find in which someone reported whether a particular behavior (such as avoiding eye contact) occurred more or less often when people were lying than when they were telling the truth. We found 1,338 cases and analyzed them all. Happy reading!

All six of the papers in this collection were published in academic journals. For fellow social scientists, they will all have a familiar feel to them. Others who have not had training in advanced statistical methods may be puzzled to find statements such as this real one: "This hierarchically nested data structure can be analyzed using a multilevel regression approach." Not to worry, though – such jargon appears mostly only in the Results sections. All of the other sections of the papers should be readable. And even the Results sections have some real rewards, I think, even for the statistically-disinclined, such as the tables of cues to deception.

My thanks to all of the co-authors of the papers in this book, and to the many wonderful students and collaborators from whom I've learned so much over the years. Thanks, too, to everyone who has asked about this research. Because you never stopped asking, I knew it was time to assemble this collection and make it available.

If you want to know more about my deception research, or my passionate study of the place of people who are single in society and in science, check out my website, www.BellaDePaulo.com, my "Living Single" blog at *Psychology Today*, and my book, *Singled Out: How Singles Are Stereotyped, Stigmatized, and Ignored, and Still Live Happily Ever After*.

Bella DePaulo
Summerland, California
July 2009

Journal of Personality and Social Psychology, May 1996, Vol. 70, No. 5, p 979-995.

Lying in Everyday Life

Bella M. DePaulo, Deborah A. Kashy, Susan E. Kirkendol,
Melissa M. Wyer, Jennifer A. Epstein

Abstract

In 2 diary studies of lying, 77 college students reported telling 2 lies a day, and 70 community members told 1. Participants told more self-centered lies than other-oriented lies, except in dyads involving only women, in which other-oriented lies were as common as self-centered ones. Participants told relatively more self-centered lies to men and relatively more other-oriented lies to women. Consistent with the view of lying as an everyday social interaction process, participants said that they did not regard their lies as serious and did not plan them much or worry about being caught. Still, social interactions in which lies were told were less pleasant and less intimate than those in which no lies were told.

Although psychologists of many orientations have had much to say about lying (DePaulo, Stone, & Lassiter, 1985; Ford, King, & Hollender, 1988; Lewis & Saarni, 1993), the topic is hardly their exclusive domain. Interest in lying transcends most disciplinary, cultural, and historical boundaries. Analyses of lying appear in religious treatises, staid textbooks, and irreverent tabloids. Perspectives on lying are as diverse as their sources. Lying has been described as a threat to the moral fabric of society (Bok, 1978), a predictor of dire life outcomes (Stouthamer-Loeber, 1986), a social skill (DePaulo & Jordan, 1982; Nyberg, 1993), and an important developmental milestone (deVilliers & deVilliers, 1978).

Pronouncements about deceit are staggeringly varied not only because of the nature of the beast, but also because the debate on deceit has in some important ways proceeded virtually unconstrained by data. Many perspectives on deceit rest on assumptions about patterns of lying in everyday life. However, some of the most fundamental questions about everyday lies have yet to be answered with compelling data. These questions include the following: How often do people lie? What do they lie about? Whom do they lie about? To whom do they tell their lies and in what contexts? What reasons do they offer for telling their lies?

We set out to address basic questions about lying in everyday life by using a daily diary methodology that has been used successfully in the study of diverse topics in social, personality, and developmental psychology (Kashy, 1991; Reis & Wheeler, 1991; Tennen, Suls, & Affleck, 1991). We asked participants to keep records of all their social interactions, and all of the lies that they told during those social interactions, every day for a week. They also described their partners in their social interactions, the targets of their lies, and their reasons for telling their lies. We collected these data from two very different samples of participants.

Our theoretical orientation to the study of lying in everyday life was drawn from perspectives on identity, self-presentation, and impression management from sociology (Goffman, 1959), linguistics

(Brown & Levinson, 1987), and social psychology (Schlenker & Weigold, 1989). From these perspectives, the "self" that is presented to others in everyday social life is characteristically an edited and packaged one. In nondeceptive presentations, the editing serves to specify and highlight the aspects of the self that are most relevant to the interaction at hand, without being designed to mislead. By comparison, the defining characteristic of the deceptive presentation is that it is purposefully designed to foster a falsef impression.

Many of the same goals that motivate nondeceptive presentations also motivate deceptive ones. These include the claiming of desired identities, the support of other people's claims to desired identities, and the exchange of enhancing and supportive emotions, preferences, and opinions. When reality is kind (e.g., when people want to present themselves as generous and caring when they really do have a long history of charitable contributions and benevolent acts), these goals can be accomplished nondeceptively; however, under less propitious circumstances, it becomes more tempting to lie. Because these kinds of goals are so fundamental to ordinary social discourse, and because reality is often unkind, we expected to find that lying is a fact of social life. We anticipated that our participants would describe lying as an everyday occurrence rather than as an extraordinary or unusual event.

In the popular press, as well as in the literature on ethics, lying often is described as a selfish act. People lie, it is assumed, to get jobs, promotions, raises, good grades, and better commissions. We, too, believe that lies are more often told to serve the self than to benefit others. However, we think that lies are less often told in the pursuit of goals such as financial gain and material advantage and instead are much more often told in the pursuit of psychic rewards such as esteem, affection, and respect.

We also think that the portrayal of everyday lies as disruptive of social life and hurtful to the targets of the lies is in need of modification. In keeping with the perspective described by Goffman (1959) and other social interaction theorists, we think that many of the lies of everyday life are told to avoid tension and conflict and to minimize hurt feelings and ill-will (Lippard, 1988; Metts, 1989). We think that people lie frequently about their feelings, preferences, and opinions and that when they do so, they are far more likely to feign a positive appraisal than a negative one.

If we are correct in assuming that lies are a fact of social life, then we should find that they are of only minor cognitive or emotional significance to the people who tell them. As with other well-practiced behaviors, everyday lies should require little planning. We expect people to describe their lies as not serious, to report low levels of distress before and after telling their lies, and to report little desire to undo their lies if they could. We also think that they will feel little concern about the possibility of getting caught and instead will expect to be believed.

Although lying is a commonplace strategy for managing impressions and social interactions, it is less common than nondeceptive techniques. It is a more extreme form of impression management that involves the deliberate fostering of a false impression rather than the judicious editing of a true one. It is likely to occur in situations that are a bit more taxing than ones in which social interaction goals can readily be accomplished in nondeceptive ways. Furthermore, in this culture, lying is generally condemned. Several consequences might follow from these circumstances. First, social interactions in which lies are told will differ in undesirable ways from those in which no lies are told; specifically, they will seem less pleasant and less intimate. Second, people will show some avoidance of the most direct modes of social interaction when telling lies; for example, they might prefer telling their lies in a letter or by telephone instead of in face-to-face interactions. Finally, people might feel a twinge of distress while they are telling their lies that they did not feel just before or immediately afterward.

Just as people are unrealistically optimistic about so many other aspects of their lives (Taylor, 1989), so, too, might they be optimistic about their lying. At the end of their week of recordkeeping, we asked participants how often they think they lie relative to other people their age. We expected participants to say that on the average, they tell fewer lies than do others.

Sex Differences in Lying

The cumulative results of hundreds of studies converge to support the theoretical statement (e.g., Bakan, 1966) and popular perception that women are the socioemotional specialists in American culture. Women interact in more intimate ways with other people than do men (Reis, in press). They self-disclose more (Dindia & Allen, 1992) and give more social support—especially emotional support—to others (Reis, in press). They also are warmer nonverbally; they smile and gaze more at their listeners, approach others more closely, and touch others more, and their facial expressions are especially expressive and legible (Hall, 1984; see also DePaulo, 1992, for a self-presentational interpretation). It has been argued that many sex differences can be attributed to the differential distribution of men and women into different social roles and that when men and women occupy the same roles, they will behave similarly (Eagly, 1987). The evidence for this position is compelling with regard to agentic behaviors such as dominance and leadership (Eagly, 1987), but less so for communal behaviors such as agreeableness and quarrelsomeness. In a pair of studies of men and women in their occupational roles, Moskowitz, Suh, and Desaulniers (1994) found that women were more communal (more agreeable and less quarrelsome) than men and that this sex difference was not qualified by social role: Women were equally more communal than men whether they were in a supervisory, subordinate, or collegial role.

Women are not only more likely to offer intimacy in their interactions with others, but they also are more likely to receive it. Both men and women regard their interactions with women as being more meaningful than their interactions with men (Reis, in press), they self-disclose more to women (Dindia & Allen, 1992), they are nonverbally warmer to women (Hall, 1984), and they offer women more social and emotional support (Reis, in press).

It has been suggested that the most pronounced differences between men and women should occur not when they are interacting with each other, but instead when they are in same-sex pairs or groups. Maccoby (1990) noted that sex segregation is pervasive throughout childhood (and continues to be important even in adulthood) and that in segregated same-sex groupings, males and females learn characteristic ways of interacting. There is some supportive evidence for this position. For example, sex differences in dominance and friendliness (Moskowitz, 1993), in communal behaviors (Moskowitz et al., 1994), and in nonverbal behaviors (Hall, 1984) all have been found to be more pronounced in same-sex than in opposite-sex interactions. The interactions that are most conducive to intimacy, then, may be those in which women are interacting with other women.

The intimacy that characterizes interactions involving women seems at first blush to be completely inconsistent with lying. Self-disclosure, for example, is the process of revealing oneself to others, whereas lying is a process of falsifying and concealing. Social support is a process of offering kindness, comfort, and aid to others, whereas lying involves a unilateral decision to withhold valid information. One hypothesis that might follow from this construal is that women will lie less often than men, particularly when they are interacting with other women.

9

There is, however, some evidence that is inconsistent with the prediction that women, more so than men, will refrain from telling lies. For example, in a study in which men and women talked about paintings that they detested with the art students who had painted them, women were more likely than men to lie about their opinions of the paintings (DePaulo & Bell, 1993). They were not, however, any more inclined than men to communicate untruthfully when the paintings were ones that they liked or when the paintings were ones that were created by other artists. The pattern of deceit in this study suggested that the women's lying may have been motivated by their concern for the artists; they seemed to be lying to avoid criticizing the artists and hurting their feelings. On the basis of this study as well as the results from a psychologically similar paradigm in which children received a disappointing gift (Cole, 1986; Saarni, 1984), DePaulo, Epstein, and Wyer (1993) suggested the possibility that one of the ways that women foster intimacy and supportiveness in their interactions with others is by telling lies. The specific prediction is that women, relative to men, tell more of the kinds of lies that are intended to benefit other people, lies that are flattering, comforting, and protective. The research we report provides a broad-ranging test of that hypothesis as it pertains to the many different lies of everyday life.

To learn whether women lie more or less than men, and whether the kind of lying that occurs when women are with other women differs from that which occurs when men are involved, it is essential to know whether women have the same number of opportunities to lie to men and women as do men. Every social interaction is an opportunity to tell a lie, and it has been amply demonstrated that rates of socializing differ markedly in different kinds of dyads and groups (e.g., Reis & Wheeler, 1991). If, for example, it were found that women told twice as many lies as men, this finding would have much different implications if women also interacted with other people twice as often as men did, compared with equally often or half as often. Although there have been several previous studies in which participants kept records of their lies for a specified period of time (e.g., Camden, Motley, & Wilson, 1984; Lippard, 1988), there are none that we know of that also included a measure of opportunities to lie.[1]

Method

Participants

Participants in Study 1 were 30 male and 47 female undergraduates who participated in partial fulfillment of a requirement for an introductory psychology course. They ranged in age from 17 to 22 (M = 18.69 years, SD = 0.91 years). Sixty-four were White, 9 were Black, and 4 described themselves as "other" than White or Black. The 77 participants did not include 1 man who completed only 2 days of the 7-day record-keeping assignment.

Participants in Study 2 were 30 men and 40 women who were recruited via advertisements posted at a local community college, from lists of people who had taken continuing education courses, and from lists of names selected randomly from the area telephone directory. They ranged in age from 18 to 71 (M = 34.19 years, SD = 12.49 years). Sixty-seven were White and 3 were Black. Other demographic information was based on 53 of the 70 participants; 17 were inadvertently given an incomplete questionnaire. Of those who did answer the complete questionnaire, 81% were employed, 57% were married, 47% had children, and 34% had no more than a high school education. The 70 participants in Study 2 did not include 1 man who said that he had recorded only about 10% of his social interactions and 5% of his lies.

Procedure

Phase 1: Introduction to the study

The Study 1 participants and the participants from Study 2 who were recruited from the community college initially responded to notices describing the research that were posted in an academic building. The study was described as one in which they would keep records of their social interactions and communications for 7 days. In Study 1 the notice indicated that participants would receive partial course credit for their participation, and in Study 2 it indicated that participants would be paid $35. Study 2 participants recruited from continuing education lists or from the phone directory were sent letters with the same description of the research; they then were contacted by telephone about a week later.

All participants attended an initial 90-min meeting in which the study and the procedures were explained. (Participants also completed several individual-differences measures reported in Kashy & DePaulo, 1996 .) In Study 1, these were group sessions attended by 10–15 participants at a time. The Study 2 sessions were conducted individually or in small groups.

Participants were told that they would be recording all of their social interactions and all of the lies that they told during those interactions every day for a week. It was noted that their role in this research was especially important in that they would be the observers and recorders of their own behavior. The investigators explained that they did not condone or condemn lying; rather, they were studying it scientifically to learn the answers to some of the most fundamental questions about the phenomenon. They encouraged the participants to think of the study as an unusual opportunity to learn more about themselves.

The key terms were then explained to the participants. A "social interaction" was defined as "any exchange between you and another person that lasts 10 min or more ... in which the behavior of one person is in response to the behavior of another person." This definition, plus many of the examples used to clarify the definition, were taken or adapted from the ones used in the initial studies involving the Rochester Interaction Record (RIR) (Wheeler & Nezlek, 1977). We did add an exception to the 10-min rule, which was that for any interaction in which participants told a lie, they also were to fill out a social interaction record, even if the interaction lasted less than 10 min. (For the college students and community members respectively, 8.9% and 10.5% of their lies were told during interactions lasting 10 min or less.)

To explain what participants should count as a lie, it was noted that "a lie occurs any time you intentionally try to mislead someone. Both the intent to deceive and the actual deception must occur." Many examples were given. Participants were urged to record all lies, no matter how big or how small. They were instructed that if they were uncertain as to whether a particular communication qualified as a lie, they should record it. (At the end of the study, two of the investigators independently read through all of the lie diaries and agreed on the few that did not meet the definition and excluded them.) The definition that we gave participants was interpreted broadly as encompassing any intentional attempts to mislead, including even nonverbal ones. The only example of a lie they were asked not to record was saying "fine" in response to perfunctory "How are you?" questions. Participants completed one deception record for every lie that they told.

Participants were instructed to fill out the forms (social interaction records and deception records) at least once a day. The forms were then collected by the experimenters at several different times throughout the week. Participants also were given pocket-sized notebooks and encouraged to write reminders of their social interactions and their lies as soon as possible after the events had taken place. They could then use their notes as a memory aid if they did not complete their social interaction and deception records until later in the day. The notebooks were not collected.

Several additional steps were taken to encourage the reporting of all lies. First, participants were told that if they did not wish to reveal the contents of any of the lies that they told, in the space on the deception record in which they were to describe their lie, they could instead write "rather not say." That way, we would still know that a lie was told as well as other information about the lie and the social interaction in which it was told (from the other parts of the records that the participants completed). Second, we instructed participants that if they did not completely remember everything about a lie that they told, they should still fill out as much of the information on the form as they could. Third, we told participants that if they remembered a lie from a previous day that they had not recorded, they should still turn in a form for that lie.

The importance of accuracy and conscientiousness in keeping the records was emphasized throughout the session. To ensure anonymity, participants chose their own identification number, which they used throughout the study. Participants did not write their names on any of the forms. At the end of the session, the investigators reviewed the amount of time it would take to complete all phases of the study and encouraged participants to terminate their participation at that point if they no longer had the interest or the time to participate fully. They were offered credit or payment even if they chose not to continue. All participants elected to continue.

Participants were given typed copies of all of the instructions and definitions they had been given during the session. This instruction booklet also included names and phone numbers of members of the research team whom they could contact at any time with any questions. Appointments also were made with each participant to meet with a researcher in approximately 3 days to drop off completed social interaction forms and check on any questions related to the study. Researchers also were available to collect forms at other times. Appointments also were made with all of the Study 1 participants to return once more at the end of the 7-day recording period to complete a final set of measures. Study 2 participants were shown an envelope and instructions that would be mailed to them at the end of the study, so that they could complete the same measures.

Phase 2: Recording social interactions and lies

During the 7-day recording period, which began the day after the introductory session, participants completed a social interaction record for all of their social interactions and a deception record for all of their lies.

The social interaction record was adapted from the RIR (Wheeler & Nezlek, 1977). On each record, participants wrote their identification number, the date, the time, and the duration of the interaction. For interactions involving three or fewer other people, participants recorded the initials and the sex of each of those persons. For interactions with more than three other people, participants simply recorded the total number of male and female interaction partners. Participants then indicated how intimate the interaction was on a 9-point scale ranging from superficial (1) to meaningful (9). They also rated the quality of the interaction on a scale with endpoints labeled unpleasant (1) and pleasant (9) and indicated the degree to which the participant influenced the other person(s) more (1) or the other person(s) influenced the participant more (9). They also indicated whether the interaction took place in writing, by telephone, or face to face.

Printed on the same page as the social interaction record was the deception record. Participants again indicated the initials and gender of the person or people to whom they told their lie. Below this were spaces to "Briefly describe the lie" and "Briefly describe the reason why you told the lie." Next were nine 9-point rating scales. Participants rated their degree of planning of the lie on a scale with endpoints labeled completely spontaneous (1) and carefully planned in advance (9). They then indicated the importance of not getting caught, from very unimportant (1) to very important (9). On the next three scales, they reported their feelings before the lie was told, while telling the lie, and after the lie was told on a scale with endpoints labeled very comfortable (1) and very uncomfortable (9). They also rated the seriousness of the lie—very trivial, unimportant lie (1) to very serious, important lie (9)—and the target's reaction to the lie—didn't believe me at all (1) to believed me completely (9). Finally, they answered two questions—"How would the target have felt if you told the truth instead of the lie?" and "How would you have felt if you told the truth instead of a lie?"—on scales with endpoints labeled much better if I told the truth (1) and much worse if I told the truth (9).

Phase 3: Additional measures

After the completion of the 7-day recording period, participants were asked to respond to one more set of measures. First, they were asked to fill out a form (not relevant to this article) describing the characteristics of each of the persons with whom they had interacted. Next, participants were given photocopies of each of their deception records and they answered two questions about each lie: "Was this lie ever discovered?" (no, not yet; don't know; or yes) and "If you could relive this social interaction, would you tell the lie again?" (no or yes).

Next, participants completed a questionnaire on which they indicated, on 9-point scales, how successful they thought they were at lying and how frequently they thought they had lied relative to what they had expected and relative to other people their age. They also indicated the percentage of their social interactions and their lies that they actually had recorded. (We urged them to be honest about this because it would help us to know the correct answers to these questions even if the percentages were low.) Finally, they indicated the average amount of time they had spent each day filling out all of the social interaction forms and the deception records.

The Study 1 participants returned to the laboratory to complete these forms. Afterward, they were interviewed by one of the investigators who tried to determine the extent to which the participants had understood and complied with the procedure and believed the information they had been given about the research. This extensive interview uncovered no problems with the procedure. Therefore, in Study 2, all of the forms from this phase of the study were mailed to the participants, and a written debrief (plus payment) was included in the package.

Coding the Lies

Developing the taxonomy

The development of a taxonomy of lies was a multistep process in which we (a) developed a preliminary taxonomy and codebook on the basis of previous taxonomic efforts, our own theoretical framework, and pilot testing; (b) coded a sample of 100 lies from the first study and modified the taxonomy as necessary; (c) trained research assistants to code all of the lies from both studies according to the new taxonomy; (d) reviewed all of the coding for consistency, adding necessary clarifications to the codebook; and (e) trained a coder in the use of the final taxonomy, including practice at coding 50 sample items. The reliabilities (kappas) reported in Table 1 were based on the relationship between that person's codings of 215 lies drawn about equally from the two studies and the actual codings of those lies (from Steps c and d) that were used in the analyses.

Kinds of lies

Participants' open-ended descriptions of their lies and their reasons for telling them were classified in four different ways. The content, type, and referent of the lie were coded primarily from the description of the lie itself. The reasons for the lie were coded from participants' self-described reasons for telling their lies. Subcategories of the kinds of lies, definitions, reliabilities, and examples are shown in Table 1 .2

Table 1
Taxonomy of Lies

Kind of lie	Definition	Examples
	1. Content	
Feelings	Lies about affects, emotions, opinions, and evaluations pertaining to people, objects, or events. Includes feigning feelings and appraisals that are more positive or less negative than they are, as well as the converse of feigning less positivity or more negativity (.85).	"Told her her muffins were the best ever."
Achievements, knowledge	Lies about achievements, accomplishments, failures, shortcomings, knowledge, and lack of knowledge (.71).	"I told him I had done poorly on my calculus homework when I had aced it."
Actions, plans, whereabouts	Lies about what the liars did, are doing, or are planning to do, or about where they were or where they are (.65).	"Said I would go out with him sometime but I won't."
Explanations, reasons	Lies about liars' reasons or explanations for their behavior (.49).	"I told him I didn't take out our garbage because I didn't know where to take it."
Facts, possessions	Lies about facts about objects, events, or people, or about possessions (.64).	"Told him my father was an ambassador."
	2. Reason[a]	
Self-centered	Lies told to protect or enhance the liars psychologically, or to advantage or protect the liars' interests; lies told to elicit a particular emotional response that the liars desired (.69). The lies told for *psychological* reasons included lies told to protect the liars from embarrassment, loss of face, or looking bad; from disapproval or having their feelings hurt; from worry, conflict, or other unpleasantness; lies told to protect the liars' privacy; to make the liars appear better (or just different) than they are; and to regulate the liars' own feelings, emotions, and moods (.68). Lies told for reasons of *personal advantage* included lies told for the liar's personal gain, to make things easier or more pleasant for the liars, or to help them get information or get their way; lies told to protect liars from physical punishment or to protect their property, assets, or safety; lies told to protect the liars from loss of status or position or to protect them from being bothered or from doing something they preferred not to do (.67).	(**Psychological**): LIE: "I told her Ted and I still liked each other when really I don't know if he likes me at all." REASON: "Because I'm ashamed of the fact that he doesn't like me anymore." (**Personal advantage**): LIE: "Lady on phone asked if a number was my current phone number. I said yes when in fact it isn't." REASON: "I want to make it hard for her to find me; they are after me for money."

(*continued on next page*)

(Table 1 *continued*)

Kind of lie	Definition	Examples
	2. Reason (continued)	
Other-oriented [b]	Lies told to protect or enhance other persons psychologically or to advantage or protect the interests of others (.68). The lies told for *psychological* reasons included lies told to protect another person from embarrassment, loss of face, or looking bad; from disapproval or having their feelings hurt; from worry, conflict, or other unpleasantness; lies told to protect another's privacy; to make other people appear better (or just different) than they are; and to regulate another person's feelings, emotions, or moods. The lies told for *another person's advantage* included lies told for another person's personal gain, to make things easier or more pleasant for others, to be accommodating, or to help them get their way; lies told to protect others from physical punishment or to protect their property, assets, or safety; lies to protect others from loss of status or position or to protect them from being bothered or from doing something they preferred not to do.	(**Psychological**): LIE: "Told her she looked well, voice sounded good when she looks less well than a few weeks ago." REASON: "Not to add worry as she undergoes chemotherapy treatments." (**Another person's advantage**): LIE: "Lied about cost per square foot." REASON: "To make money for the company."
	3. Type[c]	
Outright	Total falsehoods; lies in which the information conveyed is completely different from, or contradictory to, the truth (.50).	"I told my mother that I don't drink beer at college."
Exaggeration	Lies in which liars overstate the facts or convey an impression that exceeds the truth (.42).	"Exaggerated how sorry I was to be late."
Subtle	Lying by evading or omitting relevant details and by telling literal truths that are designed to mislead. Also includes behavioral or nonverbal lies (.60).	"He and I discussed sexual acts that I had performed, but he assumed that they had been performed with a woman."

(*continued again on next page*)

(Table 1 *continued* again)

4. **Referent**[d]		
Liar	Lies that refer to something about the lie teller, such as something the liar did or felt. Includes lies in which the liars state or imply their preferences or opinions (.68).	"I led a girl to believe that I was a model with a New York agency."
Target	Lies that refer to something about the target of the lie (.72).	"Told customer it was her color."
Other person	Lies that refer to something about a person or persons other than the liar or target (.63).	"Said this guy liked her when he really hates her guts."
Object, event	Lies that refer to something about an object, event, or place (.64).	"Disagreed when she told me my drawing was good even though I thought it was."

Note. Reliabilities (kappas) are indicated at the end of each definition.

[a] A third category of "neither self-centered nor other-oriented" was also coded, but those results are not relevant to this article. That category includes lies told to control an interaction, to create an effect (e.g., to entertain), to conform to conventions, or to simplify a response. Also coded but not included in the analyses were instances in which participants said they did not know why they told the lie.

[b] Lies told to bother or annoy others or to cause them psychological damage (e.g., Lie: "Told him the boss wanted to talk to him, but he really didn't." Reason: "So he'd look like a fool.") were not included. Only .84% of the lies in Study 1 and 2.39% of the lies in Study 2 were of this nasty variety.

[c] Understatements, in which liars "play down" the truth or give less than honest impressions (e.g., "Said I did OK on an exam – I got an A"), also were coded but were excluded from the analyses because of poor reliability (k = .14).

[d] Lies were coded into as many of the four categories as they fit.

Results

Rate of Lying

Table 2 shows the basic descriptive data on the number of lies, social interactions, and partners for the participants in both samples. As predicted, lying was an everyday event. College students reported lying in approximately one out of every three of their social interactions, and people from the community lied in one out of every five social interactions. Table 2 also shows the basic statistics separately for men and women and for dyadic lies in which men and women told lies to men or women. For the key variable of number of lies per social interaction, there were no significant effects involving sex of the participant or target.

Table 2
Descriptive Statistics for Number of Lies, Social Interactions (SIs), and Partners

All Participants

Variable	College	Community
Number of lies told		
Mean per day (SD)	1.96 (1.63)	0.97 (0.98)
Maximum per week	46	30
Median per week	11	4.5
Total lies in sample	1,058	477
Number of participants who told no lies	1	6
% Lies in dyadic SIs	61	72
Number of social interactions		
Mean per day (SD)	6.63 (2.37)	5.76 (2.60)
% SIs that were dyadic	61	70
Number of lies per social interaction[a]	.31 (0.28)	0.20 (0.22)
Number of partners[b,c]		
Mean per week (SD)	14.79 (6.33)	13.76 (8.68)
% to whom lies were told	38	30

By Sex of Participant

	College		Community	
	Men	**Women**	**Men**	**Women**
Mean no. lies per day	1.84	2.04	0.66	1.21
Mean no. SIs per day	6.00	7.03	5.90	5.67
Mean no. lies per SI[d]	0.32	0.30	0.16	0.23

By Sex of Participant (first letter) and Sex of Partner (second letter) in Dyadic Interactions[b,c]

	College				Community			
	MM	**MF**	**FM**	**FF**	**MM**	**MF**	**FM**	**FF**
Mean no. lies per day	0.54	0.52	0.42	0.88	0.30	0.22	0.32	0.50
Mean no. SIs per day	1.93	1.44	1.38	3.01	1.99	2.29	1.91	1.90
Mean no. of lies per SI[e]	0.30	0.34	0.30	0.31	0.20	0.17	0.22	0.29
Mean no. of partners	7.38	5.53	5.39	10.43	9.37	6.70	4.58	7.45
% partners to whom lies were told	35	40	38	40	24	27	34	33

Note. M = male; F = female.

[a] Computed by dividing, for each participant, the total number of lies by the total number of social interactions, then averaging across participants. Because different participants had different numbers of social interactions, the values are not identical to dividing the group-level mean for the total number of lies by the group-level mean for the total number of social interactions.

[b] Includes only partners from dyadic interactions.

[c] Computed for each participant and then averaged across participants.

[d] Sex of participant differences were not statistically significant.

[e] Sex of participant, sex of partner, and the interaction were not statistically significant.

Self-Perceptions of Lying

When we asked participants at the end of the study how successful they thought they were as liars, they generally rated themselves as fairly successful (see Table 3). Participants also said that they lied less frequently than they expected, and, as we predicted, they also said that they lied less frequently than others their age. For both samples, the mean was significantly lower than the midpoint of the scale, t (76) = 2.57, p = .01, for the college students, and t (70) = 2.22, p = .03, for the community members. In the community sample, the men (compared with the women) thought that they lied especially less frequently than others their age, t (68) = 1.98, p = .05. No other sex differences were significant.

Table 3
Self-Perceptions of Lying

Variable	College			Community		
	Overall	**Men**	**Women**	**Overall**	**Men**	**Women**
Overall perceptions						
Success at lying						
M	6.53	6.57	6.51	5.76	5.47	5.98
SD	2.03	2.08	2.02	2.01	2.30	1.76
Lied more than expected						
M	4.45	4.20	4.62	4.50	4.40	4.58
SD	1.86	2.06	1.73	1.89	2.04	1.78
Lied more than others[a]						
M	3.66	3.43	3.81	3.80	3.43	4.08
SD	1.57	1.63	1.53	1.37	1.36	1.33
Correlations with self-perceived frequency relative to others[a]						
No. of lies	.31**	.14	.41**	.38**	.37*	.35*
No of lies per social interaction	.19	.17	.20	.36**	.39*	.32*

Note. Responses were made on 9-point scales, with higher numbers indicating more of the quality.
[a] Responded to the question, "Compared with others your age, how often do you lie?"
*p < .05. **p < .01.

To determine whether participants' self-perceptions would be consistent with their actually lie-telling behavior, we correlated their answers to the question about how frequently they thought they lied relative to others their age with the actual number of lies that they told and with the number of lies that they told relative to the number of social interactions. As shown in Table 2 , all of these correlations were positive and many were significant. (Tests of the differences between correlations for men and women were not significant.) Therefore, there was some correspondence between participants' perceptions of their lying and their actual rate of lying.

Comparing Social Interactions in Which Lies Were or Were Not Told

To compare qualities of the interactions when lies were and were not told, for each participant a mean score on each interaction measure was computed across all interactions involving lies. A second set of means was computed averaging over all interactions that did not involve lies. Correlated t tests were then conducted on the participants' average responses. As predicted, participants in both studies described the interactions in which they told no lies as more intimate and more pleasant than the interactions during which they lied (see Table 4). Both the social interactions that included lies and those that did not were overwhelmingly face-to-face interactions. Interactions by telephone were less frequent, and communications in writing were the least frequent. Still, as predicted, the relative use of closer communication modalities varied significantly according to whether lies were or were not being told. For both studies, the interactions during which lies were told (compared with those during which no lies were told) were relatively more likely to involve the more distant modality of the telephone and relatively less likely to involve the closer modality of face-to-face interaction. An exception to our predictions was that there were no differences in the use of written communication as a function of whether lies were or were not told.

Table 4

Mean Characteristics of Social Interactions in Which Lies Were or Were Not Told

	College			Community		
Variable	**No Lies**	**Lies**	*t*(74)	**No Lies**	**Lies**	*t*(61)
Intimacy[a]	5.46	5.01	2.95*	5.75	4.94	4.62*
Pleasantness[a]	7.00	6.37	6.14*	6.69	5.86	5.37*
Other person's influence[a]	5.02	4.64	4.06*	4.83	4.78	0.42
Duration (hr)	0.98	0.88	1.33	1.02	0.92	1.00
Modality (%)						
Writing	1.46	1.29	0.43	0.56	0.38	0.61
Telephone	6.70	13.63	3.44*	9.13	27.68	4.82*
Face to face	91.83	85.08	3.28*	90.31	71.94	4.77*

[a] Responses were made on a 9-point scale, with higher numbers indicating more of the value.

*p < .01.

Kinds of Lies

Similarities between the studies

Table 5 shows the percentages of each kind of lie for each category of content, reason, type, and referent for both studies. The relative frequencies of the different subcategories of lies were highly similar for the two studies. For the 14 subtypes taken together, the correlation between the percentages for the college sample and the community sample was .95 (df = 12), p = .0001.

Table 5

A Taxonomy of Lies: Percentages in Each Category

Variable	College		Community	
	M	SD	M	SD
Content of the lies				
Feelings	37.42	25.93	29.53	29.97
Achievements	15.84	16.87	17.14	24.89
Actions, plans, whereabouts	27.49	25.57	27.69	27.27
Explanations	10.28	14.76	11.17	15.49
Facts, possessions	8.97	12.99	14.55	23.46
Reasons for the lies				
Self-centered	45.48	27.73	56.68	31.24
Other-oriented	25.74	24.42	24.45	27.20
Types of lies				
Outright	67.63	24.85	59.18	33.28
Exaggeration	14.74	19.30	9.23	17.80
Subtle	8.62	13.18	23.19	28.48
Referents of the lies				
Liar	88.29	16.05	90.79	19.25
Target	22.63	19.44	24.55	27.12
Other person	21.85	19.46	22.54	23.73
Object or event	33.52	24.24	50.33	29.47

Note. Within the referent category, lies were coded into as many subcategories as were relevant. Within the other categories, lies were coded into only one subcategory. Percentages do not sum to 100 for the categories with mutually exclusive codings because some of the lies could not be classified and because the percentages were computed for each participant (number of lies in that category divided by the total number of lies) and then averaged across participants.

Content of the lies

The results for the coding of the content of the lies show that for both studies, people reported lying most often about their feelings; their actions, plans, and whereabouts; and their achievements and knowledge (see Table 5). We predicted that when participants lied about their feelings, they would pretend to feel more positively than they really did more often than they would pretend to feel more negatively. To test this, we created subcategories of "feelings." The positive subcategory included lies in which people pretended to like someone or something more than they really did; faked a positive emotion that they did not really feel; pretended to have a more positive opinion than they actually did; and pretended to be more interested in a topic or a person or an event than they actually were. When people claimed that they did not mind something, when in fact they did, that, too, was included in the faking positive subcategory. The faking negative subcategory included the parallel negative categories (e.g., lies in which people pretended to dislike someone more than they really did). (The kappa reliabilities for these subcategories were .93 for faking positive and .66 for faking negative.)

For each participant we computed the number of fake positive lies told and the number of fake negative lies told. These totals were then divided by the total number of lies told and used in a mixed-model analysis of variance (ANOVA), in which sex of participant was a between-subjects variable and faking positive versus faking negative was a within-subjects variable. (Because this analysis included nondyadic lies in which partners were sometimes both men and women, as well as dyadic lies, sex of partner was not included as a variable.) For the means that we report, we multiplied the proportions by 100 to produce percentages.

The main effect for type of faking was significant for both studies, $F(1, 74) = 57.95$, MSE = 0.027, p < .001, for the college students, and $F(1, 62) = 40.03$, MSE = 0.039, p < .001, for the community members. On average, 25.23% of college students' lies involved faking positive, and 2.98% of their lies involved faking negative. For the community sample, the corresponding values were highly similar: The mean for faking positive was 23.79 and that for faking negative was 1.19. In addition, a nearly significant interaction between sex of participant and direction of faking emerged only for the college sample, $F(1, 74) = 3.69$. MSE = 0.027, p = .06, such that women were more likely to fake positive than were men (the means for fake positive for men and women were 19.33 and 28.87, respectively; those for fake negative for men and women were 3.63 and 2.58, respectively).

To determine whether the content of the lies varied with the sex composition of the dyad, we created separate variables for each kind of lie for each kind of dyad. For the feelings variable, for example, the number of lies about feelings that men told to other men was divided by the total number of lies that men told to other men; comparable variables then were computed for male–female (MF), female–male (FM), and female–female (FF) dyads. The resulting values were the dependent measures in the ANOVAs in which sex of the participant was a between-subjects variable and sex of partner was a within-subjects variable.[3] As shown in Table 6 , there were no significant effects for any content category that were consistent across the two studies.

Table 6

Kinds of Lies: Percentages in Each Type of Dyad

Variable	Mean				F		
	MM	MF	FM	FF	Sex of participant	Sex of partner	Same vs. opp. sex
Content							
Feelings							
College	18.18	44.33	45.21	43.60	2.92*	6.60**	8.45***
Community	29.06	30.65	28.87	30.07	0.00	0.03	0.00
Achievement							
College	21.42	16.65	12.61	14.93	1.08	0.09	0.73
Community	17.72	8.06	16.96	18.28	0.56	0.46	0.80
Actions, plans							
College	37.84	20.19	19.36	23.51	1.91	2.03	5.30**
Community	21.01	36.57	23.52	35.06	0.00	3.74*	0.08
Explanations							
College	15.87	13.92	10.27	12.92	0.41	0.01	0.38
Community	12.17	8.33	18.36	9.79	0.45	1.59	0.23
Facts, etc.							
College	6.68	4.91	12.57	5.04	0.81	1.73	0.66
Community	20.03	16.39	9.53	5.76	3.14*	0.42	0.00
Reasons							
Self-centered							
College	66.02	57.65	49.95	35.00	5.75**	4.27**	0.34
Community	57.39	51.11	59.41	42.63	0.10	2.85*	0.59
Other-oriented							
College	7.76	17.68	21.60	35.41	5.72**	7.87***	0.20
Community	19.19	22.69	17.82	41.84	1.34	4.69**	2.61
Types of Lies							
Outright							
College	63.72	62.45	77.50	69.54	2.02	0.87	0.48
Community	39.70	68.52	69.27	71.82	3.19*	4.10*	2.87*
Exaggeration							
College	14.59	13.24	11.54	13.04	0.09	0.00	0.16
Community	13.33	3.89	10.36	4.59	0.05	2.82*	0.17
Subtle							
College	15.50	12.36	6.52	10.51	1.34	0.03	1.85
Community	34.89	20.19	12.96	18.81	1.83	0.51	2.75
Referents							
Liar							
College	96.32	81.30	94.56	91.91	1.77	7.17***	3.51*
Community	84.03	88.89	86.61	96.85	0.74	2.60	0.33
Target							
College	14.12	26.75	32.35	26.68	2.17	0.39	2.71
Community	21.23	17.04	19.99	35.35	1.47	0.78	2.38
Other person							
College	17.51	14.92	11.99	30.01	1.04	4.36**	7.77***
Community	25.51	32.50	26.20	24.35	0.19	0.12	0.37
Object, event							
College	46.08	29.55	23.19	29.78	2.82*	1.30	7.00***
Community	47.39	41.67	50.17	42.90	0.05	0.57	0.01

Note. Means are for dyadic interactions. M=male. F=female. 1st letter = sex of participant; 2nd letter = sex of partner. For college, the *df*s for the F ratios were 1, 51; for community, 1, 40. *p<.10. **p<.05. ***p<.01.

Reasons for the lies

We predicted that participants would tell more self-centered lies than other-oriented lies but that women would tell relatively more other-oriented lies and relatively fewer self-centered lies than would men. A mixed-model ANOVA (sex of participant, self- vs. other-oriented lies) showed that the predicted main effect for type of reason was significant for both studies, $F(1, 74) = 18.62$, MSE = 0.100, $p < .001$, for the college students, and $F(1, 62) = 21.68$, MSE = 0.143, $p < .001$, for the community members. For the college students, 45.53% of the lies were self-centered, compared with 25.74% that were other-oriented. For the community sample, the corresponding percentages were 56.68 and 24.45. The prediction that the women would tell relatively more other-oriented lies than the men was supported only for the college sample, $F(1, 74) = 5.67$, MSE = 0.100, $p = .02$ (for the community sample, $F < 1$). For the college men, 50.57% of their lies were self-centered, compared with 15.25% that were other-oriented; for the women, the corresponding percentages were 42.42 and 32.21, respectively.

We also predicted that of the self-centered lies that participants told, more of them would be told for psychological reasons, such as those relevant to self-presentational and emotional concerns, than for the pursuit of personal material advantage or personal convenience. To test this, we created subcategories of self-centered lies (as described in Table 3). We then divided the number of lies each participant told for psychological reasons (and then for reasons of personal advantage) by the total number of lies the participant told and entered these two values as a repeated measures variable (psychological and personal advantage) in ANOVAs that also included sex of participant as a between-subjects variable. As predicted, participants in both studies told more lies for psychological reasons than for reasons of personal advantage; for the college students, $F(1, 74) = 4.27$, MSE = 0.055, $p = .04$, and for the community members, $F(1, 62) = 7.71$, MSE = 0.101, $p = .007$. The means were 26.78 (SD = 20.83) and 18.61 (SD = 22.24) for psychological lies and personal advantage lies, respectively, for the college students, and 36.72 (SD = 31.26) and 19.95 (SD = 22.69) for the community members, respectively. Neither the participant sex main effect nor the interaction between reason and participant sex was significant for either sample.

To determine whether there would be sex composition effects in the reasons participants described for telling their dyadic lies, we computed Sex of Participant (between-subjects) × Sex of Partner (within-subjects) ANOVAs on the two major categories of reasons: self-centered and other-oriented. As shown in Table 6 , men told significantly more self-centered lies in the college student study and nonsignificantly more in the community study. Women told significantly more other-oriented lies in the college student study and nonsignificantly more in the community study. There were indications in both studies that participants told more self-centered lies to men than to women (p s = .04 and .10 for the college and community studies, respectively). Participants in both studies told significantly more other-oriented lies to women than to men. An analysis adding to the ANOVA a within-subjects variable with self-centered and other-oriented as levels produced a significant Partner Sex × Self–Other interaction for both studies, $F(1, 51) = 8.76$, MSE = 0.077, $p = .005$, for the college study and $F(1, 40) = 4.94$, MSE = 0.133, $p = .03$, for the community study. Therefore, the degree to which participants told relatively more self-centered lies to men, and relatively more other-oriented lies to women, was significant in both studies. The Sex of Participant × Self–Other interaction was significant only for the college study, $F(1, 51) = 7.86$, MSE = 0.192, $p = .007$.

The pattern of means for both studies suggested that the dyads in which women lied to other women stood out from the others both in the low number of self-centered lies and the high number of other-

28

oriented lies. Contrasts comparing the FF dyads with the average of the other three dyad types generally were significant. Women were especially likely to tell other-oriented lies to other women, $F(1, 94) = 8.69$, MSE $= 0.082$, $p = .004$, for Study 1, and $F(1, 78) = 7.11$, MSE $= 0.104$, $p = .009$, for Study 2. In the college student study, women were especially unlikely to tell self-centered lies to other women, $F(1, 94) = 7.42$, MSE $= 0.129$, $p = .008$. This tendency was in the same direction, although not significantly so, in the community sample, $F(1, 78) = 1.77$, MSE $= 0.155$, $p = .19$. Comparison of the differences between the percentage of self-centered lies and the percentage of other-oriented lies also indicated that the FF dyads were markedly different from the others in both studies. The means (self-centered minus other-oriented) for MM, MF, FM, and FF, respectively, were 58.35, 39.97, 28.34, and -0.42 for the college students and 38.20, 28.43, 41.59, and 0.79 for the community members. The contrast comparing the FF dyads with the three others was significant for both studies, $F(1, 94) = 11.31$, MSE $= 0.294$, $p = .001$, for Study 1, and $F(1, 78) = 4.87$, MSE $= 0.395$, $p = .03$, for Study 2. In summary, across both studies, in dyads that included men, participants told many more self-centered lies than other-oriented lies. By contrast, in the dyads that included only women, the rates of self-centered and other-oriented lies were virtually identical.

Types of lies

By far, the largest category of types of lies in both samples was outright lies (see also Lippard, 1988). Sex of Participant × Sex of Partner ANOVAs on the dyadic lies produced just one (unpredicted) significant effect (see Table 6).

Referents of the lies

The vast majority of lies in both samples were about the liars. Sex of Participant × Sex of Partner ANOVAs on each of the four referent variables produced several significant findings (see Table 6). For example, the college students tended to tell more lies about people other than the liar or target to women than to men, but a significant interaction indicated that this was true only for the female participants. A contrast comparing the FF dyads with the other three kinds was significant, $F(1, 94) = 8.89$, MSE $= 0.048$, $p = .004$. In Study 2, the same contrast was significant for lies about the target, $F(1, 78) = 4.16$, MSE $= 0.094$, $p = .04$. In both instances, the lies about other people were more prominent in the FF dyads than in the other three.

Correlations Among the Kinds of Lies

What are the relationships among different kinds of lies? To answer this, we computed correlations using lies as units of analysis. (We did not compute correlations within categories, such as the different kinds of contents, because the codings were mutually exclusive.) For example, we looked at whether lies that were about feelings (coded as 1 if they were and 0 if they were not) tended to be self-centered lies (coded as 1 if the lie was self-centered and 0 if it was not). Because the sample sizes were so large (usually 1, 058 for Study 1 and 477 for Study 2), most of the correlations were significant. However, the degrees of freedom based on those sample sizes were not the appropriate ones because lies told by any one participant were not independent. To be conservative, we report here only the correlations that reached an absolute value of at least .20 for both studies.[4]

Lies about feelings tended to be other-oriented lies (r s $= .36$ and $.50$ for Studies 1 and 2, respectively, and $.47$ and $.52$ when just faked positive feelings were counted); they also tended not to be self-centered lies (r s $= -.29$ and $-.42$, and $-.23$ and $-.39$ for positive only). Lies about feelings also tended to be about the target person (r s $= .36$ and $.43$, and $.38$ and $.45$ for positive only). Lies

29

about the target person tended to be other-oriented lies (r s = .36 and .38) and tended not to be self-centered lies (r s = −.24 and −.31). Finally, lies about achievements tended not to be outright lies (r s = −.22 and −.23).

Characteristics of the Lies

Table 7 shows the characteristics of the lies as described by the participants using the 9-point rating scales and categories that were provided to them. The results underscore our contention that the lies of everyday life are mostly "light" lies that are not associated with much rumination or distress and that are generally successful. Participants said that they did not regard their lies as serious and that the level of distress they felt before, during, or after they told their lies was not high. Although they said that it was not important to them to avoid getting caught and that they did not put much planning into their lies, they thought that the targets believed them at the time that they told their lies, and, a week or so later, there were fewer than one in four of their lies (sometimes far fewer) that they knew for sure had been detected. These seemed to be lies of little or no regret: For more than 70% of the lies in both samples, participants said that if they could relive the situation, they would tell the lie again.

Table 7

Characteristics of the Lies

Variable	College		Community	
	M	**SD**	**M**	**SD**
Planning	2.95	1.29	3.12	1.76
Importance of avoiding detection	4.04	1.63	4.10	1.52
Distress before	3.56	1.66	4.09	1.78
Distress during	4.14	1.64	4.65	1.78
Distress after	4.03	1.58	4.54	1.76
Seriousness	3.34	1.40	3.08	1.34
Target believed	6.72	1.34	6.84	1.33
Protect target	5.84	0.99	5.97	1.29
Protect self	5.49	1.08	5.50	1.48
Would you tell the lie again? (% yes)	72.75	24.00	82.10	21.71
Was lie discovered? (%)				
No	59.44	27.97	57.41	34.73
Don't know	15.66	16.12	23.00	30.19
Yes	22.78	21.67	14.85	22.79

Note. The first nine variables were rated on 9-point scales, with higher numbers indicating more of the characteristic.

Participants also tended to describe their lies as protective of the targets and of themselves; they claimed that both they and the targets of their lies would have felt a bit worse if the truth had been told instead of the lie. However, they also described greater protectiveness toward the target than toward themselves. They said that the targets especially would have felt even worse if the truth had been told instead of the lie. The difference between participants' mean ratings on the "protect" scale and their mean ratings on the "protect other" scale was significant for both studies, t (75) = 2.48, p = .02, for Study 1, and t (63) = 3.01, p = .004, for Study 2.

To test our prediction that participants would feel more distressed while telling their lies than they would before or after they had told them, we compared participants' mean ratings of "distress during" to their mean ratings of "distress before"; similarly, we compared distress after with distress during and distress after with distress before. As predicted, participants felt more uncomfortable during the telling of their lies than they had just before they told them, t (75) = 5.45, p = .0001, for Study 1, and t (63) = 4.08, p = .001, for Study 2. However, their level of distress did not drop significantly from the time that they told their lies to the time directly afterward; therefore, after they had told their lies, they continued to feel significantly more uncomfortable than they had before, t (75) = 3.71, p = .0004, for Study 1, and t (63) = 2.40, p = .02, for Study 2.

To test for sex of participant and sex of partner effects (using dyadic lies only),5 we used a multilevel approach in which interactions were nested within partners and partners were nested within subjects (Bryk & Raudenbush, 1992; Kenny, Kashy, & Bolger, in press). This analysis approach involved a series of hierarchically nested regressions. For example, consider the relationship between participant sex, partner sex, and the variable seriousness (i.e., how serious the participant reported the lie to be). In the first step, a regression equation was computed for each participant with interaction partner as the unit of analysis. In this regression, the mean seriousness score for all interactions with each partner was computed and served as the outcome measure. Partner sex (coded as males = −1 and females = 1) was the predictor variable. From these regressions, an intercept and a beta weight were derived for each participant; the intercept measured the average level of seriousness across all of the participant's partners, and the beta weight estimated the relationship between partner sex and the degree to which the participant felt the lie was serious (i.e., Were lies told to men considered to be more serious than lies told to women?).

The second step involved computing two regression equations, each of which had the participant as the unit of analysis. In the first, the intercepts from the first-step regressions were the criterion scores and participant sex was the predictor variable. This analysis yielded an estimate of the relationship between participant sex and seriousness in general. In the second regression equation, the beta weights from the first-step regressions were the criterion scores and, again, participant sex was the predictor variable. This analysis of the beta weights yielded an intercept that was the average effect of partner sex on seriousness. In addition, the analysis yielded a regression coefficient that summarized the impact of the interaction between participant sex and partner sex on seriousness.6

Table 8 shows the means for the four dyad types of all of the lie characteristics for both studies, as well as the significance tests. Two effects stand out as significant or nearly significant in both studies and in the same direction. First, the partner sex effect showed that when the participants were lying to women, they said that they were more likely to be protecting the target than when they were lying to men. That is, they thought that the women to whom they told their lies would have felt even worse if they had heard the truth instead of a lie. Second, the interaction of participant sex with partner sex on the distress-before variable showed that participants felt more distressed when they were about to lie to someone of the opposite sex than when they were about to lie to a same-sex target. Closer inspection of the means for the college students, however, indicated that this was so only for the female liars. In fact, once again, it was the FF dyad that differed most strikingly from the other three. The college students who felt least distressed before telling their lies were the women who were about to lie to another woman. The same pattern of means (and significance levels) occurred for the other two distress variables. College men's discomfort did not differ depending on whether their lies were to men or to women, but women felt less distress before, during, and after their lies when lying to other women. Other effects that were significant for just one sample are shown in Table 8 .

Table 8

Characteristics of Lies Told in Each Type of Dyad

Variable	Mean				F		
	MM	MF	FM	FF	Sex of Participant	Sex of Partner	Same v opp sex
Planning[a]							
College	4.22	3.42	3.48	3.01	2.96*	9.25***	0.61
Community	3.55	4.12	4.08	3.45	0.02	0.01	2.53
Importance of avoiding detection[a]							
College	4.56	5.33	4.65	4.19	1.70	0.38	6.18**
Community	3.85	3.43	4.85	4.72	9.47***	0.55	0.14
Distress before[a]							
College	4.50	4.47	4.57	3.60	0.83	4.90**	4.39**
Community	3.44	4.20	4.76	4.47	2.88*	0.64	3.21*
Distress during[a]							
College	4.52	4.86	5.14	4.00	0.09	4.41*	15.55***
Community	4.13	4.15	5.19	5.31	7.06**	0.05	0.03
Distress after[a]							
College	4.50	4.57	5.02	3.88	0.05	6.42**	8.10***
Community	3.73	3.95	4.84	5.11	8.12***	0.72	0.01
Seriousness[a]							
College	3.74	4.61	3.88	3.12	3.74*	0.07	14.53***
Community	3.13	2.76	3.67	3.66	4.83**	0.61	0.59
Target believed[a]							
College	5.92	6.82	6.16	6.81	0.12	8.50***	0.21
Community	6.46	5.88	6.33	6.83	0.73	0.01	2.33
Protect target[a]							
College	5.26	6.11	5.81	6.04	1.08	6.29**	2.05
Community	5.86	6.42	6.01	6.65	0.33	3.47*	0.02
Protect self[a]							
College	4.71	5.62	5.76	5.54	2.81*	3.20*	8.99***
Community	5.78	5.48	5.94	5.99	0.85	0.25	0.48
Would you tell lie again?[b]							
College	67.58	60.50	59.81	70.98	0.05	0.23	4.64**
Community	77.03	73.20	73.17	69.61	0.23	0.19	0.00
Was it discovered?[c]							
College	1.84	1.63	1.78	1.59	0.22	6.00**	0.03
Community	1.57	1.92	1.91	1.68	0.13	0.14	3.05*

Note. The means are for dyadic interactions. M=male. F=female. 1st letter = sex of participant; 2nd letter = sex of partner.

[a] Rated on 9-point scales, with higher numbers indicating more of the quality.

[b] Percentage saying yes.

[c] Answers were coded as 1 = no, 2 = don't know, and 3 = yes. The percentages of participants who said yes were 27.68, 17.73, 31.20, and 11.52, respectively, for the MM, MF, FM, and FF dyads for the college study and 10.69, 18.70, 15.51, and 12.38 for the community study.

* $p < .10.$ ** $p < .05.$ *** $p < .01.$

Discussion

Lying Is a Fact of Daily Life

The studies reported here provide some of the first data, and by far the most extensive data, on some of the most fundamental questions about lying in everyday life. As we expected, lying is a fact of daily life. Participants in the community study, on the average, told a lie every day; participants in the college student study told two. One out of every five times that the community members interacted with someone, they told a lie; for the college students, it was one out of every three times. Of all of the people the community members interacted with one on one over the course of a week, they lied to 30% of them; the college students lied to 38% of the people in their lives.

Lies Are Told for Psychic Rewards

What is the nature of these lies that people tell every day? We set out to devise a taxonomy of lies, guided by the literature dating as far back as St. Augustine, by theoretical considerations and by the kinds of lies that actually did appear in the participants' diaries. Most previous attempts to categorize lies have posited two different kinds of taxonomies, one of the types of lies (e.g., outright lies vs. exaggerations) and another of the motives for the lies. We, too, found that these taxonomies were important, but they left unaddressed two other questions that are readily answered from people's descriptions of their lies: What is the content of the lies (e.g., Are they about feelings? achievements?) and what is the referent of lies (e.g., Do people lie mostly about themselves, about the person to whom they are telling the lie, about other people, or about impersonal topics such as objects or events?).

The multifaceted taxonomies we created allow a more differentiated answer to the age-old issue of the alleged selfishness of liars and their lies. One simple measure of liars' self-centeredness is the frequency with which they lie about themselves—their own feelings, opinions, achievements, actions, and possessions. The answer to this question is straightforward: Liars lie overwhelmingly about themselves. Although many lies are about the liar and someone or something else, more than 80% of the lies that participants told in both studies were at least in part about themselves.

But what about motive—were these lies told to serve the liars' own self-interests? According to participants' own descriptions of their reasons for telling their lies, the lies were in fact mostly self-serving ones (see also Camden et al., 1984). In both studies, about twice as many lies were told to benefit the liars as to benefit other people. Were these self-centered lies told specifically in the pursuit of material gain or personal convenience? To be conservative, we defined lies of "personal advantage" broadly because from our viewpoint, we expected them to occur relatively infrequently. From our perspective on lying as a behavior that serves everyday social interaction functions, such as self-presentation and emotion regulation, we predicted that self-centered lies would more often be told in the pursuit of psychic (rather than materialistic) benefits. That is, we expected people to lie to make themselves appear kinder or smarter or more honest than they believe themselves to be and to protect themselves from embarrassment or disapproval or conflict. In fact, in both studies, many more of participants' lies were told for psychological reasons than for reasons of personal advantage or convenience.

Other People Count, Too

Although participants told far more lies to benefit themselves in some way than to benefit others, still the number of other-oriented lies was not trivial. In both studies, close to one out of every four lies that participants told were told to benefit other people. Paralleling the lies that participants told for themselves, the lies told to benefit others were lies that protected them from embarrassment or worry or from having their feelings hurt. For every lie that they told, we asked participants to indicate (on rating scales) the degree to which they were protecting their own feelings by telling the lie (i.e., the degree to which they would have felt even worse if they had told the truth instead of the lie) and the degree to which they were protecting the other person's feelings. On this measure, participants in both studies described themselves as more concerned with the feelings of the targets of their lies than with their own feelings.

There was one other way in which liars' concerns about the targets of their lies became evident. At the top of the list of the contents of people's lies was the category of feelings. No content category in either study occurred more often than that of emotions, opinions, evaluations, and preferences. Furthermore, when people lied about their feelings, they overwhelmingly pretended to feel more positively, or more agreeably, than they did in fact. Importantly, these lies about feelings were disproportionately about the target person, and they also tended to be other-oriented lies and not self-centered ones. Lies about feelings, then, were about and for the target person.

Little Lies Are of Little Consequence

Because we expected lying to be an everyday social interaction process, as it was in fact, we also expected it to be infused with little cognitive or emotional baggage. In both studies, participants did indeed describe their lies in matter-of-fact ways. They said that their lies were generally not serious ones. They noted that they put little effort into planning them and did not worry much about the possibility of being caught. Instead, at the time of their lies, they reported that they expected to be believed. At the end of the study when we showed them their descriptions of each of their lies and asked them if, to their knowledge, the lies had been discovered, they reported that most of them had not been. Participants also reported at that point that they experienced little regret about their lies; when asked if they would tell the lie again if given a second chance, more than 70% said that they would. We are not suggesting that all of the lies of everyday life are little lies of little consequence; there was variability in all of our measures. However, the majority of them do seem to fit that description.

The Smudge

Although we think that lying serves basic social interaction functions such as impression management, emotion regulation, and social support, it is different in important ways from other nondeceptive means for achieving those goals. For example, when people use lying for impression management, they are not just editing their self-presentations to best fit the circumstances; instead, they are fashioning new and untrue selves. When people use lying to provide social support, the comfort they are offering is false; there is no genuine empathy behind the caring words. We think that these facts of lying, together with the morally perilous place that lying occupies in American culture, will leave their marks on the liars and on the social interactions in which they sprinkle their lies. First, we expected the liars to feel more distressed during the telling of their lies than just before or just after. In fact, participants in both studies felt more uncomfortable during their lies than they had just before. Their discomfort was a bit more enduring than we anticipated though; just after telling their lies, participants continued to feel their twinge of distress.

Second, we thought that the social interactions during which lies were told would be experienced as less pleasant and less intimate than those during which only the truth was conveyed. The results of both studies supported those predictions too. Finally, we thought that people might shy away from the closer communication modalities when they were telling lies. And, in fact, when participants in both studies were lying, they were relatively less likely to interact face to face than when they were telling the truth, and they were relatively more likely to communicate by telephone.

But Can We Believe Them?

It was important to us to elicit from our participants highly accurate and complete records of their lies. We took many steps to facilitate that. We explained what we meant by lying in great detail and gave participants printed definitions. We described our own perspective on lying as morally neutral. We described their role in the research as more akin to that of co-investigators than objects of our scrutiny. We continually emphasized the importance of accuracy and exhaustiveness and offered them the opportunity to withdraw from the study with compensation if they were not willing or able to participate conscientiously. We arranged the mechanics in ways that we thought would facilitate accuracy and thoroughness, too, from the small notebooks that we gave them to our safeguards of anonymity and our continuous availability to pick up forms and answer questions.

At the end of the study, we reassured the participants that it was fine if they had not recorded all of their social interactions or all of their lies and that it would help us to interpret the data more accurately to know what percentage of their social interactions and their lies they actually had recorded. Participants' answers to these questions were encouraging: On the average, they said that they had recorded about 86% and 89% of their social interactions (in Studies 1 and 2) and 89% and 92% of their lies. They also said that they had spent an average of 43 and 31 min a day keeping their records.

Still, despite our best efforts and our participants' claims of accuracy and thoroughness, our guess is that the 1,535 lies that we analyzed in these two studies was not the precise number of lies that the participants really did tell. Because of lapses in memory and conscientiousness, participants may have neglected to record some of their lies. There also may have been times when they did not even realize that they had told a lie. It seems likely, then, that participants actually told more lies than they recorded. If so, this would only strengthen our position that lying is an everyday behavior.

But are the kinds of lies that participants recorded biased in some way? The most plausible direction of this bias is that participants overreported their trivial and altruistic lies and underreported their serious and self-centered ones. We have no way of knowing whether this did in fact occur. However, the fact that participants described about twice as many self-centered lies as other-oriented ones suggests at least some willingness to own up to selfish motives. We also were encouraged by the similarities in the profiles of the kinds of lies that were described in the two studies. If participants biased their reports of their lies, they did so in uncannily similar ways in the two very different samples.

Sex Differences in Lying

The literature on sex differences has underscored the role of women as the socioemotional specialists in American culture. Compared with men, women give and receive more intimacy, more self-disclosures, more emotional support, and more friendly and warm nonverbal behaviors. We suggested that two kinds of predictions might follow from these sex differences. First, because lying seems so at odds with a generous, open, and revealing style of interacting, perhaps women lie much less frequently than do men. We found no evidence at all for this position.

Our alternative prediction was that women would not tell more lies overall than men would but that they would tell more of the kinds of lies that are intended to benefit other people rather than themselves. With regard to this prediction, we were partly right. In the college student study, women told significantly more other-oriented lies than did men and significantly fewer self-centered lies. The more important effect, however, was that the practice of telling kind lies was more characteristic of the dyads in which women were interacting with other women than it was of the dyads in which men were involved as liars, targets, or both. Across both studies, when men were involved in the dyads, participants told anywhere from twice as many self-centered lies as other-oriented ones to eight times as many. However, when only women were involved, the percentage of self-centered lies was virtually identical to the percentage of other-oriented ones.

Because we asked our participants to report only their lies and not their truths, we cannot know whether the sex differences in lying that we found would have been equally characteristic of truth telling. In studies of sex differences that were not specifically about deception, similar kinds of findings have been reported. For example, the results of research on self-presentational motives in everyday social interaction complement our findings on the distribution of self-centered lies in different dyad types. When women interact with each other, they are less likely to report self-promotional motives (e.g., trying to appear talented and smart) than when they interact with men or when men interact with either women or men (Leary et al., 1994).

That women have a way of interacting with each other that is different from the way they interact with men, and especially different from the way that men interact with each other, is an idea that has been developed in anthropology and sociolinguistics as well as in psychology (see Maltz & Borker, 1982, for a review). Maltz and Borker (1982) suggested that there is a "world of girls" with its own cultural traditions that is separate from the "world of boys"; each of these cultures is learned by boys and girls during the period of childhood when boys and girls socialize almost exclusively with children of their own gender. In all-girl groups, girls learn to use language to develop and sustain interpersonal bonds characterized by closeness and equality. For example, they learn to acknowledge each other's points and to express agreement with each other. This distinctive communication style seems to continue even into adulthood (e.g., Carli, 1989).

A culture in which people are expected to express agreement, show support, and protect other people's feelings, however, poses a difficult dilemma to its members. What are they to do when in fact they do not agree that the other person is blameless, when they are not having a good time at her party, or when they do not like her muffins? They can try to tell the truth tactfully, or they can try to tell a small truth that covers a bigger lie (e.g., they might say that the muffins sure look pretty). These strategies are risky, however. The truth that was meant to be tactful might feel hurtful to the target, and the target might wonder why a person with a mouthful of muffin and bite marks in what is left is commenting on how pretty the muffin looks.

We suspect that when women find themselves in dilemmas like these, they do not make much of an effort to come up with tactful and truthful alternatives to their lies. Our guess is that to them, it is not so much a dilemma as a question of values, and with regard to topics such as parties, muffins, and even controversial issues, other people's feelings matter more to them than the truth. Our suggestion is not that women lie to spare other people's feelings more than men do, because sometimes they do not; they mostly lie only to spare other women's feelings.

There was one other way in which the kinds of lies that women told to each other differed from the kinds of lies told when men were involved. In the women-only dyads, lies were disproportionately about people. It the community study, lies were about the target, and in the college student study, they were about people other than the liar or target. We already know from previous research that relative to men, women spend more of their time socializing with people (Reis, 1986), thinking about people (McAdams & Constantian, 1983), and perhaps also reminiscing about people (Ross & Holmberg, 1990). We can now add to that profile the finding that women—when they are with other women—also are more inclined to tell lies about people.

If we are to take most seriously those results that were in the same direction and statistically significant (or nearly so) in both studies, then the data seem to be telling us that to understand the psychology of lying in everyday life, it will be more useful to look to the sex composition of the dyads, or even the sex of the targets of the lies, than to look to the sex of the participants (see also Deaux, 1984). Two effects of the sex of the targets of the lies are especially noteworthy. First, in both studies, participants told relatively more self-centered lies and relatively fewer other-oriented lies to men than to women. Part of this effect is the dyad effect just described; that is, the percentage of self-centered lies is lower, and the percentage of other-oriented lies is higher, in the dyads with only women than in any of the other three dyad types. However, the target sex effect also occurs. That is, although men do not tell as many other-oriented lies to women as other women do, or as few self-centered ones, they do tell relatively more other-oriented lies and relatively fewer self-centered lies to women than they do to men.

There was one other way in which both men and women claimed to be trying to protect women with their lies. In both studies, participants said that the women to whom they told their lies, more so than the men, would have felt even worse if the truth had been told instead. In their inclinations to tell relatively more self-centered lies to men, and relatively more other-oriented and protective lies to women, participants seemed to be using their lies to impress men and to shield and reassure women.

Different Samples, Similar Results

Because the goals of our research included the collection of basic descriptive data about lying, we considered it important not to limit our participants to college students. Our aim in recruiting community members was not to find a representative community sample but to recruit a different and more diverse group of people than our college student group. If we could replicate our findings across two highly dissimilar groups, then we would feel much more confident about their generalizability. Many of the community members were married, had children, and were employed; a substantial percentage of them had no more than a high school education. In these ways, they were much different from the college students.

The results from the two groups were in many ways strikingly similar. Consistent with our theoretical perspective, lying in both groups was an everyday event. Also, both the college students and the community members described their everyday lies as causing them little preoccupation or regret. The relative frequencies of the many different kinds of lies were reassuringly similar across the two groups too. We were, however, intrigued by the fact that by every measure of rate of lying, the community members seemed to lie less often than the college students. Because the community members differed in many unsystematic ways from the college students, it is not appropriate to interpret these differences at this point. However, the data do point to the potential value of longitudinal studies of lying in everyday life (cf. Reis, Lin, Bennett, & Nezlek, 1993).

Not All Lies Are Little

Our conclusions about lying are limited to the lies of everyday life, which are mostly little lies. Serious lies, which are often deep breaches of trust, occur too, but they are far less common. They are not a fact of everyday social life. To learn about them requires a different methodology. The results of the study of serious lies will be vastly different from the ones reported here. For example, serious lies are often of great cognitive and emotional significance, and the mark they leave on the lives of the liars and the targets is more than just a smudge (DePaulo, Ansfield, Kirkendol, & Boden, 1996). A complete psychology of lying must include the study of both little and big lies.

Our conclusions also are importantly qualified by the fact that we queried only the liars. The people to whom these lies were told may have a different point of view about just how little or inconsequential these lies really are or how grateful they feel for the "protection" when others lie to spare their feelings (cf. Bok, 1978). However, as empiricists, we should not presume, in the absence of data, that the targets' perspectives will necessarily be harsher than those of the liars. Many people may prefer not to hear that their muffins are grainy or that they look like a blimp; they may prefer kind lies not only to unkind truths but even to noncommittal silences. That is for them to say.

Finally, our data do not address the question of the cumulative impact that even little lies might have over time. Once again, however, we issue the empiricists' caution not to presume the outcome of such an investigation. Those who consistently say what they think others want to hear, even when they do not really believe those things themselves, may be seen as liars, politicians, or valued colleagues and friends. That is for us to find out.

References

Bakan, D. (1966). The duality of human existence: An essay on psychology and religion. Chicago: Rand McNally.

Bok, S. (1978). Lying: Moral choice in public and private life. New York: Vintage Books.

Brown, P., & Levinson, S. C. (1987). Politeness: Some universals in language usage. Cambridge, England: Cambridge University Press.

Bryk, A. S., & Raudenbush, S. W. (1992). Hierarchical linear models: Applications and data analysis methods. Newbury Park, CA: Sage.

Camden, C., Motley, M. T. & Wilson, A. (1984). White lies in interpersonal communication: A taxonomy and preliminary investigation of social motivations. *Western Journal of Speech Communication*, 48, 309-325.

Carli, L. L. (1989). Gender differences in interaction style and influence. *Journal of Personality and Social Psychology*, 56, 565-576.

Cicchetti, D. V. & Sparrow, S. A. (1981). Developing criteria for establishing interrater reliability of specific items: Applications to the assessment of adaptive behavior. *American Journal of Mental Deficiency, 86,* 127-137.

Cole, P. M. (1986). Children's spontaneous control of facial expression. *Child Development, 57,* 1309-1321.

Deaux, K. (1984). From individual differences to social categories: An analysis of a decade's research on gender. *American Psychologist, 39,* 105-116.

DePaulo, B. M. (1992). Nonverbal behavior and self-presentation. *Psychological Bulletin, 111,* 203-243.

DePaulo, B. M., Ansfield, M. E., Kirkendol, S. E., & Boden, J. M. (1996). Serious lies: First person accounts. Manuscript in preparation.

DePaulo, B. M., & Bell, K. L. (1993). Lying kindly. Unpublished manuscript.

DePaulo, B. M., Epstein, J. A., & Wyer, M. M. (1993). Sex differences in lying: How women and men deal with the dilemma of deceit. In M. Lewis & C. Saarni (Eds.), Lying and deception in everyday life (pp. 126–147). New York: Guilford Press.

DePaulo, B. M., & Jordan, A. (1982). Age changes in deceiving and detecting deceit. In R. S. Feldman (Ed.), Development of nonverbal behavior in children (pp. 151–180). New York: Springer-Verlag.

DePaulo, B. M., Stone, J. I., & Lassiter, G. D. (1985). Deceiving and detecting deceit. In B. R. Schlenker (Ed.), The self and social life (pp. 323–370). New York: McGraw-Hill.

deVilliers, J. G., & deVilliers, P. A. (1978). Language acquisition. Cambridge, MA: Harvard University Press.

Dindia, K. & Allen, M. (1992). Sex differences in self-disclosure: A meta-analysis. *Psychological Bulletin, 112,* 106-124.

Eagly, A. H. (1987). Sex differences in social behavior: A social role interpretation. Hillsdale, NJ: Erlbaum.

Ford, C. V., King, B. H. & Hollender, M. H. (1988). Liars and lies: Psychiatric aspects of prevarication. American Journal of Psychiatry, 145, 554-562.

Goffman, E. (1959). The presentation of self in everyday life. Garden City, NY: Doubleday/Anchor Books.

Hall, J. A. (1984). Nonverbal sex differences: Communication accuracy and expressive style. Baltimore: Johns Hopkins University Press.

Hample, D. (1980). Purposes and effects of lying. *Southern Speech Communication Journal, 46,* 33-47.

Kashy, D. A. (1991). Levels of analysis of social interaction diaries: Separating the effects of person, partner, day, and interaction. Doctoral dissertation, University of Connecticut, Storrs, CT.

Kashy, D. A. & DePaulo, B. M. (1996). Who lies. *Journal of Personality and Social Psychology, 70,* 1037-1051.

Kenny, D. A., Kashy, D. A., & Bolger, N. (in press). Data analysis in social psychology. In D. T. Gilbert , S. T. Fiske , G. Lindzey (Eds.), The handbook of social psychology. (4th ed.). New York: McGraw-Hill.

Leary, M. R., Nezlek, J. B., Downs, D., Radford-Davenport, J., Martin, J. & McMullen, A. (1994). Self-presentation in everyday interactions: Effects of target familiarity and gender composition. *Journal of Personality and Social Psychology, 67,* 664-673.

Lewis, M., & Saarni, C. (Eds.). (1993). Lying and deception in everyday life. New York: Guilford Press.

Lippard, P. V. (1988). "Ask me no questions, I'll tell you no lies": Situational exigencies for interpersonal deception. *Western Journal of Speech Communication, 52,* 91-103.

Maccoby, E. E. (1990). Gender and relationships: A developmental account. *American Psychologist, 45,* 513-520.

Maltz, D. N., & Borker, R. A. (1982). A cultural approach to male-female miscommunication. In J. J. Gumperz (Ed.), Language and social identity (pp. 196–216). Cambridge, England: Cambridge University Press.

McAdams, D. P. & Constantian, C. A. (1983). Intimacy and affiliation motives in daily living: An experience sampling analysis. *Journal of Personality and Social Psychology, 45,* 851-861.

Metts, S. (1989). An exploratory investigation of deception in close relationships. *Journal of Social and Personal Relationships, 6,* 159-179.

Moskowitz, D. S. (1993). Dominance and friendliness: On the interaction of gender and situation. *Journal of Personality, 61,* 387-409.

Moskowitz, D. S., Suh, E. J. & Desaulniers, J. (1994). Situational influences on gender differences in agency and communion. *Journal of Personality and Social Psychology, 66,* 753-761.

Nyberg, D. (1993). The varnished truth. Chicago: University of Chicago Press.

Reis, H. T. (1986). Gender effects in social participation: Intimacy, loneliness, and the conduct of social interaction. In R. Gilmour & S. Duck (Eds.), The emerging field of personal relationships (pp. 91–105). Hillsdale, NJ: Erlbaum.

Reis, H. T. (in press). The interpersonal context of emotions: Gender differences in intimacy and emotional support. In D. Canary & K. Dindia (Eds.), Sex differences /similarities in communication. Hillsdale, NJ: Erlbaum.

Reis, H. T., Lin, Y.-C., Bennett, M. E. & Nezlek, J. B. (1993). Change and consistency in social participation during early adulthood. *Developmental Psychology, 29,* 633-645.

Reis, H. T. & Wheeler, L. (1991). Studying social interaction with the Rochester Interaction Record. *Advances in Experimental Social Psychology, 24,* 269-318.

Ross, M. & Holmberg, D. (1990). Recounting the past: Gender effects in the recall of events in the history of a close relationship. *Self-inference processes: The Ontario Symposium,* Vol. 6, 135-152.

Saarni, C. (1984). An observational study of children's attempts to monitor their expressive behavior. *Child Development, 55,* 1504-1513.

Schlenker, B. R., & Weigold, M. F. (1989). Goals and the self-identification process: Constructing desired identities. In L. A. Pervin (Ed.), Goal concepts in personality and social psychology (pp. 243–290). Hillsdale, NJ: Erlbaum.

Stouthamer-Loeber, M. (1986). Lying as a problem behavior in children: A review. *Clinical Psychology Review, 6,* 267-289.

Taylor, S. E. (1989). Positive illusions. New York: Basic Books.

Tennen, H., Suls, J. & Affleck, G. (1991). Personality and daily experience. *Journal of Personality, 59,* 3.

Turner, R. E., Edgley, C. & Olmstead, G. (1975). Information control in conversations: Honesty is not always the best policy. *Kansas Journal of Sociology, 11,* 69-89.

Wheeler, L. & Nezlek, J. B. (1977). Sex differences in social participation. *Journal of Personality and Social Psychology, 35,* 742-754.

Footnotes

1. In Camden, Motley, and Wilson's (1984) study, 20 college students recorded "white lies" for a 2-week period; they were asked to describe no more than 20 lies. In Lippard's (1988) study, 74 college students recorded all instances of deception for a 3-week period. There also are several studies in which participants were allowed to choose a lie (Hample, 1980) or a conversation (Turner, Edgley, & Olmstead, 1975) or a situation (Metts, 1989) to describe. We cannot know from these studies how the results may have been biased by the particular examples that participants chose to discuss.

2. A more complete description of the development of the taxonomy, and additional examples of all of the kinds of lies, are available from Bella M. DePaulo.

3. To determine whether the lies that were told to just one person differed in kind from the lies that were told to more than one person, we computed two values for each participant. First, for only dyadic interactions, the number of lies falling into a particular category (i.e., lies about feelings, explanations, outright lies, etc.) divided by the total number of lies told in dyadic interactions was calculated. A similar value for only those interactions involving multiple partners also was computed. These values then were entered into paired t tests contrasting the dyadic lies with the multiple-partner lies. For the undergraduate sample, only one significant difference emerged, indicating that lies referring to the target were more common in dyadic interactions than in multiple partner interactions, $t(64) = 2.71$, $p < .01$. The mean percentage for dyadic lies was 25.99%, and for multiple partner lies it was 17.80%. None of the other tests approached statistical significance ($p > .10$). For the community sample, there also was a significant difference in the same direction between dyadic and nondyadic interactions in the percentage of lies that referred to the target, $t(41) = 2.06$, $p = .05$ (M s = 27.31 and 18.97 for dyadic and multiple, respectively). Significant differences for lies referring to another person, $t(41) = 3.07$, $p < .01$, and to objects and events, $t(41) = 2.05$, $p = .05$, also emerged for the community sample, such that people told lies referring to other people more often in dyadic interactions ($M = 29.04$) than in nondyadic interactions ($M = 13.29$), whereas they told lies about objects and events less often in dyadic ($M = 45.98$) than in nondyadic interactions ($M = 54.92$).

4. We did not use participants as units because those who told no lies of a given kind would have been omitted from correlations involving that kind of lie, even though nonoccurrence of a kind of lie is relevant data.

5. To determine whether the characteristics of the lies that were told to just one person differed from the characteristics of the lies that were told to more than one person, we computed for each participant in each study two means for each characteristic, one for only dyadic lies and one for lies told to multiple targets. We then computed correlated t tests on these pairs of means. Only two effects were significant. In Study 1, participants said that they were trying to protect themselves more with their dyadic lies (M s = 5.57 and 5.23 for dyadic and multiple, respectively), $t(64) = 2.67$, $p = .01$. In Study 2, participants said they felt more distress before telling their dyadic lies (M s = 4.79 and 4.49 for dyadic and multiple, respectively), $t(41) = 2.00$, $p = .05$.

6. We did not use the multilevel approach to analyze the kinds of lies for two reasons. First, the outcome measures were categorical instead of continuous. Second, the multilevel approach would have dropped from the analyses data from participants who told no lies of a given kind.

Journal of Personality and Social Psychology, May 1996, Vol. 70, No. 5, p 1037-1051

Who Lies?

Deborah A. Kashy, Bella M. DePaulo

Abstract

Seventy-seven undergraduates and 70 demographically diverse members of the community completed 12 individual-differences measures hypothesized to predict lie-telling in everyday life and then kept a diary every day for a week of all of their social interactions and all of the lies that they told during those interactions. Consistent with predictions, the people who told more lies were more manipulative, more concerned with self-presentation, and more sociable. People who told fewer lies were more highly socialized and reported higher quality same-sex relationships. Manipulative people, less highly socialized people, and people with less gratifying same-sex relationships also told especially more self-serving lies, whereas people with higher quality same-sex relationships told relatively more other-oriented lies.

In a pair of diary studies of lying in everyday life, DePaulo, Kashy, Kirkendol, Wyer, and Epstein (1996) noted that, over the course of a week, people reported telling anywhere from 0 to 46 lies. Who were those people who told dozens of lies in their day-to-day lives? Did they differ from those who told hardly any lies at all? Is there a lie-telling personality type?

Studies of personality and lying have come in several varieties. For example, there are numerous studies in which people were instructed or induced to lie and to tell the truth, and their success at fooling others with their verbal and nonverbal cues was assessed (e.g., DePaulo, Blank, Swaim, & Hairfield, 1992; DePaulo & Rosenthal, 1979; Keating & Heltman, 1994; Riggio & Friedman, 1983). This literature has much to say about the kinds of people who can succeed at lying when asked to try, but it is silent on the perhaps more interesting question about the kinds of people who repeatedly take it upon themselves to tell lies. Another approach to the study of personality and lying is to design a situation that tempts people to lie and then observe whether personality predicts who actually does lie (e.g., Exline, Thibaut, Hickey, & Gumpert, 1970). Most of those studies have been imaginative, but the light that they shine is a focused beam that illuminates only the specific kinds of situations that have been modeled. To learn whether there are personality predictors of lie-telling in the broad domain of everyday life requires a very different methodology. A daily diary methodology, in which people record all of their social interactions and all of the lies that they tell during those interactions, seems particularly well suited to the task.

Scholars of many stripes, including sociologists (e.g., Barnes, 1994), psychologists (e.g., Saarni & Lewis, 1993), and philosophers (e.g., Nyberg, 1993), have commented on the harsh view of lying that seems prevalent in Western society. Solomon (1993), for example, noted that "throughout the history of philosophy, deception has been assumed to be a vice, honesty a virtue. ... [This] philosophical championing of honesty is an accurate reflection of popular morality. Lying, for philosophers and laymen alike, is wrong" (pp. 31–32). Our own perspective on lying is akin to that of Nyberg (1993), who argued that lying is "publicly condemned" at the same time that it is "privately practiced by almost everybody" (p. 7). On the basis of the literatures on identity and impression management from sociology (e.g., Goffman, 1959), linguistics (e.g., Brown & Levinson, 1987), and social psychology (e.g., Schlenker & Weigold, 1989), as well as our own previous research (DePaulo et al., 1996), we believe that lying is an everyday social interaction process. Lying is a fact of social life rather than an extraordinary or unusual event. People tell lies to accomplish the most basic social interaction goals, such as influencing others, managing impressions, and providing reassurance and support. Each of these goals, when valued deeply, provides a motivation for lying.

In the present research, we examined six individual-differences dimensions that we expected to be especially important predictors of lying in everyday life. We hypothesized that high rates of lying would be characteristic of people who are manipulative, concerned with the impressions they make on other people, insecure, and sociable and that low rates would be characteristic of those who are highly socialized and whose interpersonal relationships are especially satisfying. We also thought that personality would predict the kinds of lies that people tell. For example, although we believed that people with satisfying interpersonal relationships would tell fewer lies overall, we also thought that when they did lie, relatively more of their lies would be altruistic or other oriented (lies that served to protect or benefit other persons) and fewer would be selfish or self-centered (lies that served to protect or benefit the liar).

Manipulativeness

Lying can be used instrumentally to achieve social interaction goals such as winning friends and influencing people. This manipulative use of lying is at the heart of the personality construct of Machiavellianism. People high in Machiavellianism view others cynically, show little concern for conventional morality, and openly admit that they will lie, cheat, and manipulate others to get what they want (Christie & Geis, 1970; Falbo, 1977). Interpersonally, they are scheming but not stupid. They do not exploit others when their victims might retaliate (Christie & Geis, 1970), and they do not cheat when they are likely to get caught (Bogart, Geis, Levy, & Zimbardo, 1970). In interview situations, it is clear that those high in Machiavellianism are ambitious and dominating, but they also seem relaxed, talented, and confident (Cherulnik, Way, Ames, & Hutto, 1981). In competitive situations, they walk away with far more than their fair share of the spoils (Christie & Geis, 1970), yet they are liked more than people low in Machiavellianism (Cherulnik et al., 1981) and are preferred as partners (Christie & Geis, 1970).

A related construct called "social adroitness" (Jackson, 1976, 1978) captures the interpersonal aspects of manipulativeness more purely (apart from the intrapersonal aspects such as cynical attitudes) and more subtly and with less jarringly negative connotations. We predicted that people high in manipulativeness would tell more lies overall than low scorers—and especially more self-serving lies—but that they would not tell any fewer altruistic lies. Manipulative people tend to be aware of their own manipulations, and so we also predicted that at the end of the study, when we asked them to compare their lie-telling with other people's, they would report that they lie more often and more successfully than others.

Impression Management

From our perspective on lying as a fact of social life, perhaps the most important individual-differences predictor of lie-telling is a concern with the impressions of oneself that are being conveyed to other people. Two personality constructs—public self-consciousness (Fenigstein, Scheier, & Buss, 1975) and other-directedness (Briggs, Cheek, & Buss, 1980), seem to capture especially well a persistent attention to other people and what they think, as well as a high level of

46

motivation to make a good impression. In contrast to manipulative people who try to mold others to suit their own agendas, people who are publicly self-conscious and other directed try to mold themselves to suit others (Ickes, Reidhead, & Patterson, 1986). We think that one of the ways they do this is by lying. To seem to be the kind of person whom others might like, these people claim to be the kind of person they are not. The "other" orientation of people who are publicly self-conscious and other directed is not an altruistic concern about the needs and desires of other people but, rather, a self-interested concern with the kinds of self-presentations that others might find endearing. Therefore, we predicted that these people would tell more lies overall, and perhaps more lies to benefit themselves, but not more to benefit others. The direction of these predictions is the same as for manipulativeness, but the presumed motivational basis is different (Ickes et al., 1986).

Self-Confidence

People who tell self-centered lies are often trying to appear different than they think they really are (DePaulo et al., 1996). For example, people lie to seem kinder, wiser, more talented, more motivated, and even more moral than they are in fact (cf. Buss & Briggs, 1984). These kinds of self-centered lies may well be spoken by those who cannot accept themselves as they are. They are lies born of insecurity. We think that insecurity also predicts the telling of altruistic lies. When people tell other-oriented lies, they are often claiming to like other people, to agree with them, to approve of their actions, and to appreciate their tastes and their talents more than they actually do (DePaulo et al., 1996). It takes self-confidence to say what you really feel when that is not what the other person wants to hear. This is exactly what people low in self-esteem and high in social anxiety lack. Our prediction, then, was that people low in social self-esteem and high in social anxiety would tell more lies overall, including more self-centered lies as well as more other-oriented lies.

Socialization

If scholars are correct in suggesting that there is widespread public condemnation of lying in Western society, then people who have more strongly internalized that cultural worldview (i.e., those who are more highly socialized) are likely to tell fewer lies overall, and especially fewer lies to benefit themselves, than people who are less highly socialized. Because honesty and integrity are self-definitional to people who most strongly embrace the prevailing cultural wisdom, such people not only may tell fewer lies than others but may realize that they do. To assess individual differences in this domain, we used Jackson's (1976, 1978) Responsibility scale, which was "explicitly designed to measure persons along a dimension of degree of socialization" (Jackson, 1978, p. 73).

A construct related to socialization is social desirability (Crowne & Marlowe, 1960, 1964). Persons higher in social desirability claim unusual virtues (e.g., "I'm always willing to admit it when I make a mistake") and disclaim commonplace shortcomings (e.g., "I like to gossip at times"), and there is some evidence that they actually do possess more of certain qualities deemed desirable in Western culture (McCrae & Costa, 1983). For that reason, such people should tell fewer lies overall and especially fewer selfish lies. However, in addition to the kernel of truth, social desirability includes two kernels of deception (Paulhus, 1991). One is self-deception: Those higher in social desirability believe themselves to be more virtuous than they are in fact (Millham & Jacobson, 1978). The second is "other" deception: Those higher in social desirability describe themselves as more virtuous than they actually believe themselves to be. The latter component is the idea of social desirability as response set. In the present research, a negative correlation between social desirability and rate of lying could be supportive of our substantive prediction that highly socialized people tell fewer lies, but it could also suggest the possibility that people's reports of their lies are not entirely veridical but are determined at least in part by social desirability concerns.

Sociability

Our perspective on lie-telling as a fact of social life generates the prediction that people who are more drawn to social life are also more inclined to tell lies. This is not simply an artifactual prediction that people who have more opportunities to lie (because they socialize more) will tell more lies, because the measure of lie-telling that we use in our research is rate of lying, that is, the number of lies that people tell, controlling for the number of opportunities they have to tell lies (i.e., the number of social interactions that they report). The social interaction purposes that lying serves—such as making oneself look better and making other people feel better—may be especially appealing to people who are highly sociable. Sociability might predict lying for another reason, too. As people participate in the process of social interaction, including the process of telling lies, lie-telling is likely to become easier, more successful, and more habitual. Sociable people may come to lie more and to notice their lying less. Our prediction is that extraverts and people who are high in social participation will tell more lies than introverts or people low in social participation. When prodded to attend to their lie-telling behavior (as when, in the present research, recording their lies in journals), they will be surprised to discover just how many lies they tell.

Relationship Quality

Although lying and socializing might coexist amicably, lying and relating to others intimately and meaningfully probably do not. People who present themselves inauthentically are unlikely to experience their social interactions as intimate or meaningful. Our nomothetic data are supportive of this prediction. Both college students and people from the community described the interactions during which they lied as less intimate and less pleasant than the interactions during which they told only the truth (DePaulo et al., 1996). In the present study, we predicted that our idiographic results would be consistent with our nomothetic ones. That is, people who characteristically experience their relationships as especially meaningful should also report telling fewer lies. Self-serving lies should be particularly incompatible with intimacy in relationships; therefore, we also predicted that people with especially meaningful relationships would tell especially fewer self-centered lies. However, the kinds of lies that are told to protect other people's feelings and to bolster their self-images may be entirely compatible with intimacy. Therefore, people with gratifying interpersonal relationships may tell relatively more altruistic lies.

To test our predictions, we conducted two studies with two very different samples of participants: college students and a more demographically diverse group of people from the community. Participants completed the 12 individual-differences measures hypothesized to predict lying and then kept diaries every day for a week of all of their social interactions and all of the lies that they told during those interactions.

Method

Participants

Participants in Study 1 were 30 male and 47 female undergraduates who participated in partial fulfillment of a requirement for an introductory psychology course. They ranged in age from 17 to 22 years (M = 18.69, SD = 0.91). Sixty-four were White, 9 were Black, and 4 described themselves as "other" than White or Black. Participants in Study 2 were 30 men and 40 women who were recruited via advertisements posted at a local community college, from lists of people who had taken continuing education courses, and from lists of names selected randomly from the area telephone directory. They ranged in age from 18 to 71 years ($M = 34.19$, $SD = 12.49$). Sixty-seven were White and 3 were Black. Other demographic information is based on 53 of the 70 participants (17 were inadvertently given the undergraduate demographic questionnaire, which did not include questions about employment, education, marital status, or children). Of those who did answer the more extended questionnaire, 81% were employed, 57% were married, 47% had children, and 34% had no more than a high school education.

Procedure

There were three phases to the study: an initial introductory session, the 7-day recording period, and a final phase during which participants answered additional questions about their lies and their experiences in the study.

Phase 1: Introduction to the study

The Study 1 participants and the participants from Study 2 who were recruited from the community college initially responded to notices describing the research that were posted on a bulletin board in an academic building. The study was described as one in which they would keep records of their social interactions and communications for 7 days. In Study 1, the notice indicated that participants would receive partial course credit for their participation, and, in Study 2, the notice indicated that participants would be paid $35. Study 2 participants recruited from continuing education lists or from the phone directory were sent letters with the same description of the research, and then they were contacted by telephone about a week later.

All participants attended an initial 90-min meeting, conducted by one or more members of the research team, in which the study and the procedures were explained. In Study 1, these were group sessions attended by 10–15 participants at a time. The Study 2 sessions were conducted individually or in small groups. When participants arrived for this session, they spent the first 20 min answering the personality and demographic questionnaires. The study was then explained in full. Anyone who needed more time to complete the individual-differences measures did so at the end of the session.

Participants were told that they would be recording all of their social interactions and all of the lies that they told during those interactions every day for a week. It was noted that their role in this research was especially important in that they would be the observers and recorders of their own behavior. The investigators explained that they did not condone or condemn lying; rather, they were studying it scientifically and trying to learn the answers to some of the most fundamental questions about the phenomenon. They encouraged the participants to think of the study as an unusual opportunity to learn more about themselves.

The key terms were then explained to the participants. A social interaction was defined as "any exchange between you and another person that lasts 10 minutes or more ... in which the behavior of one person is in response to the behavior of another person." This definition, plus many of the examples used to clarify the definition, was taken or adapted from that used in the initial studies involving the Rochester Interaction Record (RIR; e.g., Wheeler & Nezlek, 1977). We did add an exception to the 10-min rule: For any interaction in which participants told a lie, they were to fill out a social interaction record, even if the interaction lasted less than 10 min. Copies of our adaptation of the RIR (see subsequent description) were then distributed, and participants were told how to fill out the form.

To explain what participants should count as a lie, it was noted that "a lie occurs any time you intentionally try to mislead someone. Both the intent to deceive and the actual deception must occur." More than a dozen examples of lies were given, including examples of kind and unkind lies and lies motivated by many different types of concerns. Participants were urged to record all lies, no matter how big or how small. They were instructed that if they were uncertain as to whether a particular communication qualified as a lie, they should record it. (At the end of the study, two of the investigators independently read through all of the lie diaries and agreed on the few that did not meet the definition and were therefore excluded.) The definition that we gave participants was interpreted broadly as encompassing any intentional attempts to mislead, including even nonverbal ones. The only example of a lie they were asked not to record was saying "fine" in response to perfunctory "How are you?" questions. Participants completed one deception record for every lie that they told. Sample records (see subsequent description) were distributed, and the investigators explained how to fill them out.

Participants were instructed to fill out the forms (social interaction records and deception records) at least once a day; it was suggested that they set aside a particular time or set of times to do so. The forms were then collected by the experimenters at several different times throughout the week. Participants were also given pocket-sized notebooks and urged to carry them at all times. They were encouraged to use these notebooks to write down reminders of their social interactions and their lies as soon as possible after the events had taken place. Then they could use their notes as an aid to their memory if they did not complete their social interaction and deception records until later in the day. The notebooks were not collected.

Several additional steps were taken to encourage the reporting of all lies. First, participants were told that if they did not wish to reveal the contents of any of the lies that they told, then in the space on the deception record in which they were to describe their lie, they could instead write "rather not say." That way, we as investigators would still know that a lie was told, and we would know other information about the lie and the social interaction in which it was told (from the other parts of the records that the participants completed). Participants declined to describe only 1% of their lies in the college sample and none of their lies in the community sample. Second, we instructed participants that if they did not completely remember everything about a lie that they told, they should still fill out as much of the information on the form as they could. Third, we told participants that if they remembered a lie from a previous day that they had not recorded, they should still turn in a form for that lie.

The importance of accuracy and conscientiousness in keeping the records was emphasized throughout the session. As a means of ensuring anonymity, participants chose their own identification number to be used throughout the study. Participants did not write their names on any of the forms.

At the end of the session, the investigators reviewed the amount of time it would take to complete all phases of the study and encouraged participants to terminate their participation at that point if they no longer had the interest or the time to participate fully. They were offered credit or payment even if they chose not to continue. All participants elected to continue.

Before they left, participants were given typed copies of all of the instructions and definitions they had been given during the session. This instruction booklet also included names and phone numbers of members of the research team with whom they had met and whom they could contact at any time with any questions or concerns they might have. Appointments were also made with all of the Study 1 participants to return once more at the end of the 7-day recording period to complete a final set of measures. Study 2 participants were shown an envelope and instructions that would be mailed to them at the end of the study so that they could complete the same measures.

Phase 2: Recording social interactions and lies

During the 7-day recording period that began the day after the introductory session, participants completed a social interaction record for all of their social interactions and a deception record for all of their lies. The social interaction record was adapted from the RIR (Wheeler & Nezlek, 1977). On each record, participants identified themselves and their partners, estimated the length of the interaction, and rated the interaction on measures of intimacy, quality, influence, and modality. (These social interaction variables are not relevant to the present article and are not discussed further.)

Printed on the same page as the social interaction record was the deception record. Participants indicated the initials and gender of the (s) to whom they told their lie (if there were three targets of the lie or fewer) or the number of men and number of women (if there were more than three targets). Below this was a blank space for participants to "briefly describe the lie" and another blank space for them to "briefly describe the reason why you told the lie." Next were nine 9-point rating scales. Participants rated their degree of planning of the lie on a scale with endpoints labeled completely spontaneous (1) and carefully planned in advance (9). Then they indicated the importance of not getting caught on a scale ranging from very unimportant (1) to very important (9). On the next three scales, they reported their feelings before the lie was told, while telling the lie, and after the lie was told; these scales ranged from very comfortable (1) to very uncomfortable (9). They also rated the seriousness of the lie, on a scale ranging from very trivial, unimportant lie (1) to very serious, important lie (9), and the target's reaction to the lie, on a scale ranging from didn't believe me at all (1) to believed me completely (9). Finally, they answered two questions—"How would the target have felt if you told the truth instead of the lie?" and "How would you have felt if you told the truth instead of a lie?"—on scales with endpoints labeled much better if I told the truth (1) and much worse if I told the truth (9).

Phase 3: Additional measures

After the completion of the 7-day recording period, participants were asked to respond to one more set of measures. Participants were given photocopies of each of the deception records they had completed. They answered two questions about each lie: "Was this lie ever discovered?" (participants checked one answer: no, not yet, don't know, or yes) and "If you could relive this social interaction, would you tell the lie again?" (participants checked either no or yes).

Next, participants completed a postquestionnaire assessing their experiences in the study. On 9-point scales, they indicated how successful they thought they were at lying (i.e., at not getting caught and arousing no suspicion) and how frequently they thought they had lied relative to what they had expected and relative to other people their age. They also answered several questions assessing their accuracy and diligence in completing the forms (described in DePaulo et al., 1996).

The Study 1 participants returned to the lab to complete these forms. Afterward, they were interviewed by one of the investigators. They were encouraged to ask any questions or voice any concerns and were told once again that their data would be treated confidentially. As part of this debriefing, they were informed that the goals of the research were exactly as described to them during the first session. The investigators tried to determine the extent to which the participants had understood and complied with the procedure and believed the information they had been given about the research. This extensive interview uncovered no problems with the procedure. Therefore, in Study 2, all of the forms from this phase of the study were mailed to the participants, and a written debrief (plus payment) was included in the package. Participants returned the materials in an addressed and stamped envelope that was also included in the package.

Personality Measures

Of the 12 personality measures, 4 were subscales of the Jackson Personality Inventory (JPI; Jackson, 1976, 1978), 2 were subscales of the Self-Consciousness Scale (Fenigstein et al., 1975), 2 were subscales of the Self-Monitoring Scale (Briggs et al., 1980; Snyder, 1974), 2 were subscales of a relationship quality measure (Rosenthal, Hall, DiMatteo, Rogers, & Archer, 1979), and the other 2 were separately developed measures (Christie & Geis, 1970; Crowne & Marlowe, 1960).

The four JPI subscales—Social Adroitness, Self-Esteem, Responsibility, and Social Participation—are all 20-item measures with a true–false format. Because the JPI has been less widely used than most of the other measures, we describe the validity data (later) in somewhat more detail. The subscales of the Self-Consciousness Scale—Public Self-Consciousness (7 items) and Social Anxiety (6 items) —have 5-point rating scales ranging from not at all characteristic (0) to extremely characteristic (4). The subscales of the Self-Monitoring Scale were Other-Directedness (11 items) and Extraversion (6 items). In the original Self-Monitoring Scale (Snyder, 1974) and in our research, a true–false format was used; Briggs et al. (1980) used a 5-point scale. The relationship quality subscales—Same-Sex Quality and Opposite-Sex Quality—are 7-item measures answered on 9-point scales.

Participants completed several other measures that were embedded in the preceding measures (e.g., the Acting subscale of the Self-Monitoring Scale and the Private Self-Consciousness subscale of the Self-Consciousness Scale). However, because we had no theoretical bases for formulating predictions about these measures, they were not included in our analyses.

Manipulativeness

The two measures of manipulativeness were the Machiavellianism scale (Christie & Geis, 1970) and the Social Adroitness subscale of the JPI (Jackson, 1976, 1978). The Machiavellianism scale is a 14-item measure with items typically answered on a 6-point scale ranging from disagree strongly (−3) to agree strongly (3). (Because of an error, participants in our studies reported their responses using a true–false format.) The scale was designed to measure an admitted willingness to use manipulative strategies such as lying and ingratiation, a cynical perspective on human nature, and a lack of concern with conventional morality. Items include "Never tell anyone the real reason you did something unless it is useful to do so" and "Anyone who completely trusts anyone else is asking for trouble."

The Social Adroitness scale was designed to capture some of the same interpersonal skill and style of Machiavellianism without the negative connotations. Jackson (1976) described the high scorer as "skillful at persuading others to achieve a particular goal, sometimes by indirect means; occasionally may be seen as manipulative of others, but is ordinarily diplomatic" (p. 10). Examples include "I enjoy trying to get people to do things without letting them know I'm doing it" and "I feel that I have a knack for getting the most out of people." High scorers rate themselves as diplomatic (instead of blunt) and ambitious, and their peers also rate them as ambitious.

Impression management

The two measures of concern with self-presentation were the Public Self-Consciousness subscale of the Self-Consciousness Scale (Fenigstein et al., 1975) and the Other-Directedness subscale of the Self-Monitoring Scale. People who are publicly self-conscious are chronically aware of themselves as social objects. They are concerned about their appearance and the kinds of impressions they convey to other people. Items include "I usually worry about making a good impression" and "One of the last things I do before leaving the house is look in the mirror."

People who score high on the Other-Directedness subscale are also very aware of themselves as social objects, and they tend to look to others for cues to appropriate behavior. Scale items include "Even if I am not enjoying myself, I often pretend to be having a good time" and "In order to get along and be liked, I tend to be what people expect me to be rather than anything else."

Social self-confidence

The two measures of social self-assurance were the Self-Esteem subscale of the JPI and the Social Anxiety subscale of the Self-Consciousness Scale. The Self-Esteem scale was constructed to capture the social and interpersonal aspects of self-esteem. Items include "People seem to be interested in getting to know me better" and "I have never been a very popular person" (reversed). In a multitrait–multimethod analysis of measures of global and social self-esteem (Van Tuinen & Ramanaiah, 1979), the JPI Self-Esteem measure correlated most highly with other measures of social self-esteem, such as the revised Janis–Field Feelings of Inadequacy Scale (Eagly, 1967; Janis & Field, 1959), and positively but less strongly with measures of global self-esteem such as the Coopersmith Self-Esteem Inventory (Coopersmith, 1967).

The Social Anxiety scale measures discomfort in social situations, including embarrassment, stage fright, and shyness. Items include "I don't find it hard to talk to strangers" (reversed) and "I get embarrassed very easily." The measure correlates highly with another carefully validated measure of social anxiety, the Interaction Anxiousness Scale (Leary, 1983, 1991).

Socialization

The two measures of socialization were the Marlowe-Crowne Social Desirability Scale (MCSD) and the Responsibility subscale of the JPI. The MCSD was originally designed to be a measure of a social desirability response bias in self-reports (Crowne & Marlowe, 1960). Sample items include "I always try to practice what I preach" and "I can remember 'playing sick' to get out of something" (reversed).

According to Jackson (1976), a high scorer on the Responsibility subscale "feels a strong obligation to be honest and upright; experiences a sense of duty to other people; [and] has a strong and inflexible conscience" (p. 10). Items include "I am very careful not to litter in public places" and

"Sometimes it is too troublesome to do exactly what I promised to do" (reversed). High scorers rate themselves as especially law abiding and are also rated that way by their peers (Jackson, 1978). They report more church attendance and less alcohol use and nonmedical drug use (Jackson, 1978). They are also less inclined to take ethical risks (Jackson, Hourany, & Vidmar, 1972).

Sociability

The two measures of sociability were the Social Participation subscale of the JPI and the Extraversion subscale of the Self-Monitoring Scale. Jackson (1976) described the person who scores high on the Social Participation subscale as someone who "will eagerly join a variety of social groups; seeks both formal and informal association with others; values positive interpersonal relationships; [and is] actively social" (p. 10). Items include "I like to meet as many new people as I can" and "I would rather telephone a friend than read a magazine in my spare time." High scorers rate themselves as more extraverted and are rated as more extraverted by their peers. They also score low on the Social Introversion scale of the Minnesota Multiphasic Personality Inventory (Hathaway & McKinley, 1943; Jackson, 1978).

The Extraversion subscale of the Self-Monitoring Scale includes items such as "I feel a bit awkward in company and do not show up quite as well as I should" and "At a party, I let others keep the jokes and stories going" (both reversed). Scores on this scale correlate negatively with the Shyness Scale (Cheek & Buss, 1981) and positively with a modified version of the Sociability scale of the EASI Temperament Survey (Buss & Plomin, 1975).

Relationship quality

The two measures of relationship quality were the Same-Sex Quality scale and the Opposite-Sex Quality scale, both developed in the process of validating the Profile of Nonverbal Sensitivity, which is a standardized measure of sensitivity to nonverbal cues (Rosenthal et al., 1979). The scales have also been used in subsequent work on interpersonal sensitivity and relationship quality (e.g., Rosenthal & DePaulo, 1979). Respondents indicate the degree to which their current same-sex and opposite-sex relationships are warm, honest, enduring, and generally satisfying; the degree to which they understand their friends' feelings and the degree to which their friends understand their feelings; and the quickness with which they make friends. Each scale score is the mean of those seven ratings.

Self-Centered and Other-Oriented Lies

As described in detail in DePaulo et al. (1996), the reasons participants gave for telling each of their lies were coded into the two major categories of self-centered and other oriented. (The kappas were .69 and .68.)

Self-centered lies

Self-centered lies were defined as lies told to protect or enhance the liars psychologically or to advantage or protect the liars' interests (as described subsequently). Also included were lies told to elicit a particular emotional response that the liars desired (e.g., Lie: "Exaggerated a problem I'm having with husband." Reason: "To get attention.").

The lies told for psychological reasons included lies told to protect the liars from embarrassment, loss of face, or looking bad; from disapproval or having their feelings hurt; or from worry, conflict, or other unpleasantness. They also included lies told to protect the liars' privacy; to make the liars appear better (or just different) than they are; and to regulate the liars' own feelings, emotions, and moods. Examples are as follows.

Lie: "I told her Ted and I still liked each other when really I don't know if he likes me at all." Reason: "Because I'm ashamed of the fact that he doesn't like me anymore."

Lie: "Lied about keeping a physician's appointment. Said I went to the doctor for a specific reason. That's not really why I went." Reason: "To maintain privacy."

Lie: "I don't lie." Reason: "Wanted to appear more honest."

Lie: "Overexaggerated the dullness of my weekend." Reason: "To prove a point—I have changed."

Lie: "Told her I was sick of guys and never wanted to see one again." Reason: "To make myself feel better."

The lies told for reasons of personal advantage included lies told for the liars' personal gain, to make things easier or more pleasant for the liars, or to help them get information or get their way. They also included lies told to protect the liars from physical punishment or to protect their property or assets or their safety. Lies told to protect the liars from loss of status or position or to protect them from being bothered or from doing something they preferred not to do were also included. The following are examples.

Lie: "Told parents typewriter expense would be $50–$60; really $20–$25." Reason: "So they'd pity me and send me money."

Lie: "Suggested they may want to go to the bookstore." Reason: "I wanted them to take me."

Lie: "Told him I knew something I did not know." Reason: "To obtain secret information."

Lie: "Lady on phone asked if a number was my current phone number. I said yes when in fact it isn't." Reason: "I want to make it hard for her to find me; they are after me for money."

Lie: "Said I was all caught up and doing fine on my reading." Reason: "I don't want my teaching assistant to know how far behind I am. She's the one who gives me my grade."

Lie: "Told her I couldn't babysit for her because I had to go somewhere." Reason: "Did not want to babysit. Her kids are brats."

Other-oriented lies

Other-oriented lies were defined as lies told to protect or enhance other people psychologically or to advantage or protect the interests of others (as described subsequently). Lies told to bother or annoy others or to cause them psychological damage (e.g., Lie: "Told him the boss wanted to talk to him, but he really didn't." Reason: "So he'd look like a fool.") were not included because only the more positively motivated lies fit our theoretical predictions. Only 1% of the lies in Study 1 and 2.5% of the lies in Study 2 were of the nasty variety.

The other-oriented lies told for psychological reasons included lies told to protect another person from embarrassment, loss of face, or looking bad; from disapproval or having their feelings hurt; or from worry, conflict, or other unpleasantness. They also included lies told to protect another person's privacy; to make other people appear better (or just different) than they are; and to regulate another person's feelings, emotions, or moods. Examples are as follows.

Lie: "Told my roommate I was having a great time at this party." Reason: "Didn't want her to feel bad."

Lie: "Told her she looked well, voice sounded good, when, in fact, she looks less well than a few weeks ago." Reason: "Not to add worry as she undergoes chemotherapy treatments."

Lie: "Told her I didn't know what Tricia's paper topic was." Reason: "Tricia wanted me not to tell anyone."

Lie: "I told her that she was neither promiscuous nor uninhibited to the point of not caring." Reason: "So she would not think that she was promiscuous."

Lie: "I told her she should have a lot of confidence because she was pretty." Reason: "Because she was in a depressed state because she broke up with her boyfriend."

The lies told for another person's advantage included lies told for another person's personal gain, to make things easier or more pleasant for others, to be accommodating, or to help them get their way. They also included lies told to protect others from physical punishment, to protect their property or assets, or to protect their safety. Lies to protect others from loss of status or position or to protect them from being bothered or from doing something they preferred not to do were also included. The following are examples.

Lie: "Lied about cost per square foot." Reason: "To make money for the company."

Lie: "Told them that it didn't matter what we did that night." Reason: "To be agreeable."

Lie: "Insisted I drive her to a party because it wouldn't be an inconvenience." Reason: "She is a terrible driver and a threat to herself and others."

Lie: "My roommate wasn't home." Reason: "She's screening calls."

Results

Personality Measures: Intercorrelations and Sample Comparisons

The correlations between the two measures of a given personality dimension (mean r = .43) were always bigger in absolute value than the mean correlations between those measures and the measures of all of the other dimensions (mean r = .22). Thus, the pattern of correlations supported our theoretically based grouping of the measures.

Consistent with theoretical predictions (e.g., Elkind & Bowen, 1979; Simmons, Rosenberg, & Rosenberg, 1973) and empirical indications (Tice, Buder, & Baumeister, 1985), the late adolescents were higher in public self-consciousness (M = 19.33, SD = 4.89) than the adults from the community (M = 16.70, SD = 4.35), t (144) = 3.42, p < .001. Also consistent with previous research (Reis, Lin, Bennett, & Nezlek, 1993) are the findings that the college students were more sociable than the community members: They scored significantly higher on social participation (college M = 10.78, SD = 4.94; community M = 8.24, SD = 4.65), t (144) = 3.18, p < .01, and marginally higher on extraversion (college M = 3.94, SD = 1.68; community M = 3.39, SD = 1.94), t (144) = 1.85, p = .07. The college students also scored higher on both measures of manipulativeness: Machiavellianism (college M = 10.10, SD = 2.90; community M = 8.20, SD = 3.38), t (144) = 3.65, p < .001, and social adroitness (college M = 11.25, SD = 3.37; community M = 10.18, SD = 4.12), t (144) = 1.73, p = .09. Finally, they scored higher on both measures of relationship quality: same-sex quality (college M = 6.90, SD = 1.03; community M = 6.43, SD = 1.19), t (144) = 2.58, p = .01, and opposite-sex quality (college M = 6.70, SD = 1.23; community M = 6.25, SD = 1.28), t (144) = 2.19, p = .03. The two groups did not differ significantly on self-esteem, social anxiety, other-directedness, or social desirability.

To determine whether the differences between the younger (college) and older (community) groups would be replicated within the community sample, we correlated the 12 personality variables with participant age. The results for responsibility were consistent such that the older community members scored higher than the younger ones (r = .28, p = .02). The comparable correlation for social desirability was nearly significant (r = .21, p = .09). The results for relationship quality were inconsistent with the group comparisons: The older community members rated their relationship quality more positively than did the younger ones (r = .24, p < .05, for same-sex quality and r = .25, p = .04, for opposite-sex quality). None of the other correlations with age differed significantly from zero.

Overall Rate of Lying

Correlations

Participants' overall rate of lying was computed by dividing the total number of lies that they reported telling over the course of the week by the total number of social interactions they reported. As we reported previously (DePaulo et al., 1996), the college students told 0.31 lies per social interaction and the community members told 0.20. One college student and 6 community members told no lies at all.

Table 1 shows the correlations between rate of lying and each of the 12 personality variables for the two samples. We also combined the results of the two studies using the method of adding Z values (Mosteller & Bush, 1954; Rosenthal, 1978); the resulting combined p values are also shown in Table 1. One-tailed results are typically discussed and reported in reports of meta-analyses; to be conservative, however, we use two-tailed p values.

Table 1

Correlations Between Number of Lies per Social Interaction and the 12 Personality Variables

Variable	College		Community		Combined *p*
	r	*p*	*r*	*p*	
Machiavellianism	.119	.307	.228	.058	.039
Social adroitness	.303	.008	.240	.046	.001
Public self-consciousness	.122	.292	.262	.028	.023
Other-directedness	.077	.507	.396	.001	.004
Self-esteem	.126	.279	.034	.779	.335
Social anxiety	.098	.398	-.033	.784	
Social desirability	.041	.725	-.208	.084	
Responsibility	-.160	.167	-.157	.195	.058
Social participation	.100	.389	.142	.240	.150
Extraversion	.183	.114	.198	.101	.023
Same-sex quality	-.194	.093	-.166	.170	.031
Opposite-sex quality	-.065	.578	-.032	.791	.561

Note. All *p* values are two-tailed.

We predicted that people who are more manipulative would tell more lies. All four correlations were in the predicted direction. For the college students, the correlation with social adroitness was statistically significant, but the correlation with Machiavellianism was not. Similarly, for the community members, the correlation with social adroitness was significant and the correlation with Machiavellianism was nearly significant. The combined results were significant for both Machiavellianism and social adroitness. Overall, then, our prediction was well supported: More manipulative people lie more than less manipulative people.

We also predicted that people who are more highly concerned with impression management would tell more lies. Again, all four correlations were in the predicted direction. For the community members, both correlations—with public self-consciousness and with other-directedness—were significant. Although the comparable correlations were not significant for the college students, the combined results across studies were significant for both measures. Therefore, our prediction that a concern with self-presentation would predict rate of lying was also fairly well supported.

There was no support for our prediction that people low in social self-confidence would tell more lies. Neither self-esteem nor social anxiety correlated with rate of lying, nor did either of the combined results reach significance.

Correlations with responsibility provided one test of our prediction that more highly socialized people would tell fewer lies. Although the correlations were not significant for either sample, they were in the predicted direction, and the combined p level across studies was nearly significant. The correlation of rate of lying with socia desirability was negative and marginally significant for the community sample, although it was positive and very small for the college students. Overall, the results provide weak support for the prediction that more highly socialized people would tell fewer lies.

All four correlations were in the direction of our prediction that highly sociable people tell more lies. The results for social participation, however, were not significant. For extraversion, the results for the individual studies were not significant, but the combined p level across the studies was significant. Overall, then, there was some limited support for our hypothesis that sociability predicts lie-telling.

Finally, we predicted that people who report higher quality same-sex and opposite-sex relationships would tell fewer lies. All four correlations were in the predicted direction; for opposite-sex quality, however, they were not even close to significant. For same-sex quality, the results for the individual studies were not significant, but the combined p level across the studies was significant. Our prediction, then, that people with more meaningful relationships tell fewer lies was supported primarily for same-sex relationships.

We also conducted analyses in which we controlled for a possible social desirability response style by partialing the MCSD out of the correlations between rate of lying and the 11 remaining personality measures. Controlling for social desirability weakened a few of the results for the community sample.[1] However, as we discuss later, the partialing procedure may have partialed out a bit of substance along with the style.

To determine whether any of our results were different for men and women, we also computed all correlations separately by gender and tested for gender differences. For the college student study, only one correlation differed significantly by gender. For men, the correlation between Machiavellianism and rate of lying was .436 (p = .018), whereas, for women, it was −.066 (p = .661). A test of the difference between these correlations produced a Z value of 2.16 (p = .031). For the community study, only the correlation with public self-consciousness differed significantly by gender (r = .494, p = .001, for women and r = −.115, p = .546, for men; Z = 2.580, p = .01).

Regressions

To assess whether some combination of the personality variables was more successful in predicting rate of lying than any single variable alone, we used a forward selection multiple regression procedure such that all 12 of the personality variables, as well as participant gender, were treated as potential predictor variables. For all regressions with both samples, the personality variables were first standardized and participant gender was coded (men = −1, women = 1). In the community study, we also included participant's age (also standardized) as a possible predictor variable. Consistent with the correlational results, for the college student study the resulting model included only social adroitness, b = .080, R^2 = .092, F (1, 7466) = 7.46, p = . 008. (The intercept for this model was .310.) Thus, for the college sample, social adroitness significantly predicted rate of lying such that students who were one standard deviation above the mean on social adroitness would be predicted to tell a lie in every two to three interactions (the rate of lying would be .390), whereas a person one standard deviation below the mean on social adroitness would be predicted to tell a lie in every four interactions (the rate of lying would be .230). No other predictor variable accounted for significant variation in rate of lying beyond that explained by adroitness.

For the community study, the model included both other-directedness and participant gender; these two variables accounted for 23% of the variation in rate of lying, R^2 = .227, F (2, 66) = 9.55, p < .001. The regression coefficient (b) for the standardized measure of other-directedness was .111, t (66) = 4.022, p < .001; for gender, the coefficient was .050, t (66) = 1.82, p = .073. (The intercept was .201.) Thus, those participants who were higher in other-directedness told more lies relative to the number of interactions they had. Gender explained additional variation in rate of lying over and above that accounted for by other-directedness: Women's rate of lying was higher (by about one lie in every 10 social interactions) than men's after differences in other-directedness had been controlled. In sum, the results of the regression analyses provide qualified support for our claim that two of the most important personality predictors of lie-telling are manipulativeness and a concern with impression management.

Self-Centered Lies

Correlations

According to our formulation, personality should predict not just overall rate of lying but also the kinds of lies that people tell. To learn whether certain kinds of people, when they do lie, tell disproportionately more self-centered lies, we computed a self-centered lying variable that was defined as the total number of self-centered lies divided by the total number of all lies. The correlations of that variable with each of the 12 personality variables are shown in Table 2 , along with the combined p levels.

Table 2

Correlations Between Percentage of Lies That Were Self-Centered and the 12 Personality Variables

Variable	College		Community		
	r	*p*	*r*	*p*	**Combined *p***
Machiavellianism	.296	.010	.153	.227	.007
Social adroitness	.020	.863	.152	.229	.331
Public self-consciousness	.142	.224	.083	.516	.187
Other-directedness	-.028	.810	.215	.087	
Self-esteem	-.055	.639	.027	.834	
Social anxiety	-.026	.822	.025	.842	
Social desirability	.036	.762	-.056	.660	
Responsibility	-.249	.031	-.198	.118	.009
Social participation	-.156	.182	-.077	.547	.170
Extraversion	.018	.879	.097	.444	.632
Same-sex quality	-.314	.006	-.276	.027	.000
Opposite-sex quality	-.044	.704	-.044	.732	.610

Note. All *p* values are two-tailed.

We predicted that manipulative people, people especially concerned with self-presentation, and people lacking in social self-confidence would tell more self-centered lies, whereas highly socialized individuals and people with high-quality personal relationships would tell fewer self-centered lies. All four of the correlations with manipulativeness were in the predicted direction (although one was very close to zero). The correlation with Machiavellianism for the college sample was significant, as was the combined p level for Machiavellianism across samples. Therefore, there was some support for the prediction that manipulative people would tell especially more self-serving lies.

The results for impression management were in the predicted direction for three of the four correlations and nearly significant in the community sample for other-directedness. Overall, however, support for the prediction that people concerned with impression management would tell more self-centered lies was weak. There was no support for our prediction that socially insecure people would tell more self-centered lies.

Our prediction that highly socialized people would tell fewer self-serving lies was fairly strongly supported when responsibility was the measure of socialization. For social desirability, however, the correlations were essentially zero (and, therefore, we do not report results that partial out this variable).

Support for our prediction about quality of relationships was very strong for same-sex quality but trivial for opposite-sex quality. People who describe their same-sex relationships as very meaningful tell fewer self-serving lies, but the same is not true for those who describe their opposite-sex relationships that way.

We computed all correlations separately by gender and tested for gender differences. For the college student study, there were none. For the community sample, the correlations with self-centered lying were significantly different for men and women only for social adroitness ($r = .504$, $p < .01$, for men and $r = -.076$, $p = .65$, for women). The Z value for the difference between the correlations was 2.35 ($p = .02$).

Regressions

Using a forward selection procedure, we regressed the 12 personality variables plus participants' gender (and, for the community sample, participants' age) on the proportion of self-centered lies that participants told. For the college student study, the model included 5 variables and accounted for more than 22% of the variance in the proportion of self-centered lies told, $R2 = .225$, $F (5, 69) = 4.01$, $p < .01$. As predicted, people higher in public self-consciousness told more self-centered lies, $b = .069$, $t (69) = 2.07$, $p = .042$, whereas highly responsible people, $b = -.069$, $t (69) = 2.25$, $p = .028$, and people with high–quality same–sex relationships, $b = -.102$, $t (69) = 3.12$, $p = .003$, told fewer self–centered lies. Contrary to predictions, however, social anxiety tended to predict self–centered lying negatively in the regression analysis, $b = -.062$, $t (69) = 1.79$, $p = .073$, whereas social desirability was positively (although not significantly) predictive of telling self–centered lies, $b = .053$, $t (69) = 1.60$, $p = .115$. For this regression equation, the intercept was .457. Thus, a person who was high in public self–consciousness and low in responsibility and who had poor same–sex relationships was especially likely to tell self–centered lies. Machiavellianism, although relating to rate of self–centered lying in the univariate analysis, was not a significant predictor of self–centered lying after quality of same–sex relationships had been taken into account.

For the community study, the regression results mirrored the correlational results. The model included two variables, both in the predicted direction, and accounted for about 11% of the variation in proportion of self-centered lies, $R^2 = .112$, $F(2, 60) = 3.79$, $p = .028$. Participants with high–quality same–sex relationships tended to tell fewer self–centered lies, $b = -.080$, $t(60) = 2.11$, $p = .04$, and other–directed people tended to tell more self–centered lies, $b = .059$, $t(60) = 1.54$, $p = .13$. (The intercept for this equation was .563.)

In sum, when all personality variables were entered into regression analyses, quality of same-sex relationships emerged as an important predictor of (less) self-centered lying for both samples, as it had in the zero-order correlational analyses. Consistent with our formulation, concern with impression management predicted more self-centered lying, and, for the college sample, responsibility predicted less of it.

Other-Oriented Lying

Correlations

To learn whether certain kinds of people, when they do lie, tell disproportionately more other-oriented lies, we computed an other-oriented lying variable that was defined as the total number of other-oriented lies divided by the total number of all lies. Table 3 shows the correlations between that variable and the 12 personality variables, as well as the p levels for the results combined across studies. We predicted only that people low in social self-confidence and people with high-quality interpersonal relationships would tell more other-oriented lies. We were wrong about self-confidence; there was no discernible relationship between self-esteem or social anxiety and the telling of other-oriented lies. There was some support for our other prediction. When people with higher quality same-sex relationships told lies, proportionately more of those lies were altruistic. The correlation was significant for the college sample and for the results that were combined across studies. Once again, quality of opposite-sex relationships did not predict lying.

Table 3

Correlations Between Percentage of Lies That Were Other Oriented and the 12 Personality Variables

Variable	College		Community		
	r	*p*	*r*	*p*	Combined *p*
Machiavellianism	-.109	.352	.051	.686	
Social adroitness	-.159	.173	.021	.871	
Public self-consciousness	-.132	.258	-.004	.976	.412
Other-directedness	-.082	.487	-.120	.345	.246
Self-esteem	.037	.751	-.086	.499	
Social anxiety	-.041	.728	.053	.678	
Social desirability	-.009	.941	.038	.767	
Responsibility	.071	.548	.073	.565	.405
Social participation	.156	.181	.069	.589	.184
Extraversion	-.022	.854	-.027	.832	.779
Same-sex quality	.261	.024	.151	.232	.014
Opposite-sex quality	-.053	.652	.109	.393	

Note. All *p* values are two-tailed.

When we computed the correlations separately by gender and tested for gender differences, we found no significant differences in the community study. In the college student study, only the social adroitness correlations were significantly different for men and women ($r = .299$, $p = .12$, for men and $r = -.231$, $p = .12$, for women). The Z value for the difference between the correlations was 2.19 ($p = .03$).

Regressions

We regressed the 12 personality variables, plus participants' gender (and, for the community sample, participants' age), on the proportion of other-oriented lies that participants told. For the college study, the model included as predictors same-sex quality and participant gender and accounted for 15% of the variation in proportion of other-oriented lies told, $R^2 = .150$, $F(2, 72) = 6.36$, $p < .01$. The gender coefficient, $b = .149$, $t(72) = 2.63$, $p < .01$, indicates that women were much more likely than men to tell other-oriented lies. (The intercept was .015.) In addition, people with higher quality same-sex relationships, $b = .046$, $t(72) = 1.67$, $p = .10$, told more other-oriented lies. There was no acceptable model for the community study.

Self-Perceptions of Lying

We predicted that manipulative people would describe themselves as especially successful liars and would also accurately report that they lie more often than other people. We predicted that highly socialized people would report that they lie less than other people. We also predicted that highly sociable people would be surprised by how often they lied, as indicated by their reports at the end of the study that they lied more frequently than they expected. Table 4 shows the correlations of the 12 personality variables with participants' perceptions of their success at lying and their estimates of how often they lie relative to other people.

Table 4

Correlations Between Self-Ratings of Success at Lying and Lying More Than Others and the 12 Personality Variables

| | Success at lying | | | | | Lied more than others | | | | |
| | College | | Community | | | College | | Community | | |
Variable	*r*	*p*	*r*	*p*	Combined *p*	*r*	*p*	*r*	*p*	Combined *p*
Machiavellianism	.218	.059	.113	.352	.046	-.030	.794	.266	.026	
Social adroitness	.062	.603	.278	.020	.044	.170	.142	.387	.001	.001
Public self-consciousness	.009	.940	.033	.786	.807	.042	.720	.299	.012	.042
Other-directedness	-.057	.625	.226	.060		.202	.080	.198	.101	.016
Self-esteem	.075	.519	.345	.003	.012	.120	.301	.182	.132	.072
Social anxiety	-.248	.031	-.152	.210	.016	-.099	.394	.004	.977	
Social desirability	-.059	.614	-.003	.984	.711	-.109	.348	-.149	.219	.126
Responsibility	-.033	.778	-.155	.201	.270	-.139	.232	-.202	.094	.042
Social participation	-.231	.044	.150	.216		.139	.230	.056	.648	.242
Extraversion	.142	.221	.373	.002	.002	.294	.010	.204	.090	.003
Same-sex quality	.015	.897	-.093	.444		.189	.103	-.077	.526	
Opposite-sex quality	.090	.441	-.058	.632		.050	.666	-.042	.728	

Note. All *p* values are two-tailed.

As we predicted, manipulative people did see themselves as more successful liars than others. The combined results across studies were significant for both Machiavellianism and social adroitness, and the individual correlations were significant or nearly so for Machiavellianism for the college sample and for social adroitness for the community sample. We also found that across studies, people high in social self-confidence, as measured by both scales, thought that they were more successful liars. Although we had not specifically predicted this finding, it is consistent with a large literature showing that people with high self-esteem and low social anxiety evaluate their own interpersonal skills more positively (Baumeister, 1993; Leary, 1983). Across studies, extraverts also described themselves as more successful liars than introverts. This, too, was an unexpected but not implausible finding.

There was also some support for our predictions that manipulative people would report that they lie more than others and that highly socialized people would report that they lie less than others. For Machiavellianism and social adroitness, the results were significant for the community sample; for social adroitness, they were also significant in the combined analysis. For responsibility, the results were significant or nearly so for the community sample and in the combined analyses. The correlations with social desirability were in the predicted direction but were not significant. Although we had not predicted any other correlates, we found that people who are especially concerned with impression management believe that they lie more than other people, as do extraverts. In sum, people's perceptions of their relative standing on the lie-telling dimension corresponded fairly well with their actual standing. Manipulative people, people who are especially concerned with self-presentation, and highly sociable people all tend to lie more often than other people and to realize that they do. Highly socialized people tend to lie less than others, and they know that, too.

We predicted that only highly sociable people would report, at the end of the study, that they had lied more often than they expected. This prediction was supported only for the extraverts in the college study ($r = .309$, $p = .007$). For social participation in the college student sample, the correlation was in the predicted direction ($r = .171$) but was not significant ($p = .140$). For the community study, both correlations were in the opposite direction, and neither was significant. There were no other significant correlations with the variable of lying more frequently than expected.

Characteristics of the Lies

For each participant, we calculated the mean of his or her ratings of the characteristics of the lies for each of the 11 variables: the degree to which he or she had planned the lie; importance of avoiding detection; distress before, during, and after the telling of the lie; seriousness of the lie; degree to which the other person seemed to believe the lie; degree to which he or she was trying to protect the other person or themselves with the lie; whether the lie had been discovered by the end of the study; and whether he or she would tell the lie again. We correlated each of these variables with the 12 personality variables. Although several individual correlations were significant, only one correlation was significant or nearly significant in both samples and in the same direction. Machiavellian people were more likely to say that if they could relive the situations, they would tell their lies again ($r = .220$, $p = .059$, for the college sample and $r = .268$, $p = .034$, for the community sample). Although this finding fits well with the theory and research on Machiavellianism, it is possible that it is simply a chance finding.

Discussion

As social psychologists, we could have at least entertained the possibility that personality would be of no consequence in predicting lie-telling in everyday life. Perhaps lies are elicited by situational presses or by the behaviors of particular other people. We do think that certain situations and people elicit lying. But we expected personality to predict lying as well. Our perspective on lying is that it is an everyday social interaction process used to accomplish fundamental social interaction goals such as managing impressions and influencing other people. Personality dimensions that are relevant to those goals, such as manipulativeness and a chronic concern with self-presentation, should predict lie-telling in everyday life.

Individual-Differences Predictors of Everyday Lying

Manipulativeness

Perhaps the most stereotypical view of personality and lying is that liars are selfish, scheming, and manipulative. When the results for Machiavellianism and social adroitness are considered by themselves, our data do little to debunk that view. In each individual study and in the combined analysis, the more socially adroit people told significantly more lies than the less socially adroit people. In the regression analysis for the college students, social adroitness was the one factor that significantly predicted the overall rate of lying in everyday life. Machiavellian people also told more lies (although, for the college students, this was true only for the men), and they were especially inclined to tell self-serving lies.

We also thought that manipulative people would know that they lie more than other people and would be confident of their lie-telling skills. These predictions, too, were generally supported. After a week of observing and recording their own lie-telling behavior (but, of course, not anyone else's), the socially adroit individuals in both studies and the Machiavellian types in the community study reported that they thought they told more lies than other people, and, across studies, both the Machiavellians and the socially adroit participants said that they believed themselves to be especially successful liars.

In many creative studies of Machiavellianism (e.g., Christie & Geis, 1970; Fehr, Samsom, & Paulhus, 1992; Geis, 1978) and a smaller number of studies of social adroitness (e.g., Jackson, 1976, 1978), manipulative individuals have been found to be more successful than others at persuading people and reaping competitive rewards. Our data lend added plausibility to the suggestion that one of the ways that manipulative people get what they want is by lying. What is impressive about these people is that at the same time that they are telling self-serving lies and getting their way, they still manage to be admired and even liked.

Impression management

Most central to our view of lying as an everyday social interaction process is the prediction that people who are most concerned about the impressions they convey to other people will be most likely to tell lies. Across both studies (but especially in the community study), people who were publicly self-conscious and other directed did indeed tell more lies than people who were less aware of themselves as social objects. Our prediction that they would tell especially more self-centered lies was supported only in the regression analyses: In the undergraduate study, public self-consciousness significantly predicted the telling of self-centered lies, and, in the community study, other-directedness did so, although less definitively. Although we had not predicted this, we also found that people who are concerned with the impressions they make on other people know that they lie more than others.

Social self-confidence

There was no evidence whatsoever in support of our predictions that people low in self-esteem and high in social anxiety would tell more total lies, more self-centered lies, or more other-oriented lies than their counterparts. We had argued that when people tell self-centered lies, they are often claiming a different and more impressive identity than they think they have earned, and we had suggested that these exaggerated claims are motivated by insecurity. Perhaps some of them really are. Others, however, may follow from the self-assurance that emboldens people to take a chance at claiming virtues that they do not really believe they possess. In a similar manner, the telling of some altruistic lies may be motivated by insecurity, and other lies may be motivated by social self-confidence. Our data suggest that sweeping generalizations about confidence and lie-telling are unlikely to be supported. The relationships are probably nuanced and complex, and we think they will be most precisely articulated by the fine-pointed pen of experimental research.

Socialization

Whereas manipulative people see lying as an acceptable means of getting what they want, and people concerned with self-presentation see it as a way of creating the impressions of themselves that they long for but cannot claim by simply behaving honestly, people who are highly socialized into the cultural wisdom of their society may simply see lying as wrong. The Responsibility scale that we used picks out people who are best described as "responsible, honest, ethical, incorruptible, scrupulous, dependable, conscientious, reliable, stable, [and] straightforward" (Jackson, 1976, p. 10). True to their descriptors and our predictions, these people did in fact tell somewhat fewer total lies, especially fewer self-serving lies, and they also knew that they lied less often than other people. These people are the practitioners and defenders of conventional morality. We found more of them among the community members than among the college students, and, within the community sample, they were more likely to be the older rather than the younger members.

Sociability

We thought that the functions that lying serves in everyday social interaction would be particularly important to people who are especially sociable and that such people would therefore lie at a higher rate than less sociable people. Over time, sociable people might lie more often because lying has become more practiced and more habitual. As such, it might also become less noticed. Hence, we also predicted that when sociable people are pushed to attend to their lie-telling behavior, as they were in the present investigations, they would be surprised at how often they lie and would report that they told more lies than they had expected. These predictions received some support, but it was limited. When the results of both studies were combined, extraverts did report a higher rate of lying than introverts. In the college study (but not the community study), extraverts also reported that they lied more often than they expected. Of course, we cannot know from these data alone whether the mechanisms we postulated were, in fact, responsible for the effects.

69

Relationship quality

Across both studies and all three measures of lying—total lying, self-centered lying, and other-oriented lying—the quality of people's same-sex relationships was the most consistent predictor of lying. People who described their same-sex relationships as warm, enduring, and satisfying told fewer lies overall, and especially fewer self-centered lies, than people who described their same-sex relationships in less glowing terms. We are intrigued by the fact that the quality of same-sex relationships was so reliably linked to lying when the quality of opposite-sex relationships was so consistently irrelevant to lying. We entrust the solution of this puzzle to future researchers.

Overall profile

The personality profile of the liar that has emerged from this research fits well with our perspective on lying as an everyday social interaction process. People who tell more lies than others are people who care more than others about the impressions they are creating in social life. They are also sociable sorts who are more likely to be extraverts than introverts. Although it is also the case that liars are manipulators, they are smooth and even likable manipulators rather than abrasive and alienating. In some ways, then, liars seem to be able participants in social life. But our data also suggest important qualifications to this lie-tolerant picture. For example, people who lie more than others have less gratifying same-sex relationships, and they are also less responsible. It is clear that our data cannot answer questions about the direction of causality in our findings, but it is equally clear that those questions are important and worth pursuing.

We think it is also important to acknowledge that the individual-differences predictors we have documented are the predictors of everyday lies, the vast majority of which are little lies (DePaulo et al., 1996). The personality correlates of serious lies may be very different.

Are Liars Lying About Their Lies?

To learn about the personality predictors of lying across the broad spectrum of everyday life, there is simply no methodological alternative to asking people to report their own lies. Only liars have a chance at recognizing and reporting all instances in which they deliberately mislead other people. But this methodology immediately raises the question of whether people's reports of their lies can be believed.

We took great pains to elicit accurate and conscientious reporting from our participants. We repeatedly emphasized the importance of accuracy and thoroughness, we described their role as more akin to that of a co-investigator than objects of investigation, we protected the privacy of their reports, and we remained continuously available to them to pick up their diary entries throughout the week and to answer their questions. We also conducted careful interviews at the end of the study to probe participants about the accuracy and completeness of their records, and the results of those efforts were reassuring (DePaulo et al., 1996).

Another way that we addressed the issue of self-report bias was to include a widely used measure of socially desirable responding, the MCSD. The correlation of this measure with the total number of lies told by the undergraduates was essentially zero. The correlations with the proportion of all lies that were self-centered and the proportion that were other oriented were also indistinguishable from zero in both studies. Only in the community study did the relationship between MCSD score and the total number of lies approach significance. The community members who scored higher on social desirability reported telling somewhat fewer lies. When we controlled for MCSD score in that study, a few results were somewhat weakened (such as the correlations with manipulativeness and responsibility), but others (such as the correlation with other-directedness) remained strong. We think that there were good theoretical reasons for the somewhat smaller correlations that occurred when MCSD score was partialed out of manipulativeness and responsibility. For example, a willingness to embrace socially undesirable attitudes such as a view of others as objects of manipulation is definitional to the construct of Machiavellianism. When that willingness is partialed out, so too is some of the theoretical foundation on which we based our predictions. Similarly, the Responsibility scale is a measure of degree of socialization. To some degree, so is the MCSD. So again, when MCSD score is partialed out of the correlation of responsibility with lying, some of the substantive basis for the correlation is partialed out, too.

Overall, then, we think that the MCSD results provide scant basis for the concern that people's reports of their lies were driven more by a motivation to look good than by their actual lie-telling behavior. Still, it is evident that our interpretation of the MCSD results is compromised by the multiple meanings and implications of the measure. Hindsight tells us that we should have used a purer measure of socially desirable responding, if indeed such a measure exists (McCrae & Costa, 1983).2

College Students and Community Members: Different Personality Profiles and Correspondingly Different Rates of Lying

In our other, related work (DePaulo et al., 1996), we found that the community members lied less than the college students on every measure of lying. They told fewer lies per day (0.97 vs. 1.96) and fewer lies per social interaction (0.20 vs. 0.31), and they lied to a smaller percentage of the people with whom they interacted in their day-to-day lives (30% vs. 38%). Furthermore, within the community sample, the older people lied less frequently than the younger people ($r = -.24$, $p = .044$). Interestingly, almost all of the ways in which the college students differed from the community members in personality were consistent with the finding that the college students lied more than the community members. The college students were more manipulative; they scored higher than the community members on Machiavellianism and social adroitness. They also seemed more concerned with impression management in that they scored higher on public self-consciousness. They were also more extraverted than the community members and less responsible. All of these differences predict higher rates of lying. Only the results of same-sex quality are inconsistent with this argument; college students reported higher quality same-sex relationships than the community members did, but same-sex quality predicts lower rates of lying. Even this one exception was tempered by the finding of a significant positive correlation with age for the community members. Thus, even though the community members reported lower quality same-sex relationships overall than did the college students, the older community members reported higher quality same-sex relationships than the younger ones (which, again, predicts less lying).

Because the community members differed from the undergraduates in so many ways other than their age, we cannot confidently attribute any of these effects to age. However, the findings for responsibility are especially suggestive because they were consistent across every level of analysis. People who were more responsible told fewer lies than people who were less responsible across the two samples. The community members were more responsible than the college students and told fewer lies, and the older community members were more responsible than the younger ones, and they also told fewer lies.

When 1, 500 Lies Are Not Enough

The two studies we have reported are the first to examine the personality predictors of lie-telling across the vast domain of everyday life. We are encouraged by the consistency of our findings across two strikingly different groups of people: a young, highly intelligent, and somewhat privileged group of undergraduates and a group that was far more diverse in age, education, income, and life experience. The two groups also differed markedly on 8 of the 12 individual-differences measures. Still, the two distinct sets of people told the same basic story about personality and lying: Lies are told by people who care deeply about what other people think of them. They are also told by people who are extraverted and manipulative. Lies are less likely to be told by people who are responsible and who experience gratifying same-sex relationships.

The results we have reported are based on almost 150 people and more than 1,500 lies. Still, we think that the more than 1,500 lies we collected were not quite enough. The categorization of lies as self-centered or other oriented captured a distinction of long-standing importance in philosophy and ethics, and one that was central to our own formulation of the relationship between personality and lying. But it is only one of the many psychologically meaningful ways in which lies can be classified. In our other, related work (DePaulo et al., 1996), we developed several different taxonomies of lies, and we also described more differentiated subtypes of self-centered and other-oriented lies. We have not reported the results of any of those more fine-grained classifications of lies in the present article because, at the level of the individual participant, there simply were not enough instances of most of the specific categories. In future research, it would help to extend the reporting period by at least an additional week to obtain more stable estimates of more different kinds of lies.

Small Effects, Big Implications

Although many of our results were consistent with predictions and statistically significant, the size of our effects was generally rather modest. It is important, then, to be appropriately cautious in drawing implications from these data. At the same time, however, we think that the prediction of everyday lying from personality perfectly fits Abelson's (1985) "variance explanation paradox" in which "a little is a lot." In Abelson's example, the hitting skill (batting average) of a baseball player accounts for a mere one third of 1% of the variance in whether that player will get a hit in a single time at bat. However, over the course of a season that puny percentage of the variance cumulates, and differences in batting averages among different players become highly consequential. Because lying is indeed an everyday event, even personality variables that account for just a small amount of the variance in lie-telling can be of great consequence over time.

References

Abelson, R. P. (1985). A variance explanation paradox: When a little is a lot. *Psychological Bulletin, 97*, 129-133.

Barnes, J. A. (1994). A pack of lies: Toward a sociology of lying. Cambridge, England: Cambridge University Press.

Baumeister, R. F. (Ed.). (1993). Self-esteem: The puzzle of low self-regard. New York: Plenum.

Bogart, K., Geis, F., Levy, M., & Zimbardo, P. (1970). No dissonance for Machiavellians. In R. Christie & F. L. Geis (Eds.), Studies in Machiavellianism (pp. 236–259). New York: Academic Press.

Briggs, S. R. Jr., Cheek, J. M. & Buss, A. H. (1980). An analysis of the Self-Monitoring Scale. *Journal of Personality and Social Psychology,* 38, 679-686.

Brown, P., & Levinson, S. C. (1987). Politeness: Some universals in language use. Cambridge, England: Cambridge University Press.

Buss, A. H. & Briggs, S. R. (1984). Drama and the self in social interaction. *Journal of Personality and Social Psychology,* 47, 1310-1324.

Buss, A. H., & Plomin, R. (1975). A temperament theory of personality development. New York: Wiley.

Cheek, J. M. & Buss, A. H. (1981). Shyness and sociability. *Journal of Personality and Social Psychology,* 41, 330-339.

Cherulnik, P. D., Way, J. H., Ames, S. & Hutto, D. B. (1981). Impressions of high and low Machiavellian men. *Journal of Personality,* 49, 388-400.

Christie, R., & Geis, F. L. (Eds.). (1970). Studies in Machiavellianism. New York: Academic Press.

Coopersmith, S. (1967). The antecedents of self-esteem. San Francisco: Freeman.

Crowne, D. P. & Marlowe, D. (1960). A new scale of social desirability independent of psychopathology. *Journal of Consulting Psychology,* 24, 349-354.

Crowne, D. P., & Marlowe, D. (1964). The approval motive. New York: Wiley.

DePaulo, B. M., Blank, A. L., Swaim, G. W. & Hairfield, J. G. (1992). Expressiveness and expressive control. *Personality and Social Psychology Bulletin,* 18, 276-285.

DePaulo, B. M., Kashy, D. A., Kirkendol, S. E., Wyer, M. M. & Epstein, J. A. (1996). Lying in everyday life. *Journal of Personality and Social Psychology,* 70, 979-995.

DePaulo, B. M. & Rosenthal, R. (1979). Telling lies. *Journal of Personality and Social Psychology,* 37, 1713-1722.

Eagly, A. H. (1967). Involvement as a determinant of response to favorable and unfavorable information. *Journal of Personality and Social Psychology Monographs,* 7.

Elkind, D. & Bowen, R. (1979). Imaginary audience behavior in children and adolescents. *Developmental Psychology,* 15, 38-44.

Exline, R. V., Thibaut, J., Hickey, C. B., & Gumpert, P. (1970). Visual interaction in relation to Machiavellianism and an unethical act. In R. Christie & F. L. Geis (Eds.), Studies in Machiavellianism (pp. 53–75). New York: Academic Press.

Falbo, T. (1977). Multidimensional scaling of power strategies. *Journal of Personality and Social Psychology,* 35, 537-547.

Fehr, B., Samsom, D. & Paulhus, D. L. (1992). The construct of Machiavellianism: Twenty years later. *Advances in personality assessment,* Vol. 9, 77-116.

Fenigstein, A., Scheier, M. F. & Buss, A. H. (1975). Public and private self-consciousness: Assessment and theory. *Journal of Consulting and Clinical Psychology,* 43, 522-527.

Geis, F. L. (1978). Machiavellianism. In H. London & J. E. Exner, Jr. (Eds.), Dimensions of personality (pp. 305–363). New York: Wiley.

Goffman, E. (1959). The presentation of self in everyday life. Garden City, NY: Doubleday/Anchor Books.

Hathaway, S. R., & McKinley, J. C. (1943). The Minnesota Multiphasic Personality Inventory. New York: Psychological Corporation.

Ickes, W., Reidhead, S. & Patterson, M. (1986). Machiavellianism and self-monitoring: As different as "me" and "you.". *Social Cognition,* 4, 58-74.
Jackson, D. N. (1976). Jackson Personality Inventory manual. Port Huron, MI: Research Psychologists Press.

Jackson, D. N. (1978). Interpreter's guide to the Jackson Personality Inventory. *Advances in psychological assessment,* Vol. 4, 56-102.

Jackson, D. N., Hourany, L. & Vidmar, N. J. (1972). A four-dimensional interpretation of risk-taking. *Journal of Personality,* 40, 483-501.

Janis, I. S., & Field, P. B. (1959). A behavioral assessment of persuasibility: Consistency of individual differences. In C. I. Hovland & I. L. Janis (Eds.), Personality and persuasibility (pp. 55–68). New Haven, CT: Yale University Press.

Keating, C. F. & Heltman, K. R. (1994). Dominance and deception in children and adults: Are leaders the best misleaders. *Personality and Social Psychology Bulletin,* 20, 312-321.

Leary, M. R. (1983). Understanding social anxiety. Beverly Hills, CA: Sage.

Leary, M. R. (1991). Social anxiety, shyness, and related constructs. In J. P. Robinson, P. R. Shaver, L. S. Wrightsman (Eds.), Measures of personality and social psychology (pp. 161–194). San Diego, CA: Academic Press.

McCrae, R. R. & Costa, P. T. (1983). Social desirability scales: More substance than style. *Journal of Consulting and Clinical Psychology,* 51, 882-888.

Millham, J., & Jacobson, L. I. (1978). The need for approval. In H. London & J. E. Exner, Jr. (Eds.), Dimensions of personality (pp. 365–390). New York: Wiley.

Mosteller, F. M. & Bush, R. R. (1954). Selected quantitative techniques. *Theory and method,* Vol. 1, 289-334.

Nyberg, D. (1993). The varnished truth: Truth telling and deceiving in ordinary life. Chicago: University of Chicago Press.

Paulhus, D. L. (1991). Measurement and control of response bias. In J. P. Robinson, P. R. Shaver, L. S. Wrightsman (Eds.), Measures of personality and social psychology (pp. 17–59). San Diego, CA: Academic Press.

Reis, H. T., Lin, Y.-C., Bennett, M. E. & Nezlek, J. B. (1993). Change and consistency in social participation during early adulthood. *Developmental Psychology,* 29, 633-645.

Riggio, R. E. & Friedman, H. S. (1983). Individual differences and cues to deception. *Journal of Personality and Social Psychology,* 45, 899-915.
Rosenthal, R. (1978). Combining results of independent studies. *Psychological Bulletin,* 85, 185-193.

Rosenthal, R. & DePaulo, B. M. (1979). Sex differences in eavesdropping on nonverbal cues. *Journal of Personality and Social Psychology, 37,* 273-285.

Rosenthal, R., Hall, J. A., DiMatteo, M. R., Rogers, P. L., & Archer, D. (1979). Sensitivity to nonverbal communication: The PONS Test. Baltimore: Johns Hopkins University Press.

Saarni, C., & Lewis, M. (1993). Deceit and illusion in human affairs. In M. Lewis & C. Saarni (Eds.), Lying and deception in everyday life (pp. 1–29). New York: Guilford Press.

Schlenker, B. R., & Weigold, M. F. (1989). Goals and the self-identification process: Constructing desired identities. In L. A. Pervin (Ed.), Goal concepts in personality and social psychology (pp. 243–290). Hillsdale, NJ: Erlbaum.

Simmons, R., Rosenberg, F. & Rosenberg, M. (1973). Disturbance in the self-image at adolescence. *American Sociological Review, 38,* 553-568.

Snyder, M. (1974). The self-monitoring of expressive behavior. *Journal of Personality and Social Psychology, 30,* 526-537.

Solomon, R. C. (1993). What a tangled web: Deception and self-deception in philosophy. In M. Lewis & C. Saarni (Eds.), Lying and deception in everyday life (pp. 30–58). New York: Guilford Press.

Stone, A. A., Kessler, R. C. & Haythornthwaite, J. A. (1991). Measuring daily events and experiences: Decisions for the researcher. *Journal of Personality, 59,* 575-607.

Tice, D. M., Buder, J. & Baumeister, R. F. (1985). Development of self-consciousness: At what age does audience pressure disrupt performance. *Adolescence, 20,* 301-305.

Van Tuinen, M. & Ramanaiah, N. V. (1979). A multimethod analysis of selected self-esteem measures. *Journal of Research in Personality, 13,* 16-24.

Wheeler, L. & Nezlek, J. B. (1977). Sex differences in social participation. *Journal of Personality and Social Psychology, 35,* 742-754.

Footnotes

1. Specifically, the correlations with manipulativeness, responsibility, and public self-consciousness were somewhat weakened. The partial correlations were .163 (p = .180) for Machiavellianism, .205 (p = .090) for social adroitness, and −.079 (p = .518) for responsibility. (For social adroitness, when the results were combined across samples with the partial correlations instead of the zero-order ones, the combined two-tailed p level was still significant, p = .002. For Machiavellianism, the new combined two-tailed p level was .080; for responsibility, it was .127.) For public self-consciousness, the partial correlation (.226) was nearly significant (p = .061). (The combined p level based on the partial correlations remained significant, p = .029.) The partial correlation with extraversion was very slightly strengthened to .208 (p = .086). None of the other zero-order correlations were significant or nearly significant, and none of them became so after we partialed out social desirability.

2. Another potential bias in our results may result from the element of self-selection inherent in the manner in which our sample was acquired. In both studies, participants responded to notices describing the research as a 7-day diary study. As Stone, Kessler, and Haythornthwaite (1991) have noted, people who volunteer to participate in diary research may be unrepresentative of the larger population.

Journal of Personality and Social Psychology, January 1998, Vol. 74, No. 1, p 63-79

Everyday Lies in Close and Casual Relationships

Bella M. DePaulo, Deborah A. Kashy

Abstract

In 2 diary studies, 77 undergraduates and 70 community members recorded their social interactions and lies for a week. Because lying violates the openness and authenticity that people value in their close relationships, we predicted (and found) that participants would tell fewer lies per social interaction to the people to whom they felt closer and would feel more uncomfortable when they did lie to those people. Because altruistic lies can communicate caring, we also predicted (and found) that relatively more of the lies told to best friends and friends would be altruistic than self-serving, whereas the reverse would be true of lies told to acquaintances and strangers. Also consistent with predictions, lies told to closer partners were more often discovered.

To understand the role of lying in close and casual relationships, it may be important to understand both the nature of the lies that are told in everyday life and the nature of close relationships. Over the past several decades, a handful of studies of lying in everyday life have been published (Camden, Motley, & Wilson, 1984 ; DePaulo, Kashy, Kirkendol, Wyer, & Epstein, 1996 ; Hample, 1980 ; Lippard, 1988 ; Metts, 1989 ; Turner, Edgley, & Olmstead, 1975), including most recently, the first such investigation to include a separate sample of adult participants who were not all college students (DePaulo et al., 1996). These studies have greatly increased our knowledge of the nature and frequency of lying in everyday life. They indicate that lying is a fact of daily life. In the DePaulo et al. (1996) studies, for example, in which lying was defined as "intentionally [trying] to mislead someone" (p. 981), the demographically diverse participants from the community reported telling an average of one lie in every five of their social interactions, and the college student participants reported telling a lie in every three interactions. In both groups, the participants were about twice as likely to tell lies that benefited themselves in some way (self-centered lies) than to tell lies that benefited others (other-oriented, or altruistic, lies). Of the self-centered lies, some of them were told in the pursuit of material gain or personal convenience, but far more of them were told for psychological reasons. By their own accounts, people told their everyday lies to try to make themselves look better or feel better, to protect themselves from embarrassment or disapproval or from having their feelings hurt, and to try to gain the esteem and affection of other people. Although participants told many lies about their achievements and their failures, their actions, plans, and whereabouts, and the reasons for their actions or inactions, the lies that they told most often were about their feelings. When people told other-oriented lies, they often pretended to feel more positively than they really did feel, and they often claimed to agree with other people when in fact they disagreed. In short, in everyday life, people lie about what they are really like and how they really do feel.

Rates of Lying in Close and Casual Relationships

When people talk about what is special to them about their personal relationships and about what closeness means to them (Argyle & Henderson, 1984 ; Maxwell, 1985 ; Parks & Floyd, 1996), they underscore the importance of talking, disclosing, and confiding—of "telling each other everything" (Parks & Floyd, 1996, p. 94) and of trusting that their confidences will be kept. They also describe issues of authenticity, noting that they can show their true feelings and be themselves, with no need to try to impress the other person. Although these self-reports may be idealized, the literature does offer some support for them. For example, people are more self-enhancing with strangers than with friends (Tice, Butler, Muraven, & Stillwell, 1995). Also, the relationship qualities that people value predict important relational outcomes. For example, self-disclosure predicts marital satisfaction (Hendrick, 1981), and trusting and confiding are positively correlated with the quality and enduringness of friendships (Argyle & Henderson, 1984).

People's reports of what they value in their relationships also dovetail with important theoretical statements about the significance of personal relationships. For example, Deci and Ryan (1991) believe that there are three primary psychological needs, and one of them is the need for relatedness (see also Baumeister & Leary, 1995). This need "encompasses a person's strivings to relate to and care for others, [and] to feel that those others are relating authentically to one's self" (p. 243). Similarly, Reis and Patrick (1996) argued for the profound importance of intimacy to human well-being. They define intimacy as "an interactive process in which, as a result of a partner's response, individuals come to feel understood, validated, and cared for" (p. 536). From attachment theory comes the proposition that "humans possess basic needs that are naturally satisfied by social relationships" (Hazan & Shaver, 1994, p. 10), and that the most basic need is for felt security. Feelings of security, in turn, depend largely on the answer to the question "Can I trust my partner to be available and responsive to my needs?" (p. 13). Trustworthy partners, according to Holmes and Rempel (1989), are dependable people who can be counted on to be honest and benevolent.

None of these theoretical perspectives offers explicit predictions about the rates of everyday lying in close and casual relationships. However, the prediction that lying occurs at lower rates in closer relationships would probably be consistent with all of them. Lying is by definition an inauthentic communication; as such, it cannot serve the need for genuine relatedness. When people lie about who they really are and how they really feel, they cannot elicit understanding or validation of the person they really believe themselves to be. They also cannot easily serve as targets of secure attachment, because people who lie especially often to promote their own needs are unlikely to be trusted to be responsive to other people's needs.

We predicted, then, that people will lie less often in close relationships than in casual ones. Also, because lie telling violates close relationship ideals such as openness and authenticity, we predicted that when people do lie to their close relationship partners, they will feel more distressed than when they lie to partners in casual relationships (Miller, Mongeau, & Sleight, 1986). They will feel more uncomfortable as they anticipate telling the lie, as they actually tell it, and just after they have told it.

Kinds of Lies in Close and Casual Relationships

The theoretical perspectives we described underscore the significance of authenticity and trustworthiness in close personal relationships. But they also point to the importance of caring and emotional support. One way that people might try to communicate their love and concern for the important people in their lives is by telling altruistic lies. They compliment them, pretend to agree with them, and claim to understand. The meta-messages of these lies may be supportive rather than threatening (cf. Ruesch & Bateson, 1951 ; Watzlawick, Beavin, & Jackson, 1967). By lying, the liars may be saying that they care more about the other person's feelings than the truth.

Our initial prediction was that people will tell fewer lies to closer relationship partners. We added a second prediction: When people do lie to partners in close relationships, relatively more of the lies will be altruistic than self-centered.

Beyond Closeness: Other Predictors of Lying

In addition to the emotional considerations we have described, there may also be practical reasons for a lower rate of everyday lying in closer relationships than in more casual ones. For example, the possibilities for successful deception in close personal relationships may be constrained by the knowledge that the partners share about each other. A college student can try to convince a casual acquaintance that his father is an ambassador (as one of ours did), but the same lie will not succeed with a close friend who already knows that the "ambassador" is actually a bartender. Relationship partners who have known each other for a long time may be especially likely to have, or to be perceived as having, detailed knowledge about each other's lives that would discourage many attempts at deceit.

In some instances, partners do not already know the truth that a person might be tempted to cover with a lie. Even in those cases, however, people may fear that their partners are more likely to discover the truth eventually if they are close partners, who typically interact frequently (Nezlek, 1995), than if they are only casual relationship partners. People who interact with each other on a regular basis may be vulnerable to this fear of eventual detection even if they are not emotionally close to each other.

These arguments predict that people will less often attempt to lie to their close relationship partners, to people they have known for a long time, and to people with whom they interact frequently. It also follows that when lies are told to such people, those lies are more likely eventually to be discovered. Objective evidence will surface that will betray the deceits, or the liars will become entangled in their own webs of deceit as they struggle to keep their stories consistent.

People in close relationships may also fear that their lies are more likely to be immediately transparent to close relationship partners, who may have developed a special sensitivity to their nonverbal and verbal clues to deceit, than to casual partners (Anderson, Ansfield, & DePaulo, in press). Regardless of whether this fear is justified, it can act as a deterrent to lying to close relationship partners. When people do lie to close partners, they may be less likely to feel confident that their partners believed their lies. In the present research, we asked participants to indicate whether they thought each lie had been believed at the time that they told it. Then, a week or so later, we asked whether the lie had been discovered.

Relationship partners are not always seekers of the truth. As Ekman and Friesen (1969) pointed out several decades ago, people can collaborate to maintain rather than discover each other's lies. Partners in close relationships, more so than those in casual ones, come to know each other's sensitive and taboo topics (Baxter & Wilmot, 1985). By steering clear of such treacherous turf, they can reduce their partners' temptations to lie.

Other processes could also be important in predicting rates of lying in different relationships. For example, Millar and Tesser (1988) hypothesized that people lie when their behavior violates the expectations that another person holds for them. They found support for their predictions in role-play studies of parent–child and employee–employer relationships. The violated expectations model generates a prediction at odds with our own: Because close relationship partners hold more expectations about each other than do casual partners, the rate of lying in close relationships might be higher. On the other hand, the expectations we hold about close relationship partners may be more realistic than the expectations we hold for acquaintances and strangers, and therefore they may be less likely to be violated.

Varieties of Closeness

When the study of personal relationships was just beginning, closeness was often operationalized in terms of different relationship categories (Berscheid, Snyder, & Omoto, 1989a). Marriages and parent–child relationships, for example, were sometimes assumed to be "closer" relationships than friendships. These kinds of assumptions were later questioned, as it became apparent that particular relationships within categories vary greatly in closeness, and that relationship categories vary in many important ways other than closeness. For example, romantic relationships may be uniquely characterized by certain kinds of self-presentational concerns. Relationships that are asymmetrical in power, such as those between parents and children, may also differ importantly in deception-relevant ways from those that are more symmetrical. For instance, people who have less power may be tempted to lie to those who have more power in order to obtain the resources they control (cf. Hample, 1980 ; Lippard, 1988).

In the present research, participants identified each of their interaction partners as a stranger, acquaintance, friend, best friend, romantic partner, spouse, parent, child, sibling, or other relative. To test our hypothesis that fewer lies would be told to closer relationship partners, we first considered only those relationship categories that we believed to vary primarily in closeness: strangers, acquaintances, friends, and best friends. Thus, romantic partners, spouses, parents, and other family members were not included. Our prediction would be supported if participants lied most frequently to strangers, then acquaintances, and least frequently to best friends. Second, we used three measures of closeness (described below) that are independent of relationship type, and we examined the relationship between closeness and rate of lying in analyses that included all dyadic interaction partners. Third, we tested the same links between closeness and rate of lying within each of the major relationship categories (friends, family members, acquaintances and strangers, romantic partners). In this most stringent test of our hypothesis, closeness and rate of lying should have been inversely related within every major relationship category.

Relationship researchers often assess "subjective closeness," which is a person's subjective emotional experience of "feeling close" to someone. This is usually measured on scales that ask people directly how close they feel to each of their partners. We used such a measure in the present research.

Still another measure of closeness was derived theoretically from interdependence theory. Kelley et al. (1983) hypothesized that close relationships are characterized by frequent and diverse interactions that endure over time and in which the partners influence each other's behavior and values. Berscheid, Snyder, and Omoto (1989b) developed the Relationship Closeness Inventory (RCI) to measure the frequency, strength, and diversity components of interdependence, which they summed together to form their overall index of closeness (they considered the duration of the relationship separately). The RCI is a measure of "behaving close," which is distinguishable from the subjective measures of "feeling close" (Aron, Aron, & Smollan, 1992). We did not use the RCI because it had not yet been published when our data were collected. However, we did have access to information similar to that generated by the RCI frequency subscale in the form of the number of dyadic social interactions participants reported with each of their partners (using a version of the Rochester Interaction Record [RIR]; Wheeler & Nezlek, 1977). This measure is probably a more accurate measure of interaction frequency than the RCI frequency subscale, which is based on participants' retrospective estimates of the amount of time they spent alone with each partner over the past week (Reis & Wheeler, 1991).

To assess endurance over time, we included the standard measure of relationship duration (participants' reports of the number of months or years they had known each partner). Thus, the present study measured three relationship qualities (subjective closeness, frequency of interaction, and relationship duration) as well as relationship type (e.g., friend, spouse).

We thought that all three operationalizations of closeness would predict rates of lying: People would lie less often to those relationship partners to whom they feel especially close, to those with whom they interact more frequently, and to those whom they have known for a longer time. However, because we believed that it is the emotional quality of close relationships that most strongly deters lying, we predicted that subjective emotional closeness would be the most important predictor. When the predictive power of all three types of closeness were tested together (by entering them into a simultaneous regression equation), only subjective closeness would remain a significant (negative) predictor of lying.

The Present Research

Our data are from two diary studies of lying in everyday life that were first described by DePaulo et al. (1996) and Kashy and DePaulo (1996) . DePaulo et al. (1996) presented a profile of everyday lying (e.g., the types of lies that were told, the reasons for lying, gender differences in lying), and Kashy and DePaulo (1996) reported personality predictors of lying in everyday life. The present report represents a unique contribution in its focus on everyday lying in different kinds of relationships.

In the two studies, 77 college students and 70 people from the community recorded all of their social interactions and all of the lies that they told during those social interactions every day for a week. Participants described each lie and the reason for telling it in their own words, and they also rated the characteristics of their lie-telling experiences (such as how distressed they felt while telling it and whether they thought it was believed). At the end of the week, they described the nature and closeness of their relationship with each of the persons with whom they had interacted, and they indicated for each lie whether or not it had been discovered.

The present research builds on previous research on lying in relationships in several important ways. First, it is more comprehensive than previous studies in which participants selected just one particular lie (Hample, 1980) or conversation (Turner et al., 1975) or situation (Metts, 1989) to describe. Second, it is the only research to include a measure of participants' opportunities to lie, that is, the number of social interactions they had with each partner. Previous studies that reported that people told more lies to close relationship partners than to casual ones (Hample, 1980 ; Lippard, 1988) are difficult to interpret, in that people interact more frequently with close partners than with casual ones (Nezlek, 1995). Rate of lying (number of lies per number of social interactions) is a more appropriate measure. Third, the community member sample described in this report (and in DePaulo et al., 1996, and Kashy & DePaulo, 1996) is the only group we know of in the literature on lying in everyday life that is not a group consisting solely of college students.[1] Finally, the present research is especially comprehensive in the number of ways that relationships are assessed. Relationship type was documented, and patterns of lying were compared across the different types. Closeness was operationalized in three ways: as subjective closeness, frequency of interacting, and relationship longevity. We examined the links with lying of all three operationalizations of closeness in analyses that included all relationship partners; we also looked at the same links within major relationship categories, such as family and friends.

Method

Participants

Participants in Study 1 were 30 male and 47 female undergraduates who participated in partial fulfillment of a requirement for an introductory psychology course. They ranged in age from 17 to 22 (M = 18.69, SD = 0.91). Sixty-four were White, 9 were Black, and 4 described themselves as "other" than White or Black. The 77 participants do not include one man who completed only 2 days of the 7-day record keeping.

Participants in Study 2 were 30 men and 40 women who were recruited by means of advertisements posted at a local community college, from lists of people who had taken continuing education courses, and from lists of names selected randomly from the area telephone directory. They ranged in age from 18 to 71 (M = 34.19, SD = 12.49). Sixty-seven were White and 3 were Black. Other demographic information is based on 53 of the 70 participants, as 17 were inadvertently given the undergraduate demographic questionnaire, which included no questions about employment, education, marital status, or children. Of those who did answer the more extended questionnaire, 81% were employed, 57% were married, 47% had children, and 34% had no more than a high school education. The 70 participants in Study 2 do not include one man who said that he had recorded only about 10% of his social interactions and 5% of his lies.

Procedure

There were three phases to the study: an initial introductory session, the 7-day recording period, and a final phase during which participants answered additional questions about their lies and their experiences in the study.

Phase 1: Introduction to the study

The Study 1 participants and the participants from Study 2 who were recruited from the community college initially had responded to notices posted on a bulletin board in an academic building describing the research. The study was described as one in which they would keep records of their social interactions and communications for 7 days. In Study 1, the notice indicated that participants would receive partial course credit for their participation, and in Study 2, the notice indicated that participants would be paid $35. Study 2 participants recruited from continuing education lists or from the phone directory were sent letters with the same description of the research; then they were contacted by telephone about a week later.

All participants attended an initial 90-min meeting in which the study and the procedures were explained. In Study 1, these were group sessions attended by 10–15 participants at a time. The Study 2 sessions were conducted individually or in small groups.

Participants were told that they would be recording all of their social interactions and all of the lies that they told during those interactions every day for a week. It was noted that their role in this research was especially important in that they would be the observers and recorders of their own behavior. The investigators explained that they did not condone or condemn lying; rather, they were studying it scientifically and trying to learn the answers to some of the most fundamental questions about the phenomenon. They encouraged the participants to think of the study as an unusual opportunity to learn more about themselves.

The key terms were then explained to the participants. A "social interaction" was defined as "any exchange between you and another person that lasts 10 minutes or more . . . . in which the behavior of one person is in response to the behavior of another person." This definition, plus many of the examples used to clarify the definition, were taken or adapted from the ones used in the initial studies involving the RIR (for example, Wheeler & Nezlek, 1977). We added an exception to the 10-min rule, which was that for any interaction in which participants told a lie, they were also to fill out a social interaction record, even if the interaction lasted less than 10 min. (For the college students and community members respectively, 8.9% and 10.5% of their lies were told during interactions lasting 10 min or less.) Copies of our adaptation of the RIR (see description below) were then distributed, and participants were told how to complete the form.

To explain what participants should count as a lie, we noted that "a lie occurs any time you intentionally try to mislead someone. Both the intent to deceive and the actual deception must occur." Many examples were given. Participants were urged to record all lies, no matter how big or how small. They were instructed that if they were uncertain as to whether a particular communication qualified as a lie, they should record it. (At the end of the study, two coders independently read through all of the lie diaries and agreed on the few that did not meet the definition and were therefore excluded.) The definition that we gave participants was interpreted broadly as encompassing any intentional attempts to mislead, including even nonverbal ones. The only example of a lie they were asked not to record was saying "fine" in response to perfunctory "How are you?" questions. Participants completed one deception record for every lie that they told. Sample records (see description below) were distributed, and the investigators explained how they were to be completed.

Participants were instructed to fill out the forms (social interaction records and deception records) at least once a day; it was suggested that they set aside a particular time or set of times to do so. During the week-long data collection period, the forms were collected by the experimenters at several different times. Participants were also given pocket-sized notebooks and were urged to carry them at all times. They were encouraged to use these notebooks to write down reminders of their social interactions and their lies as soon as possible after the events had taken place. Then they could use their notes as an aid to their memory if they did not complete their social interaction and deception records until later in the day. The notebooks were not collected.

Several additional steps were taken to encourage the reporting of all lies. First, participants were told that if they did not wish to reveal the contents of any of the lies that they told, then in the space on the deception record in which they were to describe their lie, they could instead write "rather not say." That way, we, as investigators, would still know that a lie was told, and we would know other information about the lie and the social interaction in which it was told (from the other parts of the records that the participants completed). The content of 11 of the lies in the college student sample and none of the lies in the community sample were described as "rather not say." Second, we instructed participants that if they did not completely remember everything about a lie that they told, they should still fill out as much of the information on the form as they could. Third, we told participants that if they remembered a lie from a previous day that they had not recorded, they should still turn in a form for that lie.

The importance of accuracy and conscientiousness in keeping the records was emphasized throughout the session. To assure anonymity, we allowed participants to choose their own identification number, which they used throughout the study. Participants did not write their names on any of the forms.

At the end of the session, the investigators reviewed the amount of time it would take to complete all phases of the study and encouraged participants to terminate their participation at that point if they no longer had the interest or the time to participate fully. They were offered credit or payment even if they chose not to continue. All participants elected to continue.

Before they left, participants were given typed copies of all of the instructions and definitions they had been given during the session. This instruction booklet also included names and phone numbers of members of the research team with whom they had met and whom they could contact at any time with any questions or concerns they might have. Appointments were made with each participant to meet with a researcher in approximately 3 days to drop off completed social interaction forms and check on any questions related to the study. Researchers were available to collect forms at other times as well. Appointments were also made with all of the Study 1 participants to return once more at the end of the 7-day recording period to complete a final set of measures. Study 2 participants were shown an envelope and instructions that would be mailed to them at the end of the study so that they could complete the same measures.

Phase 2: Recording social interactions and lies

During the 7-day recording period, which began the day after the introductory session, participants completed a social interaction record for all of their social interactions and a deception record for all of their lies.

The social interaction record was adapted from the RIR (Wheeler & Nezlek, 1977). On each record, participants wrote their identification number and the date, time, and duration of the interaction. For interactions involving three or fewer other people, participants recorded the initials and the gender of each of those persons. (They kept a list of the initials of each of their interaction partners in the small notebooks that we gave them so that they could remember the initials and use the same ones for any given person each time.) For interactions with more than three other people, participants simply recorded the total number of male and female interaction partners. Participants then completed several scales describing the quality of the interaction. (These social interaction variables, described in DePaulo et al., 1996, are not relevant to the present report.)

Printed on the same page as the social interaction record was the deception record. Participants again indicated the initials and gender of the person(s) to whom they told their lie if there were three targets of the lie or fewer, or the number of males and number of females if there were more than three targets. (This information was the same as for the social interaction record except when participants directed their lie to a subset of the people involved in the interaction.) Below this was a blank space for participants to "briefly describe the lie" and another blank space for them to "briefly describe the reason why you told the lie." Next were nine 9-point rating scales. Participants rated their degree of planning of the lie on a scale with endpoints labeled completely spontaneous (1) and carefully planned in advance (9). Then they indicated the importance of not getting caught, from very unimportant (1) to very important (9). On the next three scales, they reported their feelings before the lie was told, while telling the lie, and after the lie was told, on a scale with endpoints labeled very comfortable (1) and very uncomfortable (9). They also rated the seriousness of the lie: very trivial, unimportant lie (1), to very serious, important lie (9); and the target's reaction to the lie: didn't believe me at all (1), to believed me completely (9). Finally, they answered two questions— "How would the target have felt if you told the truth instead of the lie?" and "How would you have felt if you told the truth instead of a lie?"—on scales with endpoints labeled much better if I told the truth (1) and much worse if I told the truth (9). The three ratings of comfort and the measure of the target's belief are of primary importance to the present report.2

Phase 3: Additional measures

After the completion of the 7-day recording period, participants were asked to respond to one more set of measures. First, we gave them a list of all of the initials they had used to refer to all of their interaction partners, and we asked them to fill out a separate form for each of those persons. On the forms, participants indicated the person's age and gender. Then they completed several 15-point scales. The ones relevant to this report were responses to the questions "How close do you feel to this person?" and "How much do you like this person?" Participants' responses to those two questions were highly correlated (college: r = .84, p < .001; community: r = .81, p < .001), and so they were averaged to form our measure of closeness. Participants also indicated how long they had known the person, in years, months, and days. This was our measure of the duration of the relationship. Because the data were highly skewed, we used a square root transformation of the total number of months in our analyses. Finally, participants checked off the particular category that best described their relationship with the person (best friend, friend, acquaintance, stranger, parent or guardian, spouse, child, brother or sister, other relative), and they indicated whether the relationship was romantic or not romantic.

Next, participants were given photocopies of each of the deception records they had completed. They answered two questions about each lie: "Was this lie ever discovered?" (participants checked one answer: no, not yet; don't know; or yes) and "If you could relive this social interaction, would you tell the lie again?" (participants checked either no or yes). The results of the first question are described in this report. Participants also completed a postquestionnaire, which is not relevant to the present report (described in DePaulo et al., 1996).

The Study 1 participants returned to the lab to complete these forms. Afterward, they were interviewed by one of the investigators, who tried to determine the extent to which the participants had understood and complied with the procedure and believed the information they had been given about the research. This extensive interview uncovered no problems with the procedure. Therefore, in Study 2, all of the forms from this phase of the study were mailed to the participants, and a written debrief (plus payment) was included in the package. Participants returned the materials in an addressed and stamped envelope that was also included in the package.

Self-Centered and Other-Oriented Lies

As described in detail in DePaulo et al. (1996) , the reasons participants gave for telling each of their lies were coded into the two major categories of self-centered and other-oriented. (The kappas were .69 and .68.) A third category of "neither self-centered nor other-oriented" was also coded, but those results are not relevant to the present report. That category included lies told to control an interaction, to create an effect (e.g., to entertain), to conform to conventions, or to simplify a response. Also coded but not included in the analyses were instances in which participants said they did not know why they told the lie. Examples of self-centered and other-oriented lies are shown in Table 1 .

Table 1

Examples of Self-Centered and Other-Oriented Lies Told to People in Different Relationship Categories

Relationship Category	Lie	Reason
	Self-Centered Lies	
Nonromantic		
Best friend	I lied about something I didn't want him to know.	I told the lie so I could keep some privacy about my personal life.
Friend	I told her that I admire her uninhibited way.	So she would not think that I was a prude.
Acquaintance	I said I was not worried about my grades.	I didn't want him to think I was stupid. That I am so smart that it is easy to pull them up.
Stranger	Told customer that if she likes her jeans that way, they weren't too tight.	To sell the outfit. (I did.)
Romantic partner (not spouse)	Said I didn't mind him picking up a girl last night.	Wanted to appear untouchable.
Family		
Mother	I told her I'd been studying hard.	Because she's my mother and she'd kill me if she thought I hadn't been studying.
Father	Said we paid off all bills except standard monthly, but we haven't.	So he would co-sign for a new house I want even though he thinks it's too much money.
Spouse	I told her I had to be in D.C. to see a doctor.	Actually, I wanted to visit a friend to trade computer software.
Child	Told son to clean up room and get ready for the weekend and maybe we'd do something special.	Needed his room cleaned up.

(*continued on next page*)

(Table 1 *continued*)

Other-Oriented lies		
Nonromantic		
Best friend	I told her that I'd love for her to stay with me and my family if she wanted to when I really wanted to be alone with them.	She was lonely and I didn't want her to have to stay in the dorm by herself.
Friend	Took sides with her when I really think she was also at fault.	She's going through a divorce and I just didn't want to go against her because it's hard enough to deal with a divorce.
Acquaintance	I told her she was nice-looking even though she isn't.	To make her feel good.
Stranger	Acted like I didn't know the information she was giving me. She told me to "talk to so and so." (I already had talked to so and so.)	So she could feel helpful.
Romantic partner (not spouse)	Told him I loved the food he ordered for me when it wasn't that great.	Didn't want to make him feel bad.
Family		
Mother	I told her I didn't mind going shopping if she wanted me to.	She needs my help but wouldn't ask if she thought I didn't want to go.
Father	I hid my wife's plans to leave.	He would be hurt by the truth and my wife may change her mind.
Spouse	After sex, I pretended to have experienced orgasm.	Did not want to hurt my husband.
Child	I told my son maybe my husband was late because he had car trouble when I thought he'd stopped off for a drink.	Didn't want my son to worry.

Self-centered lies

Self-centered lies were defined as lies told to protect or enhance the liars psychologically or to advantage or protect the liars' interests (as described below). Also included were lies told to elicit a particular emotional response that the liars desired.

The lies told for psychological reasons included lies told to protect the liars from embarrassment, loss of face, or looking bad; from disapproval or having their feelings hurt; and from worry, conflict, or other unpleasantness. They also included lies told to protect the liars' privacy; to make the liars appear better (or just different) than they are; and to regulate the liars' own feelings, emotions, and moods.

The lies told for reasons of personal advantage included lies told for the liars' personal gain, to make things easier or more pleasant for the liars, or to help them get information or get their way. They also included lies told to protect the liars from physical punishment, or to protect their property or assets or their safety. Lies told to protect the liars from loss of status or position or to protect them from being bothered or from doing something they preferred not to do were also included.

Other-oriented lies

Other-oriented lies were defined as lies told to protect or enhance other persons psychologically or to advantage or protect the interests of others (as described below). Lies told to bother or annoy others or to cause them psychological damage (e.g., lie: "Told him the boss wanted to talk to him, but he really didn't"; reason: "so he'd look like a fool") were not included. Only 0.84% of the lies in Study 1 and 2.39% in Study 2 were of this nasty variety.

The other-oriented lies told for psychological reasons included lies told to protect another person from embarrassment, loss of face, or looking bad; from disapproval or having their feelings hurt; from worry, conflict, or other unpleasantness. They also included lies told to protect another person's privacy; to make other people appear better (or just different) than they are; and to regulate another person's feelings, emotions, or moods.

The lies told for another person's advantage included lies told for another person's personal gain, to make things easier or more pleasant for others, to be accommodating, or to help them get their way. They also included lies told to protect others from physical punishment, or to protect their property or assets or their safety. Lies to protect others from loss of status or position or to protect them from being bothered or from doing something they preferred not to do were also included.

Results

Sample Characteristics: Closeness, Duration, and Frequency

Because we were interested in predicting rates of lying from the quality of participants' relationships with particular other people, we included in our analyses only those lies told to just one person (dyadic lies) and omitted those lies that were told to more than one person at a time. Dyadic lies constituted 61% of the lies told by the college students and 72% of the lies told by the community members.

Table 2 shows the mean level of closeness, the mean duration of the relationship, and the mean frequency of interaction with partners in each relationship category. (Fathers are not included as a separate category in the table because only 11 community members and 15 college students reported having any dyadic interactions with their fathers over the course of the week. Fathers are, however, included in the composite category of all family members.) The college students and community members were remarkably similar in their self-reported closeness to different categories of relationship partners, both in the rank ordering of the categories and the absolute values of the means. Both groups reported extremely high levels of closeness to their best friends, family members, and romantic partners. They also reported fairly high levels of closeness to their friends and very low levels of closeness to acquaintances and strangers. The community members, who were older than the college students, reported relationships of longer duration than those of the college students in every category except strangers. The rank ordering of the relationship types by duration, however, was identical for the two groups. With regard to the frequency of their interactions, the college students reported relatively more interactions with friends than did the community members, t (137) = 4.03, p < .001, whereas the community members reported relatively more interactions with acquaintances, t (121) = 3.22, p = .002, and family members, t (112) = 6.69, p < .001.

Table 2

Mean Closeness, Duration, and Frequency of Interacting for Different Categories of Relationships

Relationship category	n[a]	Closeness[b]	Duration[c]	Duration[d]	Frequency[e]
Nonromantic					
Best friend					
College	46	13.93	3.79	5.99	5.48
Community	25	13.43	8.51	9.23	4.68
Friend					
College	77	9.90	1.41	3.29	13.29
Community	62	9.41	4.23	6.00	7.94
Acquaintance					
College	64	4.57	0.41	1.77	3.36
Community	59	4.57	2.18	3.99	6.00
Stranger					
College	14	1.42	0.04	0.51	1.36
Community	27	1.34	0.05	0.36	1.30
All friends					
College	77	10.66	1.74	3.65	16.56
Community	64	9.98	4.68	6.34	9.52
All acq/str					
College	67	4.27	0.38	1.67	3.49
Community	60	4.21	1.98	3.57	6.48
Romantic (not spouse)					
College	59	13.48	2.28	4.44	6.36
Community	28	13.31	4.35	6.54	9.18
Family					
(All)					
College	54	14.02	18.21	14.67	2.35
Community	60	13.31	20.15	14.78	8.80
Mother					
College	39	14.53	18.83	15.03	1.64
Community	22	13.58	29.00	18.50	2.27
Spouse					
Community	30	14.42	18.30	13.76	8.07
Child					
Community	23	14.15	15.30	12.49	5.43
All Partners[f]					
College	77	10.31	2.92	4.29	1.99
Community	69	9.23	6.80	7.10	2.20

Note. Means were computed by summing for each participant and then averaging across participants. Acq/str = acquaintances and strangers.

[a] Number of participants who had at least one dyadic interaction with someone in the category.

[b] 1-15 scale, with higher numbers indicating greater closeness.

[c] Years.

[d] Square root of number of months.

[e] Mean number of dyadic interactions for participants who interacted with someone in the category at least one time.

[f] Includes partners not listed in this table (family members other than mother, spouse, and child).

Correlations among the closeness, duration, and frequency of social interaction variables were computed separately for each participant, weighted by the number of partners, then averaged. (In all analyses to follow, a square root transformation was applied to the number of months of relationship longevity to form our duration measure.) Closeness was significantly correlated with duration (square root), r (76) = .52, $p < .001$, for the college students, and r (68) = .56, $p < .001$, for the community members, and with frequency, r (76) = .33, $p < .001$, for the college students, and r (68) = .43, $p < .001$, for the community members. Duration and frequency were not significantly correlated for either sample. r s = .04 and .24, respectively.3

Predicting Rate of Lying and Types of Lies From Closeness, Duration, and Frequency

One of the primary questions addressed in this study is whether the rate of lying to a partner relates to the closeness of the relationship between the participant and that partner. The rate of lying data have an unbalanced hierarchical structure such that each participant interacts with (and lies to) different partners, and some participants have interactions with many partners whereas other participants interact with relatively few partners. This hierarchically nested data structure can be analyzed using a multilevel regression approach (Kenny, Kashy, & Bolger, in press). This method of analysis involves two steps, the first of which estimates the relationship between closeness to a partner and rate of lying to that partner separately for each participant. The second step aggregates the relationship between closeness and rate of lying to the partner across participants and tests whether, across participants, the closeness and rate of lying relationship is statistically different from zero. The second step can also be used to examine whether this relationship differs as a function of participant-level predictor variables, such as participant gender.

Consider as an example the relationship between rate of lying (number of lies to the partner divided by number of social interactions with the partner) and relationship duration. Each participant generates two scores for each partner: the rate of lying to that partner and the length of time the participant has known the partner. In the multilevel modeling approach, a separate regression equation is estimated for each participant in which duration predicts rate of lying; interaction partner is the unit of analysis in each participant's regression. These regressions yield both an intercept and a slope for each participant. Interpretation of the intercepts from the multilevel approach is simplified if the predictor variable(s), relationship duration in this example, is centered around zero or standardized. The intercept estimates the participant's average rate of lying across all partners, and the slope estimates the relationship between how long a participant has known a partner and the rate of lying to that partner.

The regression coefficients (intercepts and slopes) estimated for each participant then serve as outcome measures in a second set of regression analyses that treat participant as the unit of analysis. This step of the analysis can include participant-level predictor variables, such as participant gender. In one second-step regression analysis, the intercepts from the first-step regressions are used as the criterion scores. If participant gender is used as a predictor (coded as men = −1, women = 1), this second-step regression would yield an estimate of the grand mean for rate of lying, as well as an estimate of the degree to which male participants lied more or less frequently than female participants. More important, when the slopes from the first-step regressions are used as the criterion scores and participant gender is the predictor, the second-step regression yields an intercept that estimates the average relationship between relationship duration and rate of lying for all participants.

This analysis also provides an estimate of the degree to which the relationship between relationship duration and rate of lying differs for male and female participants.

The precision of the first-step regressions is likely to vary from participant to participant for two reasons. First, some partic- ipants will have interacted with more partners than others. Second, the relationship between relationship duration and rate of lying may be more consistent for some participants than for others. The two-step regression approach used in our analyses takes these factors into account using a weighted least-squares solution in which the second step regressions are weighted by the standard errors of the first step regression coefficients.

This two-step regression approach was used to examine the relationship between each measure of closeness and rate of lying. We also used a variation on this approach to examine the unique predictive ability of each of the three closeness variables, partialing out the other two. That is, for each participant a multiple regression equation was estimated in which rate of lying to a particular partner was the criterion and subjective closeness to the partner, duration of relationship, and frequency of interaction with the partner were entered simultaneously in the first step regressions. The regression coefficients from these multiple regressions were then pooled across participants, again weighting by the standard errors of the regression coefficients. In the results and discussion below, each of the predictor variables was standardized.

Results for both the univariate and multivariate methods are shown in Table 3 .4 We also combined the results of the college and community samples using the meta-analytic technique of combining p s. When the results were not significant for one or both samples but were significant in the combined analysis, we mention the combined p in the text.

Table 3

Predicting Rate of Lying and Types of Lies From Closeness, Duration, and Frequency of Interaction

Variable	Regression with 1 relationship variable[a]		Simultaneous regr with all 3 vars[b]	
	b	*t*	*b*	*t*
Rate of lying[c]				
Closeness				
College	-.084	4.99***	-.106	5.15***
Community	-.063	3.00**	-.055	2.07*
Duration[d]				
College	-.010	0.60	.033	1.78+
Community	-.039	2.07*	.016	0.65
Frequency of interaction				
College	-.036	2.42*	-.014	0.91
Community	-.045	4.47**	.001	0.05
Self-centered lies[e]				
Closeness				
College	-.064	2.56**	-.104	2.92**
Community	.050	1.01	.076	0.71
Duration[d]				
College	-.028	0.91	-.021	0.57
Community	.023	0.41	.080	0.80
Frequency of interaction				
College	-.002	0.09	.043	1.40
Community	.030	0.73	.094	1.49
Other-oriented lies[f]				
Closeness				
College	.073	2.74**	.069	2.05*
Community	.050	1.38	.071	1.01
Duration[d]				
College	.071	2.87**	.065	1.83+
Community	-.007	0.14	-.113	1.45
Frequency of interaction				
College	.010	0.40	-.038	1.09
Community	-.001	0.04	-.057	0.90

Note. Analyses of rate of lying were based on college: n = 71 and community: n = 59. Analyses of self-centered lies were based on college: n = 41 and community: n = 21. Analyses of other-oriented lies were based on college: n = 34 and community: n = 21.

[a] Two-step regression analyses with closeness or duration or frequency entered in the first step and participant gender in the second.

[b] Simultaneous regression with closeness, duration, and frequency entered together in the first step and participant gender in the second.

[c] Number of lies told to partner divided by number of social interactions with partner.

[d] Analyses were based on square root of number of months.

[e] Number of self-centered lies told to partner divided by the total number of lies told to partner.

[f] Number of other-oriented lies told to partner divided by the total number of lies told to partner.

+ $p <$ or $= .10$.   * $p <$ or $= .05$.   ** $p <$ or $= .01$.   *** $p <$ or $= .001$.

In the analyses that included just one of the relationship variables at a time, closeness, relationship duration, and frequency of social interaction were all (negative) predictors of the overall rate of lying and were significantly so for all except duration for the college students. Participants told fewer lies to the people in their lives to whom they felt closer, to those with whom they interacted more frequently, and (for the community members) to those whom they had known for a longer time. However, when all three variables were entered simultaneously, only closeness remained a significant predictor of lying. For both groups, partic- ipants lied less often to the people to whom they felt closer. The relationship variables did not interact significantly with either participant gender or partner gender.

The proportion of lies that were self-centered was not significantly predicted by either duration or frequency. For the college student sample, it was predicted by closeness: When participants told lies to the people in their lives to whom they felt especially close, relatively fewer of those lies were self-centered ones. However, a significant interaction of closeness with participant gender, t (40) = 2.24, p = .031, indicated that it was primarily for the men that closeness was a negative predictor of the proportion of self-centered lies (for men, the coefficient for closeness predicting rate of lying was −.12); for women, there was essentially no relationship (b = −.008). No other interactions with gender were significant.

As predicted, closeness was a positive predictor of the rate of telling other-oriented lies. When participants did tell lies to the people to whom they felt especially close, relatively more of those lies were other-oriented ones. This effect was in the same direction for both samples and was significant for the college students and in the combined analysis (the combined p = .006). The only other significant predictor of the telling of other-oriented lies was duration: For the college students (only), the longer they had known another person, the more likely it was that the lies they told to that person would be other-oriented ones.[5]

For some family members, the duration of the relationship is sometimes equal to the participant's age. Therefore, for all results involving relationship duration, we recomputed them deleting family members. For rate of lying in the single-variable regression, the result for duration that was significant for the community sample became nonsignificant when family members were excluded, b = −.028, t (54) = 1.24, p = .22. For the simultaneous regression, the result for duration for the college sample that was marginally significant became nonsignificant, b = .025, t (68) = 1.27, p = .21. For predictions of self-centered lies for the community sample, the result for the single-variable regression for duration that was in the unpredicted direction (positive) became negative, though not significantly so, b = −.041, t (18) = 0.97, p = .34. In the simultaneous regression, the b for duration for the community sample also became slightly negative, b = −.015, t (10) = 0.18, p = .86. For predictions of other-oriented lies for the college sample, the result for duration in the single-variable regression dropped from significant to nearly significant, b = .048, t (29) = 1.76, p = .09. For the community sample, the result for duration in the single-variable regression that was in the unpredicted direction (negative) became positive and significant, b = .075, t (20) = 2.14, p = .04. For the simultaneous regression for the community sample, the result for duration also switched from negative to slightly positive, b = .032, t (11) = 0.58, p = .57. In sum, when analyses involving relationship duration were recomputed deleting family members, the results for rate of lying became slightly weaker, but the results for self-centered and other-oriented lying generally became somewhat more consistent with predictions.

Lying in Different Kinds of Relationships

Table 4 shows the overall rate of lying and the proportions of lies that were self-centered and other-oriented separately for each of the different kinds of relationship. In these analyses, we separated romantic relationships and family relationships from other relationships. We predicted that within the latter category, the overall rate of lying would be lowest for best friends, next lowest for friends, then acquaintances, and would be highest for strangers. In that closeness systematically decreased from best friends to strangers (see Table 2), this was another test of the closeness hypothesis, only with romantic and family ties removed. The ordering of the means for both groups was generally as predicted by the closeness hypothesis. The overall rate of lying increased systematically from best friends and friends to acquaintances and strangers. The linear trend was tested using a multilevel regression approach in which a regression equation was computed for each participant using the level of the relationship as a predictor (best friend = 4, friend = 3, acquaintance = 2, and stranger = 1) and the rate of lying to partners in that relationship category as the criterion. The test of the linear slope was significant for both groups, $t(41) = 2.83$, $p = .007$, for the college students and $t(24) = 2.15$, $p = .042$, for the community members.

Table 4

Rate of Lying and Types of Lies in Different Categories of Relationships

Relationship category	Rate of lying[a]		Self-centered lies[b]		Other-oriented lies[c]	
	Mean	n	Mean	n	Mean	n
Nonromantic						
Best friend						
College	27.96	46	37.28	23	36.67	23
Community	17.03	25	50.00	7	42.86	7
Friend						
College	27.62	77	38.16	61	28.29	61
Community	26.06	62	42.84	37	42.78	37
Acquaintance						
College	48.21	64	56.40	43	13.72	43
Community	32.86	59	55.78	36	24.27	36
Stranger						
College	77.38	14	54.54	11	18.18	11
Community	55.56	27	54.49	13	26.28	13
All friends						
College	27.47	77	38.31	63	30.22	63
Community	21.71	64	42.18	38	44.46	38
All acq/str						
College	48.31	67	58.26	44	14.39	44
Community	35.34	60	54.85	39	23.72	39
Romantic (not spouse)						
College	34.33	59	47.27	37	28.22	37
Community	31.78	28	64.22	17	19.61	17
Family						
(All)						
College	31.53	54	48.96	24	34.38	24
Community	15.36	60	60.77	29	18.94	29
Mother						
College	46.37	39	58.33	20	31.67	20
Community	30.08	22	66.67	9	11.11	9
Spouse						
Community	9.85	30	46.50	10	16.50	10
Child						
Community	8.08	23	65.48	7	34.52	7

Note. Acq/str = acquaintances and strangers.

[a] Number of lies divided by number of social interactions multiplied by 100.

[b] Number of self-centered lies divided by total number of lies multiplied by 100.

[c] Number of other-oriented lies divided by total number of lies multiplied by 100.

We combined best friends and friends into a category called "all friends," and compared the rate of lying to that category with the rate of lying to the category of acquaintances and strangers combined. This test was significant for both groups (see Table 5). The college students and the community members told more lies per social interaction to acquaintances and strangers than to their friends. Comparisons of the category of all family members to the acquaintance plus stranger composite yielded a significant result for the community members, who reported a lower rate of lying to their family members than to acquaintances and strangers. The effect was in the same direction for the college students, and it was significant in the combined analysis ($p = .003$). Finally, the rate of lying to family members did not differ significantly from the rate of lying to all friends for either sample.

Table 5

Comparison of Lies Told to Family, Friends, and Acquaintances and Strangers

Comparison	Rate of lying[a]		Self-centered lies[b]		Other-oriented lies[c]	
	t	n	*t*	n	*t*	n
Friends versus acq/str						
College	2.75**	67	1.78+	39	3.00**	39
Community	2.20*	55	2.12*	25	3.29**	25
Acq/str versus family						
College	1.39	48	1.31	17	1.69	17
Community	2.99**	51	0.27	16	0.03	16
Friends versus family						
College	0.42	54	1.49	22	0.46	22
Community	1.24	55	1.11	18	2.09*	18

Note. Acq/str = acquaintances and strangers.

[a] Number of lies divided by number of social interactions multiplied by 100.

[b] Number of self-centered lies divided by total number of lies multiplied by 100.

[c] Number of other-oriented lies divided by total number of lies multiplied by 100.

$+ p <$ or $= .10$. $* p <$ or $+ .05$. $** p <$ or $= .01$.

Although participants in both groups reported high levels of closeness to their romantic partners and to their mothers, the rates of lying in both of these categories were fairly high. Both the college students and community members told about one lie in every three of their social interactions to their romantic partners (not including spouses). The rate of lying to mother was especially high for the college students and approached the level of one lie in every two social interactions. In contrast, the rates of lying to spouses and children were the lowest of all: The community members told less than one lie in every 10 social interactions to them.

We could not compute the linear contrast on the proportions of all lies that were self-centered or other-oriented, because the number of participants who told those kinds of lies to partners in several different relationship categories was too small. However, we did compute the critical comparison between all friends and the acquaintance and stranger composite. This comparison was significant or nearly so for both samples and for both kinds of lies. As predicted, participants told proportionately fewer self-centered lies and proportionally more other-oriented lies to their friends than to acquaintances and strangers.

To determine whether the key relationship between closeness and overall rate of lying (shown in Table 3) would also occur within each of the relationship categories, we computed regressions using closeness as a predictor of number of lies per social interaction for the categories of (a) best friends and friends, (b) acquaintances and strangers, and (c) all family members. The n s for these analyses are necessarily smaller than those in Table 3 because only a subset of the relationship categories is included each time. In addition, the n s are reduced because some participants did not have multiple interactions within a relationship category (or did not lie to anyone in that relationship category) and were therefore not included in the analyses of that category. Also, participants who assigned identical closeness ratings to all of their partners within a given category had to be excluded as well. Consequently, we did not have sufficient n s to compute these regressions for the all family category for the college students (we had an n of 14 for the community sample). The other n s, for the college and community samples respectively, were 70 and 38 for best friends and friends, and 22 and 25 for acquaintances and strangers.

For four of the five slopes that we could compute, the predicted negative relationship between closeness and rate of lying occurred. Only for the all family category in the community sample was the slope positive, $b = .011$, but the effect was tiny, $t (13) = 0.10$, $p = .92$. For the category of all friends, the b s were $-.015$ and $-.040$ for the college and community samples. Although neither of these effects reached significance ($p s = .26$ and $.12$), the combined p was nearly significant ($p = .058$). Similarly, within the category of acquaintances and strangers, the b s were $-.067$ and $-.064$, which were individually nonsignificant ($p s = .20$ and $.21$) but nearly significant when combined ($p = .071$). In sum, within all of the major relationship categories, except the family category for the community sample, the key finding that fewer lies were told to closer relationship partners was replicated. That the significance levels were not as impressive as in the analyses using all of the data is attributable to the reduced power.

Perhaps what is important about lying in relationships is not the rate of lying, but whether any lies at all are told to a particular relationship partner. To examine this possibility, we looked at the percentage of partners within each category to whom any lies at all were told. For the college students, these percentages were 66, 44, 36, and 38, respectively, for the strangers, acquaintances, friends, and best friends. For the community members, the corresponding values were 47, 34, 30, and

33. (The percentage for the category of all family members was identical for both samples, 34.) In both samples, participants told lies to a smaller percentage of their best friends and friends than to acquaintances and strangers; for the college students, $t(67) = 1.72$, $p = .090$, for the community members, $t(57) = 2.12$, $p = .038$ (combined $p = .008$). The linear trend testing the prediction that participants would tell the greatest percentage of lies to strangers, next greatest to acquaintances, and lowest to best friends was nearly significant in each sample, $b = -.051$, $t(47) = 1.80$, $p = .078$, for the college students, and $b = -.078$, $t(27) = 1.96$, $p = .06$, for the community members, and was significant in the combined analysis ($p = .010$). In sum, considering the percentage of partners to whom any lies were told instead of the number of lies per social interaction does not change the conclusion that lying decreases as relationship closeness increases.

Predicting Characteristics of the Lies From Closeness, Duration, and Frequency

Multilevel regression analyses were used to predict characteristics of the lies (e.g., degree of planning, importance of avoiding detection) using relationship closeness, relationship duration, and frequency of interaction as predictors. As described earlier, in this analysis a separate regression was computed for each participant, treating partner as the unit of analysis. In this case, however, the criterion was the average rating of a lie characteristic to a particular partner, averaging across all lies told to that partner. The predictor was the variable measuring closeness of the relationship (standardized) with the partner. As before, the second step of the analysis involved predicting the regression coefficients from the first step, using participant gender as the predictor. This analysis resulted in an average regression coefficient estimating the relationship between the lie characteristic variable and the closeness measure (see Table 6), as well as an estimate of the interaction between participant gender and partner closeness in predicting the lie characteristic.

Table 6

Predicting Characteristics of the Lies From Closeness, Duration, and Frequency of Interaction

Lie characteristic	Closeness *b*	Duration *b*[a]	Frequency *b*
Distress before			
College	.179*	.171	.328
Community	.110	.376+	-.725+
Distress during			
College	.060	.202+	.419*
Community	.023	.427	-.697+
Distress after			
College	.131	.233*	.377+
Community	.115	.265	-.509+
Target believed			
College	-.282**	-.182	.012
Community	.040	.116	.124
Was it discovered?			
College	.092**	.017	-.049
Community	.092	.189	-.345*

Note. The regression coefficients (*b*s) above were computed using standardized predictor variables.
[a] Analyses were based on square root of number of months.
+ $p <$ or $= .10$.   * $p <$ or $= .05$.   ** $p <$ or $= .01$.

Table 6 shows the regression coefficients for the predictions of the characteristics of the lies for the two samples. We predicted that participants would feel more distressed about the lies that they told to their closer relationship partners. For the key variable of subjective closeness, all six results (distress before, during, and after, for the college and community samples) were in the predicted direction. For distress before, the b s were significant for the college students and in the combined analysis (p = .04), and for distress after, the combined result was nearly significant (p = .06). Generally, then, the participants did feel more uncomfortable about the lies they told to the people to whom they felt emotionally closer, though most of the individual results (before combining) were not significant.

The duration of the relationship was a consistent predictor of participants' distress across both samples. The college students and the community members felt more distressed before (combined p = .02), during (combined p = .02), and after (combined p = .01) the telling of their lies to the people they had known longer. However, when these analyses were recomputed omitting family members, all of the results became nonsignificant.

The results for frequency were in different directions for the two samples. The college students tended to feel more distressed about the lies that they told to the people with whom they interacted more frequently. The community members tended to feel less distressed about their lies to those people.

We also predicted that participants would feel less confident that their lies had been believed when the targets of those lies were closer relationship partners. For the college students, the result for subjective closeness was as predicted. No other effects were significant.

Finally, we predicted that the lies would be more likely to have been discovered by the end of the study when they had been told to partners to whom the participants felt emotionally closer, whom the participants had known longer, and with whom they interacted more frequently. For subjective closeness, the results were in the predicted direction for both groups and were significant for the college students and in the combined analysis (p = .01). For relationship duration, the results were in the predicted direction but not significant. (This was also true when family members were excluded from the analyses.) For frequency, the results were in the direction contrary to predictions and were significant for the community members and in the combined analysis (p = .05). There were no significant interactions with participant gender for any of the lie characteristics.

In sum, the results for the characteristics of the lies were strongest and most consistent with predictions for the measure of subjective closeness. Participants tended to feel more distressed before and after telling lies to people to whom they felt emotionally closer. At the time that they told their lies, the college students were especially unlikely to think that their subjectively closer relationship partners believed those lies. And across both groups, participants reported that the lies they told to their subjectively closer relationship partners were more likely to have been discovered by the end of the study.

Characteristics of Lies in Different Kinds of Relationships

We computed the mean level of each lie characteristic separately for each of the three relationship category composites: all friends, acquaintances plus strangers, and all family members. We then did pairwise comparisons and combined the p values across the two samples. For the comparisons of friends with acquaintances and strangers, there were no effects that were significant and consistent across the two groups. For the college students, one effect was consistent with predictions: They thought that their friends were less likely to have believed their lies than were acquaintances and strangers, t (37) = −2.36, p = .02. For the comparisons of lies told to family members versus acquaintances and strangers, participants' feelings of distress during and after the telling of their lies were in the same direction for both samples and were significant in the combined analysis. As predicted, participants felt more distressed during and after the telling of their lies to family members, relative to acquaintances and strangers. For distress during, for the college students, t (15) = 2.38, p = .03; for the community members, t (15) = 1.62, p = .13; and the combined p = .01. For distress after, for the college students, t (16) = 1.29, p = .22; for the community members, t (15) = 1.92, p = .07; and the combined p = .03. Finally, for comparisons of lies told to family members with lies told to friends, only one effect was significant: The college students said that they felt more distressed while lying to family members than to their friends, t (21) = −2.72, p = .01.

Discussion

Closeness Predicts Lower Rates of Everyday Lying

Among the qualities that people value most in their close personal relationships are the self-disclosure and confiding that occur in those relationships, the freedom they feel to be themselves (Argyle & Henderson, 1984 ; Maxwell, 1985 ; Parks & Floyd, 1996), and their trust that their partners will care about them and be responsive to their needs. The same characteristics predict the quality and durability of personal relationships (Argyle & Henderson, 1984 ; Hendrick, 1981). Those characteristics are also described as deeply significant in some of the most influential theoretical statements about close relationships (e.g., Bowlby, 1988 ; Deci & Ryan, 1991 ; Hazan & Shaver, 1994 ; Holmes & Rempel, 1989).

In contrast, the lies that people tell in their everyday social interactions violate just those ideals. When people tell everyday lies, they pretend to be different kinds of people than they believe they really are, and they profess feelings that they are not actually experiencing and opinions they do not in fact embrace (DePaulo et al., 1996). We therefore expected to find lower rates of lying to closer relationship partners. The data were strongly supportive of that prediction. In both studies, when we examined the relationship between closeness and rates of lying for all of the people with whom the participants interacted, we found that the participants told fewer lies per social interaction to the people to whom they felt closer. Participants also told fewer lies to the people with whom they interacted more frequently, and for the community members, they told fewer lies to the people they had known longer. But when all of these relational aspects—closeness, frequency of interacting, and relational duration—were considered simultaneously, it was subjective closeness that emerged as the only significant predictor of rates of lying. It was also subjective closeness that most consistently predicted participants' feeling of discomfort about their lies. Participants felt more distressed before and after telling lies to partners to whom they felt emotionally closer.

Our position, then, is that everyday lies violate the nature of close relationships. If people's presentations of themselves to another person are so distorted as to be deliberately misleading, and if they hide and fake their feelings and opinions a bit too often, then their relationship with that person may no longer be a close one. Ideally, close relationships should provide some insulation from the need to present oneself dishonestly. People in close relationships know each other's weaknesses and annoyances as well as their strengths and charms, and yet they still value and care about each other.

Reis and Patrick's (1996) account of the intimacy process highlights the importance of feeling understood and validated. Perhaps those feelings are what separate relationships that are emotionally close from those that are characterized only by longevity or by frequent contacts. Duration of the relationship and frequency of interaction by themselves provide little protection from the risks of honestly presenting one's true and vulnerable self.

Pragmatic Deterrents to Lying

Although we believe that the emotional deterrents to lie telling in close relationships are most important, we think that there are important practical considerations as well. Partners in emotionally close relationships believe that they develop special sensitivities to each other's verbal and nonverbal cues and that they are therefore especially likely to see through each other's lies (Anderson et al., in press). Even in instances when close relationship partners believe that they might get away with their lies when they first tell them, they may still fear that the lies will be detected eventually or that the work of maintaining the lies would not be worth the effort. There are also certain lies that simply cannot be told to close relationship partners, who are already knowledgeable about the truth of the matter. All of these kinds of factors could have helped to account for our finding that people told fewer lies per social interaction to their closer relationship partners.

If participants were in fact deterred from telling lies that they believed had little chance of remaining undetected by their close relationship partners, then perhaps the lies they did tell were more successful. But that did not occur. The college students thought that their emotionally closer relationship partners were less likely to have believed their lies at the time they were told. They and the community members, considered together, also reported that the lies they told to their closer relationship partners were more likely eventually to have been discovered. We had predicted that lies would also be more often discovered by partners the participants had known for a long time, and by partners with whom the participants interacted frequently. We were wrong on both counts. We thought that frequent interactions would provide frequent opportunities to discover the lies and that longevity would provide relationship partners with an accumulated knowledge about each other that would also increase the odds that lies would eventually come undone. But neither opportunity nor knowledge may matter much if emotional investment is lacking. Perhaps relationship partners need to care about knowing the true facts and feelings of each other's lives in order to turn opportunity and knowledge into insight and lie-detection success.

The Special Place of Altruistic Lies in Close Relationships

In underscoring the link between honesty and closeness, we are not denying the presence and importance of deception in personal relationships (see also DePaulo, 1992 ; Parks, 1982). Even in relationships with spouses, for which the rate of lying was lower than for any other adult category, lies were told in nearly one out of every 10 social interactions. Efforts to eliminate totally all everyday lies from close personal relationships would probably be misguided. For instance, a little bit of light lying might serve important privacy needs for individuals in close relationships.

Other important functions of lying were suggested by the special place that altruistic lies seem to hold in close relationships. Although lying in general, and—in some analyses—self-centered lying in particular, occurs at lower rates in closer relationships, other-oriented lying occurs at relatively higher rates. People who tell the kinds of other-oriented lies that involve faking agreement with their partner's opinion or course of action may be conveying the message that they are on their partner's side. In discussing the importance of talk to the maintenance of relationships, Duck (1994) argues that talk serves to demonstrate a "symbolic union" between the relationship partners. Our data suggest that when partners in close relationships are not in fact united in their views, they may still pretend that they are.

Other kinds of altruistic lies serve to protect other people's faces and feelings. These are the kinds of other-oriented lies that may help to convey the caring and concern that have been deemed so essential to the processes of intimacy (Reis & Patrick, 1996), relatedness (Deci & Ryan, 1991), and attachment (Bowlby, 1988).

We had a hint from our earlier work with this data set that other-oriented lies might play a special role in successful relationships (see also Metts, 1989). In our analyses of individual differences in everyday lying (Kashy & DePaulo, 1996), we found that individuals who reported greater satisfaction with their same-gender relationships characteristically (across all of the people with whom they interacted) told relatively more other-oriented lies than self-centered ones. Of course, that finding was about the ways in which particular individuals differ from each other as liars. We could not have known from that finding alone whether it would follow that people tell relatively more altruistic lies than self-centered ones to their closer relationship partners. Conceptually, though, the findings complement each other.

Perhaps we should have recognized another precursor to our findings in a process that has been shown to predict effective relationship functioning. That process is accommodation (Rusbult, Yovetich, & Verette, 1996). It occurs when people who are the target of a relationship partner's inconsiderate, humiliating, or otherwise destructive behavior do not articulate or act on the intense negative emotion that they experience. Instead, they behave constructively, and express sentiments that are kinder than the ones they really feel. Rusbult and her colleagues believe that this process involves a "transformation of motivation." We believe that it also involves deception.

When, in the process of accommodation, individuals set aside their own self-interest and instead behave more constructively, the target of their altruism is not so much their relationship partner as the relationship itself (Rusbult et al., 1996). But perhaps the liars are beneficiaries as well. Aron and his colleagues have argued that in close relationships, individuals behave as if some or all of the characteristics of their partner are also, at least in part, their own. That is, they feel more of a oneness or union with their partner (Aron, Aron, Tudor, & Nelson, 1991). One implication is that acts that benefit the partner are also experienced as beneficial to the individuals themselves. This casts a new light on our findings. It suggests that people may tell relatively more other-oriented lies to their closer relationship partners because they are more likely to feel personally benefited by those lies.

Our argument has been that people tell relatively more altruistic lies in their closer personal relationships because they care more about their partners' feelings in those relationships. These lies, we believe, communicate understanding, validation, and caring—the essential components of intimacy. But in their discussion of the process of developing and maintaining intimacy, Reis and Patrick (1996) noted that partners can validate each other's experiences without necessarily agreeing with their point of view. The implication, it seems, is that it should be possible to communicate caring and concern without lying. This lofty ideal may be admirable, but it is not always easy to achieve. If you really think your friend was at fault in her disastrous relationship with her husband, and that your best friend, who is dying of cancer, looks even worse than she did a few weeks before, how do you communicate those sentiments in a caring, validating, loving—and honest—way?

The Problem With Mothers and Lovers

There were some important exceptions to our findings that closeness predicted lower rates of lying. Participants reported very high levels of closeness to their mothers and to their romantic partners (who were not spouses). Levels of closeness to mothers and lovers were about as high as for best friends, and even higher than for friends. Yet the rates of lying to these partners were not especially low. Participants in both studies told about one lie in every three social interactions to their romantic partners, and community members lied at about the same rate to their mothers. The college students lied in almost every other interaction they had with their mothers. We think that these exceptions occurred because closeness is not the only important predictor of lying. Lying may also be predicted by the power of the targets of the lies (Hample, 1980 ; Lippard, 1988), and by their interpersonal attractiveness and appeal. For college students especially, mothers still control significant resources and privileges, and so students lie in order to obtain those things. Children of all ages may also continue to care about what their mothers think of them, and so self-presentational lies continue to be prevalent even among the adults from the community sample.

Romantic partners who are not spouses present a different set of lures for lies. People may want very much to impress their romantic partners and to be loved and admired by them, but they may be insecure about whether they will succeed. This, too, is a recipe for deceit. Uncertain about whether their "true selves" are lovable enough to attract and keep such appealing mates, people present themselves as they wish they were instead of how they believe they are in fact. Our explanations of the mother and lover problems are speculative, though, and in need of further testing.

Lying and Relationship Development

In comparing the rates of lying to different categories of relationship partners, we were especially struck by the differences between romantic partners who were or were not spouses. People lied in about one out of every three of their interactions with their romantic partners who were not spouses, but in less than one in ten of their interactions with their spouses. As intimate relationships deepen and romantic partners become spouses, do the rates of lying decrease along the way? Or are those romantic relationships that ultimately result in marriage characterized by greater honesty from the outset? Longitudinal studies would help to elucidate these and other possible explanations.

Is the Truth Bias Really a Bias?

One of the most robust findings in the literature on deception–detection is a truth bias: When presented with equal numbers of truths and lies to judge, people characteristically believe that more of the messages are truths than lies (DePaulo, Stone, & Lassiter, 1985). This truth bias is even stronger for close relationship partners, such as relatives and friends, than it is for strangers (Buller, Strzyzewski, & Comstock, 1991 ; Millar & Millar, 1995 ; see also Levine & McCornack, 1992 ; McCornack & Parks, 1986 ; for a review, see Anderson, Ansfield, & DePaulo, in press). Within the experimental paradigms in which the truth bias has been documented, it is indeed an error: People identify more of the messages as truths than lies when in fact the numbers are identical. But in the real world, truths are more common than lies (DePaulo et al., 1996). The present research has shown that rates of truth telling are not equivalent across relationships but are higher in closer relationships. Using real-world base rates as criteria, the stronger truth bias in closer relationship categories should not be regarded as a mistake (Funder, 1987).

Little Lies, Big Lies

Millar and Tesser's (1988) model of violated expectations holds that people tell lies when their behavior violates other people's expectations for them. Because close relationship partners have more expectations for each other, the likelihood that expectations will be violated and lies will be told is greater in close relationships than in casual ones. Our findings that fewer lies are told in close relationships are inconsistent with the Millar and Tesser (1988) predictions. Perhaps we were wrong in thinking that a greater number of expectations implies a greater likelihood of expectancy violation; if the expectations are accurate, then they may be violated only rarely. Another possibility is that the violated expectations model may be a more powerful predictor of serious lies than of the everyday lies that were the focus of the present research. Serious lies are often told to cover seriously bad behaviors, such as infidelities (DePaulo, Ansfield, Kirkendol, & Boden, 1997). In those instances, the truth (e.g., that an infidelity occurred) may seem to the liar to pose a greater threat to the relationship than a lie, which the liar might hope will never be discovered (cf. McCornack & Levine, 1990). In everyday lies, in contrast, it is the lie that is more threatening. One person's poor grades, for example, pose less of a threat to a friendship than the person's denial that the grades are poor or that she or he is concerned about them. In short, we believe that the relationship between closeness and lying will depend on whether the truth or a lie would pose a greater threat to the relationship. In the domain of serious lies, it is often the truth that would hurt the most and force a renegotiation of the relationship; in that domain, then, close relationships may be breeding grounds for deceit.

Methodological Issues

In this research, we asked people to tell us about an aspect of their own behavior that is considered socially undesirable in their culture. It is important, then, to address the question of whether we can believe these self-reports of lies. The validity issue is one that concerned us deeply from the outset. We did everything we could think of to try to elicit accurate and thorough reports. For example, we had an extensive initial meeting with the participants in which we explained what counted as a lie in great detail and in which we emphasized the importance of accuracy and conscientiousness. We collected participants' diary entries several times throughout the week so that they would record their own behavior soon after it occurred, and we assured them that their anonymity would be protected (see DePaulo et al., 1996, for further details). So far as we know, no prior study of lying in everyday life instituted such procedures for encouraging accuracy.

Several aspects of our findings reassure us of the validity of participants' reports. First, participants reported a high rate of self-centered lying. They did not try to convince us that all or even most of their lies were altruistic. Second, in this report as well as our previous ones (DePaulo et al., 1996 ; Kashy & DePaulo, 1996), the most important findings were impressively similar across the two samples. If participants were misrepresenting their lying, they were doing so in strikingly similar ways in the two very different groups.

Still, it is possible that some motivations were shared by the two groups and thus produced similar, but invalid, results. For example, it is possible that when participants reported more altruistic motivations for the lies that they told to their closer relationship partners, they were simply rationalizing. We think that the best response to these kinds of challenges is to test them experimentally. For example, Bell and DePaulo (1996) experimentally manipulated participants' liking for an art student, who then questioned the participants about their opinions of her work. Consistent with our findings that people tell relatively more altruistic lies to the people to whom they

108

feel closer, the participants who were induced to like the artist more also told more altruistic lies to her (see also DePaulo & Bell, 1996).

Another threat to the validity of our results is that the diary methodology may be a reactive one. For example, perhaps partic- ipants who noticed that they had told many self-centered lies to some of their interaction partners felt less close to those partners as a consequence, and rated their closeness to them accordingly at the end of the study. We do not find this particular challenge troublesome, as it does not explain why we also found fewer self-centered lies to close others when closeness was operationalized by relationship category (i.e., participants told fewer self-centered lies to best friends and friends than to acquaintances and strangers). Of course, it may be possible to generate still other alternative explanations of our findings that follow from the possible reactivity of the diary methodology. Our response again is to encourage experimental tests of any hypotheses that can be tested experimentally.

At the same time, however, it is important to recognize that the most basic questions that motivated this research—e.g., do people tell fewer lies per social interaction to the people in their lives with whom they share closer emotional bonds (as research and theory on close relationships would predict)?—are not testable experimentally. People cannot be randomly assigned to be spouses, parents, or best friends. We think that the diary methodology, despite its limitations, is the best available methodology for testing theoretically motivated questions about the rates and patterns of everyday lying in close and casual relationships.

References

Anderson, D. E., Ansfield, M. E., & DePaulo, B. M. Love's best habit: Deception in the context of relationships. in pressIn P. Philippot, R. S. Feldman, & E. J. Coats (Eds.), The social context of nonverbal behavior. Cambridge, England: Cambridge University Press.

Argyle, M. & Henderson, M. (1984). The rules of friendship. *Journal of Social & Personal Relationships,* 1, 211-237.

Aron, A., Aron, E. N. & Smollan, D. (1992). Inclusion of Other in the Self Scale and the structure of interpersonal closeness. *Journal of Personality & Social Psychology,* 63, 596-612 10.1037//0022-3514 .63.4.596.

Aron, A., Aron, E. N., Tudor, M. & Nelson, G. (1991). Close relationships as including other in the self. *Journal of Personality & Social Psychology,* 60, 241-253 10.1037//0022-3514 .60.2.241.

Baumeister, R. F. & Leary, M. R. (1995). The need to belong: Desire for interpersonal attachment as a fundamental human motivation. *Psychological Bulletin,* 117, 497-529.

Baxter, L. & Wilmot, W. (1985). Taboo topics in close relationships. *Journal of Social & Personal Relationships,* 2, 253-269.

Bell, K. L. & DePaulo, B. M. (1996). Liking and lying. *Basic & Applied Social Psychology,* 18, 243-266.

Berscheid, E., Snyder, M., & Omoto, A. M. (1989a). Issues in studying close relationships: Conceptualizing and measuring closeness. In C. Hendrick (Ed.), Review of personality and social psychology: Vol. 10. Close relationships (pp. 63-91). Newbury Park, Ca: Sage.

Berscheid, E., Snyder, M. & Omoto, A. M. (1989b). The Relationship Closeness Inventory: Assessing the closeness of interpersonal relationships. *Journal of Personality & Social Psychology,* 57, 792-807.

Bowlby, J. (1988). A secure base: Parent-child attachment and healthy human development. New York: Basic Books.

Buller, D. B., Strzyzewski, K. D. & Comstock, J. (1991). Interpersonal deception: I.Deceivers' reactions to receivers' suspicions and probing. *Communication Monographs,* 58, 1-24.

Camden, C., Motley, M. T. & Wilson, A. (1984). White lies in interpersonal communication: A taxonomy and preliminary investigation of social motivations. *Western Journal of Speech Communication,* 48, 309-325.

Deci, E. L., & Ryan, R. M. (1991). A motivational approach to self: Integration in personality. In R. Dienstbier (Ed.), Nebraska Symposium on Motivation: Vol. 38. Perspectives on motivation (pp. 237-288). Lincoln: University of Nebraska Press.

DePaulo, B. M. (1992). Nonverbal behavior and self-presentation. *Psychological Bulletin,* 111, 203-243.

DePaulo, B. M. & Bell, K. L. (1996). *Journal of Personality & Social Psychology,* 71, 703-716 10.1037//0022-3514 .71.4.703.

DePaulo, B. M., Ansfield, M. E., Kirkendol, S. E., & Boden, J. M. (1997). Serious lies: First person accounts. Manuscript in preparation.

DePaulo, B. M., Kashy, D. A., Kirkendol, S. E., Wyer, M. M. & Epstein, J. A. (1996). Lying in everyday life. *Journal of Personality & Social Psychology,* 70, 979-995.

DePaulo, B. M., Stone, J. I., & Lassiter, G. D. (1985). Deceiving and detecting deceit. In B. R. Schlenker (Ed.), The self and social life (pp. 323-370). New York: McGraw-Hill.

Duck, S. (1994). Steady as (s)he goes. In D. Canary & L. Stafford (Eds.), Communication and relational maintenance (pp. 45-60). New York: Academic Press.

Ekman, P. & Friesen, W. V. (1969). Nonverbal leakage and clues to deception. *Psychiatry: Interpersonal & Biological Processes,* 32, 88-106.

Funder, D. C. (1987). Errors and mistakes: Evaluating the accuracy of social judgment. *Psychological Bulletin,* 101, 75-90.

Hample, D. (1980). Purposes and effects of lying. *Southern Speech Communication Journal,* 46, 33-47.

Hazan, C. & Shaver, P. R. (1994). Attachment as an organizational framework for research on close relationships. *Psychological Inquiry,* 5, 1-22.

Hendrick, S. S. (1981). Attachment as an organizational framework for research on close relationships. *Journal of Personality & Social Psychology,* 40, 1150-1159.

Holmes, J. G., & Rempel, J. K. (1989). Trust in close relationships. In C. Hendrick (Ed.), Review of personality and social psychology: Vol. 10. Close relationships (pp. 187-220). Newbury Park, Ca: Sage.

Kashy, D. A. & DePaulo, B. M. (1996). Who lies? *Journal of Personality & Social Psychology,* 70, 1037-1051.

Kelley, H. H., Berscheid, E., Christensen, A., Harvey, J. H., Huston, T. L., Levinger, G., McClintock, E., Peplau, L. A., & Peterson, D. R. (1983). Analyzing close relationships. In H. H. Kelley, E. Berscheid, A. Christensen, J. H. Harvey, T. L. Huston, G. Levinger, E. McClintock, L. A. Peplau, & D. R. Peterson (Eds.), Close relationships (pp. 20-67). New York: Freeman.

Kenny, D. A., Kashy, D. A., & Bolger, N. Data analysis in social psychology. in press. In D. T. Gilbert, S. T. Fiske, & G. Lindzey (Eds.), The handbook of social psychology (4th ed.). New York: McGraw-Hill.

Levine, T. R. & McCornack, S. A. (1992). Linking love and lies: A formal test of the McCornack and Parks model of deception detection. *Journal of Social & Personal Relationships, 9*, 143-154.

Lippard, P. V. (1988). "Ask me no questions, I'll tell you no lies": Situational exigencies for interpersonal deception. *Western Journal of Speech Communication, 52*, 91-103.

Maxwell, G. M. (1985). Behaviour of lovers: Measuring the closeness of relationships. *Journal of Social & Personal Relationships, 2*, 215-238.

McCornack, S. A. & Levine, T. R. (1990). When lies are uncovered: Emotional and relational outcomes of discovered deception. *Communication Monographs, 57*, 119-138.

McCornack, S. A., & Parks, M. R. (1986). Deception detection and relational development: The other side of trust. In M. L. McLaughlin (Ed.), Communication Yearbook 9 (pp. 377-389). Beverly Hills, Ca: Sage.

Metts, S. (1989). An exploratory investigation of deception in close relationships. *Journal of Social & Personal Relationships, 6*, 159-179.

Millar, K. U. & Tesser, A. (1988). Deceptive behavior in social relationships: A consequence of violated expectations. *Journal of Psychology, 122*, 263-273.

Millar, M. & Millar, K. (1995). Detection of deception in familiar and unfamiliar persons: The effects of information restriction. *Journal of Nonverbal Behavior, 19*, 69-84.

Miller, G. R., Mongeau, P. A. & Sleight, C. (1986). Fudging with friends and lying with lovers: Deceptive communication in personal relationships. *Journal of Social & Personal Relationships, 3*, 495-512.

Nezlek, J. B. (1995). Social construction, gender/sex similarity and social interaction in close personal relationships. *Journal of Social & Personal Relationships, 12*, 503-520.

Parks, M. R. (1982). Ideology in interpersonal communication: Off the couch and into the world. In M. Burgoon (Ed.), Communication Yearbook 5 (pp. 79-107). New Brunswick, NJ: Transaction Books.

Parks, M. R. & Floyd, K. (1996). Meanings for closeness and intimacy in friendship. *Journal of Social & Personal Relationships, 13*, 85-107.

Reis, H. T., Lin, Y. C., Bennett, E. & Nezlek, J. B. (1993). Change and consistency in social participation during early adulthood. *Developmental Psychology, 29*, 633-645.

Reis, H. T., & Patrick, B. C. (1996). Attachment and intimacy: Component processes. In E. T. Higgins & A. W. Kruglanski (Eds.), Social psychology: Handbook of basic principles (pp. 523-563). New York: Guilford Press.

Reis, H. T. & Wheeler, L. (1991). Studying social interaction with the Rochester Interaction Record. *Advances in Experimental Social Psychology, 24*, 269-318.

Ruesch, J., & Bateson, G. (1951). Communication: The social matrix of psychiatry. New York: Norton.

Rusbult, C. E., Yovetich, N. A., & Verette, J. (1996). An interdependence analysis of accommodation processes. In G. J. O. Fletcher & J. Fitness (Eds.), Knowledge structures in close relationships: A social psychological approach (pp. 63-90). Mahwah, NJ: Erlbaum.

Tice, D. M., Butler, J. L., Muraven, M. B. & Stillwell, A. M. (1995). When modesty prevails: Differential favorability of self-presentations to friends and strangers. *Journal of Personality & Social Psychology, 69,* 1120-1138.

Turner, R. E., Edgley, C. & Olmstead, G. (1975). Informational control in conversations: Honesty is not always the best policy. *Kansas Journal of Sociology,* 11, 69-89.

Watzlawick, P., Beavin, J. H., & Jackson, D. D. (1967). Pragmatics of human communication: A study of interactional patterns, pathologies, and paradoxes. New York: Norton.

Wheeler, L. & Nezlek, J. B. (1977). Sex differences in social participation. *Journal of Personality & Social Psychology,* 35, 742-754.

Footnotes

1. The college students in the Metts (1989) study included adult reentry students, but they constituted less than a third of the sample and their data were not analyzed separately.

2. Results from the other measures can be obtained from the authors.

3. Other studies in the literature have also reported descriptive data about relationship characteristics. For example, the mean number of social interactions per day reported by our college students, 6.6, is very similar to the number reported by Reis and Wheeler (1991) for Americans, 6.9. Our community members reported an average of 5.8 social interactions per day. Similarly, in a longitudinal study, Reis and his colleagues noted that participants reported more social interactions per day as college students, 6.9, than they did nearly a decade later, 5.1 (Reis, Lin, Bennett, & Nezlek, 1993). With regard to the correlations among different relationship qualities, our correlations between duration and closeness were stronger than those reported by Berscheid et al. (1989b) and Aron et al. (1991). In the studies reported in the latter article, the correlation between duration and closeness was stronger for men than for women; for women, the correlations were sometimes slightly negative. In our data, the average correlations (computed separately for each participant, omitting family members, and then averaged across participants) were very similar for men and women in the college sample (mean r = .48, n = 30, and mean r = .44, n = 47, respectively). For the community sample, there was a trend in the direction reported by Aron et al. (1992): The correlation was somewhat stronger for the men (mean r = .55, n = 30) than for the women (mean r = .39, n = 39), t (67) = 1.88, p = .06, for the test of the difference between the correlations.

4. The results shown in Table 3 were all based on dependent variables that were ratios (i.e., number of lies divided by number of social interactions; number of self-centered or other-oriented lies divided by total number of lies). We also computed alternative analyses that did not involve ratios as dependent measures. To predict rate of lying from closeness and duration, we added number of social interactions as a predictor variable and used number of lies as the dependent variable. To predict self-centered and other-oriented lying from closeness and duration, we added the total number of lies as a predictor variable, and used the number of self-centered or other-oriented lies as the dependent variable. In these analyses, only one effect that was significant using a ratio dependent variable (the effect of duration on overall rate of lying for the community sample) was not even marginally significant in the new analyses (b = −.021). All other patterns remained the same.

5. The n s decrease dramatically in the analyses of self-centered and other-oriented lying, compared with rate of lying. This is because the analyses can include only participants who told lies in at least two dyadic interactions and who told self-centered (or other-oriented) lies in some dyadic interactions and non-self-centered (or non-other-oriented) lies in other dyadic interactions.

Journal of Personality and Social Psychology, October 1996, Vol. 71, No. 4, p 703-716

Truth and Investment: Lies Are Told to Those Who Care

Bella M. DePaulo, Kathy L. Bell

Abstract

Participants discussed paintings they liked and disliked with artists who were or were not personally invested in them. Participants were urged to be honest or polite or were given no special instructions. There were no conditions under which the artists received totally honest feedback about the paintings they cared about. As predicted by the defensibility postulate, participants stonewalled, amassed misleading evidence, and conveyed positive evaluations by implication. They also told some outright lies. But the participants also communicated clearly their relative degrees of liking for the different special paintings. The results provide new answers to the question of why beliefs about other people's appraisals do not always correspond well with their actual appraisals.

In their formal roles as parents and supervisors, and in their informal roles as colleagues and friends, people often provide us with evaluative feedback. They comment on our work, our behavior, our friends, and our lovers. These appraisals are important for many reasons, including three interdependent ones. First, evaluative feedback can be of great emotional significance. Second, it can have instrumental value; for example, it can shape performance and guide important life decisions. Third, the appraisals of others—or our perceptions of them—can form and inform our sense of self (e.g., Baldwin, 1992; Felson, 1992; Jussim, Soffin, Brown, Ley, & Kohlhepp, 1992; McNulty & Swann, 1994; Mead, 1934). According to the symbolic interactionists, the self that develops is a "looking glass self" (Cooley, 1902) formed by our perceptions of others' responses to us.

The looking glass metaphor seems to imply that the question of the accuracy of perceptions is nonproblematic; we can simply look to others and see their opinion of us reflected back to us directly (Felson, 1992; Glaser & Strauss, 1964). Yet the preponderance of evidence suggests that there is considerable error in our perceptions of how others view us (e.g., DePaulo, Kenny, Hoover, Webb, & Oliver, 1987; Kenny & DePaulo, 1993). Our perceptions of others' appraisals correspond imperfectly with their actual appraisals, and our self-perceptions are more closely linked to our perceptions of how others view us than to their actual views of us (Felson, 1992).

When we err in our perceptions of how others view us, we may do so because others did not communicate their views of us openly and honestly, or because we misinterpreted their appraisals. Three elements are important: what the evaluators tried to convey (as indicated by their own reports), what they actually did convey (as indicated, for example, by transcripts of what they said), and how their communications were perceived (as indicated by people's impressions). Studies of meta-accuracy typically omit the middle element: There is no precise record of what evaluators actually said, or the record is never analyzed. In the present research we assessed all three components.

An important reason for dishonesty in evaluative communications may be that evaluators care more about the emotional impact of their feedback than its instrumental value. The feedback that supervisors can provide to floundering employees, for example, is potentially of instrumental value both to the employees and to the organization, yet supervisors are reluctant to provide feedback to those employees and often delay doing so (Larson, 1989). Honesty and openness are highly prized characteristics of friendships, yet even friends are reluctant to share their unflattering appraisals of each other (Blumberg, 1972; Mayer, 1957). The persons directly affected by bad news have the greatest need to know that news, yet people are more inclined to communicate such news to uninvolved third parties than to the targets (Felson, 1992; Tesser & Rosen, 1975).

As an individual's personal investment in an object increases, both the instrumental and the emotional significance of evaluative feedback are likely to increase as well. For example, when an art student is discussing paintings with other people, the appraisals that they can provide are more emotionally impactful and also more useful when the paintings are the art student's own work than when they are the creations of other artists. Yet we think that emotional considerations will prevail, and evaluators will be less honest about the paintings when they are the art student's own work—particularly when they dislike the work—even though it would be especially useful to the art students to know how their work really is perceived by other people. For instance, art students whose work is poor yet who never hear that from others may pursue a major or even a career to which they are ill suited.

In the present research, participants looked over a set of paintings, chose the two they liked the best and the two they liked the least, and indicated just how much they liked each of those four paintings. They also wrote out what they liked and disliked about each painting. Only then did they learn that they would be discussing those paintings with an art student who was personally invested in one of the liked and one of the disliked paintings. Those conversations were videotaped (and later transcribed). After each conversation, we asked the participants how honest and how comfortable they had been and how much liking they had tried to convey. We then showed the videotapes to judges who indicated their perceptions of the participants' honesty and actual liking for the paintings. We predicted that the participants would be more dishonest and more uncomfortable, and would exaggerate their liking more, when they were discussing the paintings that were special to the art student—especially when they disliked those paintings.

Goffman (1967, 1971) provided a perspective for understanding people's reluctance to say exactly what they feel. He argued that in order for everyday social life to proceed smoothly, it is important for people to give deference to the "faces" (identities) that others seem to be claiming. As politeness theory has documented (P. Brown & Levinson, 1987; R. Brown & Gilman, 1989; Holtgraves, 1992), people understand this and act accordingly. No one needs to tell us to be polite when discussing an ugly painting with the artist who created it. Disagreements and criticisms are face-threatening and will be communicated only very politely, if at all—but even positive communications, P. Brown and Levinson argued, can be face-threatening (e.g., compliments that cause embarrassment).

Telling people explicitly to be polite and to try to avoid hurting another person's feelings, then, should result in communications that are no different than if no instructions had been given. In both instances, people will dishonestly convey overly positive appraisals. To break down the sturdy barriers to the communication of negative evaluations, it may be important to underscore explicitly the importance of honesty. In the present research, we explicitly instructed some of our participants to be honest about their appraisals. Only from such honest evaluations, we said, could the art students really learn about other people's perceptions of art. We predicted that these instructions would dampen participants' exaggerations, relative to conditions in which participants were instructed to be polite or were given no special instructions, but we were unsure as to whether they would elicit evaluations that were totally honest.

The situation we created was a very difficult one for the participants, especially when they were discussing paintings they disliked with the art student who painted them. Bavelas and her colleagues (Bavelas, Black, Chovil, & Mullett, 1990) characterized this situation as the most common sort of "communicative avoidance–avoidance conflict: [Participants had] a choice between saying something false but kind and something true but hurtful" (p. 58). On the basis of more than a dozen experiments, Bavelas et al. concluded that, in these situations, people equivocate. They avoid answering the question that is asked, they avoid describing their own opinion, they are unclear in the answers they do give, and they sometimes even avoid addressing the person who posed the question. Bavelas et al.'s research, then, tells us what people do not say in avoid–avoid situations (or at least in role-play versions of them), but it stops short of telling us what they do say. Even their conclusions about what people do not say are based not on content analyses of the communications but on judges' global impressions.

We agree with Bavelas et al. (1990) that people prefer to avoid telling either outright lies or hurtful truths. Therefore, we predict, as they did, that the rate of telling outright lies will be low. However, we think that the rate of lying, though low, will still be responsive to our experimental manipulations. Specifically, we predict that participants will be most likely to lie when discussing paintings they dislike with art students who are personally invested in them—especially if the participants had been instructed to be polite.

In the difficult situation we created, we think that participants have two goals: They want to mislead the art student about how they feel, but they also want to be able to deny that they lied. Their communications will be governed by what we will call the defensibility postulate, that is, participants' inclination to exaggerate their liking for the paintings and to convey dishonest appraisals of them will be tempered by considerations of defensibility (see also Schlenker, 1980). Participants will craft communications which, if challenged, can be defended as either truthful or at least not clearly deceptive. In the context of this experiment, we think that one way they can do this is to amass misleading evidence. As the art student continues to probe them about their opinions of the paintings, they can mention more and more of the things that they really do like about the paintings, while being a bit more restrained in enumerating the aspects of the paintings that they really do dislike. The result is a communication that is likely to succeed in conveying a misleadingly positive impression yet can still be defended as truthful—after all, all of the positive aspects mentioned were ones that the participants really did like about the paintings. Not mentioning all of the disliked aspects, they might argue, is not dishonest—they just did not mention them.

We think that the participants will also come up with entirely new aspects of the paintings that they will claim to like—aspects that they had not written down when we first asked them to describe what they liked and disliked about the paintings. Perhaps they will tell themselves that they just noticed these new virtues of the painting during the conversation with the art student. Defensibility is especially likely to remain intact if they also notice some new aspects of the painting that they dislike. Again, though, the newly discovered disliked aspects will be far outnumbered by the new liked aspects.

The prediction made by Bavelas et al. (1990) that people will avoid stating their own opinion is consistent with the defensibility postulate and was directly tested by the coding of participants' explicit expressions of liking or disliking for the paintings. When participants are discussing a painting they dislike, especially one that is special to the art student, they might stonewall—that is, avoid making any explicit evaluations at all. They might also mention fewer aspects of the paintings that they like or dislike.

There is another very clever way that participants can defensibly imply more liking than they really do feel for the paintings, and that is by manipulating what they say about the paintings in which the art students are not personally invested. That is, at the same time that participants try to avoid saying explicitly that they dislike the art student's own paintings that they detest, they can be far less reticent in voicing their distaste for the paintings created by other art students. The strategy is one of social comparison by implication. In comparison to the negative appraisals that were explicitly stated about the other artists' work, the withholding of any explicit appraisals of the art student's own work will seem rather positive. Those communications are also defensibly positive: If pressed, the participants can claim that they did not say that they liked the art student's own work; they simply said that they did not like the other artists' work.

When we showed the videotapes of the conversations to the judges, we gave them the same information that the artists would be likely to have in the comparable real life situations. That is, the judges knew whether the paintings were special to the artists, but they did not know what the participants really did think of the paintings. They also did not know the participants' intentions— that is, whether they were making any special effort to be honest or polite.

We predicted that the judges would report some of the same things that the participants would say themselves—that the participants were less honest and less comfortable, and exaggerated more, when discussing the paintings in which the artists were more invested (cf. DePaulo & Kirkendol, 1989; DePaulo, Lanier, & Davis, 1983; DePaulo, Stone, & Lassiter, 1985b). If that were all that the judges noticed, then those results might simply reflect judges' theories about how people communicate to people who care, rather than any real discernment. However, because the judges did not know whether the participants liked or disliked a painting, if they also thought that the participants seemed especially less honest when discussing the special paintings when the participants disliked those paintings, then they would be showing some insight into participants' true feelings.

It is important to note that we asked the judges directly just how much they thought the participants really did like each of the paintings. If they discounted the participants' expressions of liking too much in the special conditions (because they knew that the participants were talking to artists who were personally invested in the paintings), they would be wrong about the participants' actual feelings (cf. Gilbert & Malone, 1995; Snyder & Frankel, 1976). If instead they were too inclined to take what the participants said at face value (e.g., DePaulo, 1992, 1994; DePaulo, Stone, & Lassiter, 1985a; Gilbert & Malone, 1995; Jones, 1990), they would again be wrong, but in a different direction. That is what we predicted. Because we expected the participants' verbal strategies to be effective in creating misleadingly positive impressions, we expected the judges to believe that the participants really did like the special paintings more than the not-special ones.

Method

Participants and Art Students

Participants were 47 male and 47 female introductory psychology students who participated for partial fulfillment of a course requirement in an experiment that was ostensibly about psychology and art. Five other participants were excluded: 2 men and 1 woman who surmised the purpose of the experiment, 1 man whose speech could not be understood, and 1 woman who completed the forms improperly. Participants were randomly assigned to the six between-subjects cells formed by the crossing of the two degrees of investment (paintings were described as the art student's favorites or her own) with the three kinds of instructions (honest, no instructions, polite). There were 7 or 8 men and 7 or 8 women in each of the cells.

Three women alternated in the role of the art student, and 3 women and 2 men served as experimenters. Preliminary analyses in which art students and experimenters were included as a factor in the design showed fewer significant effects involving the factor than would be expected by chance.

Procedure

Participants were run individually and were told that the experiment was designed to help art students learn more about how art is perceived by people who are not experts. Participants were then left alone in a room to choose the 2 paintings they liked the most and the 2 they liked the least from 19 paintings that were displayed. (The paintings had been painted by undergraduates in an introductory painting course.) Participants rated each of these 4 paintings on 9-point scales of liking, with higher numbers indicating greater liking. The experimenter then returned and gave the participant a second questionnaire on which the participant was asked to describe briefly, in an open-ended format, what he or she liked and disliked about each of the 4 paintings.

The experimenter then told the participant that he or she would now discuss the four paintings with the art student. The experimenter mentioned that the art student may have actually painted some of the paintings herself, and she would tell the participant if she had. The experimenter also informed the participant that the art student would not know that the four paintings were ones that the participant selected and that she would not ever see the participant's ratings of liking for the paintings or the brief descriptions of what the participant liked and disliked about the paintings.

The art student always claimed that one of the participant's two most favorite paintings (randomly selected) and one of the participant's least favorite paintings (also randomly selected) were special to her in some way. The two types of specialness, or degrees of investment, were randomly assigned. In the moderate investment condition, the art student claimed that the painting was one of her favorites ("This is one of my favorites"); in the high investment condition, she claimed that the painting was one of her own ("This is one that I did."). She introduced this information just before asking the participant what he or she thought of the painting.

Participants were randomly assigned to one of three instructional conditions. One third of them were instructed to be honest when discussing the paintings with the art student. Specifically, they were told:

If it turns out that the art student did paint some of these paintings, you should still be very honest in describing your own opinions about those paintings. Tell her truthfully what you liked and what you disliked about each painting you discuss, even if the paintings are ones she painted herself. This is supposed to be a learning experience for the students. For them to really learn about people's perceptions of art, they have to hear unbiased descriptions of those perceptions. They need to know what you really did like and really did dislike about each painting you discuss.

Some of the art students like to mention which ones they really liked of the ones that are NOT theirs. Again, be sure to be honest about your own opinions of the paintings. Tell her what you really think of the painting, regardless of what her opinions might be. They will learn more if they hear your true opinions.

Another third of the participants were instructed to be polite to the art student and to try not to hurt her feelings. Specifically, they were told:

If it turns out that the student did paint some of these paintings, try to convince her that you really did like the ones she painted so that her feelings won't be hurt. It is OK to mention things you dislike about her paintings when she asks, but just try to convey the impression that overall, you like the ones she did. This study is supposed to be a learning experience for the participants, but we don't want any of them to end up feeling badly because of it.

Some of the art students like to mention which ones they liked of the ones that are NOT theirs. Again, it is OK if you don't agree with her—you can say that, but just try to be real nice about it.

In the no-instructions condition, participants were not given any particular instructions about what to do.

After determining that the participant understood the instructions, the experimenter left the room, turned on a hidden video recorder, then returned with the art student. After introducing the participant to the art student, the experimenter left the room.

The art student, who was unaware of the participant's instructional condition (but did know which paintings the participants liked and disliked), then proceeded to interview the participant about each of the four paintings, in counterbalanced order. She asked the following questions about each painting, giving the participant ample time to answer each question before moving on to the next: "What do you think of it? What are some of the specific things you like about it? (Anything else?) What are some of the specific things you dislike about it? (Anything else?)" Participants were instructed by the experimenter not to ask the art student about her opinions. The art students were trained to deflect any such questions.

After the discussion of each painting, the art student left the room while the participant completed a questionnaire about the discussion. On 9-point scales, participants indicated how much liking they tried to convey to the art student, how honest and straightforward they had been, and how comfortable they felt while discussing what they liked and disliked about the painting. Participants were debriefed, and all of them signed a consent form allowing us to use their videotapes.

Judges and Videotapes

Seven male and 14 female undergraduates were recruited to rate videotapes (with sound) of the discussions of the paintings. The tapes were rated by just one judge at a time. Not all of the judges rated all of the tapes; on the average, each tape was rated by 6 men (the range was 5–7) and 12 women (11–14).

The discussions of the paintings were edited onto 17 videotapes of about 1 hr each. A nearly equal number of participants from each condition appeared on each tape. After each discussion of each painting, there was a 10-s rating pause. During the pause, judges rated the participant on 9-point scales of honesty, actual liking for the painting, degree of liking that the participant was trying to convey to the art student, and comfort, with higher numbers indicating more of each attribute. Reliabilities (alphas) were .78 for honesty, .94 for actual and conveyed liking, and .71 for comfort.

Transcripts and Coders

Exact typed transcripts were made of all of the discussions of all of the paintings. Three undergraduates coded the transcripts. One coded the conversations of half of the participants in each condition (188 conversations), and a second coded the other half. We used these codings in the analyses. The third person coded 48 of the conversations coded by the first person and 44 of the conversations coded by the second person. The conversations in each set included approximately equal numbers from each condition. The codings of the third person were compared with those of the first two to assess reliability.

Verbal Strategies

Each coder coded three verbal strategies separately for each discussion of each painting.

1. *Explicit evaluations of liking and disliking*

Coders indicated whether the participants explicitly said that they liked the paintings and whether they explicitly said that they disliked them.

2. *Total number of liked and disliked aspects that were mentioned*

Coders counted the total number of different aspects of the paintings that participants said that they liked and the total number they said they disliked. For example, if participants said they liked the color, the shading, and the originality, they would get a score of 3 for total number of liked aspects.

3. *Number of new liked and disliked aspects that were mentioned*

Coders counted the number of aspects of the paintings that participants said they liked and disliked that were different from the aspects that the participants had described in writing before they knew they would be meeting an art student. To code this variable, coders first identified each of the liked and disliked aspects that participants described in writing, then they identified the liked and disliked aspects from the transcripts of the discussions, then they compared the two sets.

Reliabilities

There were two intraclass correlations for each variable: One was the correlation between the first coder and the third, and the other was between the second coder and the third. For explicit evaluations of liking the reliabilities were .96 and .96; for explicit evaluations of disliking they were .85 and 1.00; for total number of liked aspects, .88 and .92; for total number of disliked aspects, .88 and .80; for new liked aspects, .75 and .80; and for new disliked aspects, .71 and .59.

Results

Manipulation Checks

On a manipulation check questionnaire, all participants in the honest condition indicated that their goal was to be honest about their feelings about the paintings. All participants in the polite condition indicated that their goal was to try to be nice and avoid hurting the art student's feelings. When questioned about their understanding of the instructions just before beginning the discussion of the paintings, all participants correctly reported that the art student may have painted some of the paintings (or that some were the art student's favorites) and that they would not know whether the art student had painted any of the paintings until they met her. Ninety-two of the 94 participants correctly indicated that they would be discussing the four paintings they had selected. (Because the 2 participants who initially volunteered the wrong answer corrected it after further probing, and because all of their other manipulation check data were correct, their data were retained in the analyses.) All of the participants understood that the art students would believe that the paintings picked for discussion were selected at random by the experimenter. All participants also understood that the art student would not see what they had written about the paintings.

Analyses of participants' initial ratings of their liking for the paintings indicated that they liked their two favorite paintings far more than their two least favorite ones (M s = 7.35 and 2.32). Because the paintings that were described as special to the art student were randomly assigned, participants should not have liked them any better than the ones that were not special, and in fact they did not (M s = 4.82 and 4.84; see Table 1 for significance tests).

Table 1

Effects of Participants' Liking for the Paintings and Artists' Investment on Participants' and Judges' Ratings

| | Type of Painting | | | | | | Fs (1, 82) | | |
| | **Disliked** | | | **Liked** | | | Artists' investment | Participants' liking | Inter-action |
	Not special	**Special**	Difference	Not special	**Special**	Difference			
Participants									
Comfort	6.47	5.05	1.42***	6.88	6.61	0.27	60.19***	58.69***	19.52***
Honesty	7.66	6.38	1.28***	7.99	7.98	0.01	48.50***	67.68***	47.07***
Actual liking	2.30	2.34	0.04	7.35	7.35	0.00	0.03	1392.96***	0.04
Conveyed liking	3.18	3.96	0.78*	6.44	6.79	0.35	26.89***	176.90***	2.90+
Exaggeration	0.88	1.62	0.74	-0.91	-0.56	0.35	19.94***	74.85***	1.64
Judges									
Comfort	5.85	5.75	0.10*	6.08	6.06	0.02	4.62*	73.70***	3.00+
Honesty	6.56	6.22	0.34***	6.51	6.37	0.14*	46.94***	1.17	6.65**
Actual liking	3.67	3.84	0.17+	5.91	5.98	0.07	4.85*	766.96***	1.11
Conveyed liking	4.14	4.65	0.51***	6.41	6.70	0.29**	45.19***	670.52***	4.24*
Exaggeration	0.47	0.81	0.34****	0.50	0.72	0.22***	84.72***	1.02	3.40+

Note. The special paintings were the ones in which the artists were invested. *Difference* is *not special* minus *special* for comfort and honesty, and *special* minus *not special* for actual liking, conveyed liking, and exaggeration.

$+ p < $ or $ = .10.$ $* p < $ or $ = .05.$ $** p < $ or $ = .01.$ $*** p < $ or $ = .001.$

Design and Measures

Data were analyzed with a mixed-design analysis of variance (ANOVA). The between-subjects factors were the instructional manipulation (participants were told to be honest or polite or they were given no instructions) and artists' degree of investment in the special paintings (those paintings were described as either the artists' favorites—the moderate investment condition, or as their own work—the high investment condition). The within-subjects factors were the artists' investment in the paintings (they were invested in the special paintings and not invested in the not-special ones) and the participants' liking for the paintings (disliking or liking).[1]

Participants' reports of how honest and straightforward they had been in their discussions were highly correlated, r (92) = .86, p < .001, and so they were averaged to form a single measure of honesty. The measure of participants' actual liking for the paintings was their ratings of their liking for each of the paintings before they knew that they would be meeting an art student. Their reports of how much liking they had tried to convey to the art student were collected after the discussions. We assessed the degree to which the participants had exaggerated their liking by subtracting participants' actual liking for each painting from the degree of liking that they tried to convey. The other dependent measure was participants' ratings of their comfort during each of the discussions. Similarly, for the analyses of the judges' impressions, dependent measures were judges' perceptions of the participants' honesty, comfort, actual liking for the paintings, and degree of liking that they seemed to be trying to convey. We computed exaggeration scores by subtracting perceptions of actual liking from perceptions of conveyed liking.

Participants' Self-Reports and Judges' Impressions

Paintings that were liked and disliked, special and not special

As we predicted, the main effect of investment was significant for all relevant dependent measures (see Table 1 for statistical tests and significance levels). When the paintings were special to the art students (second and fifth columns of Table 1), compared to when they were not (first and fourth columns), the participants reported being more uncomfortable and more dishonest. They also tried to convey more liking, and they exaggerated their liking more. Similarly, all main effects of liking for the painting were significant. Participants said they were less comfortable and less honest when discussing the paintings they disliked than the ones they liked. They tried to convey more liking for the paintings they liked, but they exaggerated their liking more for the paintings they disliked (i.e., they tried to convey more liking than they really did feel). In fact, according to their self-reports, participants actually understated their liking for the liked paintings. Also as predicted, the effects of the artists' investment on participants' honesty and comfort depended significantly on whether the participants liked the paintings. Participants were significantly less honest and less comfortable when discussing the special paintings than the not-special ones only when they disliked the paintings.

The judges also thought that the participants were more uncomfortable and dishonest when discussing the special paintings than the not-special ones and that they tried to convey more liking, and more exaggerated liking, for the special paintings. The differences in honesty and conveyed liking that they noted were even more striking when the participants disliked the paintings than when they liked them.

There was a significant main effect of investment, but no significant interaction with liking for the painting, on judges' impressions of participants' actual liking for the paintings. Participants liked the special paintings almost exactly the same as the not-special ones. The judges did not know this, and from watching the tapes, their impression was that the participants really did like the special paintings even more than the not-special ones.[2]

There was one other way in which the judges' impressions departed from the participants' self-reports. The participants said they exaggerated their liking for the disliked paintings but understated their liking for the liked paintings. The judges thought that the participants were always exaggerating their liking (especially so for the special paintings). Tests of whether the exaggeration (or understatement) scores differed from zero were significant for all four paintings for the participants' self-reports (all p s ≤ .05 or smaller) and the judges' impressions (all p s < .001).

Finally, although the judges were not told whether the participants liked the paintings, their impressions of the discussions of the liked and disliked paintings were accurate. They thought the participants really did like the liked paintings more, and were trying to convey more liking for them, and that they felt less comfortable discussing the disliked paintings.

Honesty and politeness

Did the participants who were instructed to be honest or to be polite behave and feel differently than those who were left to their own devices? Significant main effects of the instructional manipulation for the measures of honesty, $F(2, 82) = 8.42$, $p < .001$, MSE = 6.92, and exaggeration, $F(2, 82) = 4.66$, $p = .01$, MSE = 4.89, indicated that they did. The means for self-reported honesty in the honest, no-instructions, and polite conditions, were 7.71, 7.85, and 6.95, respectively. The difference between the honest and the no-instructions conditions was not significant. The difference between the no-instructions and the polite conditions was significant, $F(1, 82) = 14.31$, $p < .001$. In their reports of their own honesty, then, participants given no special instructions were more similar to the participants instructed to be honest than to those who were urged to be polite. The judges' impressions of the participants' honesty showed the same thing, $F(2, 82) = 3.03$, $p = .05$, MSE = 0.85. The judges thought that the participants were no less honest in the no-instructions condition (M = 6.49) than in the honest condition (M = 6.46, F < 1), but they thought the participants were significantly less honest in the polite condition (M = 6.30) than in the no-instructions condition, $F(1, 82) = 5.33$, $p = .02$.

However, in the degree to which they reported exaggerating their liking for the paintings, participants in the no-instructions condition were more similar to participants who were told to be polite. (The uninstructed participants did not differ significantly from the polite participants [F < 1], but they did differ significantly from the honest participants, F [1, 82] = 4.30, p = .04.) In fact, participants in both the no-instructions and the polite conditions said that they tried to convey more liking than they really did feel (M s = 0.37 and 0.61 for the no-instructions and polite conditions, respectively), but participants in the honest condition said that they conveyed slightly less liking than they felt (M = −0.21).

Did the instructional manipulation influence the way the participants discussed the paintings that were or were not special to the art students? Significant interactions between the instructional manipulation and the investment variable for the measures of honesty, conveyed liking, and exaggeration, indicated that it did. As shown in Table 2 , in all three instructional conditions, participants said that they were less honest when the artists were invested in the paintings than when they were not, and they also said that they tried to convey more liking and that they exaggerated their liking more when the artists were invested. The degree to which they showed these effects, however, increased from the honest to the no-instructions to the polite condition. (See the columns in Table 2 labeled Difference.) For the exaggeration measure, for example, the degree to which participants exaggerated their liking more for the special than for the not-special paintings was only 0.08 (and not significant) in the honest condition; it increased to 0.32 in the no-instructions condition and to 1.25 in the polite condition. In fact, for all three measures, participants in the no-instructions condition were more similar to the participants in the honest condition than they were to the participants in the polite condition. Contrast analyses showed that the difference between the special paintings and the not-special ones was the same for the honest condition and the no-instructions condition for all three measures (F s < 1); but the special versus not-special difference was significantly greater in the polite condition than in the no-instructions condition for all measures (all p s = .007 or smaller).

Table 2

Effects of Instructions and Artists' Investment on Participants' and Judges' Ratings

		Instructions		
		Honest		
Ratings	*F*s (1, 82)	Not special	**Special**	Difference
Participants				
Honesty	7.42***	7.86	7.56	0.30
Conveyed liking	6.44**	4.73	4.97	0.24
Exaggeration	8.58***	-0.25	-0.17	0.08
Judges				
Actual liking	2.96+	4.86	4.84	-0.02
Conveyed liking	6.30**	5.36	5.50	0.14
Exaggeration	3.72*	0.50	0.66	0.16**
		No instructions		
Participants				
Honesty		8.09	7.59	0.50*
Conveyed liking		5.07	5.42	0.35
Exaggeration		0.21	0.53	0.32**
Judges				
Actual liking		4.77	4.86	0.09
Conveyed liking		5.23	5.64	0.41***
Exaggeration		0.46	0.78	0.32***
		Polite		
Participants				
Honesty		7.52	6.39	1.13***
Conveyed liking		4.62	5.73	1.11***
Exaggeration		-0.02	1.23	1.25***
Judges				
Actual liking		4.73	5.04	0.31**
Conveyed liking		5.24	5.88	0.65***
Exaggeration		0.51	0.84	0.33***

Note. Difference is *not special* minus *special* for honesty, *special* minus *not special* for conveyed liking, exaggeration, and actual liking.

+ $p <$ or = .10.   * $p <$ or = .05.   ** $p <$ or = .01.   *** $p <$ or = .001.

The judges also thought that the ways that the participants handled the discussions of the special (compared to the not-special) paintings were influenced by their attempts to be honest or polite. The judges thought that the participants tried to convey more liking and more exaggerated liking for the special paintings than for the not-special ones (and they tended to think that the participants really did like the special paintings more, which they did not), and they also noticed that the degree to which participants tried to favor the special paintings increased from the honest to the no-instructions to the polite condition (see Table 2).

The way that the uninstructed participants compared to the others was different for the judges' ratings than for the participants' own reports. In the self-report data, the degree to which the participants favored the special over the not-special paintings was essentially the same for the participants who were told to be honest as for those who were left to their own devices—contrary to our predictions. The judges, in contrast, thought that uninstructed participants were no different from the polite participants in the degree to which they favored the special paintings. (The F s were < 1 for exaggeration, and 2.52 and 2.51, both p s = .12, for actual and conveyed liking, respectively.) The judges also thought that the uninstructed participants were different from the honest participants in the degree to which they favored the special paintings; for conveyed liking, $F(1, 82) = 3.46$, $p = .07$, and for exaggeration, $F(1, 82) = 4.82$, $p = .03$.

Finally, the instructional manipulation was especially important to the way the participants dealt with the artists' investment when the paintings were ones the participants disliked. The three-way interaction of instructions, investment, and liking for the painting was significant for participants' reports of their honesty, $F(2, 82) = 12.23$, $p < .001$, $MSE = 1.59$. As shown in Table 3 , when participants liked the paintings (see last three columns of the table), the instructions they received had virtually no effect in any of the conditions on how honest they were about the special compared to the not-special paintings. However, when participants disliked the paintings (first three columns of Table 3), they admitted to being less honest about the ones that were special to the artists compared to the ones that were not. This difference was significant in every instructional condition, but it increased from the honest (M = 0.50) to the no-instructions (M = 0.94) to the polite condition (M = 2.38). Once again, the uninstructed participants, in their self-reports, were more similar to the participants who were told to be honest than to those who were told to be polite. The difference between special and not special was not significantly greater in the uninstructed condition than in the honest condition, $F(1, 82) = 1.89$, $p = .17$, but it was significantly greater in the polite condition than in the uninstructed condition, $F(1, 82) = 20.25$, $p < .001$.

Table 3

Effects of Instructions, Participants' Liking for the Paintings, and Artists' Investment on Participants' and Judges' Ratings

	Type of Painting					
Ratings and instructions	**Disliked**			**Liked**		
	Not special	*Special*	Difference	Not special	*Special*	Difference
Participants:						
Honesty						
Honest	7.58	7.08	0.50*	8.14	8.04	0.10
No instructions	7.90	6.96	0.94***	8.28	8.22	0.06
Polite	7.48	5.10	2.38***	7.55	7.67	-0.12
Judges						
Honesty						
Honest	6.52	6.39	0.13	6.54	6.37	0.17+
No instruct.	6.67	6.31	0.36***	6.58	6.42	0.16+
Polite	6.49	5.97	0.52***	6.42	6.33	0.09
Conveyed liking						
Honest	4.27	4.30	0.03	6.46	6.71	0.25+
No instruct.	4.01	4.59	0.58***	6.45	6.69	0.24+
Polite	4.15	5.07	0.92***	6.32	6.70	0.38**

Note. The special paintings were the ones in which the artists were invested. *Difference* is *not special* minus *special* for honesty and *special* minus *not special* for conveyed liking.
+ $p <$ or $= .10$. * $p <$ or $= .05$. ** $p <$ or $= .01$. *** $p <$ or $= .001$.

The judges also noticed that it was especially difficult for the participants to discuss the special paintings truthfully when the participants disliked the paintings but were trying to be polite about them, $F(2, 82) = 3.27$, $p = .04$, MSE = 0.28. As shown in Table 3 , the degree to which the participants seemed to be more dishonest when discussing the disliked paintings that were special to the artists (compared to the disliked paintings that were not special) increased from the honest to the no-instructions to the polite condition. The same pattern occurred for judges' perceptions of the liking that participants seemed to be trying to convey, $F(2, 82) = 4.74$, $p = .01$, MSE = 0.54. When the participants disliked the paintings, the judges thought that they seemed to be trying to convey especially more liking for the special than for the not-special paintings and that this tendency increased from the honest to the no-instructions to the polite condition. Again, the judges, in contrast to the participants, thought that the uninstructed participants were more similar to the participants who were told to be polite than to the participants told to be honest. For perceptions of honesty, the special versus not-special difference for the disliked paintings was not significantly smaller in the no-instructions condition than in the polite condition, $F(1, 82) = 1.57$, ns, but it was nearly significantly greater in the no-instructions condition than in the honest condition, $F(1, 82) = 3.25$, $p = .07$. For the measure of conveyed liking, the corresponding values were $F(1, 82) = 3.03$, $p = .08$, and $F(1, 82) = 7.93$, $p = .006$.

Verbal Strategies

Design

The design for the analyses of participants' verbal strategies was the same as for the participants' self-reports and the judges' ratings, except that one within-subjects factor of professed affect (liking–disliking) was added. For the measure of explicit evaluation, the levels were (a) whether the participants explicitly said that they liked the painting and (b) whether they explicitly said that they disliked it (see Cochran, 1950, and Rosenthal & Rosnow, 1991, for the use of ANOVA with dichotomous dependent variables). For total aspects mentioned and for new aspects mentioned, the levels were number of liked aspects mentioned and number of disliked aspects mentioned.

Initial likes and dislikes

To be sure that participants did not like more aspects of the special paintings than the not-special ones even before they met the art students, we analyzed the number of liked and disliked aspects of all of the paintings that participants had described in writing. The interaction of investment with number of liked versus disliked aspects was not significant ($F < 1$). Thus, participants began by listing almost exactly the same number of likes and dislikes for the special paintings as for the not-special ones.

Professed affect

The main effect of professed affect was significant for all three measures. Across the discussions of all of the paintings, the participants were almost twice as likely to say that they liked a painting (M = 0.44) than to say that they disliked it (M = 0.24), even though all participants actually liked the exact same number of paintings that they disliked, $F(1, 82) = 56.09$, $p < .001$, MSE = 0.13. They also mentioned many more things that they liked than disliked about the paintings (M s = 5.26 and 3.61),

F(1, 82) = 66.49, p < .001, MSE = 7.64, and of the aspects of the paintings that they mentioned but had not originally listed, significantly more of them were aspects that they liked than disliked (M s = 3.26 and 2.04), F(1, 82) = 43.01, p < .001, MSE = 6.47.

Liked and disliked paintings

Participants had more difficulty communicating truthfully about the paintings that they disliked than about the ones that they liked. The interactions between professed affect and liking for the paintings were significant for all three measures. As shown in Table 4 , when participants liked a painting, they said so 81% of the time; however, when they disliked a painting, they said so explicitly only 48% of the time, F(1, 82) = 353.70, p < .001, MSE = 0.19. When participants liked a painting, they mentioned many more things about it that they liked than that they disliked, but when they disliked a painting, they mentioned fewer than one more thing about it that they disliked than liked, F(1, 82) = 217.25, p < .001, MSE = 5.05. Similarly, when discussing a painting that they liked, participants mentioned 4.18 additional things about it that they liked that they had not already listed, compared to only 1.33 new things that they disliked; in contrast, the number of new liked and disliked aspects that participants generated when the painting was disliked hardly differed (2.34 and 2.75), F(1, 82) = 114.39, p < .001, MSE = 4.33.

Table 4

Participants' Verbal Strategies Used in Discussing the Disliked and Liked Paintings

	Participants' liking for the paintings		
Verbal Strategy	**Disliked**	**Liked**	Difference
Explicit evaluation[a]			
Liked	0.08	0.81	0.73***
Disliked	0.48	0.00	-0.48***
Total aspects mentioned			
Liked	3.84	6.67	2.83***
Disliked	4.62	2.61	-2.01***
New aspects mentioned			
Liked	2.34	4.18	1.84***
Disliked	2.75	1.33	-1.42***

[a] Proportion of participants who explicitly said that they liked or disliked the paintings.
*** $p <$ or $= .001$.

Stonewalling was indicated by the main effect for liking for the painting for the measures of explicit evaluation, $F(1, 82) = 30.37$, $p < .001$, $MSE = 0.09$, and total number of aspects mentioned, $F(1, 82) = 7.87$, $p = .007$, $MSE = 4.09$. These results showed that participants not only had a hard time telling the truth about the disliked paintings, but they also had a hard time saying anything at all. When participants disliked a painting, they were less likely to make any explicit evaluation (whether positive or negative) than when they liked it (M s = 0.28 and 0.41 for disliked and liked paintings, respectively). Participants also mentioned fewer things that they liked or disliked when they disliked a painting (M = 4.23) than when they liked it (M = 4.64).

Not-special and special paintings

Professed affect interacted significantly with investment, and in the predicted direction, for all three measures. As shown in Table 5 , when the paintings were special to the art students (compared to when they were not), the participants were relatively more likely to say that they liked them and relatively less likely to say that they disliked them, $F(1, 82) = 7.83$, $p = .006$, $MSE = 0.13$. Similarly, when the paintings were special, compared to when they were not, the participants mentioned relatively more things that they liked about them and relatively fewer things that they disliked, $F(1, 82) = 13.14$, $p < .001$, $MSE = 4.22$. Similarly, the participants thought of relatively more new things to like about the special paintings than about the not-special ones, and relatively fewer things to dislike, $F(1, 82) = 5.70$, $p < .05$, $MSE = 3.55$. Thus, the ways in which the participants discussed the special versus the not-special paintings paralleled the ways they discussed the liked versus disliked paintings. It is important to note that the interactions of professed affect with investment were not qualified by participants' liking for the painting (except for one higher order interaction involving instructions, discussed next). That means, for example, that participants used their strategy of mentioning many more liked than disliked aspects (of the special paintings) just as much when discussing the paintings they disliked as the paintings they liked.

Table 5

Participants' Verbal Strategies Used in Discussing the Not-Special and Special Paintings

	Artists' investment		
Verbal Strategy	Not special	**Special**	Difference
Explicit evaluation[a]			
Liked	0.41	0.48	0.07*
Disliked	0.28	0.21	-0.07*
Total aspects mentioned			
Liked	5.02	5.49	0.47*
Disliked	3.92	3.30	-0.62**
New aspects mentioned			
Liked	3.09	3.42	0.33+
Disliked	2.20	1.88	-0.32

Note. The special paintings were the ones in which the artists were invested.

[a] Proportion of participants who explicitly said that they liked or disliked the paintings.

+ $p <$ or $= .10$.   * $p <$ or $= .05$.   ** $p <$ or $= .01$.

Honesty and politeness

A main effect of instructions on explicit evaluations indicated that the more polite the participants were instructed to be, the less likely they were to offer any explicit evaluation at all, $F(2, 82) = 3.30$, $p < .05$, $MSE = 0.10$. The means for the honest, no-instructions, and polite conditions were 0.38, 0.35, and 0.30, respectively. The instructional manipulation also moderated the way the participants explicitly evaluated the paintings that were or were not special to the art students. There was a significant interaction among the instructional manipulation, investment, liking for the painting, and professed affect, $F(2, 82) = 4.84$, $p = .01$ (see Table 6). If participants were being completely honest, then they would explicitly say that they disliked the paintings that they actually did dislike and that they liked the paintings that they actually did like. That is, the numbers in the middle two columns of Table 6 would all be exactly 1.00. But none of them were. The numbers were fairly high for the liked paintings; when participants really did like the paintings, between 69% and 91% of them explicitly said that they did. And virtually none of them ever said that they disliked any of those paintings. Neither the artists' investment in the paintings nor the instructions the participants had been given made much of a difference. But when participants disliked the paintings, they often refrained from saying so explicitly, and both the instructions and the artists' investment mattered to them.

Table 6

Effects of Instructions, Participants' Liking for the Paintings, and Artists' Investment on Participants' Explicit Evaluations

Instructions	Disliked paintings		Liked paintings	
	Professed liking	Professed disliking	Professed liking	Professed disliking
Honest				
Not special	.09	.56	.81	.03
Special	.03	.62	.91	.00
Difference	-.06	.06	.10	-.03
No instructions				
Not special	.00	.64	.83	.00
Special	.16	.40	.79	.00
Difference	.16*	-.24***	-.04	.00
Polite				
Not special	.03	.47	.69	.00
Special	.16	.22	.81	.00
Difference	.13+	-.25***	.12+	.00

Note. The special paintings were the ones in which the artists were invested.

Entries are proportions of participants who explicitly said that they liked or disliked the paintings.

+ $p <$ or $= .10$. * $p <$ or $= .05$. *** $p <$ or $= .001$.

134

As shown in Table 6 , participants strayed farthest from the truth when they disliked a painting that was special to the artist and they were trying to be polite about it. When instructed to be honest, 62% of the participants explicitly acknowledged that they disliked the painting that was special to the artist; among the uninstructed participants, only 40% did so, and among those participants urged to be polite, only 22% did so. (All differences among these three numbers were significant [p s < .01 or smaller].) In the no-instructions and polite conditions, 16% of the participants told outright lies: They explicitly said that they liked the painting that they had already indicated in writing that they hated. (In the honest condition, 3% of the participants did this.)

It is also informative to compare the relative percentages of participants who explicitly said that they liked and disliked the detested special paintings in each condition. In the honest condition, 59% more of the participants said that they disliked than liked the painting that they did in fact dislike. In the no-instructions condition the difference was 24%, and in the polite condition it was only 6%.

Participants' explicit evaluations of the disliked paintings that were not special to the artists showed that participants used the predicted strategy of evaluation by implication. Participants were somewhat less likely to say explicitly that they disliked the disliked paintings when they were instructed to be polite than when they were instructed to be honest, but this drop from honest to polite was far less precipitous when the paintings were not special to the artist (56 to 47) than when they were special (62 to 22). The converse occurred for explicit statements of liking—the outright lies. Participants in the polite condition (and the no-instructions condition) told polite lies about the paintings they disliked that were special to the art student: 16% of them said that they liked those paintings, compared to 3% in the honest condition. In contrast, when the disliked paintings were not special to the artist, 3% of the participants in the polite condition (and none in the no-instructions condition) explicitly said that they liked them, compared to 9% in the honest condition.

In sum, then, when participants were trapped in the challenging situation of trying to be polite about work they disliked that was special to the artists with whom they were interacting, they manipulated both their evaluation of the work in which the artists were invested and their evaluation of the other artwork in which the artists had no investment. They refrained from saying explicitly that they disliked the paintings that were special to the artists. At the same time, they were much less restrained when it came to condemning the paintings that were not special.[3]

Discussion

A Looking Glass or a Reversible Figure?

Decades of research relevant to the reflected appraisal process have indicated that our perceptions of others' views of us are not strongly related to their actual views and that our self-perceptions are more highly related to our perceptions of others' appraisals than to their actual appraisals (Felson, 1992). We began with two possible explanations for the poor fit between actual and perceived appraisals. First, people may not be open and honest in communicating their appraisals. Second, we may misperceive those appraisals.

The present study strongly supported the first explanation. The participants refrained from saying how they really did feel about the paintings, especially when they disliked them. By itself, this finding is hardly new. From the literatures on performance appraisals (Fisher, 1979; Larson, 1984,

1986, 1989), the MUM effect (Tesser & Rosen, 1975), and lying in everyday life (DePaulo, Kashy, Kirkendol, Wyer, & Epstein, 1996; see also Folkes, 1982), as well as the literatures that followed more directly from the symbolic interactionist tradition (Blumberg, 1972; Felson, 1992; Swann, Stein-Seroussi, & McNulty, 1992), we already knew that there are formidable barriers to the direct communication of appraisals—especially negative ones—to the persons they concern. What our work has shown that is new is (a) the powerful impact on appraisals of the target person's personal investment in the object of the appraisals, (b) the difficulty of eliciting totally honest evaluations, and (c) the value of the defensibility postulate in predicting the verbal strategies people use in dodging the truth. Perhaps even more important, our findings suggest that (d) when we look to others for their appraisals, what we see is neither a looking glass nor a hopelessly distorted image, but a reversible figure.

Truth and investment

Among the many motives that have been postulated to account for the reluctance to convey negative evaluations, concern with the target person's feelings is perhaps the one that is most consistently cited and supported. If the target person's feelings are most important, then the more the target person cares about the object of evaluation, the less likely that person should be to hear a truthful appraisal, especially when the truth would hurt. This is so, we predicted, even though the instrumental value of honest appraisals should also increase with the target person's personal investment. Our study was the first to manipulate target persons' personal investment, and our findings were strongly supportive of our predictions. Across virtually every measure, communications were more dishonest when the target persons cared about the objects of the appraisals than when they did not.

Is the truth ever told to those who care?

We predicted that, when left to their own devices, people are practitioners of politeness (P. Brown & Levinson, 1987). We are the first to test people's strategic use of polite dissembling by directly instructing some of the participants to behave as politeness theory predicts they would and then comparing their behavior to that of participants given no special instructions. We thought that the uninstructed participants would convey appraisals of the paintings the art students cared about that were just as distorted and dishonest as those conveyed by the participants who were explicitly instructed to be polite and avoid hurting the art student's feelings. According to the judges' perceptions, this is what usually happened. The participants' reports, however, were often at odds with our prediction. The self-reports of the uninstructed participants were usually more similar to those of the participants urged to be honest than to those urged to be polite.

We are inclined to trust the judges' perceptions. The participants in the uninstructed condition may have been motivated to describe themselves as honest. (The polite participants, in contrast, had an excuse for being dishonest—they were following instructions.) The judges had no investment in perceiving the participants as either honest or dishonest, and they made their ratings without any awareness of the participants' instructional conditions. We also trust the judges' perceptions more because they were more in line with the results of our objective measures of what the participants actually said. The results were clearest for our measure of outright lies about the disliked special paintings. The percentage of participants who explicitly said that they liked the paintings that they had already told us that they detested was identical in the no-instructions and the polite conditions (16%); in the honest condition it was lower (3%). The same pattern is evident in the percentage of participants who refrained from saying explicitly that they disliked the detested paintings when they were special compared to when they were not special. In the honest condition, this withholding of an explicit negative evaluation was equally likely for the special as for the not-special paintings, but in the uninstructed and the polite conditions participants were significantly more likely to refrain from saying that they disliked the detested painting when it was special than when it was not. Furthermore, the magnitude of this difference between the special and not-special paintings was virtually identical for the uninstructed and polite participants (Table 6).

In that the participants who were urged to be honest told virtually no lies about the special paintings they disliked, and were no more likely to withhold their explicit negative evaluations of the special paintings than of the not-special ones, were they evenhanded in their discussions of the special and not-special paintings in every other way, too? If so, that would indicate that there is an easy way to elicit totally honest feedback—urge others to tell the truth and give them a compelling reason for doing so (e.g., it is only by hearing totally honest reactions that art students can learn how others really do perceive particular paintings). According to the participants' self-reports, they usually were evenhanded. The one important exception occurred when they were describing the paintings they disliked; in that condition they admitted that they were significantly less honest about the special paintings than the not-special ones (Table 3). The judges, too, thought that the honest participants were usually just as honest when discussing the special paintings as they were when discussing the not-special ones. But again, there was an important exception. The judges thought that the honest participants exaggerated their liking more when they were discussing the special paintings than the not-special ones (see Table 2).

Another condition in which it may have been possible for all participants to be just as honest about the special paintings as the not-special ones was when they liked the paintings. According to their self-reports, participants were in fact evenhanded in their discussions of the special and not-special paintings when they liked the paintings. On no measure did they report significantly less truthfulness. The judges, however, did think there were some differences. For example, they thought that the participants were trying to convey significantly more liking, and that they were exaggerating their liking more, for the paintings they liked that were special to the artists than for the liked paintings that were not special (see Table 1). The objective measures of what the participants really did say lend support to the judges' views. The strategy of amassing positive evidence preferentially for the special paintings (relative to the not-special ones) was just as evident when the participants liked the paintings as when they disliked them. In this study, then, there was essentially no condition under which art students who cared about the paintings heard totally honest feedback about them.

The defensibility postulate

When participants give a painting one of the lowest possible ratings on the liking scale and then tell the art student that they like that painting, it is hard for them to defend that statement as truthful. For that reason, our defensibility postulate predicted that outright lies would occur infrequently, as in fact they did. But they also occurred exactly when we expected them to—when the participants were discussing paintings they disliked that were special to the art student, and especially when they were given no special instructions or were instructed to be polite.

The strategy of amassing misleadingly positive evidence when one's true opinion is negative is one that was noted in passing nearly four decades ago in a study of the self-restraint of friends (Mayer, 1957). In the present context, participants practiced this strategy by mentioning many aspects of the special paintings that they really did like while mentioning relatively few aspects that they actually disliked. The resulting communications are highly defensible in that the positive qualities that the participants mentioned were ones that they really did like. Although participants were not equally forthcoming about the qualities they disliked, they did not deny disliking those qualities (which would not be defensible); they simply refrained from mentioning them.

The mentioning of new positive qualities that were not initially listed is a riskier strategy, but one that perhaps can work if participants convince themselves that they really do like these newly discovered aspects that they simply had not noticed previously. Credibility is added if the participants also notice some new aspects of the paintings that they dislike, though our prediction is that they will discover fewer of these new disliked aspects than liked aspects when the paintings are special. The results supported that prediction, too.

We believe that future research will show that the strategy of amassing misleading evidence is widely used. Most objects of evaluation—for example, personalities, appearances, job performances, paintings, and journal articles—are complex stimuli that routinely elicit both positive and negative reactions. It is a fairly simple matter, then, when put on the spot to voice one's opinion, to reel off one positive comment after another.

Also as predicted by the defensibility postulate, participants used the very clever strategy of evaluation by implication. By explicitly stating their disliking for the paintings created by other artists, while refraining from stating their disliking for the art student's own work, they implied a favorable social comparison. They appeared to like the art student's own work more than the other artists' work. They never exactly said that, however, so their communications can be defended as truthful.

In contexts in which it is possible for evaluators simply to avoid communicating their appraisals, we think that they will often do just that. In the performance appraisal literature, for example, it has been noted that supervisors sometimes delay giving negative feedback (Larson, 1989). Even when complete avoidance is no longer possible, evaluators still manage to convey less than the whole truth. For example, both supervisors (Larson, 1986) and football coaches (Felson, 1981) hedge by conveying specific appraisals rather than global ones. In the present research, we found that participants stonewalled by offering fewer explicitly evaluative comments and mentioning fewer aspects of the paintings that they liked or disliked when they were discussing paintings they disliked than ones they liked.

The reversible figure

Our results suggest an unanticipated answer to the question of why our perceptions of others' appraisals are not strongly related to others' actual appraisals: Participants described the paintings in ways that allowed the art students a choice as to what to hear and what to believe.

When discussing disliked paintings that the artists cared about, participants exaggerated their liking, withheld explicit expressions of disliking, and even told some outright lies. This gave the art students the opportunity to think that the participants really did like those paintings. But the participants also dropped some blatant hints as to their relative degrees of liking for the different paintings that the artists cared about. For example, they did not even try to convey as much liking for the paintings they disliked as for the ones they liked. They rated the disliked special paintings a 2 on the 9-point scale at the beginning of the study, and they tried to convey a rating of 4 to the art students. Although this was substantially higher than the liking they really did feel, it was still significantly lower than the degree of liking they tried to convey for the special paintings they really did like—a 7.

By biasing their appraisals of the special paintings in a positive way—by mentioning relatively more things that they liked about them and relatively fewer things that they disliked about them, relative to the not-special paintings—the participants again handed the artists the option of believing that they really did like their paintings. Still, the ratio of liked to disliked aspects that the participants communicated was not as lopsided as when they were describing paintings that they really did like.

Participants' explicit evaluations also allowed for interpretive flexibility. Sixteen percent of the uninstructed and polite participants explicitly said that they liked the special paintings that they actually hated. However, that number was dramatically lower than the 80% of the uninstructed and polite participants who explicitly said that they liked the special paintings that they really did like.

One of the most important qualifications of the symbolic interactionist model that has emerged from research is that the link from metaperception to self-perception is not unidirectional. Although it is true, as the symbolic interactionists have long maintained, that our perceptions of how others view us can influence our self-concept, it is also true that our self-concept can influence our beliefs about how others view us (Felson, 1992; Jussim et al., 1992; McNulty & Swann, 1994). The present research shows how the latter effect might occur. The feedback that people receive, even in the very difficult situations like the ones we created in this research, is unlikely to be totally dishonest and univalent. Instead, it is complex and multifaceted, offering plausible evidence for very different interpretations. This leaves lots of room for self-perceptions to influence the interpretation that is selected.

Qualifications

Our results are qualified in three ways. First, we recruited only women as artists, to keep the size of the study manageable. What was not known then, but is known now, is that people tell more lies to protect the other person's feelings when they are talking to women than to men (DePaulo et al., 1996). If we had included male artists, the overall rate of lying would probably have been lower. But we think that the key relationship between truth and investment would have remained unaffected. Still, that is a question for future research.

Second, we argued that participants were being less than truthful when they were more effusive about the special paintings than the not-special ones, after indicating in their initial ratings of the paintings that they liked the special and not-special paintings just the same. However, it is possible that over the course of the conversations, participants changed their minds about the special paintings and really did come to like them more. However, even if the process were one of genuine attitude change rather than strategic dissembling, the consequences for the artists remain the same: They heard evaluations of the paintings they cared about that were strikingly more positive than they would have heard if the paintings were not special to them. They could not count on gleaning equally glowing appraisals from evaluators who did not know, or did not care, whether the paintings were special to them.

In fact, although we have argued that lies are told to those who care, we must also acknowledge that sometimes brutal truths are told instead. In our paradigm, this did not occur. Perhaps participants would have told the truth if they cared more about the long-term consequences for the artists of hearing misleading feedback, rather than the short-term consequences of hurting the artists' feelings and feeling badly for having done so. Some evaluators are in roles that demand that they pay attention to the long-term consequences. Pre-med advisors, for example, are duty bound to warn their low-achieving advisees that their career plans may be unrealistic. Still, we suspect they would often find a way to do so politely. Perhaps evaluators will be harshly critical when they are intellectually insecure (Amabile, 1983). But even this effect, we think, is likely to occur only when the evaluators are either protected by anonymity or when they do not need to deliver their feedback to the person they are criticizing in a face-to-face interaction. We think that naked truths will be told when the conventions of polite society have not yet been fully internalized (as in the story of the emperor's new clothes), or when they have been temporarily abandoned, as when adults are caught in the throes of anger or hatred. Other possibilities are better left to research than to speculation.

References

Amabile, T. M. (1983). Brilliant but cruel: Perceptions of negative evaluators. *Journal of Experimental Social Psychology, 19,* 146-156.

Baldwin, M. W. (1992). Relational schemas and the processing of social information. *Psychological Bulletin, 112,* 461-484.

Bavelas, J. B., Black, A., Chovil, N., & Mullett, J. (1990). Equivocal communication. Newbury Park, CA: Sage.

Blumberg, H. H. (1972). Communication of interpersonal evaluations. *Journal of Personality and Social Psychology, 23,* 157-162.

Brown, P., & Levinson, S. (1987). Politeness: Some universals in language usage. Cambridge, England: Cambridge University Press.

Brown, R. & Gilman, A. (1989). Politeness theory and Shakespeare's four major tragedies. *Language in Society, 18,* 159-212.

Cochran, W. G. (1950). The comparison of percentages in matched samples. *Biometrika, 37,* 256-266.

Cooley, C. H. (1902). Human nature and the social order. New York: Scribner's.

DePaulo, B. M. (1992). Nonverbal behavior and self-presentation. *Psychological Bulletin, 111,* 203-243.

DePaulo, B. M. (1994). Spotting lies: Can humans learn to do better. *Current Directions in Psychological Science, 3,* 83-86.

DePaulo, B. M., Kashy, D. A., Kirkendol, S. E., Wyer, M. M. & Epstein, J. E. (1996). Lying in everyday life. *Journal of Personality and Social Psychology, 70,* 979-995.

DePaulo, B. M., Kenny, D. A., Hoover, C., Webb, W. & Oliver, P. (1987). Accuracy of person perception: Do people know what kinds of impressions they convey. *Journal of Personality and Social Psychology, 52,* 303-315.

DePaulo, B. M., & Kirkendol, S. E. (1989). The motivational impairment effect in the communication of deception. In J. Yuille (Ed.), Credibility assessment (pp. 51–70). Norwell, MA: Kluwer Academic.

DePaulo, B. M., Lanier, K. & Davis, T. (1983). Detecting the deceit of the motivated liar. *Journal of Personality and Social Psychology, 45,* 1096-1103.

DePaulo, B. M., Stone, J. I., & Lassiter, G. D. (1985a). Deceiving and detecting deceit. In B. R. Schlenker (Ed.), The self and social life (pp. 323–370). New York: McGraw-Hill.

DePaulo, B. M., Stone, J. I. & Lassiter, G. D. (1985b). Telling ingratiating lies: Effects of target sex and target attractiveness on verbal and nonverbal deceptive success. *Journal of Personality and Social Psychology,* 48, 1191-1203.

Felson, R. B. (1981). Self and reflected appraisals among football players: A test of the Meadian hypothesis. *Social Psychology Quarterly,* 44, 116-126.

Felson, R. B. (1992). Coming to see ourselves: Social sources of self-appraisals. *Advances in group processes,* Vol. 9, 185-205.

Fisher, C. D. (1979). Transmission of positive and negative feedback to subordinates: A laboratory investigation. *Journal of Applied Psychology,* 64, 533-540.

Folkes, V. S. (1982). Communicating the reasons for social rejection. *Journal of Experimental Social Psychology,* 18, 235-252.

Gilbert, D. T. & Malone, P. S. (1995). The correspondence bias. *Psychological Bulletin,* 117, 21-38.
Glaser, B. G. & Strauss, A. L. (1964). Awareness contexts and social interaction. *American Sociological Review,* 29, 669-679.

Goffman, E. (1967). Interaction ritual: Essays on face-to-face behavior. Garden City, NJ: Anchor.

Goffman, E. (1971). Relations in public. New York: Harper & Row.

Holtgraves, T. (1992). The linguistic realization of face management: Implications for language production and comprehension, person perception, and cross-cultural communication. *Social Psychology Quarterly,* 55, 141-159.

Jones, E. E. (1990). Interpersonal perception. New York: Freeman.

Jussim, L., Soffin, S., Brown, R., Ley, J. & Kohlhepp, K. (1992). Understanding reactions to feedback by integrating ideas from symbolic interactionism and cognitive evaluation theory. *Journal of Personality and Social Psychology,* 62, 402-421.

Kenny, D. A. & DePaulo, B. M. (1993). Do we know how others view us? An empirical and theoretical account. *Psychological Bulletin,* 114, 145-161.

Larson, J. R. Jr. (1984). The performance feedback process: A preliminary model. *Organizational Behavior and Human Performance,* 33, 42-76.

Larson, J. R. Jr. (1986). Supervisors' performance feedback to subordinates: The impact of subordinate performance valence and outcome dependence. *Organizational Behavior and Human Decision Processes,* 37, 391-408.

Larson, J. R. Jr. (1989). The dynamic interplay between employees' feedback-seeking strategies and supervisors' delivery of performance feedback. *Academy of Management Review,* 14, 408-422.

Mayer, J. E. (1957). The self-restraint of friends: A mechanism in family transition. *Social Forces,* 35, 230-238.

McNulty, S. E. & Swann, W. B. Jr. (1994). Identity negotiation in roommate relationships: The self as architect and consequence of social reality. *Journal of Personality and Social Psychology, 67,* 1012-1023.

Mead, G. H. (1934). Mind, self, and society. Chicago: University of Chicago Press.

Rosenthal, R., & Rosnow, R. L. (1991). Essentials of behavioral research (2nd ed.). New York: McGraw-Hill.

Schlenker, B. R. (1980). Impression management. Monterey, CA: Brooks/Cole.

Snyder, M. L. & Frankel, A. (1976). Observer bias: A stringent test of behavior engulfing the field. *Journal of Personality and Social Psychology, 34,* 857-864.

Swann, W. B. Jr., Stein-Seroussi, A. & McNulty, S. E. (1992). Outcasts in a white lie society: The enigmatic worlds of people with negative self-conceptions. *Journal of Personality and Social Psychology, 62,* 618-624.

Tesser, A. & Rosen, S. (1975). The reluctance to transmit bad news. *Advances in experimental social psychology,* Vol. 8, 193-232.

Witt, C. L., Bell, K. L., & DePaulo, B. M. (1996). Sex differences in deceptiveness: Real or perceived ?Unpublished manuscript.

Footnotes

1. Sex of participant also was included as a factor in the design, but the results of that factor are not of central relevance to the theme of the present report and therefore are not included. They are currently available from Bella M. DePaulo and will be reported in a subsequent article that will include several studies in addition to the data from this research (Witt, Bell, & DePaulo, 1996). The significant effects for participant sex that did occur in the present research generally indicated that the overall effects were characteristic of both the men and the women, but they were even more characteristic of the women. For example, the judges believed that both the men and the women were trying to convey more liking for the special paintings than for the not-special ones, but they saw a bigger difference for the women than for the men. The degree-of-investment factor was included to test whether our predictions for investment would be qualified by degree of investment. Although those results will not be presented, significant interactions did occur for participants' self-reports and judges' impressions. In all instances, the interactions indicated that the effects of investment were even stronger when the art students were highly invested in the paintings (the paintings were their own work) than when they were moderately invested in them (the paintings were their favorites). Complete results are available from Bella M. DePaulo.

2. We thought that if our judges had instead been completely unaware of the most important constraint in the present research—when the participants were and were not talking to artists who cared—they might have been even more taken by participants' expressions of liking. To test this, we prepared exact typed transcripts of the four conversations of 8 of the participants in the no-instructions and polite conditions who were talking to the artists about paintings that were or were not the artists' own. We recruited 65 raters (32 men and 33 women) to report their impressions of how much the participants really did like the paintings in each conversation, on the same 9-point scale used by our judges. Approximately half of the raters (n = 33) rated the conversations with the same information that our judges had—that is, they knew when the artists claimed that the paintings were their own. For the other raters (randomly assigned), that critical information was removed from the transcripts. The key interaction between whether the paintings were or were not special, and whether the judges knew that they were special, was significant, $F(1, 61) = 33.54$, $p < .001$, MSW = 0.94. When the paintings were not special, raters perceived almost exactly the same amount of liking when they knew that they were not special (M = 4.75) as when they did not know that (M = 4.79). However, when the paintings were special and the raters knew that they were, they thought that the participants liked those paintings much less (M = 4.66) than when they did not have that information (M = 5.40). That is, raters discounted some of the liking that participants expressed when they knew that the participants were talking to an artist who cared. The

implication for understanding the ratings made by our judges, who did know when the paintings were special, is that they may have (inaccurately) perceived even greater differences in liking between the special and not-special paintings if they had not had that crucial information.

3. An example of a truthful answer to the question "What do you think of it?" was given by a participant discussing a disliked painting that was one of the artist's favorites: "It's ugly. It's just ugly." An example of a truthful message about a liked painting that was one of the artist's favorites was: "I liked it. This was, this was my second favorite of the group. Um, it was the, the detail that was put into, uh, some of the, you know, the, the nuances in color, the way the black is done. And um, and it was, uh, yeah, I really liked it overall." An example of an answer that was coded as a lie (i.e., the participant claimed to like a disliked painting) was given by a participant discussing a painting that was the artist's own work: "I like this one." All participants had more to say about each painting when asked additional questions, but these were their complete answers to the artist's first question ("What do you think of it?"). Over the entire course of the discussion of each painting, participants spoke an average of 217 words.

Psychological Bulletin, March 1992, Vol. 111, No. 2, p 203-243

Nonverbal Behavior and Self-Presentation

Bella M. DePaulo

Abstract

Because of special characteristics of nonverbal behaviors (e.g., they can be difficult to suppress, they are more accessible to the people who observe them than to the people who produce them), the intention to produce a particular nonverbal expression for self-presentational purposes cannot always be successfully translated into the actual production of that expression. The literatures on people's skills at using their nonverbal behaviors to feign internal states and to deceive are reviewed as they pertain to the question of whether people can overcome the many constraints on the translation of their intentions into expressions. The issue of whether people's deliberate attempts to regulate their nonverbal behaviors can be detected by others is also considered.

The study of nonverbal behavior has a distinguished place in the history of science. Beginning with Charles Darwin (1872/1965), who wrote the ground-breaking piece, the Expression of the Emotions in Man and Animals, some of the most eminent scientific scholars, such as Wundt, Boring, Titchener, Gordon and Floyd Allport, and even Hull, have written about nonverbal expressive behavior (Goldstein, 1983). In the writings of some of these scientists, as well as in the work of many others who have contributed to the vast literature on nonverbal behavior, there is often a bias. Many of these scholars have been interested in nonverbal behaviors that are spontaneous and unregulated expressions of internal states, such as emotions and traits.[1] Nonverbal behavior can reflect such states, and the accumulated wisdom of the field should indeed be informative about these matters. However, from a social psychological perspective, perhaps one of the most interesting aspects of nonverbal behavior is that it is only rarely totally unregulated. In social interactions, people more often exert some control over their nonverbal expressive behavior. This attempted control is not always conscious, and it is not always successful, but it is pervasive. In this article, a particular type of deliberate regulation is considered: the control of nonverbal behavior for self-presentational purposes.

Erving Goffman, of course, is one who did recognize the self-presentational significance of expressive behaviors. In his provocative analysis of the presentation of self in everyday life (Goffman, 1959), he pointed out that the behaviors that a person "gives off," expressive behaviors that are taken to be genuinely and unselfconsciously reflective of something about the person, can be purposefully controlled so as to convey particular impressions (see also Goffman, 1963, 1971, 1974). His analysis was based on many casual observations and anecdotes but not much experimental data. It is now possible, 3 decades later, to present a more systematic, empirically based account of the (nonverbal) presentation of self in everyday life.

The self-presentational perspective offers coherence to a vast literature on nonverbal communication that too often has seemed sprawling, amorphous, and atheoretical. The questions posed by those who study language without words have often been quite intriguing in and of themselves; unfortunately, however, they have too often remained by themselves; rather than joining hands with other questions in an organized conceptual structure. In this review, the self-presentational perspective provides that structure. Dozens of studies that were generated from other frameworks or from no particular framework are reconstrued self-presentationally.

The study of nonverbal behavior, even when it has been pursued from a self-presentational perspective, has generally neglected what may well be one of the most important issues in the field: the question of when nonverbal behaviors can and cannot be willfully produced. Typically, it is assumed that the production of desired nonverbal expressions is nonproblematic. That issue, then, is bypassed, and the field moves along to other questions. An example of such a question is, "If aspiring executives want to convey nonverbally an impression of competence, how should they do so?" And the typical sort of answer is that they should (for example) speak in an unwavering tone of voice. And that is the end of it. But for the would-be executives, it is really just the beginning. They may care so deeply about sounding competent that their motivation to do so may itself undermine the firmness of their voice. Or, they may be so sure that they already sound confident, that they do not invest the effort necessary to make that ring of confidence loud enough for all to hear.

Motivation and confidence are just two of a wide array of factors that can undermine or enable the successful production of nonverbal behaviors for self-presentational purposes. Although there have been statements here and there about the difficulty of producing a particular nonverbal behavior (e.g., Ekman, 1985) or about a certain kind of psychological factor that can undermine nonverbal performance (e.g., Schlenker & Leary, 1982), nowhere is there an attempt at a comprehensive analysis of the potential difficulties involved in creating nonverbally the kind of impression one most wants to convey. That issue will be at the center of this review. Such a question, about the conditions under which people can purposefully regulate their nonverbal behaviors for self-presentational purposes, leads directly to the complementary question of the conditions under which others can tell that nonverbal behaviors are being deliberately regulated. That issue is also addressed. But first, the parameters of the fields of nonverbal behavior and self-presentation are described, and the implications of a self-presentational perspective for the study of nonverbal behavior is specified.

Scope of This Review

The opening sections of this review delineate the fields of nonverbal behavior and self-presentation and their intersection. First, the key constructs of nonverbal behavior and self-presentation are defined, and examples of self-presentational uses of nonverbal behaviors are described. The question "why non verbal behavior" or "why only nonverbal behavior" is also addressed. It is argued that there is a set of properties that characterize nonverbal behaviors more accurately than they characterize verbal behaviors and that these properties have important implications for the effectiveness with which self-presentational goals can be implemented.

Second, the scope of self-presentation is discussed. It is argued that the scope is quite broad, though not all-encompassing. The breadth of the self-presentational perspective derives from the range of targets of self-presentational attempts, the levels of awareness at which self-presentational strategies may be enacted, and the kinds of performances that can aptly be considered self-presentational. There are, however, nonverbal behaviors that are not self-presentational; those are discussed, too.

146

It is in the next set of sections that the key issue is discussed, namely, that the intention to regulate a particular nonverbal expression for self-presentational purposes cannot always be translated successfully into the actual production of that expression. It is proposed that there are three phases during which the production of self-presentationally relevant nonverbal behaviors can be disrupted. The first is the point at which intentions to regulate one's nonverbal behaviors are formed. It is argued that because of cultural or situational norms, intentions to produce certain kinds of nonverbal performances are rarely formed. The second and perhaps most important phase, which is discussed in greatest detail, occurs during the translation of self-presentational intentions into nonverbal behaviors. Sometimes intentions cannot be translated into nonverbal behaviors because the behaviors are too difficult to produce at will. Other impediments are more personal; for example, self-presenters may lack the requisite abilities or experiences, or they may be constrained by the structure of their face or the pitch of their voice or even by their own preferred styles of interacting. Constraints are also imposed by motivation and by emotion, by spontaneous expressiveness, and by lack of confidence. All of these are reviewed. The third phase occurs after the nonverbal performance has been completed; at that point, there are constraints on the effectiveness with which performances can be appraised and then modified in the future.

Can people overcome the many constraints on the translation of their intentions into actions and succeed at regulating their nonverbal expressions so as to achieve their self-presentational goals? This question is addressed in two sections. In the first, the literature on people's skills at using their nonverbal behaviors to convey particular impressions that may or may not be consistent with their actual feelings is reviewed. The second starts with the assumption that the kinds of factors that undermine (and enable) effective nonverbal performances are differentially characteristic of different kinds of people. Therefore, using the theoretical discussion of those factors, it should be possible to predict individual differences in the use of nonverbal behaviors for self-presentational purposes. Examples of individual differences that are especially germane to self-presentation, such as age, sex, physical attractiveness, and public self-consciousness, are discussed.

Much of the literature on nonverbal communication is about specific individual nonverbal behaviors, such as smiling or gaze, as opposed to the constellations of behaviors that make up nonverbal expressions, such as facial expressions of anger. The study of the role of individual nonverbal behaviors in the self-presentational process presents special challenges. Those challenges are considered, and to illustrate the major points, the literature on one particular nonverbal behavior (smiling) is reviewed in detail.

Next, the question of whether the reading of nonverbal behaviors (as opposed to the enactment of them) can serve self-presentational purposes is considered. Then, the important question of detectability of self-presentational attempts is addressed. This issue is approached at two levels. One is the aggregate level. The kinds of questions at this level are of the sort that are likely to be posed by experimental social psychologists. They ask whether people generally act differently, nonverbally, under different self-presentational contingencies. But detectability might also be addressed at a more micro or individual level, in a way that might be of special interest to clinical practitioners and to laypersons. The questions at this level are about specific nonverbal behaviors enacted by particular people at particular points in time, and the central issue is whether it is possible to know whether such behaviors are being deliberately regulated for self-presentational purposes.

Finally, the view of the relationship of emotions to nonverbal behaviors that is implicit in this review is compared with several other perspectives. It is argued that the present perspective is compatible with views of nonverbal behaviors as serving social motives or as ways of regulating person–environment interactions.

Nonverbal Behaviors and Their Special Significance for Self-Presentation

Nonverbal Behaviors and Their Self-Presentational Uses

Nonverbal cues are a motley crew. Examples include such diverse behaviors as facial expressions; bodily orientations, movements, and postures; vocal cues (other than words); aspects of physical appearance; interpersonal spacing; and touching. Some theorists (e.g., Knapp, 1978) also include attire and even the arrangement and decoration of rooms and other spaces. Nonverbal cues are sometimes called nonverbal expressive behaviors. Often, nonverbal expressions are taken to be expressions of emotions; indeed, among the important information that can be conveyed by nonverbal behaviors is information about emotion. But nonverbal behaviors can convey many other kinds of information, too, such as information relevant to opinions, moods, values, personality dispositions, psychopathologies, physical states such as fatigue, and cognitive states such as comprehension or befuddlement. Thus, people can use their nonverbal behaviors—or try to—to claim a variety of self-relevant characteristics.

Self-presentation is a matter of regulating one's own behaviors to create a particular impression on others (Jones & Pittman, 1982), of communicating a particular image of oneself to others (Baumeister, 1982), or of "showing oneself [to an audience] to be a particular kind of person" (Schlenker & Weigold, 1989). People can use many strategies to convey particular impressions to others that do not necessarily involve nonverbal expressive cues. For example, University of Virginia students who are proud of their association with the university and want new acquaintances to know that they are "U VA" students can simply mention this fact as they exchange pleasantries. Similarly, students who want to impress each other with their independence can slip into the conversation stories about eating dinner alone in crowded dining halls and feeling comfortable doing so (B. M. DePaulo, LeMay, & Epstein, 1991). If they want to get their favorite professors to like them, they can tell them what great lecturers they are or offer to run the projector for the next movie (E. E. Jones, 1964; E. E. Jones & Wortman, 1973). And an athlete who has just lost an important race but does not want to be seen as a talentless runner can tell the coach and the fans that his or her leg was really sore (e.g., C. R. Snyder & Higgins, 1988).

Many of these self-presentational goals can be accomplished nonverbally. Students who want to broadcast their association to the university, for example, can wear U VA sweatshirts and drink from U VA mugs. In fact, research has shown that this type of basking in reflected glory occurs more frequently after the hometown team has won than after it has lost (Cialdini et al., 1976). Students who want to ingratiate themselves to their professors can nod and smile and don an expression of utter fascination throughout each lecture (cf. Purvis, Dabbs, & Hopper, 1984; Rosenfeld, 1966). And athletes who want to claim that their legs are sore rather than slow can limp perceptibly as they leave the track (cf. Berglas & Jones, 1978; Jones & Berglas, 1978). Of course, verbal and nonverbal strategies can also be used together, as when the athlete winces in pain as she mentions the stiffness in her leg.

The Special Significance of Nonverbal Behaviors for Self-Presentation

There are numerous reasons why nonverbal behaviors should be of special interest to scholars of the dynamics of self-presentation. They include the following:

148

Nonverbal behavior is irrepressible

From a social psychological perspective, one of the most interesting properties of nonverbal cues in social interaction is that they are irrepressibly impactful. Try as they might, people cannot refrain from behaving nonverbally. If, for example, they try to be as passive as possible, they are likely to be perceived as unexpressive, inhibited, withdrawn, and uptight (cf. B. M. DePaulo & Kirkendol, 1989; see also J. A. Hall, Roter, & Katz, 1987). And even if they do succeed in quieting their dynamic nonverbal cues (such as their facial expressions and body movements and postures), their static nonverbal cues will still speak loudly. Relatively permanent physical features such as head size and shape, body build, physical attractiveness, and skin color have an immediate and important influence on the impressions perceivers form.

It is futile to hope, then, that one can manage to convey nonverbally no particular impression at all simply by interacting in blithe obliviousness to one's own nonverbal behaviors. Others will form some impression that is based in some manner on the nonverbal behavior they are observing, whether one wants them to or not and whether they want to or not (cf. Kleck & Strenta, 1980). The best one can hope for is to control the nature of that impression.

Nonverbal behavior is linked to emotion

Most major theorists of emotion and emotion expression (e.g., Buck, 1984; Ekman, 1972, 1977; Izard, 1977; Tomkins, 1962) posit that there are hard-wired links between the elicitation of certain basic emotions and the triggering of facial muscles that produce expressions of those emotions. (Challenges to this point of view are discussed at the end of this article.) When they suddenly become fearful, for example, people find that nonverbal indicants of fear begin to appear on their faces involuntarily. There is no analogous process whereby a particular, predictable set of words begin to be formed at the same time. For this reason, the kind of information that is conveyed by nonverbal behavior is sometimes more intensely and inescapably personal than is the information that is conveyed by verbal behavior. This is not to say that nonverbal behaviors convey emotions whereas verbal behaviors do not, for this is certainly untrue (e.g., Krauss, Apple, Morency, Wenzel, & Winton, 1981). Nor is it to say that nonverbal behaviors necessarily communicate emotions more often or even more efficiently than do verbal behaviors, though the latter is sometimes true. Rather, the point is that there may be certain automatic links between the elicitation of emotion and the expression of emotion that are present for nonverbal, but not verbal, behavior. Unless people can deliberately override those links (an issue that is discussed in more detail later), they will wear the emotions they are experiencing on their faces and in their voices.

Although there are other possible interpretations (e.g., Fridlund, 1991a), the fact that facial expressions of the basic emotions are fundamentally the same across cultures (e.g., Ekman, 1972; Izard, 1971) is consistent with the position that there may be automatic links between the experiencing of the basic emotions and the expression of those emotions.[2] The complement of this is that there are also cross-cultural consistencies in the perceptions of facial expressions of emotions (e.g., Ekman et al., 1987; Keating et al., 1981). From an ecological perspective (e.g., Buck, 1988; McArthur & Baron, 1983), it has been argued that emotional expressions are directly perceived, that is, that the perceptual apparatus is hard-wired to pick up emotional information without needing any additional contribution of higher order cognitive processes. The implications for self-presentation could be substantial. People who can simulate expressions of the basic emotions even when they are not actually experiencing those emotions can tap into the very powerful perceptual structures of their interaction partners. (See Buck's 1984 discussion of "voluntary expression initiation.") When a social actor dons an expression that closely approximates the real thing, it may be directly perceived as such by the other parties to the interaction. Those people may experience an immediate sense of knowing how the actor feels. They may be unlikely to question either the genuineness of the actor's expression or the trustworthiness of their understanding of that expression.

Nonverbal behavior is less accessible to actors than to observers

In most ways, people know more about themselves, and they know it more directly, than others could ever know. Awareness of nonverbal behaviors is an important exception to this rule. People never see their own facial expressions exactly as others do. Even if they were to stand in front of a mirror as they interact, they would see only a mirror image of their faces; they would not see their facial expressions in the exact same way that their interaction partner would. The tone of a person's voice also sounds different to her or him than it does to others. Because of the mechanics of the situation (i.e., the sound waves travel a different route to the speaker's ears than to the listener's), this is necessarily true. In contrast, when speakers communicate with words, both they and their listeners ordinarily hear the exact same words.

In interpersonal interactions, then, people never know as much about their own nonverbal behaviors as do the people with whom they are interacting. They do have access to internal cues that others do not, such as feedback from their own muscle movements, but these cues are only indirectly informative about how their nonverbal behaviors appear to others. Interactants sometimes provide feedback about people's expressive behaviors, either directly or indirectly (Ekman & Friesen, 1969), and through this "social biofeedback" process (Buck, 1988), people can glean further hints as to how their expressive behaviors appear to others. But this feedback, too, is only indirectly informative. When people are trying to convey a particular impression of themselves to others, this inaccessibility of their own nonverbal behavior provides both flexibility and constraint. Because they cannot see their faces or hear their voices the way others do, they are deprived of an important source of on-line information about the kinds of impressions they may be conveying. This may make it difficult for them to regulate their behavior on a moment-to-moment basis so as to convey just the right impression. And over the long term, they may develop odd or irritating nonverbal mannerisms of which they are completely unaware. Therein lies the constraint. However, the same inaccessibility provides people with a ready excuse for behaviors that create an undesired impression. For example, the admonition "Don't look at me like that" can be countered with the incredulous "Like what? I don't know what you mean." And it may indeed be the case that the person was unaware of how his or her face appeared. However, it is also possible that the person knew quite well what impression his or her facial expression would convey but also knew that if challenged, he or she could hide behind a facade of ignorance.

Nonverbal behavior is off-the-record

Many nonverbal behaviors are off-the-record of the actor who produced them, because of the inaccessibility described above. But they are in other senses off-the-record to all parties to an interaction: the actor, the interaction partner, and any other observers. In commenting on an interaction, it is more difficult to describe a facial expression or a tone of voice than it is to recount the words that were spoken. Parties to a social interaction might ask each other to repeat their words, but they never ask each other to repeat their facial expressions, voice tones, or body movements or gestures. Furthermore, even if they did "catch" the nonverbal expression the first time and could hold it in their minds, they still could not seek further clarity about its meaning by looking it up in a dictionary To the self-presenter, this elusiveness of nonverbal behavior contributes further to the flexibility with which it can be used. People might take a chance at expressing something nonverbally that they would be reluctant to express verbally; should pangs of regret set in, they can deny that the behavior ever occurred or that it had the meaning being attributed to it.

Nonverbal behavior communicates unique meanings

That words can communicate meanings that would be nearly impossible to convey nonverbally is hardly in doubt. (Imagine explaining Einstein's theory of relativity using only your face.) Poets and novelists would have us believe that the same is true for nonverbal expressions: They can convey meanings and emotions that could never be adequately expressed in words. Should empirical research come down on the side of the poets, the implication for self-presentation will be that certain identity-relevant impressions can be conveyed only nonverbally.

Nonverbal behavior occurs quickly

Many nonverbal reactions occur almost instantaneously. When perceivers see someone get hurt, or hear someone say something that was clearly painful to disclose, they can convey an empathic nonverbal reaction immediately. In contrast, it would take a bit longer to formulate and convey an appropriately empathic verbal response. The quickness of the nonverbal reaction will probably underscore its sincerity (or perceived sincerity). The slower verbal mode is more vulnerable to perceiver attributions of deliberateness and disingenuity.

Not all of these special characteristics are equally apt descriptions of all nonverbal behaviors. For example, all of these characteristics are accurate descriptions of facial expressions, and most of them aptly characterize body orientations, movements, and postures and tone-of-voice cues. Interpersonal spacing, however, may be just as accessible to actors as to observers, and it may also be fairly easy to describe (i.e., it is not off-the-record except in that people's judgments of the distance between themselves and other people are imperfect). Analogously, touching is hardly irrepressible: Under ordinary circumstances, most people can refrain from touching others if they so desire. To cite just one more example, changes in physical attire can rarely be accomplished with the same speed that can characterize facial expressions or voice tones. Therefore, nonverbal behaviors vary systematically in the number of these attributes that characterize them. It may be—although this point is speculative—that the study of nonverbal behaviors characterized by more, rather than fewer, of these attributes will be most illuminative of self-presentational processes because the enactment and interpretation of such behaviors may be most problematic.

Note also that not all of the special characteristics of all nonverbal behaviors distinguish them from verbal behaviors. As noted above, verbal behaviors, like nonverbal behaviors, can communicate unique meanings, though the unique meanings conveyed by words may be different from those conveyed without words. Still, the package of attributes as a whole better characterizes nonverbal behaviors than verbal behaviors, and several of the attributes are never characteristic of verbal behaviors.

The special qualities of nonverbal behaviors should add up to an absolution of responsibility for the self-presenter. People are probably not held accountable for behavior that is irrepressible, that can be triggered quickly and automatically, that is inaccessible to them and elusive to others, and that has meanings that cannot be conveyed in any other way. Observers are not totally naive to the possibility that nonverbal behaviors can be deliberately regulated, but they seem generally to be more "taken" by the spontaneity and trustworthiness of such behaviors (Schneider, Hastorf, & Ellsworth, 1979). Direct tests of these assumptions should be conducted.

The second, and perhaps even more important, implication of the special characteristics of nonverbal behaviors for the self-presentational process is that many nonverbal behaviors are not readily or effectively produced or controlled. Sometimes, for example, people do not know which nonverbal behaviors to enact to convey a desired impression. But this limitation is equally characteristic of verbal behaviors: Sometimes people do not know which words to choose to convey a desired impression. There is a more fundamental level, however, at which verbal behaviors are almost perfectly controllable whereas many nonverbal behaviors are not. If a person wants to say a particular word, ordinarily he or she can simply and straightforwardly do so. Producing certain nonverbal behaviors (as is discussed more fully later) can be far more problematic. This characteristic is differentially applicable to different nonverbal behaviors; that is, nonverbal behaviors vary systematically along a continuum of controllability (e.g., Ekman & Friesen, 1969; Rosenthal & DePaulo, 1979a, 1979b). An open posture, for example, is easier to produce than is a high-pitched tone of voice. Those nonverbal behaviors that are difficult, but perhaps not impossible, to control may be most important to our understanding of the self-presentational process because of the special challenges they pose to self-presenters.

Scope of Self-Presentation

Targets of Self-Presentations

Self-presentation to target persons and observers

Typically, the person to whom the self is presented is the other person in the interaction. Thus, the aspects of self that are presented are edited in such a way as to create the desired impression on that particular person. An example comes from a study in which women were interviewed by a male employer who was known to be either traditional or liberal in his attitudes toward women (von Baeyer, Sherk, & Zanna, 1981). The women who interviewed with the more traditional man presented themselves in a more feminine way than did those who interviewed with the more liberal employer. Other research has shown that women (and men), when faced with no particularly strong self-presentational demands, convey nonverbally a degree of femininity that corresponds with their self-ratings of femininity (Frable, 1987; Lippa, 1978b). The von Baeyer et al. (1981) findings suggest that these expressions can be edited so as to appear even more feminine to a traditional male and less feminine to a liberal male.

Sometimes expressive behaviors that seem to be directed toward an interaction partner are actually performed for the benefit of others who are not part of the interaction at all but are simply observing it. Goffman's (1971) discussion of "tie-signs" describes just such a situation. Tie-signs are behaviors used by people in a relationship to make clear to others the nature of that relationship. Members of a couple who are attending a party, for example, might hold hands and gaze at each other; and if, during the course of the event, they drift apart from each other, they might periodically check back. All of these behaviors announce the "withness" of the twosome (Scheflen, 1974) to others in the gathering.

Behaviors interpreted as tie-signs were observed in a naturalistic study of couples waiting in movie lines (Fine, Stitt, & Finch, 1984). The woman in the couple was approached by an interviewer who proceeded to ask her either intimate or nonintimate questions. The behavior of the man of the couple was observed. When the interviewer asked the woman personal questions, the man was much more likely to gaze at the woman he was with and to orient his body toward hers than when the interviewer asked impersonal questions. And when the interviewer was a man, the male member of the couple was especially unlikely to orient away from the interaction. The authors hypothesized that the men were underscoring the couple's togetherness and that they were especially inclined to do so under the more threatening circumstances (i.e., when the interviewer was another man or was someone who asked personal questions).

Self-presentation to reference others and to the self

It can be argued that nonverbal behaviors that occur in private are unlikely to be self-presentational. But exceptions have been postulated. It has been suggested, for example, that even when people are by themselves, their behavior may be guided by the characteristics and values of people who are important to them (e.g., Greenwald & Breckler, 1985; Schlenker & Weigold, 1989). A boy with a toothache, for example, might think about his father's admonition to be brave, and consequently, he might try to squelch his facial expressions of pain. This is an example of self-presentation to reference others, who are not physically present. This sort of self-presentation could even occur with regard to fictitious others, such as imaginary playmates. Self-presentation to self has also been postulated (e.g., Greenwald & Breckler, 1985; Schlenker & Weigold, 1989) and could occur if, for instance, the boy had internalized the importance of being brave and tried to don an expression of stoicism to convince himself that he was living up to his ideals.

Although the concepts of self-presentation to self and to reference others may at first blush seem difficult to operationalize, encouraging data have already been published. Baldwin and Holmes (1987) asked subjects to visualize the faces of different categories of significant others (e.g., either friends or parents) and found systematic effects on their self-evaluations and on their self-ratings of enjoyment of sexually provocative literary passages. Although expressive behaviors were not measured, it would be a straightforward extension of the research to do so. Muscle movements likely to be indicative of smiling (assessed by electromyographic (EMG) measures taken over the relevant facial muscles) were measured in two studies of implicit audience effects. In one (Fridlund et al., 1990), subjects who imagined enjoying themselves in the presence of other people showed more EMG activity than those who imagined enjoying themselves alone, even when levels of self-reported happiness were equated in the two conditions. Thus, subjects seemed to smile more in the "presence" of others, even when those others were present only in their imagination. In the other study (Fridlund, 1991b), subjects watching pleasant videotapes showed more facial EMG indicative of smiling when they knew that a friend of theirs was in a nearby room than when they were watching by themselves. Again, the implicit (though not physical) presence of another person augmented nonverbal expressive movements.

Self-presentation to intimates and nonintimates

That people often try deliberately to convey particular impressions of themselves when they first meet other people (especially people they regard as powerful or attractive) is not really in doubt. A study conducted in bars and restaurants cleverly captured a bit of this purposeful self-presentation as it occurs in newly developing relationships (Daly, Hogg, Sacks, Smith, & Zimring, 1983). Men and women were unobtrusively observed in restrooms, and the amount of time they spent preening (fixing their hair, straightening their clothes, looking at themselves in the mirror) was recorded. They were then interviewed about the nature of their relationship with the person they were sitting with in the establishment. These relationships ranged from first dates through marriages and long-term same-sex friendships. True to conventional folk wisdom, people in newer relationships spent more time preening than did people in more established relationships.

Does this mean that self-presentational considerations are less important in longer standing or more intimate relationships than in less developed relationships? Probably not. Although people may become less concerned with the superficial aspects of their self-presentations (such as their hairstyle) as their relationships deepen and become more secure, they may become more concerned with the images they convey of weightier aspects of themselves, such as their ability to be caring and committed over long periods of time. These kinds of self-presentations can be conveyed nonverbally, too. Over the long term, couples come to face different life tasks, such as parenting and caring for elderly relatives. As these transitions into new roles occur, the members may become concerned with conveying new images of themselves to their partner (e.g., the good mother). Even in the absence of major life changes, people may feel that they have changed or want to change in important ways. As this occurs, they may try to convey this new image of themselves to a partner who has become accustomed to an older image and may be resistant to the change. Self-presentational concerns may also become intensified in the face of a serious threat to the relationship, such as spousal infidelity. In such instances, the betrayed spouses may try to make themselves more attractive to their partner, or they may try to convey or even exaggerate the extent to which they feel hurt. Even in stable long-term relationships, with no immediate threats, changes, or transitions into different life roles, self-presentational considerations can be important, and they can be important even with regard to superficialities. If, for example, a wife becomes so unconcerned about her appearance in front of her husband that she neglects to brush her hair for days at a time, her husband might regard this as a disturbing comment on her regard for him and for their relationship. (See Schlenker, 1984, for a more extensive discussion of self-presentational considerations in relationships.)

Deliberate, Nondeliberate, and Once-Deliberate (or Once-Learned) Behaviors

When people unexpectedly experience a very intense stimulation (for example, when they accidentally step into an icy puddle), an emotional expression is likely to appear instantly on their face, and the intensity of the expression, at the moment when it first appears, is unlikely to be affected by the presence of other people (e.g., Craig & Patrick, 1985). Another situation in which the presence of others is likely to have little impact on expressive behavior is when a person is completely absorbed in an interesting or challenging task (E. E. Jones & Pittman, 1982; Schlenker, 1980). Subjectively self-aware people (e.g., Duval & Wicklund, 1972) become so wrapped up in the ongoing activity that it never enters their mind to monitor their expressive behavior to control the impressions that such behavior might convey. Their expressive behavior, then, is not deliberate and not self-presentational.

Or is it? It has been suggested (Jones & Pittman, 1982; Schlenker, 1980) that there are many behaviors that were once produced deliberately but then after years of practice eventually became habitual. Girls from traditional families, for example, may be taught to "sit like a lady." For years, they might practice this deliberately, perhaps even looking at themselves in a mirror to ascertain that their posture is indeed sufficiently ladylike. Eventually, conscious monitoring is no longer necessary. Even when, 30 years later, the girl has grown into an astro-physicist who is alone in her study totally absorbed in a challenging intellectual puzzle, she will have automatically assumed the posture of a lady. At that point, the expressive behavior is no longer deliberate, but it is arguably different from other expressive behaviors that never were purposefully regulated.

Posture is a relatively discrete and circumscribed behavior; however, more extensive and dynamic patterns of nonverbal behaviors can also, after much practice, become habitual. Efron's (1941) classic study of the gestures of Italian and Jewish immigrants, and the ways in which those gestures changed as the immigrants became assimilated, is a suggestive example of this process. The Italians and Jews initially used very different styles of hand, head, and body movements in their conversations with others of the same ethnicity. The Italians, for example, used very expansive movements but rarely touched their conversation partners; the Jews, in contrast, used more constrained movements, but often touched the other person. A generation later, however, the offspring of these two sets of immigrants who had cut many of their traditional ties used conversational expressive styles that more closely resembled those of the American subgroups to which they had become assimilated than those of their parents. It is not clear from Efron's study, however, whether these first-generation offspring deliberately practiced the new gestures, and at first used them primarily in their interactions with Americans, or whether they were learned entirely out of awareness.

An important mechanism governing the deliberate management of nonverbal behaviors is what Ekman (1972) called display rules. Display rules are cultural norms governing the management of emotional expressions. They indicate which emotions should be conveyed, depending on the situation, the person who is communicating the emotion, and the person to whom the emotion is being communicated. For example, the ritual look of delight on the face of the first runner-up as the new Miss America is announced is a product of the display rule that dictates that losers should mask their sadness with an expression of joy for the winner. In studies of the readability of spontaneous and posed facial expressions, it has been found that positive emotions are generally easier to read from people's faces than are negative emotions (Buck, 1984; Wagner, MacDonald, & Manstead, 1986; but see also Gallois & Callan, 1986). Wagner et al. (1986) have suggested that this finding may be an example of the operation of a "residual display rule" (to communicate pleasant affects and suppress negative ones) that remains in evidence even when people believe that they are alone and unobserved.

Spontaneously produced nonverbal behaviors that never were consciously practiced or controlled may appear to naive observers to be quite similar to overlearned, habitually produced nonverbal behaviors. Yet the two classes of behaviors have different origins, different developmental histories, different elicitors, and different neurological substrates. In theory, then, they should be distinguishable. Examples of spontaneously produced nonverbal behaviors include those that result from the elicitation of the basic emotions. One implication of the hard-wired links that may exist between the elicitation of basic emotions and the triggering of the facial muscles associated with those emotions (discussed above) is that facial expressions of the basic emotions never need to be practiced nor do they even require any observational learning. These expressions appear whenever the relevant emotions are elicited, unless they are muted or altered by deliberate attempts at regulation. (As M. Lewis & Michalson, 1985, have suggested, it is possible that in infancy, the experience and expression of emotion are not synchronized from the outset. Some degree of maturation, for example, may need to occur first.) Although the particular events that elicit the basic emotions vary from culture to culture and even from person to person, the triggering of the facial muscles that occurs once the emotions are elicited does not vary (Ekman, 1972). Another characteristic of spontaneous facial expressions of the basic emotions is that they are often quite brief in duration. Unless the emotion elicitor is itself particularly long lasting or particularly intense, the facial expression triggered by the elicitor will appear and disappear rather quickly.

Nonverbal expressive behaviors that result from learning and practice are very different. The kinds of nonverbal expressive behaviors that will be deliberately practiced (or even picked up out of awareness) are not hard-wired and will vary with individual-difference and social learning factors such as reward and punishment contingencies and particular histories of observational learning. These behaviors bear the stamp of particular personalities and particular lives. For example, a teenager who admires a popular rock star might deliberately try to simulate his mannerisms. If practiced often enough, such mannerisms might take on the appearance of a personal style. Unlike genuinely spontaneous behaviors that appear and disappear quickly, these mannerisms may seem to be ever present. They may also appear to be occurring spontaneously and unselfconsciously. Yet these once-learned nonverbal behaviors are responsive to interpersonal contingencies in ways that genuinely spontaneous nonverbal behaviors are not. If, for instance, the teen were to spend an evening with peers from a different clique who think the rock star is dumb, the mannerisms might suddenly vanish. And over time, as the popularity of the rock star fades, so too will the teen's idolatrous mannerisms.

Issues of Accuracy and Honesty

The definition of self-presentation as a deliberate (or once-deliberate) attempt to convey a particular impression of oneself does not imply that self-presentations are necessarily deceptive (E. E. Jones, 1990; E. E. Jones & Pittman, 1982; Schlenker, 1980, 1984, 1987). To be sure, they can be. People can and do on occasion deliberately try to convey the impression that they are a different kind of person than they in fact believe themselves to be. Often, the attempt is to claim a more positive identity (such as a kinder or gentler one) than is deserved, but there can also be advantages to claiming negative images (such as more intimidating or dependent ones), and so these, too, are occasionally embraced (E. E. Jones & Pittman, 1982).

Probably vastly more common than the claiming of an image that people believe to be totally uncharacteristic of themselves is the editing of the images that are presented. Some people may, for example, believe that they are most accurately described as dependent in some ways but independent in others. In interactions with people who value independence and when in situations in which independence is especially appropriate, they may choose to emphasize their independence; in other types of contexts, they might instead emphasize their dependence. In both kinds of situations, they can present aspects of themselves that are genuine. It is not that what they are presenting is feigned, but that it is only part of what they might have presented (Schlenker, 1984).

Ekman and Friesen (1975) have made similar distinctions with specific reference to the management of facial expressions of emotions. People can, they maintain, manage their facial expressions by outright falsification. But they can also use two milder management techniques: the qualification of an expression that is accomplished by adding an expression that comments on the expression just produced (e.g., showing a sad face, then smiling soon afterwards to indicate that the sadness is bearable) and the modulation of the intensity of the expression. In qualifying and modulating, people are not claiming different emotions than the ones they are experiencing; instead, they are merely editing the public presentations of their felt emotions.

In the absence of any clear reason to think otherwise, people seem to believe that others see them quite similarly to how they see themselves (B. M. DePaulo, Kenny, Hoover, Webb, & Oliver, 1987; Kenny & DePaulo, 1991). They assume that their personalities, as they construe them, are readily apparent to others, even when they have not made any special effort to make them apparent. But when it becomes especially important to them to come across as exactly the kind of person that they believe they really are, then the process is probably not left to chance. Instead, people try deliberately to make their identities, as they construe them, perfectly clear to others (cf. Cheek & Hogan, 1983; Hogan, 1982; Leary & Kowalski, 1990). The process is one of deliberate control of expressive behaviors for self-presentational purposes, but the goal is accuracy rather than dissimulation or exaggeration or shading of the truth.

There are other situations, too, in which people deliberately regulate their nonverbal behavior in an attempt to enhance the correspondence between their self-perceptions and their self-presentations. For example, models of self-awareness and self-regulation (e.g., Carver & Scheier, 1981; Duval & Wicklund, 1972) suggest that when people direct their attention toward themselves, they become more aware of their own personal standards and values and more likely to try to behave in accord with those values. There are individual differences in the tendency to be inner directed rather than outer directed (e.g., Fenigstein, Scheier, & Buss, 1975), in the degree to which a self-image of autonomy is valued over a self-image of social conformity (Schlenker & Weigold, 1990), and in the importance that is attached to acting consistently with one's own values (e.g., M. Snyder, 1979). These, too, will be important predictors of whether deliberate attempts at self-presentation will serve to augment or to undermine the consistency between traits or other internal states and the nonverbal behaviors taken to be expressive of those states (see also Lippa, 1983).

Uses of Nonverbal Behaviors That Are Not Self-Presentational

The domain of self-presentation as defined thus far is quite broad. It includes presentations to self and to reference others as well as the more theoretically and empirically tractable presentations to target persons and observers. Similarly, it includes behaviors that were deliberately enacted and practiced until they came to appear spontaneous as well as behaviors that are being deliberately enacted at the moment without the benefit of much prior practice. Despite this apparent breadth of definition, there are important categories of nonverbal behaviors that are not self-presentational.

A few of these were mentioned previously. For example, initial reactions to intense stimuli are unlikely to be self-presentational. Nonverbal behaviors emitted in private settings (e.g., while watching television by oneself), along with those that occur while a person is involved in a very absorbing task, are also unlikely to be self-presentational. In these examples, though, the possibilities of self-presentation to self or reference others (e.g., Fridlund, 1991a, 1991b; Fridlund et al., 1990), as well as the possibilities that the behaviors are habitual remnants of those that were once produced deliberately, need to be ruled out.

In studies in which subjects watch mildly pleasant or unpleasant slides, their facial responses to the slides can be so indistinct that observers watching their faces have no idea whether the slides the subjects are viewing are pleasant or unpleasant. Yet electrodes attached to the subjects' face can pick up different EMG activity during the pleasant as compared with the unpleasant slides (Cacioppo, Petty, Losch, & Kim, 1986; see also Cacioppo, Martzke, Petty, & Tassinary, 1988). The behaviors picked up by the EMG recordings, which are too subtle to be noticed by untrained observers, are of no self-presentational significance, because observers cannot be impressed by behaviors they cannot detect. There are two exceptions. One would occur if a person were trying to convey a particular impression nonverbally but succeeded only in producing a behavior too weak or too fleeting to be identifiable by others. Another exception would be the nonverbal behaviors that occur as part of presentations to self or to reference others; these would not need to be discernible to observers to be self-presentational.

Other examples of nonverbal behaviors that are not self-presentational occur during conversations. Turn switching in conversations often proceeds smoothly and effortlessly. Each person seems to know exactly when the other person will stop speaking and yield the floor, yet neither person ever says, "Okay, you can speak now," or "Wait, I'm not finished." Instead, these wishes are communicated nonverbally, with behaviors known as turn signals (Duncan & Fiske, 1977) or regulators (Ekman & Friesen, 1969). For example, the person about to yield the floor typically stops gesturing, begins speaking a little less loudly, stretches out the last word, and looks toward the other person (Cappella, 1985; Duncan & Fiske, 1977). These nonverbal behaviors that serve as conversational traffic signals are not self-presentational.

Nonverbal behaviors can also be used to illustrate and clarify a verbal message, as when a person motions to the left while giving directions to a befuddled tourist (e.g., Cohen, 1977). Nonverbal behaviors called emblems (Ekman, 1976) have direct verbal translations and can be used in place of words, as when a friend asks his roommate from across a noisy room how the University of Virginia fared in the basketball game and the roommate holds up two fingers in the shape of a V to indicate that Virginia won. Nonverbal gestures can also be used in the service of a particular task (cf. Patterson, 1983), as when a batting coach, in teaching a Little Leaguer how to choke up, puts his or her hands over the child's and moves them across the bat. All of these kinds of nonverbal behaviors are produced deliberately, but none of them are self-presentational.

People can deliberately regulate their nonverbal behaviors so as to simulate a particular personality or a particular cognitive process (such as comprehension) or even a particular pathology (e.g., Braginsky, Braginsky & Ring, 1969), but those behaviors that are spontaneous and unselfconscious expressions of personality (e.g., Allport, 1937; Frable, 1987; Lippa, 1978b), cognitive processing (e.g., Kahneman, 1973; Kenner, 1984; Rinn, 1984), or psychopathology (e.g., Boice & Monti, 1982; Ellgring, 1986; Feldman, Philippot, & Custrini, 1991; Pitman, Kolb, Orr, & Singh, 1987; Scherer, 1979; Singer & Spohn, 1956) are not self-presentational.

Most examples of nonverbal behaviors that are not self-presentational, though, can take on self-presentational significance with just a little adjustment. For example, if the roommate wanted to convey not just the information that Virginia had won but also the impression that he was proud of this victory, he might produce Vs with both hands and shake them high in the air, Richard Nixon style, for all to see. And if the batting coach wanted not only to show the player how to choke up but also to convey that she or he was a no-nonsense coach, then the coach might communicate the instructions in a stern and mirthless manner.[3]

Implications of the Self-Presentational Perspective

Numerous implications follow from the self-presentational perspective as it is construed in this review. Some of these implications depart importantly from those of other perspectives. It is predicted that the literature on nonverbal behavior, though often generated from perspectives other than the self-presentational one (or from no particular theoretical framework at all), will be consistent with these implications:

- People try to regulate their nonverbal behaviors. They are rarely content to allow their nonverbal behaviors to be spontaneous and unselfconscious expressions of their dispositions or feelings or other internal states.
- Attempts at nonverbal regulation are often guided by self-presentational goals. That is, people use their nonverbal behaviors in attempts to claim identities that they find desirable

and that they think others will find believable (e.g., Schlenker, 1980; Schlenker & Weigold, 1989).

- When contextual cues vary in self-presentationally relevant ways, nonverbal behaviors should vary also. For example, when people are dependent on others to achieve their goals, they should act differently toward them nonverbally than when they can get what they want completely independently.

- The regulation of nonverbal behaviors for self-presentational purposes is learned. Therefore, nonverbal skills and strategies should vary systematically with important units of socialization such as culture, gender, and age. Similarly, personality differences that are of special self-presentational significance, such as differences in self-monitoring, need for approval, and public self-consciousness, should also be powerful predictors of nonverbal abilities and styles.

- Adults generally have the skills necessary to regulate their nonverbal behavior successfully for self-presentational purposes.

- Nonverbal skills are not homogeneous. Instead, patterns of skills should be predictable from self-presentational considerations. For example, there are many more occasions in social life during which people attempt to convey emotions or attitudes or evaluations that are more positive than they really feel than ones in which people attempt to convey appraisals that are more negative than they really feel. Therefore, it should follow that attempts at feigning positivity are more often effective than are attempts at feigning negativity. This prediction differs from one that might follow from component-skills models that are often proposed in developmental psychology and cognitive psychology. According to those models, the success of a performance can be predicted from the degree to which people have mastered the enactment and coordination of the individual components that constitute the performance. The argument here is not that the component-skills perspective is unimportant; in fact, the sections on factors that constrain and enable nonverbal performances are entirely compatible with such a model. Instead, the argument is that self-presentational considerations are important, too; in some instances, they offer explanations as to why particular components are unlikely to be practiced and developed.

- People's success at using their nonverbal behaviors to attain self-presentational goals is attributable not only to their own skill but also, perhaps even more importantly, to perceivers' lack of skill or their willingness to go along with others' identity-relevant claims. In most domains, perceptions of reality become increasingly accurate over the course of development, so that by adulthood, people understand fundamental aspects of their world, such as space, time, and causality, in a reasonably insightful (though usually imperfect) way. Perceptions of certain self-presentational aspects of the social world differ dramatically from this accuracy model. As Goffman (1959) pointed out, people claim certain identities in their social interactions, and perceivers tend to honor those claims. They tend to take other people's self-presentations at face value, rather than trying to see through them, and they expect the same latitude in return (see also E. E. Jones, 1979).Several predictions follow from this construal. One is that when people are feigning an affect or opinion or disposition that is at odds with their true internal state (as they view it), perceivers read whatever it is that people are trying to convey more than they read what is really true. Another is that this tendency to see what others want one to see rather than what is in fact true may in some instances be more characteristic of adults than of children. Thus, in the self-presentational domain, socialization can result in decrements rather than enhancements in accuracy of perception. Third, although one might expect spontaneous communications to appear particularly natural, veridical, and therefore readable, the prediction from the self-presentational perspective is that the contents of such communications (e.g., feelings of happiness or sadness) can be read more easily when they are posed than when they are

159

expressed spontaneously. A fourth prediction (for which there are currently no relevant data) is that in the course of everyday social interactions, perceivers will often fail to realize that other people's nonverbal behaviors are being deliberately regulated. They will understand in the abstract that such regulation occurs but will often miss the signs of it during specific ongoing interactions. When asked directly to compare several behaviors, they may be able to tell that regulated behaviors appear somewhat less spontaneous than unregulated ones, but without such a prod, the distinction is likely to go unnoticed.

- There will be important limitations to the kinds of identities that people can successfully claim. People can vary their self-presentations effectively, but only within a certain range. Many of the limitations will be imposed by social reality. For example, although any competent adult should be able to simulate extraversion, people who really are extraverts should be able purposefully to convey an impression of extraversion more effectively than can people who really are introverts. Analogously, people should be less successful at feigning an emotion that is at odds with the emotion they are actually experiencing if their experienced emotion is strong rather than weak. In general, then, the social world is more tolerant of the editing of conveyed identities, so that they depart only slightly from the social actor's actual experiences, than of the complete fabrication of new identities.

Linking Self-Presentational Intentions to Nonverbal Actions

One approach to the study of nonverbal behavior and self-presentation is to document the self-presentational meanings attributed by perceivers to various nonverbal behaviors and expressions. One could, from this perspective, review the nonverbal cues that are most likely to convey impressions of liking and of status, for example. Several extensive and insightful reviews of this nature have already been published (e.g., Burgoon, Buller, & Woodall, 1989; Edinger & Patterson, 1983; Schlenker, 1980). From these reviews, it is possible to glean answers to questions such as "if I want to try deliberately to convey to another person the impression that I really like him, which nonverbal behaviors should I use to do so?" In some instances, once the answer to such a question is learned, the translation of that knowledge into the actual enactment of the nonverbal behavior is straightforward. For example, if it were discovered that one way to convince a person that you like him is to show him the "A-OK" gesture whenever he suggests something, then anyone physically capable of making such a gesture could use it—and probably successfully—when trying to communicate liking. The same is true for most other instances of nonverbal emblems.

More interesting theoretically are the many instances in which the translation of self-presentational intentions into the actual production of nonverbal behaviors is not at all straight-forward. One of the primary goals of this article is to provide a theoretical analysis and empirical review of constraints on the translation of self-presentational intentions into nonverbal actions. There are many reasons why self-presentational intentions cannot always be translated successfully into the desired nonverbal behaviors or expressions. Sometimes the expressions that people would like to enact are ones that they simply cannot produce. Other times, the expressions are ones that they could produce under optimal conditions, but the prevailing circumstances are undermining rather than enabling. For example, situations that arouse debilitating levels of motivation or emotion, as well as those that shake a person's confidence, can sever the link between self-presentational intentions and nonverbal actions. Emotion is a particularly important constraining factor with regard to nonverbal self-presentations, because the hardwired links that may exist between the elicitation of emotion and the expression of emotion pose particularly daunting challenges to those who would try to work against their emotions by feigning an emotion that differs from the one they are actually experiencing.

Nonverbal performances can be constrained even before self-presentational intentions are formed. This can happen, for example, if certain kinds of nonverbal self-presentations are so counternormative that intentions to produce such performances are unlikely ever to be formed. For instance, if a priest during a solemn ceremony were marrying a man he suspected to be a philanderer, he would be unlikely even to think of rolling his eyes or snickering as the miscreant said "I do." Even after a self-presentational intention has been translated into a nonverbal performance, there can be constraints on the accuracy of people's appraisal of their performance and on their ability to modify their current and future self-presentations in light of the outcomes of their prior performances. All of these constraints are reviewed next.

Constraints on the Use of Nonverbal Behaviors for Self-Presentational Purposes

The formulation of self-presentational intentions, the enactment of nonverbal behaviors, and the link between the two can be rendered problematic at several points. First, various factors can constrain the kinds of intentions that are formed. Second, many factors can disrupt the actual translation of intentions into actions. And third, some factors limit the effectiveness with which people evaluate and modify their performances. Although each factor is discussed under only one of these three phases, many are relevant to several phases. For example, knowledge of display rules governing the use of nonverbal behaviors is relevant not only to the kinds of self-presentational intentions that are likely to be formulated but also to the kinds of appraisals that are likely to be made of performances that have already been enacted.

Most of the factors that constrain nonverbal performances can also function in enabling ways, so that they enhance the likelihood of self-presentational success. For example, although motivation to create a particular impression can become so intense that it disrupts effective performance, it can also fuel efforts to learn more about the targets of one's self-presentation. Such knowledge eventually may translate into more precisely tailored, and thereby more effective, self-presentations. The focus of the present section is on factors that can limit self-presentational success; however, the ways in which these factors can enable effective performance are also discussed.

Constraints on the Formulation of Intentions to Enact Particular Nonverbal Self-Presentations

Cultural and situational norms or conventions can be powerful enough to prevent certain kinds of nonverbal self-presentations from ever being considered. Thus, they constrain the kinds of intentions that are formed. Individual differences in appreciation of these norms, and in knowledge of the ways in which different nonverbal self-presentations are likely to impact on others, can similarly guide or constrain the kinds of self-presentations that are likely to be selected.

Cultural or situational norms influence nonverbal behaviors in obvious ways when the norms refer directly to nonverbal expressive behaviors (as captured in the concept of display rules). But cultural and situational norms can also impact on nonverbal behaviors in more indirect ways, as for example when they dictate that the experiencing of certain emotions would be inappropriate in certain contexts; if these "feeling rules" (Hochschild, 1979) are taken seriously, then the overt expressions of the inappropriate feelings are less likely to be produced.

Cultural constraints

There are important differences across cultures in the degree to which expressiveness in general is expected or tolerated and in the more specific norms about who should or should not express which emotions or attitudes in which situations. This cross-cultural hypothesis posits a difference not in innate reactions to the elicitation of emotions, but in the kinds of overt expressions of emotions that are encouraged or allowed. This point was nicely demonstrated in a study in which Japanese and American participants watched neutral and stressful films while alone, then discussed those films with the experimenter (described in Ekman, 1972, and Ekman, Friesen, & Ellsworth, 1982). When the participants were alone, the facial expressions of the Japanese and the Americans were very similar. But when the interview commenced, the Japanese were far more likely than the Americans to put on a happy face when discussing the distressing films.

Norms for expressiveness also vary within subcultures (e.g., P. Miller & Sperry, 1987), families (e.g., Halberstadt, 1991), and perhaps other groups as well, such as organizations (e.g., P. J. DePaulo, DePaulo, Tang, & Swaim, 1989). In each of these contexts, when norms proscribe certain kinds of nonverbal self-presentations, participants are less likely to consider attempting such self-presentations and more likely to feel uncomfortable if they do decide to attempt them. The long-term effects of such norms may even be that skills at enacting such self-presentations atrophy (if indeed they ever develop in the first place); participants then would not be able to produce the relevant nonverbal behaviors even if they did want to do so.

Situational constraints

Within cultures, some situations severely constrain the types of nonverbal behaviors that may appropriately be displayed. In Western cultures, for example, gleeful laughter is highly inappropriate at funerals, and tearful indignation would not be the expected response from the target of a surprise birthday party. In these kinds of situations, display rules dictate the nonverbal expressions that are appropriate. When people conform to these dictates, as most do, little is revealed about them as individuals (E. E. Jones & Davis, 1965). Certainly, there is room for maneuvering even within these strong situational constraints. People occasionally do, for example, deliberately dramatize the depth of their grief at funerals. But the opportunities for varied self-presentations are fewer than in most other situations.

Situations can also enable or indulge certain nonverbal self-presentations. For example, at a crowded disco filled with frenzied dancers, someone who ordinarily is reserved might instead feel sufficiently disinhibited to try out a very different style of dancing wildly to the music.

Knowledge

To use nonverbal behaviors successfully for self-presentation, people need to have some basic knowledge of the relationship between nonverbal behaviors and internal states, of the kinds of nonverbal behaviors that are appropriate to use at particular times and in particular situations, and of the kinds of reactions and interpretations that particular nonverbal behaviors are likely to elicit from others. In some situations, people may not know what type of impression to try to convey; it may simply be unclear to them what type of self-presentational strategy would best serve their goals. The abstract understanding of display rules and of other regularities governing the use and interpretation of nonverbal expressive behaviors is separate from the ability to produce such behaviors. The latter factor, considered next, is also important.

Constraints on the Translation of Self-Presentational Intentions Into the Actual Production of Nonverbal Behaviors

Ability, practice, and experience

Once people know what impression they would like to convey, and also know (even if only implicitly) which nonverbal behaviors they need to produce to convey that impression, they still need to have a certain set of enactive abilities to succeed. For example, they need to be able to control the muscles involved in producing the desired expressions. For some types of muscles (see below), this can be difficult even under optimal conditions. Under more taxing circumstances, such as when people are experiencing an intense emotion that they are trying to hide, they may need to find a different way of approaching the task other than trying directly to control the relevant muscles. For example, they might try to modify their experience of the emotion itself, such as by mentally reliving emotional experiences that are inconsistent with the emotion being experienced (Hochschild, 1983; Stanislavski, 1948/1965). The abilities to generate alternative strategies and to enact them successfully are important skills that are likely to vary from individual to individual (e.g., Dodge, 1989; Harris, 1989; McCoy & Masters, 1990; Moore, 1984).

Many, though not all, nonverbal self-presentational abilities can be improved by practice and experience. For example, there is some evidence that experienced salespeople are very effective liars. In a study (P. J. DePaulo & DePaulo, 1989) in which salespeople delivered pitches for products that they liked and disliked, the same kinds of judges who were generally successful at detecting the lies of less experienced liars were totally unsuccessful at detecting the lies of the experienced salespeople. They were unsuccessful even when given hints that typically help people to detect the lies of inexperienced liars, for example, hints to pay special attention to the speaker's tone of voice (B. M. DePaulo, Lassiter, & Stone, 1982). There is also evidence that the reason these hints were not useful is that the salespeople were skilled at controlling their nonverbal expressive behaviors so that they did not reveal their true feelings (P. J. DePaulo & DePaulo, 1989). Politicians, too, seem to be adept at managing their facial expressions in ways that elicit favorable responses from their constituents (McHugo, Lanzetta, Sullivan, Masters, & Englis, 1985; Sullivan & Masters, 1988). There is anecdotal evidence that accomplished poker players are also especially talented at regulating their nonverbal behaviors (Hayano, 1980).

Constraints on the controllability of particular nonverbal behaviors and cues

Physical characteristics such as body type, physical attractiveness, head shape and size, skin coloring, and facial wrinkles can powerfully influence perceivers' impressions. These factors can be a source of enormous frustration to self-presenters, because there is so little that can be done to change most of them.

Research on some physical characteristics, such as attractiveness, is voluminous and is reviewed in detail elsewhere (e.g., Hatfield & Sprecher, 1986). A more recent example is the work generated from an ecological perspective on baby-facedness (Berry & McArthur, 1986). Adults vary systematically in the degree to which their face looks like the face of a baby (big, round eyes; small chin; high eyebrows, and so forth). It has been hypothesized that adults who have baby-type faces will be perceived as having baby-type traits. And in fact, in a study in which the presence or absence of baby-type features was systematically manipulated, perceivers thought the more baby-faced adults were more naive, more honest, warmer, and kinder (Berry & McArthur, 1985; see also Brownlow & Zebrowitz, 1990). In a study of the ramifications of baby-facedness in the legal system, it was found that more baby-faced defendants were less often perceived as guilty of charges of intentional criminal behavior and more often perceived as guilty of charges of negligent criminal behavior. Even when they were seen as guilty of negligent criminal acts, though, they were given lighter sentences (Berry & Zebrowitz-McArthur, 1988). Similar kinds of effects have been documented for vocal qualities. For example, adult speakers with childlike voices are perceived as warmer, weaker, and less competent than speakers with more adultlike voices (Montepare & Zebrowitz-McArthur, 1987).

Although relatively permanent physical characteristics such as baby-facedness often constrain nonverbal self-presentations, they can also be enabling to people inventive enough to learn to make optimal use of them. For example, baby-faced people may learn, in response to a stinging accusation, to adopt a particularly poignant look of innocence that works far better for them than it ever could ever work for someone with a less babyish countenance.

In contrast to the relatively static physical characteristics, dynamic cues such as facial expressions and hand movements and gestures provide primarily for flexibility in the pursuit of self-presentations, because many of them are readily controlled. There are, however, important exceptions (Rinn, 1984). In his discussion of facial cues to deceit, Ekman (1985) pointed to several facial muscle movements that the vast majority of people cannot produce at will. An example is the raising and pulling together of the eyebrows that occurs reliably when people are afraid. Because fewer than 10% of adults can produce these movements deliberately, there will be limitations on the degree to which people can convincingly convey an impression of fearfulness when they are not really afraid. Fearfulness is just one example of a larger category of emotions that people have difficulty feigning: the category of negative emotions. The problem that people have with expressing negativity is one that now has been documented across a variety of methodologies and subject populations (e.g., Morency & Krauss, 1982; Shennum & Bugental, 1982). This asymmetry in the ease of expression of positive as compared with negative affects is probably an example of the undermining effects of cultural and situational prohibitions on expressive abilities. Because there are so many more situations in which people are encouraged to feign positive emotions than ones in which they are urged to feign negative emotions and because people are reluctant to communicate harsh evaluations (e.g., Blumberg, 1972; Felson, 1980; Tesser & Rosen, 1975), skill at enacting the negative displays may never develop fully. This is just what the self-presentational perspective predicts.

Level and range of expressive cues

Most people are limited in the range of identities they can convincingly claim. An important aspect of this limitation is the constraint imposed by the level and range of expressive cues that a person can command. A man with a very high pitched voice, for example, may find it difficult to convey the impression of being a gruff task-master who barks orders at cowering subordinates. The example is not just hypothetical. Empirical work suggests that men with more dominant-appearing faces advance to higher ranks in the military (Mazur, Mazur, & Keating, 1984; see also Lee & Ofshe, 1981). Like physical characteristics, the level and range of expressive cues can also be enabling of effective self-presentations for people who appreciate the potential of their particular expressive profiles for the types of identities they can claim most convincingly.

There is ample empirical documentation of the constraints imposed by individual differences in expressive profiles. For example, in a study of the legibility of people's facial expressions, it was found that people's faces that were easy to read when they were watching one kind of pleasant slide were also easy to read when they were watching another kind of pleasant slide; observers could tell in both cases that they were watching something pleasant. However, when the same people were watching unpleasant slides, their faces were more difficult to read; observers often mistakenly thought the people were again watching pleasant slides (Zuckerman, Larrance, Hall, DeFrank, & Rosenthal, 1979). This effect has been replicated numerous times (e.g., Kraut, 1982; Wallbott & Scherer, 1986) and is now known as the demeanor bias. Some people simply have pleasant faces, and they tend to appear pleasant even under unpleasant circumstances. This is why the demeanor bias is a constraint: It limits the kinds of impressions that people can convey effectively.

There is also an honesty/dishonesty demeanor bias. Some people simply look like honest people, even when they are telling lies (Bond, Kahler, & Paolicelli, 1985; Zuckerman, DeFrank, Hall, Larrance, & Rosenthal, 1979). Other people, such as those who are socially anxious, characteristically look dishonest, even when telling the truth (Riggio, Tucker, & Throckmorton, 1987). There is a demeanor effect for voices, too, for both pleasantness/unpleasantness (Zuckerman, Larrance, Hall, DeFrank, & Rosenthal, 1979) and honesty/dishonesty (Zuckerman, DeFrank, Hall, Larrance, & Rosenthal, 1979). In fact, the honesty/dishonesty demeanor effect is stronger for voices than for faces (Zuckerman, Larrance, Spiegel, & Klorman, 1981), and people have more trouble controlling their tone of voice than their face when they try to lie.

Personal style

Although Gordon Allport made some of the earliest and most influential contributions to our understanding of expressive behaviors (e.g., Allport, 1937; Allport & Vernon, 1933), he was not a great believer in successful regulation and control of such behaviors. He acknowledged that people might try deliberately to disguise their expressive behaviors, but he was willing to concede this only for specific behaviors or for short periods of time. When it came to what he referred to as "style," or the totality and complexity of all of a person's expressive behaviors taken together, he did not think that purposeful disguise was even a possibility. In Allport's (1937) words, "Style ... develops gradually from within; it cannot for long be simulated or feigned" (p. 493). Several studies (reviewed below) have shown that people actually can simulate a whole constellation of cues suggestive of a personality type very different from their own; Allport's hypothesis, as yet untested empirically, suggests that they would not be able to maintain such a deception for long. Abraham Maslow (1949) has made much the same suggestion.

Personal style can also impose constraints on self-presentational performances in more specific ways. For example, certain kinds of people seem to favor certain styles of interacting with others. One of the best-documented examples of this is from the domain of social anxiety. People who are socially anxious often adopt defensive and protective social interaction strategies, especially under conditions of evaluative pressure (e.g., Arkin, Lake, & Baumgardner, 1986; DePaulo, Epstein, & LeMay, 1990; Greenberg, Pyszczynski, & Stine, 1985; Schlenker & Leary, 1982, 1985). This retreat to the comfort of one's habitual style can be an impediment to self-presentational success in situations in which more assertive and acquisitive styles are more appropriate. More generally, to the extent that one's preferred or habitual personal style constrains or conflicts with the goals of one's immediate self-presentational attempt, the less successful that attempt is likely to be.

Motivational constraints

Even those people who can command a range of expressive behaviors and who understand when it might be most propitious to attempt to convey a particular impression will not convey that impression if they simply do not care enough to do so. Conveying the right impression at the right

165

time and the right place can be an effort, and people sometimes are not motivated to make that effort. Motivation may be important at every point in the self-presentational process, from the acquisition of knowledge about nonverbal behaviors and the appropriate contexts for the display of such behaviors to the production of those behaviors and the pursuit of information regarding the effect that they had on others. People who are dispositionally motivated to use nonverbal behaviors effectively for self-presentational purposes may be especially successful at doing so, because they have sought much useful information and have diligently practiced and refined their skills.

However, motivation can instead be an impediment to self-presentational success, as when motivated people become too emotional (see below) or when they try too hard to control all of their verbal and nonverbal behavior (e.g., B. M. DePaulo & Kirkendol, 1989; see also Baumeister & Scher, 1988; Heckhausen & Strang, 1988). For example, when people are especially motivated to succeed in getting away with their lies, their lies become, paradoxically, more obvious to observers (e.g., B. M. DePaulo & Kirkendol, 1989; B. M. DePaulo, Kirkendol, Tang, & O'Brien, 1988; B. M. DePaulo, Lanier, & Davis, 1983; B. M. DePaulo, Stone, & Lassiter, 1985b). The lies told by motivated liars are not revealed verbally, but nonverbally. The role of emotion may be important here, too. Motivated liars are emotional liars, and therefore they must grapple with the difficult problem of controlling the nonverbal cues to the emotions they are experiencing. Sometimes they try to do this by suppressing their behavior. These attempts can backfire, though, in that people who are trying to suppress their expressive behaviors sometimes look and sound like they have something to hide. Another strategy that motivated liars might use is to try deliberately to control all of their verbal and nonverbal behaviors. This strategy, too, though, is likely to fail, because the specific components of nonverbal performances are unlikely to be available to conscious awareness (cf. Polanyi, 1962). The strategy may be especially counterproductive when used by people who are characteristically not very self-focused, such as those who are low in self-consciousness (Baumeister, 1984; Baumeister & Showers, 1986).

Even when people are not trying to lie, motivation can sometimes be debilitating to effective nonverbal performance (e.g., B. M. DePaulo et al., 1990). This has been most compellingly documented in the literature on social anxiety. Social anxiety occurs when people are highly motivated to create a particular impression on others but insecure about their ability to do so (e.g., Leary, 1983; Schlenker & Leary, 1982, 1985). There are many nonverbal manifestations of this anxious yearning, including nervous behaviors such as fidgeting and stuttering, disaffiliative behaviors such as letting longer silences develop, and image-protective behaviors, which are behaviors that are sociable in a safe way, such as nodding and smiling and listening without interrupting (Schlenker & Leary, 1982). These are not the behaviors that are likely to characterize the performances of skilled impression managers.

Emotional constraints

Emotions can undermine self-presentational efforts because of the automatic links, described earlier, between the elicitation of the basic emotions and the nonverbal expression of those emotions. For example, a person who suddenly becomes very afraid will only with great difficulty convince an onlooker that he is actually quite calm and composed. He can try to suppress or mask the facial actions triggered by the fear, but fragments of these movements might "leak" out anyway (Ekman, 1985). He may try to speak in a steady manner, but his voice might quiver and his pitch might rise uncontrollably.

From an individual differences perspective, emotionality (or affect intensity) is an important dimension of temperament (e.g., Buss & Plomin, 1975; Goldsmith et al., 1987; Thomas & Chess, 1985; Thomas, Chess, & Birch, 1968). Dispositionally emotional people tend to respond to affect-provoking stimuli intensely and to experience emotions deeply (Flett, Boase, McAndrews, Pliner, & Blankstein, 1986; Larsen & Diener, 1987). In emotionally provocative situations, attempts to suppress the overt expression of emotions or to cover emotions with expressions of different emotions should be more problematic for people whose emotional reactions are characteristically more intense than for those whose reactions are typically more muted. At the same time, however, the strength of their feelings should be distinctly advantageous to affectively intense people who want to communicate their feelings to others either clearly and honestly or in an exaggerated manner.

The personality profile of affectively intense people indicates that such people tend to be extraverted, sociable, active, and arousable (Larsen & Diener, 1987). Thus, it is probably fairly easy for such people to convey positive impressions of outgoing friendliness in their interactions with others. Perhaps others notice that their emotions are apparent from their nonverbal behaviors and see this as indicative of an openness that invites gregariousness and maybe even closeness. At this point, however, this is purely speculative; the role of nonverbal expressiveness as a link between affect intensity and the impressions that are conveyed in social interaction is in need of empirical exploration.

Emotionality can be construed not just in terms of intensity of affect but also with regard to the range of emotions typically experienced (Sommers, 1981; Sommers & Scioli, 1986). The links between emotional range and nonverbal self-presentations have not yet been established, but it is likely that emotional range will function primarily as an enabling factor, so that people who typically experience more different kinds of emotions can more effectively convey a wider variety of impressions than can those who tend to experience a more narrow range of emotions. However, it is also possible that emotional range will constrain a person's ability to convey a single impression or emotion unambivalently.

Spontaneous expressiveness

There are consistent individual differences in spontaneous expressiveness, which is the degree to which feelings and emotions are readable from nonverbal behaviors when people are not trying deliberately to convey their feelings (e.g., Buck, 1984; Notarius & Levenson, 1979).[4] These can be measured by paradigms such as those used by Buck (1979, 1984), in which people are videotaped surreptitiously while watching emotion-evoking slides and those tapes are then shown to judges who try to discern the slides the people were watching, or by the use of various personality scales that tap this trait (Manstead, 1991). Whereas affect intensity refers to the ease with which emotions can be triggered and the intensity which they are experienced, expressiveness describes the link between the experiencing of an emotion and the nonverbal expression of the emotion. People who are spontaneously expressive are not necessarily more emotional (King & Emmons, 1990); in fact, such people may be dispositionally less physiologically reactive than those who are not so outwardly expressive (e.g., Buck, 1979, 1984; H. E. Jones, 1935; Lanzetta & Kleck, 1970; Prideaux, 1922). But the emotions that they do experience, regardless of how weak or intense, are more likely to appear on their face, and perhaps in their voice, than are the emotions of people who are less expressive.

Because the links between the elicitation of emotions and the nonverbal expression of those emotions are presumably stronger for people who are spontaneously expressive, the job of hiding those nonverbal expressions, when that is deemed desirable, is more difficult for them (cf. Kraut,

1982). An interesting example of this effect was reported in a study in which expressive and unexpressive people learned that they had just defeated two competitors (Friedman & Miller-Herringer, 1991). The participants heard this information either when they were alone or in the presence of the other competitors. Most participants looked much less jubilant when they were in front of their competitors than when they were alone. But the suppression of gloating was apparently more difficult for the expressive people; they looked much more gleeful than did the unexpressive people when others were present.

Although spontaneous expressiveness can be constraining, there are also many ways in which it can be self-presentationally advantageous. First, spontaneously expressive people tend to be skilled at posing emotions nonverbally. When they are experiencing no particular emotions, they can use their face and voice to convey the impression that they actually are experiencing certain affects and emotions (Buck, 1975; Cunningham, 1977; Tucker & Riggio, 1988; Zuckerman, Hall, DeFrank, & Rosenthal, 1976; Zuckerman, Larrance, Hall, DeFrank, & Rosenthal, 1979). They are also skilled at deceiving, when the deception task does not demand that they work against strong emotions (B. M. DePaulo, Blank, Swaim, & Hairfield, in press). They should also be skilled at conveying emotions that they really are experiencing in a legible or exaggerated way.

Second, expressive people are liked better than unexpressive people. This is a highly replicable finding, which has been documented for people who are spontaneously expressive (e.g., Sabatelli & Rubin, 1986), for those who are skilled at posing nonverbal expressions (e.g., Friedman, DiMatteo, & Taranta, 1980), for those who describe themselves as emotionally expressive (e.g., Friedman, Riggio, & Casella, 1988) or as extraverted (e.g., Riggio & Friedman, 1986), for people who are from expressive families (Halberstadt, 1984), and for people who have expressive facial features (Cunningham, 1986). It has also been documented in a study in which the measure of expressiveness was the frequency of socially oriented nonverbal behaviors exhibited by people in face-to-face interactions (Shrout & Fiske, 1981).

Third, across numerous studies, expressive people often appear more attractive than unexpressive people and never appear less attractive (B. M. DePaulo et al., in press; Friedman et al., 1988; Larrance & Zuckerman, 1981; Riggio, 1986; Sabatelli & Rubin, 1986). Perhaps they simply are endowed with greater physical beauty. But there may be more to it than that. When unexpressive people try to act in a particularly expressive way, they appear more attractive than when they try to act in a particularly inhibited way. Thus, their attempts to be expressive enhance their attractiveness. Expressive people, in contrast, appear just as attractive when they are trying to be expressive as when they are trying to be inhibited, and in both cases, they appear more attractive than unexpressive people. Expressive people, then, seem to know how to regulate their attractiveness so that they can manage to appear beautiful even under difficult conditions that make others look less physically appealing (B. M. DePaulo et al., in press).

Fourth, Buck (1989) has suggested that people who are expressive may "turn on" the expressive behavior of others. Their expressiveness encourages others to be open and expressive in return. Certainly, this is one of the rules of verbal expressiveness; one person's level of self-disclosure is generally matched or reciprocated by the target of that disclosure (e.g., Cappella, 1981; Cozby, 1973). Analogously, unexpressiveness dampens the expressiveness of others. For example, normal people who are interacting with schizophrenics, who tend to be expressively inhibited, are themselves less expressive than when they are interacting with other normals (Krause, Steimer, Sanger-Alt, & Wagner, 1989). Even infants appear to be more expressive when their mothers are facially expressive than when they are reserved (Kaye & Fogel, 1980; see also Jones, Collins, & Hong, 1991).

The salience of the nonverbal behaviors of expressive people probably also serves to elicit more explicit feedback about those behaviors and the internal states that they may or may not reflect (Buck, 1988). Through this mechanism, expressive people, by their very expressiveness, contribute to their own "emotional education" (Buck, 1989) and probably also to the further development and refinement of their nonverbal self-presentational skills.

Expressive people also seem able, wittingly or unwittingly, to influence the emotions of others. In dyadic and group interactions, the moods of the less expressive people are influenced by the moods of the more expressive people (Friedman & Riggio, 1981; Sullins, 1991). Perhaps this occurs in part because expressive people are generally more noticeable than are unexpressive people (Sullins, 1989).

In the field of medicine, physicians who can pose emotions nonverbally are advantaged in that they tend to have more satisfied patients (DiMatteo, 1979; Friedman, DiMatteo, & Taranta, 1980). In education, expressive teachers are evaluated much more positively by their students than are unexpressive teachers (e.g., Abrami, Leventhal, & Perry, 1982; Basow & Distenfeld, 1985). In the domain of athletics, there are attributional advantages to being expressive. Athletes who are outwardly expressive are perceived as having exerted more effort than those who are not expressive, and after failure, the expressive athletes are seen as having more ability and as being less responsible for their failure than are the unexpressive athletes (Rejeski & Lowe, 1980).

In many ways, then, spontaneous expressiveness is an powerful predictor of self-presentational outcomes. Its importance is also underscored by its stability across time and across situations (Notarius & Levenson, 1979). Reliable individual differences in expressiveness may be apparent even in infancy (Buck, 1984; Field & Walden, 1982). And in a longitudinal study of individual differences in inhibition (not specific to nonverbal inhibition), Kagan and his colleagues found evidence of inhibited and uninhibited styles that are consistent from age 2 until at least age 7 (e.g., Kagan, Reznick, Snidman, Gibbons, & Johnson, 1988). Moreover, the kinds of personality variables that are correlated with expressiveness are replicable from study to study and are similar in studies of children (Buck, 1975, 1977) and in studies of adults (Friedman, DiMatteo, & Taranta, 1980; Friedman, Prince, Riggio, & DiMatteo, 1980; Friedman, Riggio, & Segall, 1980; Riggio, 1986). These variables include extraversion, popularity, dominance, impulsiveness, and playfulness. Finally, although both expressive and unexpressive people can modify their overall levels of expressiveness so as to become more expressive or less expressive at will, expressive and unexpressive people each have their own domain of expressiveness. Unexpressive people, when trying to be expressive, are not able to appear as expressive as expressive people when the latter are acting naturally. Similarly, expressive people, when trying to be unexpressive, are not able to appear as inhibited as unexpressive people when the unexpressives are acting naturally (DePaulo et al., in press).

In summary, spontaneously expressive people create more favorable impressions on others, probably without even trying. When they do try to convey particular impressions, they are especially successful at doing so, as long as they are not trying to convey an impression that is at odds with a strong emotion that they are experiencing. The profiles of expressive people are similar to those of affectively intense people, although much more is known about the self-presentationally relevant correlates and consequences of expressiveness than of emotionality.

People who believe that they can succeed in conveying the impressions they want to convey probably really will succeed more often than those who are less confident. This seems to be true both for people who are dispositionally confident (e.g., Leary, 1983; Schlenker & Leary, 1982) as well as for people in whom high expectations for success have been experimentally induced (e.g., B. M. DePaulo et al., 1991). It is not entirely clear why confidence has this effect, but several explanations seem plausible. For example, people who are confident may become less emotional in difficult situations, and their composure might then help them to convey their desired impressions successfully. Confidence might also help people to avoid self-defeating strategies. For instance, instead of paying close attention to their own nonverbal behaviors in challenging interpersonal situations, which can sometimes impair performance, confident people might instead pay attention to the reactions of others.

Confidence, then, will almost always be an enabling factor with regard to effective self-presentations. However, it can become constraining or undermining at its extreme, in that people who are overconfident may not mobilize the effort necessary to convey just the right impressions (Schlenker & Leary, 1985).

Constraints on Appraisals and Modifications of Self-Presentations

The self-presentational process does not end with the production of a particular nonverbal performance. There are still possibilities for modifying that performance as the interaction continues and to learn from it after it has ended. On-line modifications in nonverbal communications are constrained by the limitations in awareness discussed earlier; that is, because people cannot see or hear their own nonverbal behaviors exactly as others do, it may be difficult for them to fine-tune their self-presentations. The appraisals of the effectiveness of their nonverbal productions may also be in error. Suggestive evidence for this comes from the finding that people think that they are more skilled at controlling their own expressive behavior while lying than most other people are at controlling theirs (Zuckerman, Koestner, & Driver, 1981). Even when people are correct in their intuitions about what their expressive behaviors look or sound like, they may still err in their guesses about how others might interpret those behaviors (cf. B. M. DePaulo et al., 1987; Kenny & DePaulo, 1991).

Skill at Conveying Impressions Nonverbally

Can people overcome the many constraints on the execution of their self-presentational intentions and manage effective nonverbal performances? By adulthood, do they have (for example) the necessary knowledge, ability, experience, and confidence to make successful nonverbal claims to the identities they value? The assumption of the self-presentational perspective is that they do. Many studies are pertinent to this question, including those that have assessed people's skill at communicating various emotions and attitudes nonverbally. These include studies of the ability to pose particular affective states as well as studies of skill at deceiving. Before those studies are reviewed, I consider the issue of the legibility of totally unregulated nonverbal expressions. Research on spontaneous expressiveness indicates whether people's nonverbal behaviors are likely to reveal their internal states even when they are not trying to control those behaviors. To the extent that spontaneous expressions are legible, the task of deliberately exaggerating those expressions is eased, but the task of muting those expressions or covering them with entirely different expressions is complicated.

Legibility of Spontaneous Nonverbal Expressions

The results of studies in which people are surreptitiously videotaped in emotionally impactful situations (e.g., Kleck & Mendolia, 1990; Kraut, 1982; Wagner et al., 1986; Zuckerman et al., 1976; Zuckerman et al., 1979) are quite consistent. Typically, the affects or emotions that subjects are experiencing are apparent from their facial expressions. The spontaneous revealingness of nonverbal behaviors is not limited to expressions of positivity and negativity nor of the basic emotions. Whether children understand a lesson or are confused by it, for example, is also evident from their faces (Allen & Atkinson, 1978). Amusement can be read from faces, too (Edelmann & Hampson, 1981). Nonverbal revealingness is not limited to facial expressions. Similarly accurate inferences about affects and emotions can be made from the tone of voice (e.g., Cunningham, 1977; Scherer, 1986; Zuckerman et al., 1979). And observers who can see people's body movements as well as their facial expressions can tell when those people are feeling embarrassed (Edelmann & Hampson, 1981).

Together, the studies of spontaneous expressiveness indicate that nonverbal behavior can convey information about people's experiences even when they are not trying purposefully to make their experiences evident to others. There are qualifications to this conclusion, of course. For example, in the Wagner et al. (1986) study in which happiness, anger, and disgust were communicated accurately, fear, sadness, and surprise were not. Also, there are certain spontaneously produced nonverbal behaviors (e.g., sneezing) that are unlikely to be valid indicators of any psychologically interesting process or state. The number of such behaviors, however, may be surprisingly small. Coughing, for example, appears to be psychologically meaningful (Pennebaker, 1980).

Nonverbal Posing Skill

Studies of people's ability to pose certain states nonverbally are very similar to studies of spontaneous communications, except that in the posing studies, people are instructed to try deliberately to convey the impression that they are experiencing a certain state, such as fear. Sometimes they really are experiencing that state (e.g., they are watching a scary movie); other times they are simply instructed to pose an expression that would convey an impression of fear. Virtually every study of this nature has shown that people can successfully make clear to others, using only nonverbal cues, the internal state that they actually are experiencing and that they can also convey to others the impression that they are experiencing a particular internal state when in fact they are not. A variety of nonverbal behaviors can be managed in this way, including facial expressions (e.g., Jaeger, Borod, & Peselow, 1986; Kraut, 1982; Wallbott & Scherer, 1986; Zaidel & Mehrabian, 1969; Zuckerman et al., 1976; Zuckerman, Larrance, Hall, DeFrank, & Rosenthal, 1979; Zuckerman, Lipets, Koivumaki, & Rosenthal, 1975), tone of voice cues (e.g., Apple & Hecht, 1982; Scherer, 1986; Wallbott & Scherer, 1986; Zaidel & Mehrabian, 1969; Zuckerman, Larrance, Hall, DeFrank, & Rosenthal, 1979; Zuckerman et al., 1975; see also Williams & Stevens, 1972), body movements and postures (e.g., Cunningham, 1977), and even gait (Montepare, Goldstein, & Clausen, 1987). Furthermore, when people are deliberately trying to convey an impression of a state that they are not really experiencing, their nonverbal behaviors convey that impression to others even more clearly and effectively than when they really are experiencing the state but are not trying purposefully to communicate it to others (e.g., Zuckerman et al., 1976; Zuckerman, Larrance, Hall, DeFrank, & Rosenthal, 1979). That is, consistent with the implications of the self-presentational perspective, people's posed expressions are more legible than their spontaneous expressions.

Buck (1984) has suggested that when people attempt to pose nonverbal expressions of emotions, they can tap into hardwired structures that are already in place for the spontaneous expressions of those emotions. They do not need to learn to produce those expressions in the way that they would need to learn to form expressions of states that are not prewired. Such a mechanism could help to account for the success with which such expressions are produced.

Skill at Deceiving

Research on deception takes the posing results one step further and asks whether people can convey nonverbally the impression that they are experiencing something very different from what they really are experiencing. For example, can they take a taste of a bitter solution and lead observers to believe that they just sipped something sweet (e.g., Feldman, Jenkins, & Popoola, 1979; Feldman & White, 1980)? Can they smell something pleasant and convince another person that they the odor is actually disgusting (Kraut, 1982)? Can they listen to a totally incomprehensible lesson and assume a look of complete understanding (Allen & Atkinson, 1978)? Can they talk about someone they despise and still convey the impression that they really like that person (B. M. DePaulo & Rosenthal, 1979; B. M. DePaulo, Rosenthal, Green, & Rosenkrantz, 1982; Zuckerman, Amidon, Bishop, & Pomerantz, 1982)?

When they can use nonverbal cues in concert with verbal cues to convey false impressions, people are generally successful at managing the impression that they are experiencing something different than what they really are experiencing. As predicted by the self-presentational perspective, then, perceivers generally believe the affects or attitudes that people are faking, rather than seeing through to the ones they are really feeling (e.g., B. M. DePaulo, Stone, & Lassiter, 1985a). There is some evidence that the same thing occurs when nonverbal cues are used alone to accomplish the deceit, but the evidence is more scarce and less reliable (Zuckerman, DePaulo, & Rosenthal, 1981).

Perceivers, though, are not totally hoodwinked. Although they tend to see others as basically honest, even when they are lying, they can see a difference in truthfulness between truths and lies. Lies seem less truthful to them than do truths. Furthermore, even though perceivers believe, for example, that a woman who is just pretending to like a man really does like him, they can tell that her liking is less intense than when she is honestly conveying her fond feelings for a man she really does like (e.g., B. M. DePaulo et al., 1985a).

When people try to assume an entire constellation of behaviors indicative of a wholly different personality type than their own, the results are quite similar. An example comes from a study in which extraverts and introverts tried to come across both as introverted and as extraverted in simulated teaching demonstrations (Lippa, 1976). Judges who viewed the videotapes of the lessons believed that the people who were just pretending to be extraverts were more extraverted than the people who really were extraverts but were pretending to be introverts. Again, though, the perceivers were not completely fooled. They could tell that the people who were feigning extraversion were not as extraverted as the extraverts who were trying to make their extraversion apparent and that the people who were feigning introversion were not as introverted as the introverts who were trying to make their introversion apparent. These results are entirely consistent with the results of an analogous study of expressiveness (reviewed earlier), which showed that unexpressive people could not manage to appear as expressive as expressive people and the expressives could not manage to appear as inhibited as the unexpressives (B. M. DePaulo et al., in press). Both sets of results are supportive of the assumption of the self-presentational perspective that there are constraints on the degree to which people can claim identities that are different from their "true" identities as they perceive them.

In the Lippa (1976) study, as in most of the other studies of posing and deceiving, the participants were not involved in face-to-face interactions. The participants were pretending to be teaching, but no students were actually present. In contrast, Toris and DePaulo (1984) used a simulated job interview format in which introverts and extraverts tried to come across as introverted or extraverted in successive sessions with different interviewers. The interviewers' task was to try to determine whether the applicants really were introverted or extraverted. The participants in this study were especially adept at feigning a different personality type. Interviewers believed that the applicants were the types of persons they were pretending to be, rather than the types of persons they really were. And they saw no difference in extraversion between genuine and dissimulated displays of extraversion nor between genuine and dissimulated displays of introversion. This study raises the possibility that perceivers are even more likely to be taken by people's deceptive self-presentations when engaged in dynamic face-to-face interactions than when forming impressions in a more passive way, as when observing others from a distance or viewing them on a videotape. And in fact, Gilbert and his colleagues have found that cognitively "busy" perceivers, compared with more passive perceivers, tend to take others' self-presentations at face value (Gilbert, Krull, & Pelham, 1988; see also Baumeister, Hutton, & Tice, 1989; Gilbert & Krull, 1988).

Across many studies, perceivers are quite consistent in their tendency to judge others as basically truthful and to believe the feelings or attitudes that others are trying to convey rather than those that they really do hold (B. M. DePaulo et al., 1985a). This occurs even though perceivers often know that the persons they are observing may be lying some of the time. Of course, in these paradigms, perceivers do not know when the people they are observing are lying and when they are telling the truth. Differentiating truth from deceit is a complex task and calling someone a liar (or even just suspecting, in one's own mind, that another person is being deceitful) is an emotionally charged and interpersonally hazardous act (e.g., B. M. DePaulo, 1981). Perhaps it should not be surprising, then, that in these paradigms, perceivers give the people they are observing or interacting with the benefit of the doubt.

There is a related set of studies on the "correspondence bias" (see E. E. Jones, 1979, 1986, 1990, for reviews) that makes perceivers' task even more straightforward. In some of those paradigms, perceivers read essays that were written by target persons. The essays were randomly assigned to the target persons; thus, the positions espoused in the essays bore no systematic relationship to the target person's true attitudes. Furthermore, perceivers were told that the essays were assigned in this arbitrary manner. Still, they inferred that the target person's true attitude was consistent with the attitude in the essay. Many artifactual explanations of this correspondence bias have been ruled out, and the effect has been replicated in countless paradigms (E. E. Jones, 1990). Ross (1977) calls the effect the "fundamental attribution error"; E. E. Jones (1990) believes that it is the most robust and replicable effect in social psychology. Goffman (1959) might say that it is a matter of honor; people honor each other's identity claims. By adulthood, this inclination may be so habitual that, in the ordinary course of events, it is rarely undone. In fact, consistent with the implications of the self-presentational perspective, there is even evidence that the tendency to read people's feigned feelings more than their felt ones may actually increase with age (B. M. DePaulo, Jordan, Irvine, & Laser, 1982).

There is some evidence that in simulating a particular personality disposition, what people do is to present an exaggerated version of the expressive behaviors that characterize such a disposition. For example, extraverts tend to speak more quickly than do introverts. When feigning extraversion, people speak even more quickly than do genuine extraverts, and when feigning introversion, they speak even more slowly than real introverts do (Feldstein & Sloan, 1984). An analogous finding has

173

been described in the clinical literature. People who are trying to fake particular disorders sometimes adopt the strategy of presenting an even more extreme set of symptoms than would characterize someone who really was afflicted with the relevant malady (Pankratz, 1988). Other examples of overshooting the mark can be gleaned anecdotally. For example, Pankratz (personal communication, December 2, 1988) has pointed out that female impersonators seem almost to caricature what it is like to walk or talk or dress like a woman (see also McConnell-Ginet, 1978).

When people present themselves in a way that does not correspond to their self-concept, they generally want their false presentations to be believed. For example, people who see themselves as introverted might sometimes try to act extraverted because they believe that it would be advantageous in certain contexts to appear to be an extravert. Occasionally, however, people feel compelled to present themselves deceptively against their wishes. Examples of this from the political arena are mistreated hostages who are pressured to make videotapes in which they proclaim their well-being. Can people in such situations, while saying appropriately deceptive things, use their nonverbal behaviors to make it clear to others that they are lying? Can they similarly make it clear when they are telling the truth? The one study conducted on this topic did not involve hostages; however, the study did make it clear that it is possible, for undergraduates at least, to manage their own facial expressions and tone of voice cues in a way that purposefully betrays their own verbal deceptions (Zuckerman, DeFrank, Hall, Larrance, & Rosenthal, 1979).

Sensitivity in the Deployment of Skills

Much of the research on nonverbal self-presentational skills has involved paradigms in which participants are instructed to try to convey particular impressions. It therefore addresses the question of whether people can create such impressions when asked to try to do so. However, as Cappella (1988) has pointed out, there is much more to effective self-presentation than the mere production of the relevant behaviors on demand. Self-presentation most often occurs during social interactions; thus, issues of timing (e.g., Davis, 1982), appropriateness, and sensitivity to the context and to the motives of the other interactants are also important.

Research on motor mimicry provides an apt example of skill at producing nonverbal behaviors in a sensitive way. Examples of motor mimicry, such as cringing when other people are in pain and smiling when they are happy, have generally been regarded as indicative of processes such as empathy or vicarious emotional responding (Bavelas, Black, Lemery, & Mullett, 1986). The assumption has been that these responses are expressions of the internal state of the person doing the mimicking. In contrast, Bavelas and her colleagues (Bavelas et al., 1986) have argued that whereas motor mimicry may in part reflect internal states, it also has important communicative functions. In their research, an experimenter winced in pain after dropping a heavy object on his already-injured hand. Several seconds later, he turned either toward the participant or the other experimenter. Consistent with the hypothesis that participants' facial expressions of pain serve a communicative function, those expressions increased over time in the condition in which the pained experimenter faced the participant and decreased in the condition in which he faced the other experimenter. The difference in the occurrence of pain expressions across the two conditions was especially striking at the exact point at which the injured experimenter did or did not look at the participant. Furthermore, when videotapes of the participants' expressions were shown to judges who were unaware of the orientation of the experimenter, they perceived the expressions of the participants who ended up face-to-face with the injured experimenter as more knowing and more caring than the expressions of the other participants. It appears from this study, then, that people can regulate the timing and the qualitative aspects of their nonverbal expressions to fit the nuances of the interaction.

174

Skill at regulating nonverbal behaviors for self-presentational purposes can include skill not only in regulating the expressive behaviors themselves but also in setting up the situation so that nonverbal behaviors will have their desired impact. This skill, too, requires exquisite sensitivity to contexts and to motives. It may be just this sort of skill at setting the stage that accounts for much of the success of con artists (e.g., Blum, 1972; Maurer, 1940).5

In summary, the literatures on the abilities to pose expressions of internal states that may or may not be present, to feign states that are different from those actually experienced, and to time the production of these nonverbal expressions in contextsensitive ways suggest that people are often remarkably successful at managing their nonverbal self-presentations, despite the many potential impediments to their performances. There are, though, important individual differences in these skills. I review those next.

Predicting Individual Differences in the Use of Nonverbal Behaviors for Self-Presentational Purposes

By considering the factors that constrain and enable the use of nonverbal behaviors for self-presentational purposes (reviewed above) and the degree to which those factors characterize different kinds of people, it should be possible to predict individual differences in the degree to which people try deliberately to use nonverbal behaviors for self-presentational purposes and in their success at so doing. Age differences and sex differences may be the most powerful individual-difference predictors of the use of nonverbal behaviors for self-presentational purposes; they are reviewed first. Then several other examples of important self-presentationally relevant individual differences are considered, that is, physical attractiveness, self-monitoring, need for approval, and public self-consciousness.

Age

With age come increases in several of the factors that facilitate, rather than constrain, the effective use of nonverbal behaviors for self-presentational purposes. These include knowledge, ability, practice, experience, and motivation.

As children grow older, they acquire more knowledge about the hows, whens, wheres, and whys of expressive behavior (e.g., Saarni, 1990). For example, they learn more about internal states and the nonverbal behaviors that typically correspond to those states. Importantly, they also show a rudimentary grasp, beginning as early as the preschool years, of the fact that people's expressive behaviors do not always correspond to their internal states (e.g., Harris, Donnelly, Guz, & Pitt-Watson, 1986) and that one of the reasons they do not correspond is that people can purposefully control their nonverbal behavior so as to convey a misleading impression (e.g., Gnepp & Hess, 1986). With age, children's comprehension of the complexities of this process becomes increasingly sophisticated (e.g., Gnepp & Hess, 1986; Saarni, 1988).

Over the course of development, children also learn more about the situational and cultural conventions governing the use of nonverbal behaviors, and they learn more about how different kinds of people are likely to react to different kinds of self-presentations. They undoubtedly acquire this knowledge in part because social punishments and rewards are increasingly meted out contingent on the deftness with which children adhere to expressive conventions and fine-tune their self-presentations to other people's feelings and needs.

As children learn about the norms of expressiveness in contexts in which others care about their mastery of this cultural wisdom, their own motivation to practice these rules and to learn even more about them grows. Meanwhile, they become more skilled at controlling their facial musculature so as to produce an array of expressions at will (Ekman, Roper, & Hager, 1980; Fulcher, 1942; Kwint, 1934), and they also become more adept at perspective taking (e.g., Higgins, 1981; see also Feldman, White, & Lobato, 1982; Shennum & Bugental, 1982) and emotional self-regulation (Harris, 1989; McCoy & Masters, 1990) and more facile in the generation of alternative strategies for producing desired self-presentational outcomes.

The fact that the incidence of social smiling increases during the preschool years (Cheyne, 1976), at least in Western cultures, is suggestive evidence that children are not only understanding more about the management of expressive behavior but also attempting more of that management in their own interactions. As they progress through the school years, children use display rules more often, more spontaneously, and more effectively. For example, on opening a brightly wrapped present and finding a drab baby toy, older children (for whom the toy is especially inappropriate) are more likely than younger ones to look and sound pleased with their gift (Saarni, 1984; but see also Cole, 1986). Other suggestive evidence of children's use of nonverbal behaviors for self-presentational purposes comes from studies of the strategic use of crying (Blurton-Jones, 1967), the use of "winning" facial expressions in conflict situations (Camras, 1982) and in situations in which children might try to convey an impression of competence (Zivin, 1982; see also Allen & Atkinson, 1978), and the deliberate suppression of expressions of anger (Cummings, 1987).

When preschoolers are asked to try to pose with their faces emotions that they are not actually feeling, girls become better and better at this with age (Zuckerman & Przewuzman, 1979). Throughout the childhood years, both boys and girls also become more talented deceivers. Some interesting demonstrations of this involved Feldman's drink-tasting paradigm, in which subjects sample sweetened and unsweetened drinks while trying to convince another person that they like both drinks. At the youngest ages tested (first graders), children's true reactions to the drinks leaked out: It was clear from their faces that they were not enjoying the unsweetened drinks. Seventh graders, in contrast, looked just as pleased with the unsweetened drinks as with the sweetened ones. College students took this charade a step further: From their faces, one would have thought that the sugarless samples were even tastier than the sweet ones (Feldman et al., 1979).

The socialization of the expression of emotions may well begin in infancy. Malatesta and Haviland (1982) have shown that in mother–infant interactions, infants display expressions suggestive of a wide array of emotions (see also Izard, Huebner, Risser, McGinnes, & Dougherty, 1980); mothers, however, model mostly just expressions of positive emotions. Perhaps it should not be surprising, then, that studies of children indicate that socially acceptable emotions are more readily read from their faces than are less acceptable emotions (Buck, 1984; Morency & Krauss, 1982; Shennum & Bugenthal, 1982; see also Ekman, Roper, & Hager, 1980). In fact, some studies find that this continues to be true even of adults (Buck, 1984).

Although many of the lessons of socialization are presumably conveyed fairly uniformly within a given culture, others are more specific to particular subgroups, such as families. Expressive conventions vary systematically from family to family, and these variations have important implications for the development of expressive skills within the family unit. Children from more emotionally expressive families, for example, are more adept at expressing certain emotions nonverbally than are children from less expressive homes (Halberstadt, 1983, 1986, 1991). Another telling example of subgroup variation in the training of emotional expressiveness is the differential socialization of the sexes (see below).

In summary, then, the story of development is in most ways a tale of ever-broadening opportunities. Children become more knowledgeable, more skillful, and more motivated with regard to the use of nonverbal behaviors for self-presentational purposes. This will usually mean that they can be more and more successful in that domain when they want to be.

Age does, however, bring a few potential impediments to expressive control. Over the course of the preschool years, girls (but not boys) become more spontaneously expressive (Buck, 1977), which can make it difficult for them to feign emotions that are different from the ones they are feeling. Also, children's growing awareness of the norms and sanctions of social life make them more prone to emotions that can prove disruptive to effective self-presentations. For example, when older children try to lie, they might experience more guilt and shame than do younger children. They then face the challenging task of concealing not only the lie itself but also the distress they are feeling about telling the lie. Socialization also quite likely inhibits the development of certain skills, such as the ability to communicate negative emotions (e.g., Morency & Krauss, 1982; Shennum & Bugental, 1982). In addition, socialization sensitizes children to situational and cultural conventions in ways that eventually will constrain the type and range of self-presentations that children and young adults will attempt to convey. As children develop a distinctive and stable personal style, that too can constrain the kinds of identities that they will try to claim nonverbally.

Little research exists on the continued development of nonverbal self-presentational skills across later adult years. There is evidence, though, that affect intensity decreases between the ages of 16 and 68 (Diener, Sandvik, & Larsen, 1985). Perhaps this decline helps to account for the findings that older women's facial expressions are more blended and fragmented than those of younger women (Malatesta & Izard, 1984) and that elderly adults are more successful than are young adults at using their facial expressions to fool others in the drink-tasting paradigm (Parham, Feldman, Oster, & Popoola, 1981).

Sex

Differences in ability, motivation, and spontaneous expressiveness all converge to produce what may be one of the most pervasive and important of all individual differences in the use of nonverbal behavior for self-presentational purposes: sex differences.

As early as 3 months of age, there are indications that girls may develop differently than boys in the expressive domain. For example, in interactions with their mother, infant girls show more facial expressions that look like expressions of interest than do boys (Malatesta & Haviland, 1982). By adulthood, a myriad of cues suggest that women are, nonverbally, more involved in their interpersonal interactions than are men (J. A. Hall, 1984, see also Exline, 1963). For example, women have more expressive and more legible faces than do men. They also smile more than men do, gaze at their listeners more, and are gazed at more. They approach others more closely and are approached more closely than others. They tend to touch others more and to be touched more (Stier & Hall, 1984; but see J. A. Hall & Veccia, 1990; Major, Schmidlin, & Williams, 1990, for some qualifications). Their body movements are also more involved and more expressive. If women were purposefully trying to convey the impression of being sociable, likable, and interested in the other person, they could hardly do better than this. Still, it is not clear from these data alone whether women try deliberately to achieve these effects, whether they try deliberately to do so early in their lives and then come to act that way habitually, or whether it simply feels more natural and more comfortable to them to behave that way for reasons that are not tied to self-presentational considerations and never were.

In addition to being more involved nonverbally than are men, women also are more open in the expression of their emotions and personality. At least three lines of evidence indicate this. First, studies of facial expressions show that women are more spontaneously expressive than are men (J. A. Hall, 1984; see also Buck, Baron, & Barrette, 1982; Buck, Baron, Goodman, & Shapiro, 1980). Women also describe themselves as more emotionally expressive than men in self-report studies (Brody, 1985). Second, research on deception indicates that when lying, women are less likely than are men to use the strategy of "hamming" (B. M. DePaulo & Rosenthal, 1979). Hams are people who, for example, when pretending to like someone they actually despise, will appear to like that person even more than someone they genuinely like. Observers tend to believe faked affects more than the genuine, covered-up ones (B. M. DePaulo et al., 1985a); thus, hamming is generally an effective way to deceive. In that women use this strategy less than do men, their true feelings are sometimes more accessible to others than are men's. Third, women's self-descriptions, particularly on the self-monitoring scale, also suggest greater openness. High self-monitors act like different people in different situations, whereas low self-monitors act more consistently with their own self-perceived personalities across situations (Snyder, 1979). Women tend to score lower on the scale than do men, suggesting, in effect, that they wear their personality on their sleeve (Rosenthal & DePaulo, 1979a).

An open and expressive style has many self-presentational advantages: Other people tend to find it endearing, and they often reciprocate the intimacy that it seems to offer (see above). The evidence to be reviewed next tentatively suggests that women may be especially concerned with self-presentational issues. Perhaps, then, there are motivational underpinnings to their open and involving nonverbal style. Women may realize, at some level, that it is interpersonally advantageous to be, or to appear to be, open, involved, and expressive.

There are indications that women may be more interested than are men in gaining social approval (Block, 1978; Huston, 1983; Millham & Jacobson, 1978) and in avoiding disapproval (Crowne & Marlowe, 1964). They may be more likely to experience self-presentationally relevant emotions such as shame and embarrassment, and these differences are sometimes apparent even before the preschool years (H. Lewis, 1971; see also M. Lewis, Stanger, & Sullivan, 1989). Like men, women realize that punishments and rewards are contingent on the situational appropriateness of the emotions they express, but for women, these expectations are even stronger than they are for men (Graham, Gentry, & Green, 1981).

Behavioral evidence, too, suggests that women may in certain ways be more concerned with self-presentational considerations than are men. For example, they spend more time preening in rest rooms (Daly et al., 1983), they are more interested in clothes (Solomon & Schopler, 1982), and across the life span, they are more concerned about their body weight, physical appearance, and eating habits (Pliner, Chaiken, & Flett, 1990). When females are engaged in face-to-face interactions in the drink-tasting paradigm, it appears from their faces that they like the drinks more than males do, even though they appear to like the drinks somewhat less than the males do when they think that no one can see them (Feldman et al., 1979). In the disappointing gift paradigm, too, girls put on a happy face much more frequently than do boys (Cole, 1986; Saarni, 1984); this effect occurs even for 3-year-olds (Cole, 1986).

When women decide deliberately to use their nonverbal behaviors for self-presentational purposes, they may have more of the relevant abilities at their disposal than do men. They can pose emotions with their faces more skillfully than can men (J. A. Hall, 1984), and they know it (Zuckerman & Larrance, 1979). They also speak less haltingly and with fewer speech errors than do men (J. A. Hall, 1984).

In summary, women are nonverbally more involved and more open in their interpersonal interactions than are men. Their faces are more spontaneously expressive, and when they want to use their faces to pose a particular emotion, they can do so more successfully. From an early age, their behavior suggests that they may be especially concerned with making good impressions and avoiding making bad ones, though certainly there will be exceptions. (Perhaps men, in contrast, are relatively more concerned with maintaining privacy and control.) Generally, these qualities probably serve women well in their interpersonal lives. But there are hazards as well. For example, in situations in which people are trying to create a good impression by lying, women's lies are more detectable from their nonverbal cues than are men's (B. M. DePaulo & Kirkendol, 1989; DePaulo et al., 1988). It is probably both their greater motivation to succeed in such situations and their greater spontaneous expressiveness that undermine their deceptive attempts. More speculatively, women might be at a disadvantage when it is socially appropriate to be distant and stern rather than open and engaging.

Physical Attractiveness

Physically attractive people are better at communicating emotions spontaneously with their facial expressions (Sabatelli & Rubin, 1986), and they are also better at posing emotions with their faces (Larrance & Zuckerman, 1981). When they care about telling an effective lie, they are more successful at controlling their nonverbal behaviors than are less attractive people; that is, they are less vulnerable to the motivational impairment effect (B. M. DePaulo et al., 1988). The contributing factors seem to be confidence and ability. Attractive people have higher expectations for success in social situations (Abbott & Sebastian, 1981; Cash & Begley, 1976). They are probably also accustomed to being the targets of attention. Thus, they may be more practiced and skilled at controlling their nonverbal behaviors, and they may also be less self-conscious about those behaviors. Ordinarily, in emotionally charged situations, spontaneous expressiveness can be a hindrance to deception success. But for physically attractive people, who are confident, practiced, and unselfconscious, it seems not to get in the way.

Self-Monitoring, Need for Approval, and Public Self-Consciousness

High self-monitors are people who "monitor and control the images of self they project to a great extent ... carefully observe their own performances and adjust their behavior to convey the desired image, acting like different people depending on the situation and their audience" (Snyder, 1987, pp. 4–5). Low self-monitors, on the other hand, "typically express what they really think and feel" (Snyder, 1987, p. 5). Both motivation and ability seem to be important components of self-monitoring. When they are about to lie to another person, high self-monitors will try to obtain more information about that person to construct a more effective lie, and they do this even when there are costs to procuring the information (Elliott, 1979). When it comes time actually to tell their lies, those high self-monitors who are especially skilled actors deftly control the pacing of their speech: They speak at the same rate when they are lying as they do when they are telling the truth (Siegman & Reynolds, 1983). Self-monitors are also more skilled at posing emotions, both with their faces and with their voices (Riggio & Friedman, 1982; M. Snyder, 1974).

179

High self-monitors modify their own expressive behaviors more than do lows in social (compared with nonsocial) situations. For example, on learning that they have just defeated their competitors at a task, highs exude jubilation with victory gestures when they are alone, but they are much more subdued when the competitors are there with them; the expressive behaviors of the lows are more similar across the two situations (Friedman & Miller-Herringer, 1991). In contexts in which the appropriate behavior might be to act similarly across situations, then it is the high self-monitors, rather than the lows, who show more cross-situational consistency. For example, many teachers believe that they should convey to all students the impression that they expect them to succeed, even though those expectations may actually be true only of the smarter or more motivated students. One might, then, expect high self-monitors, compared with lows, to behave more similarly when interacting with students for whom they have high versus low expectations for success. And in fact, high self-monitors do convey to observers fairly similar impressions of their expectations for their students' success, regardless of their actual expectations. In contrast, low self-monitors who are also dispositionally very expressive convey clearly to others their different levels of expectations for the different students they teach (Sullins, Friedman, & Harris, 1985; see also Lippa, 1978a).

There are some indications that high self-monitors are sensitive to global variations in the requirements of different situations, roles, and audiences, rather than being especially attuned to moment-to-moment variations in interpersonal contingencies (Dabbs, Evans, Hopper, & Purvis, 1980). The latter type of sensitivity may be more characteristic of people who score high on the Social Desirability Scale (Crowne & Marlowe, 1964). People who are especially sensitive to the approval of others rarely interrupt when others are speaking (Feldstein, Alberti, BenDebba, & Welkowitz, 1974, cited in Harper, Wiens, & Matarazzo, 1978), and they are not very adept at communicating negativity with their face or voice (Zaidel & Mehrabian, 1969). Moreover, when conversing with others, the intensity of their speech is especially likely, over time, to converge with the intensity of their partner's speech (Natale, 1975).

Another individual-difference dimension of obvious relevance to self-presentation is public self-consciousness, which is "an awareness of and a responsivity to the impressions that are being made on others" (Scheier & Carver, 1981, p. 198; see also Fenigstein et al., 1975). The key component of high public self-consciousness is probably the motivational one; highs care more than do lows about the impressions they are conveying to others. This may be why people high in public self-consciousness blush more than lows, because blushing seems to have the effect of muting the negativity of others' reactions to one's own embarrassing behaviors (Leary & Meadows, 1991). The importance of the motivational component may also be evident in the findings that women who are high in public self-consciousness wear more makeup (L. C. Miller & Cox, 1982) and that both men and women who are publicly self-conscious are more interested in clothes (Solomon & Schopler, 1982). There is also suggestive evidence that people high in public self-consciousness have a more accurate appreciation of the kinds of self-presentational strategies that are (or are not) likely to create positive impressions (Holtgraves & Srull, 1989). Perhaps this understanding is born of their motivation to learn what impresses others. It is possible, though, that their motivation is at times too intense, and then serves to undermine rather than facilitate their interpersonal goals. It may be just this mechanism that accounts for the finding that highs appear less credible than lows when attempting to deceive (Riggio, Tucker, & Throckmorton, 1987; Riggio, Tucker, & Widaman, 1987).

Specific Nonverbal Behavioral Cues

Limitations to the Study of Specific Nonverbal Cues

Much of the discussion so far has focused on nonverbal expressions, which are complex sets of specific behaviors that can covary with particular emotions or states (e.g., vocal expressions of happiness, facial expressions indicating comprehension). But much of the literature on nonverbal communication concerns individual behaviors, such as gazing or smiling or leaning. From that tradition, much has been learned about the specific nonverbal cues that are correlated with (a) affects or attitudes, such as liking and dominance, (b) discrete emotions, such as happiness and sadness, (c) cognitive states, such as exerting mental effort and paying close attention, (d) personality traits, such as extraversion and shyness, and (e) pathologies, such as anxiety and depression. Much has also been learned about the nonverbal behaviors that correlate with perceptions of these states. Thus, for example, it has been shown in this literature which nonverbal cues covary with actual liking and which ones covary with people's perceptions of liking.

The self-presentational significance of the correlates of perceptions is much clearer than is the significance of the correlates of actual states. If, for example, physicians were interested in learning about the specific nonverbal behaviors they could use to come across as likable, they would do better to learn about the behaviors that people take to be signs of liking than to learn about the behaviors that really do occur when one person likes another. Part of the ambiguity inherent in the literature on actual cues lies in the fact that it is often impossible to determine from the studies whether the cues were deliberately produced to convey a particular impression. For example, when people who claim to like the person with whom they are interacting are observed to smile, lean forward, and gaze into the other person's eyes, it is not clear whether they are purposefully behaving that way to make their liking clear to the other person or whether these are unmonitored and unselfconscious expressions of that liking.

There are other ambiguities, too, in the study of individual nonverbal cues (some of which also characterize the study of nonverbal expressions). Most important, perhaps, is the fact that there are no perfect one-to-one correspondences between particular nonverbal behaviors and specific states or meanings. For instance, although people who like each other often gaze into each other's eyes, they do not always do so; and though gazing is often interpreted as a sign of liking, it is not always construed in this way.6 Thus, the conclusions that can be drawn about the correlates of specific nonverbal behavioral cues will always be conditional and probabilistic.

Another limitation is that the relationships between particular behaviors and specific states or meanings are sometimes quite small ones. It might be possible, for example, to show that crossing the legs at the knees instead of at the ankles has an effect on people's perceptions, but the effect may well be trivial in magnitude, even if statistically significant.

From a self-presentational perspective, a more interesting limitation of the specific cues approach is that people rarely regulate their behavior at that level. Instead of trying deliberately to lean forward, smile, and gaze, people probably instead try to convey an impression of liking, with the leaning and smiling and gazing following from that, perhaps even out of their awareness. There are exceptions to this generalization, of course. During election years, for example, presidential candidates are sometimes coached on the precise regulation of specific nonverbal behaviors. (During the 1988 election, Roger Ailes, George Bush's media consultant, was quoted in News-week [Warner & Fineman, 1988, p. 19] as telling Bush, during rehearsal for one of the debates, "There you go with that f——ing hand again. You look like a f——ing pansy!") There is a risk to attempting to regulate behaviors at this level, which is that the regulated behaviors are likely to appear wooden and unnatural. Techniques such as those used by the Stanislavski school of acting, in which actors are urged to try to bring to mind an experience similar in affective tone to the one they are trying to portray, are more likely to be effective (cf. Ekman, 1985).

Knowledge of the shortcomings of the specific cues approach can be used constructively to select for study cues that are especially likely to prove illuminating about the processes of self-presentation. Cross-cultural research, starting with Darwin's (1872/1965) contribution and proceeding through the important work of Izard (1971) and of Ekman (1972) and to the more recent studies of Keating, Ekman, and their colleagues (Ekman et al., 1987; Keating et al., 1981), provides insights into the kinds of behaviors that are likely to be used and interpreted consistently across cultures. In fact, some of the behaviors that show cross-cultural regularities also exhibit intriguing parallels even across species (e.g., Zivin, 1985). Behaviors that exhibit such stability are likely to be worthy of further study.

Other behaviors are likely to provide productive avenues for research because their hypothesized relationships to particular mental states and to particular perceptions are firmly rooted in theory. For example, in their model of social anxiety (as mentioned earlier), Schlenker and Leary (1982) predicted that three different kinds of behaviors should be characteristic of the socially anxious: nervous behaviors such as fidgeting and speaking disfluently, disaffiliative behaviors such as contributing infrequently to conversations, and image-protecting behaviors, which are innocuous behaviors such as nodding, smiling, and listening attentively.

Still other behaviors are worthy of special scrutiny because they are likely to be particularly reliable indicators of certain conditions or states. For example, Ekman (1985) has argued that certain facial muscles are rarely subject to willful control. Thus, the movement of such emotion-relevant muscles is more likely to indicate the presence of the corresponding emotion than is the movement of other muscles that covary with the emotion (and perhaps even have hard-wired links to components of the emotion) but can be controlled voluntarily.

To illustrate the study of a specific nonverbal behavior from a self-presentational perspective, research on smiling will be reviewed. Smiles meet the requirements outlined above, in that there are demonstrated cross-cultural regularities in the interpretation of smiling, there are theoretical formulations predicting the use of smiling, and there are reliable facial muscles that produce smiling when the appropriate emotion is present but that are less likely to be active when it is not.

Smiling and Self-Presentation

Salience of smiles

Smiles occur with great regularity in social life, and they are very salient signals. Darwin (1872/1965) believed that the expression of smiling became associated with happiness because it is so different in appearance from the expression of negative emotions. In fact, compared with other emotional-relevant behaviors, smiles are especially easy to recognize, even when they appear only very briefly and when the smiler is far away (Hager & Ekman, 1979; see also Simpson & Crandall, 1972).

Smiles are also very potent interpersonal cues. In a study of people's emotional responses to videotapes of President Reagan's expressive displays, McHugo and his colleagues (McHugo et al., 1985) found that when Reagan put on a happy or reassuring face, he moved his viewers—even the anti-Reaganites—to smile in return. For other politicians, too, their happy facial expressions seem to engender in their electorate more positive emotional responses and more favorable attitudes (Sullivan & Masters, 1988). The smiles of those who talk about the candidates appear to be similarly effective. For example, a network broadcaster who smiled more frequently when discussing Reagan than Mondale during the 1984 presidential campaign had viewers who were more likely to vote for Reagan than Mondale; the same voting pattern did not occur for the viewers of the other two network broadcasters, who did not smile differentially on any one candidate (Mullen et al., 1986). In legal contexts, smiles can soften the evaluations made of transgressors; especially when the infractions are minor, transgressors are judged more leniently when they smile than when they do not (Forgas, O'Connor, & Morris, 1983). And in many mildly uncomfortable situations in everyday social life, smiles can be used to apologize, neutralize, and appease (e.g., Elman, Schulte, & Bukoff, 1977; Goldenthal, Johnston, & Kraut, 1981; Mackey, 1976; van Hooff, 1972). But smiles can also enrage instead of mollify. For instance, married couples who use smiles and other seemingly positive visual behaviors in combination with very negative tone of voice cues tend to be more poorly adjusted than couples who communicate less often in this manner (Noller, 1982).

Responsiveness of smiling

Smiling is exquisitely responsive to moment-to-moment variations in the social context. Smiles that are reciprocated, for example, differ markedly in duration from those that are not; reciprocated smiles persist, whereas nonreciprocated ones vanish almost instantly (Duncan, 1983). Bugental (1986) has reported a similar effect in a study of women's interactions with unresponsive and responsive boys: The women's smiles faded more quickly if they were interacting with the unresponsive boys.

Stability of sex differences in smiling

There are some remarkably reliable individual differences in the use of smiling. Foremost among these is a sex difference. Women smile much more than men do. This is true when they are interacting face-to-face in the laboratory (Dovidio, Brown, Heltman, Ellyson, & Keating, 1988; J. A. Hall, 1984), when they are observed unobtrusively in naturalistic settings (Halberstadt & Saitta, 1987), and even when they are depicted in advertisements (Halberstadt & Saitta, 1987; see also Goffman, 1979). Women who are especially feminine are particularly likely to smile, and men who are especially masculine are especially unlikely to smile (LaFrance & Carmen, 1980). Thus, womens smiles might less reliably indicate positive affect than do men's. One piece of suggestive evidence is the finding that the distressing combination of a positive facial expression and a negative tone of voice is more likely to be used by wives than by husbands (Noller, 1982). Another is an observation from the literature on parent–child interactions that mothers' smiles occur even in combination with verbal content that is negative, whereas fathers' smiles occur more selectively in combination with congruent verbal content (Bugental, Love, & Gianetto, 1971). However, in a study of college students who were describing intense emotional experiences, the women's smiles were more consistent with the verbal content of their descriptions (Halberstadt, Hayes, & Pike, 1988).

Cross-cultural consistencies in interpretations of smiling

With regard to the impressions it conveys, smiling seems to have a pervasive primary meaning. The meaning, of course, is happiness. It is a meaning that is shared panculturally (Ekman, Friesen, & Ellsworth, 1972; Izard, 1971; Keating et al., 1981). This is, unsurprisingly, likely to be an accurate interpretation, as there is evidence that the wearer of a smile is often happier than someone who is not smiling, even when both are thinking similarly positive thoughts (e.g., McCanne & Anderson, 1987; see also Ekman, Friesen, & Ancoli, 1980; for a different perspective, see Fridlund, 1991a).

Multiple meanings of smiling

Although happiness may be the "first" meaning of smiling, there are many other kinds of smiles in addition to smiles of genuine happiness (e.g., Keating, 1985). Ekman (1985) has described 19 varieties. Several of these are smiles indicative of emotions other than happiness, such as fear and contempt. Other kinds of smiles are distinctly inter-personal; these include flirtatious smiles, compliance smiles, coordination (cooperative) smiles, and listener response smiles. The social aspects of smiling are quite striking (Fridlund, 1991a). In fact, Kraut and Johnston (1979) forwarded the argument, on the basis of a series of studies, that smiles are more reliably associated with social motivation than with emotional experience. For example, they found that bowlers who had just rolled a strike or a spare smiled less when facing the pins and watching them fall than when they turned to face their friends. Similarly, they found that an emotional variable—pleasant versus unpleasant weather—was a less potent predictor of a pedestrian smiling than was a social variable—whether the pedestrian was alone or with another person. Of course, social and emotional experiences are often intertwined, as many emotional experiences occur in the presence of others and are occasioned by their actions or by the smiler's attempts to influence their actions or affects (cf. Ekman, Davidson, & Friesen, 1990).

Multiple interpretations of smiling

Just as the production of smiles is governed by different emotions and different goals, so too is the interpretation of them qualified in many ways. For example, although smiling transgressors are generally evaluated more generously than are nonsmiling transgressors (Forgas, 1987; Forgas et al., 1983), smiling transgressors who are also very physically attractive (compared with those who are less attractive) are held more responsible for their transgressions (Forgas, 1987). Another example concerns the finding (mentioned above) that mothers' smiles are less reliably associated with positive verbal messages than are fathers'; children seem to be sensitive to this, for when they are interpreting inconsistent combinations of verbal and nonverbal cues, they are more likely to discount a woman's smile when it contradicts other cues than a man's (Bugental, Kaswan, & Love, 1970; Bugental, Kaswan, Love, & Fox, 1970).

Self-presentational uses of smiling

The salience of the smile, its potency in interpersonal interactions, and a set of meanings characterized by considerable consistency but not inconsiderable subtlety and ambiguity together suggest that as a self-presentational strategy, smiling has great potential.

Is that potential realized? That is, is there any evidence that smiling is used deliberately for self-presentational purposes? Dale Carnegie (1936) certainly believed that it should be. One of his six

184

rules for winning friends was a simple one-word suggestion: "Smile" (p. 72). More recently, Hochschild (1983) has suggested that smiling is a very important component of the job of flight attendants, who note that both management and passengers seem to expect (and want) this from them.

With regard to the empirical literature, some of the evidence for the self-presentational use of smiling is merely suggestive. For example, people who are motivated to have warm and close interactions with others smile more than do those whose intimacy motivation is lower (McAdams, Jackson, & Kirshnit, 1984). This could suggest that such people are using smiling as a way of conveying to others that they are the kinds of people who favor intimate exchanges. But they could instead be spontaneous, unregulated expressions of those desires. Another example comes from a study involving women who attributed their caregiving outcomes either to ability or to luck; in interactions with children, the women who felt relatively powerless (subject to the vagaries of luck) flashed smiles onto their faces much more rapidly than did the women who felt more powerful (Bugental, 1986). Bugental speculated that the more rapid onset of smiles may have been indicative of an ingratiating self-presentational style, which these women used to acknowledge their own feelings of powerlessness.

Also interpretable from a self-presentational perspective are two studies in which participants interacted with partners who were expected to be either friendly or unfriendly (in one study) or similar or dissimilar to the participants (Ickes, Patterson, Rajecki, & Tanford, 1982). Participants tended to smile frequently both when their partners were expected to be friendly and when they were expected to be unfriendly (compared with a control condition of no expectations), and they also smiled frequently regardless of whether they expected their partners to be similar or dissimilar to themselves. In the friendly and in the similar conditions, participants' smiles may have been unself-conscious expressions of their genuine liking. In the unfriendly and dissimilar conditions, however, participants may have been using smiling strategically to convince the other person of their own friendliness and likability and to elicit similar friendliness in return.

More direct evidence of the use of smiling for self-presentational purpose comes from studies in which participants were led to believe that they should try to ingratiate, and those in which participants were directly instructed to try to gain (or avoid) the approval of others. In an example of the former type of study, participants either were or were not told that they would soon have to ask another person for help (Lefebvre, 1975). Those who believed that they would have to try to obtain the other person's help smiled more at that person than did those who had no help-seeking expectations. Similarly, participants in a different study who were told directly to try to gain their partner's approval smiled more at that person than did the participants who were instructed to try to avoid their partner's approval (Rosenfeld, 1966).

Also relevant to the question of whether people use smiling for self-presentation is the issue of whether people smile when they are lying, especially when they are lying to cover negative feelings. A meta-analysis of 19 studies in which smiling was assessed during deceptive and truthful communications suggested that liars do not smile any more frequently than truth tellers and, in fact, may even smile slightly less (Zuckerman, DePaulo, & Rosenthal, 1981). However, in those studies, smiling was usually treated as a unitary category, and different types of smiles were not identified. More recently, Ekman and his colleagues (Ekman, Friesen, & O'sullivan, 1988) have argued that smiles indicative of genuine enjoyment can be distinguished from other false smiles. In a microanalysis of their earlier study (Ekman & Friesen, 1974) in which nurses watched pleasant or gruesome films while trying to convince an interviewer that all of the films were pleasant, Ekman and Friesen found that the nurses who were trying to cover up their negative reactions to the gruesome films did indeed show relatively fewer genuine enjoyment smiles and more false smiles than did those who were honestly describing their reactions to the films that really were pleasant. To discriminate these smiles, however, requires special training. Laypersons cannot do so on their own. Instead, they often seem to believe that people who are smiling in any way are less likely to be lying than are those who are not smiling (e.g., Ruback, 1981; Zuckerman, DePaulo, & Rosenthal, 1981; however, see also Riggio, Tucker, & Widaman, 1987). Smiling can, then, be used effectively to convince others of one's own truthfulness.

Self-Presentation and Skill at Reading Nonverbal Cues

The study of the deliberate use of nonverbal behaviors for self-presentational purposes is primarily a study of the production of nonverbal cues. It is possible that the interpretation of nonverbal cues also serves self-presentational purposes, but that is more difficult to establish convincingly. For example, aggressive boys are biased toward seeing negativity and dominance in their interpretations of ambiguous nonverbal messages (Nasby, Hayden, & DePaulo, 1980). By declaring that seemingly innocuous communications really are hostile or threatening, these boys may be underscoring their cynical view of the world. However, other interpretations of this result are equally plausible.

In another suggestive study (B. M. DePaulo, Brittingham, & Kaiser, 1983), people were helped either appropriately or inappropriately and soon thereafter had an opportunity to reciprocate to their helpers. People who were helped appropriately were especially sensitive to the nonverbal need cues of the person who had helped them and thus were able to reciprocate the help in an appropriate way. Their accuracy in reading the helper's cues (which they did not evidence when they were helped inappropriately) may have been a way for them to convey to the helper the impression that they were grateful and sensitive people. Again, however, many other interpretations are plausible, too.

A final example, which may be somewhat more compelling than the others, comes from the research on sex differences in nonverbal decoding skills. Women tend to be more accurate interpreters of nonverbal cues than are men (J. A. Hall, 1984), but the degree to which they outperform men varies systematically with the kinds of cues they are trying to interpret. Women are especially more skilled than men at decoding overt cues that other people probably want them to understand (such as facial expressions that are not intended to be deceptive) but are not any more skilled than men at detecting covert cues (such as discrepant and deceptive messages) that others might prefer that they not detect (Rosenthal & DePaulo, 1979a, 1979b). One interpretation of these results is that by their pattern of nonverbal decoding sensitivities and insensitivities, women are conveying to others their desire to be interpersonally accommodating, that is, to see what others want them to see but not what others do not want them to see. They are, in Goffmanesque style, going along with other people's self-presentations. Although this interpretation is speculative, it is bolstered by a variety of related findings. For example, this pattern of apparent nonverbal accommodatingness becomes increasingly evident throughout the adolescent years (Blanck, Rosenthal, Snodgrass, DePaulo, & Zuckerman, 1981), suggesting perhaps that women are being socialized to read cues in this way. Also, women who are more personally and interpersonally vulnerable (e.g., lower in self-esteem and social adroitness, uncomfortable with hostility and with asking for help) are especially likely to show this pattern of reading overt cues better than covert cues (Rosenthal & DePaulo, 1979a). Perhaps these kinds of women are especially motivated to convince others that they are accommodating and "easy" interaction partners.

Can the Deliberate Use of Nonverbal Behaviors for Self-Presentational Purposes Be Detected?

Detectability of Self-Presentational Efforts: The Aggregate Level

The question of whether self-presentational uses of nonverbal behaviors can be detected can be addressed at two levels. First, at the aggregate level, one can ask whether people's nonverbal behavior is generally different when self-presentational motives are likely to be differentially operative. The strategies include (among others) the same ones described above for ascertaining whether smiling is used deliberately for self-presentational purposes. One can, for example, examine nonverbal behavior as a function of individual-difference variables that are likely to be relevant to self-presentational motives. This approach was discussed earlier. Or one could investigate whether people's nonverbal behavior is different in private than in the presence of others and whether differences in the characteristics of the particular others who are present will affect the types of nonverbal behaviors that are displayed. One could also create situations that vary systematically in the self-presentational motives they are likely to elicit, or most directly, one could simply manipulate experimental instructions so that different participants are told to try to achieve different self-presentational goals. These aggregate level approaches are discussed in this section.

In this section and the next, the focus will be primarily on methods of discerning deliberateness that have already been applied directly to the nonverbal domain. Other approaches are also possible. For example, the literature on automatic and controlled processes raises the possibility of examining the relative effects of attentional load on nonverbal performances hypothesized to vary in the degree to which they are being deliberately regulated (e.g., Paulhus, Graf, & van Selst, 1989; Schlenker & Weigold, 1989). From systems theory comes the notion of equifinality, suggesting that if a nonverbal behavior is being regulated in the service of a self-presentational goal, then if that approach to achieving the goal is blocked, some other approach will be attempted (e.g., von Bertalanffy, 1968). Research on equilibrium models of nonverbal interaction indirectly suggests that such an approach could be promising (e.g., Argyle & Dean, 1965; Burgoon et al., 1989).

Nonverbal behavior in private and in public

In numerous studies, the presence, involvement, or visual accessibility of another person or persons has been manipulated, and the effect on the subject's expressive behavior has been observed. In all but a few such studies (Craig & Patrick, 1985; Feldman, Devin-Sheehan, & Allen, 1978), these manipulations have had noticeable effects on nonverbal expressions.

In some studies, another person (or persons) sits next to the subject, or else leaves the room, while the subject performs a task such as trying to imitate the expressions shown in photographs (Kilbride & Yarczower, 1980; Yarczower, Kilbride, & Hill, 1979) or watching slides and forming impressions of them (Yarczower & Daruns, 1982). The other person does not perform the task, and the subject's performance is in no way relevant to that person. In these studies, subjects' facial expressions are typically less intense, more ambiguous, and more difficult to read when another person is present than when the subject is alone, except when the other person is a friend (Fridlund, 1991b). A study by Kraut (1982) differed from these in that the other person was always present and was engaging in the same task as was the subject (sniffing different kinds of odors). Visual accessibility was manipulated by separating half of the subjects from the other person by a translucent screen; thus, the two people could see each other's gross movements but not the details of one another's face. In this study, too, greater accessibility of another person dampened subjects' facial expressiveness.[7]

Subjects were also less facially expressive when they believed they were being observed by another person who was behind a one-way mirror than when they believed that no such person was present (Kleck et al., 1976). However, because the subjects were male undergraduates who were receiving electric shock and the observer was described as a female peer, the observer's presence was probably more psychologically meaningful to these subjects than to the subjects in the previously described studies. Chapman and Wright (1976) used a paradigm in which children listened through headphones to humorous materials in the presence of another child who was believed to be also listening to the materials (coactor) or not listening to them (audience). The confederates (coactors and audiences) were trained to display different levels of mirth in different conditions. In this study, the confederate's mirth facilitated the subject's nonverbal expressions of mirth, particularly when the confederate was a coactor and displayed high levels of mirth. In a similar study, Foot, Chapman, and Smith (1977) showed that the facilitation of mirth was especially pronounced when the coactors were friends rather than strangers. In a study involving groups of adults (Freedman & Perlick, 1979), the confederate's mirth facilitated the subject's nonverbal expressions of mirth when the groups listened to the humorous tapes in small (high-density) rather than large rooms.

The psychological dynamics are also likely to be different in studies in which the other person is the target of the subject's expressive behaviors, rather than a bystander, observer, or coactor. In the Feldman et al. (1979) drink-tasting study, for example, subjects were instructed to convey the impression that they liked both the sweetened and the unsweetened drink to an interviewer with whom they interacted either face-to-face or by speaking into an audio tape recorder. When subjects really did like the drinks, and communicated that to an interviewer who was physically present, their facial expressions were especially positive.

In still other studies, the other person is not just a passive target of the subjects' expressions but has some stake in the information the subject is conveying. For example, in one study (Feldman, 1976), teachers were instructed always to praise their students, even though the students sometimes performed well but other times performed poorly. In one condition, the teacher and student interacted face-to-face; in the other, the student was behind a one-way mirror and could not see the teacher, although the teacher could see her. Once again, facial (and bodily) expressions of positivity were augmented in the condition in which the teachers expressed praise in a face-to-face interaction with a student who really had performed well.

Negative facial expressions can also be augmented by manipulations involving another person, as indicated by the results of a study in which an experimenter either did or did not make eye contact with a subject right after dropping a heavy monitor on his already-injured hand (Bavelas et al., 1986). When the experimenter established eye contact, the subject conveyed more intense expressions of pain.

When the socially appropriate response would be to dampen one's expressive behavior, then subjects do just that. In one study, for example (Cole, 1986), subjects received a disappointing prize from a person who remained there as the prize was conferred or left immediately. Subjects suppressed their expressions of disappointment when the person was there to observe them, and these subjects were only 3 or 4 years old. Suppression is also the socially appropriate response on learning that one has just defeated one's rivals. In fact, subjects stifle their expressions of exuberance in such situations when the defeated rivals are in the same room, compared with when they are in a different room (Friedman & Miller-Herringer, 1991).

In summary, expressiveness is dampened by the presence of other people who are not the targets of one's expressions. But when one's expressive behaviors are relevant to others, then those behaviors are regulated in socially appropriate ways in the presence of the relevant target persons. These kinds of data do not constitute definitive evidence for the operation of self-presentational dynamics, but they are consistent with that perspective.

Characteristics of the audience

A variety of studies indicate that people behave differently, nonverbally, when addressing different target persons or audiences. For example, in telephone conversations with men with whom they had either intimate or casual relationships, women talking to the intimate partner sounded more approachable, sincere, submissive, scatterbrained, feminine, and babyish to judges who heard only the women's parts of the conversation and were unaware of the relationship status of the male listeners (Montepare & Vega, 1988). In another study of telephone conversations (Steckler & Rosenthal, 1985), subjects spoke to either bosses or peers. Women's voices sounded relatively more competent when they were talking to bosses, whereas men's voices sounded more competent when they were talking to peers. On television talk shows, both men and women sound more businesslike, condescending, dominant, and unpleasant when talking to a man than to a woman (J. A. Hall & Braunwald, 1981). In a study of verbal and nonverbal communications in the courtroom, Blanck, Rosenthal, and Cordell (1985) found that judges appeared warmer, more professional, more open-minded, and less dominant when in the presence of older, more-educated jurors than in the presence of younger, less educated ones. And in a study in which participants lied and told the truth to clinical students described as experts or nonexperts at the detection of deception, the participants maintained more eye contact with the experts (Fugita, Hogrebe, & Wexley, 1980). Perhaps they believed, as do many laypersons (e.g., DePaulo et al., 1985a), that gaze aversion was a cue to deception and that expert lie detectors would be especially attuned to that cue. Even infants are sensitive to audience characteristics; when playing with toys, they were more likely to turn around and smile at their mother when she was attentive than inattentive (S. S. Jones et al., 1991; S. S. Jones & Raag, 1989), and when another adult (a stranger) was also present, they were less likely to smile at her than at their mother (S. S. Jones & Raag, 1989).

It is not clear from these studies and others like them (e.g., B. M. DePaulo & Coleman, 1986, 1987) whether the systematic differences in participants' nonverbal behaviors as a function of different audiences were the result of deliberate efforts to convey different impressions to different audiences, whether the differences were habitual remnants of behaviors that were once deliberately regulated, or whether they resulted from some other mechanism (e.g., the women really did feel more feminine when conversing with their intimate friends and were simply expressing this spontaneously). However, it is clear from these kinds of studies that people's nonverbal behaviors do sometimes vary systematically with the characteristics of the audiences and that these variations in nonverbal cue usage have implications for the ways in which the people exhibiting those cues are perceived by others.

Self-presentational relevance of the situation

In the discussion of smiling, it was noted that when people are in a situation in which they anticipate having to ask for help, they smile more than when they have no such expectation (Lefebvre, 1975). Smiling, though, is just one of a constellation of nonverbal behaviors that people use when they want to come across as likable and attractive. For example, in the Lefebvre study, participants expecting to have to ask for help also looked at their partner more frequently. And in another study in which participants had an opportunity to seek help from their partner, their posture mirrored those of their partner to a greater degree than did that of participants for whom the possibility of seeking help was not salient (LaFrance, 1985).

In some organizations, employees are explicitly encouraged to use nonverbal behaviors for self-presentational purposes. In a chain of neighborhood grocery stores in which the clerks were urged to interact positively with the customers to convey a positive organizational image, those clerks who wore more of the symbols of the organization (e.g., name tags, smocks) also displayed more positive emotional expressions (including smiling and eye contact) when interacting with customers (Rafaeli, 1989). These data illustrate in a suggestive way the impact of self-presentationally relevant cues (such as symbols of an organization that encourages friendliness) on nonverbal expressive behavior.

Explicit self-presentational instructions

Smiling is also just one of a set of nonverbal behaviors that are affected by direct instructions to try to gain the approval of another person. Under such instructions, women gesture more, men nod their heads in agreement more, and both men and women make it especially clear that they are listening attentively by using certain "backchannelling" responses, such as "mm-hmm" (H. M. Rosenfeld, 1966). Approval seekers also sit closer to the targets of their attention (H. M. Rosenfeld, 1965) and spend more time gazing into their eyes (Pellegrini, Hicks, & Gordon, 1970). Seating position is used not only to elicit liking but also to convey likability. In a study in which participants were instructed to select a seat at a rectangular table that would convey a warm and friendly impression to the other group members, participants who were the second to arrive sat right next to the first person, and those who were the first to arrive chose one of the two middle seats (Riess & Rosenfeld, 1980). In both cases, participants were decreasing the distance between themselves and the others. Analogously, participants instructed to try to appear cold and unfriendly chose seats that created the greatest possible distances between themselves and the other group members. Those instructed to come across as leaders chose one of the head positions, and those instructed to convey the impression that they were not interested in participating chose seats far away from the head position and less visually accessible to people in that position (e.g., a corner seat farthest away from the head position).

Another important self-presentational goal is self-promotion, which is an attempt to come across as extremely competent (e.g., E. E. Jones & Pittman, 1982). Subjects instructed to create an impression of competence put on noticeably different nonverbal performances than did those instructed to elicit liking. The self-promoters were less inclined than were the ingratiators to act nonverbally attentive to their partners, by nodding, smiling, and gazing, and they were more inclined to act in ways that might draw attention to themselves, such as by sitting up straight and gesturing confidently (Godfrey, Jones, & Lord, 1986). Furthermore, judges viewing videotapes of these interactions formed impressions in line with these differences: They thought that the self-promoters (compared with to the ingratiators) seemed to be trying to attract more attention to themselves and to give less attention to others. These kinds of studies provide the most direct evidence that people can and do use nonverbal behaviors in their attempts to create particular impressions on others and that these differences in behavior can be detected at the aggregate level.[8]

Detectability of Self-Presentational Efforts: The Individual Level

The second way of addressing the question of whether nonverbal behavioral attempts at self-presentation can be detected is the more difficult one. It asks whether, for a particular nonverbal behavior or expression, attempts at managing that behavior can be detected. That is, can an observer watch a particular person at a particular point in time and determine whether that person's nonverbal behavior is being deliberately regulated for self-presentational purposes? The fact that spontaneous facial expressions have different neurological underpinnings than do posed expressions (Buck, 1984, 1985; Rinn, 1984, 1991; see also Cacioppo et al., 1986) lends plausibility to the prediction that there will be observable behavioral differences as well. However, the issues are complex.

Determining whether a nonverbal behavior or expression has been spontaneously produced or deliberately managed is similar in many ways to the task of ascertaining innocence or guilt in a courtroom. The relevant evidence will come from a wide variety of sources, ranging from relatively objective evidence, which can be gathered and evaluated only by trained experts, to more subjective evidence, such as global impressions offered by untrained observers. Although the latter kind of evidence is often on the mark, in many instances it is not, and the observers' feelings of confidence are rarely good predictors of when their judgments are or are not valid (e.g., B. M. DePaulo & Pfeifer, 1986). From case to case, the collection of evidence will vary greatly in definitiveness, and few cases will be open-and-shut.

In evaluating nonverbal behaviors, the task is especially complex because the alternatives are actually more numerous than just spontaneous versus deliberate. For example, when a woman has a pleasant facial expression and tone of voice, is smiling and nodding and gazing into a man's eyes, and is leaning toward him, it is possible that she is spontaneously and unselfconsciously expressing genuine liking for him (e.g., Mehrabian, 1972). However, it is also possible that she is (a) trying deliberately to make clear to him just how much liking she really does feel, (b) trying to exaggerate the amount of liking that she feels, (c) trying to communicate less liking than she feels, (d) trying to convey the impression that she likes him, even though she feels neutral toward him (posing), (e) trying to convey the impression that she likes him, even though she dislikes him (lying), (f) communicating liking cues by mistake, when she had actually intended to communicate something else.

Perceivers who are trying to distinguish among the many possible interpretations of a particular communication can, as with most judgmental tasks, draw from base-rate information about the person and the situation. For example, they can ask themselves how this particular person is likely to feel in this particular situation, whether she is the type of person who is likely to try to convey a particular type of impression, and if so, whether she would have the necessary skill to do so successfully. They can also ask whether the situation is one that calls for a particular type of self-presentation and whether there are rewards and punishments attendant on the successful communication of that impression (in which case people might be especially likely to be trying deliberately to convey that impression, cf. E. E. Jones, Davis, & Gergen, 1961; Kraut, 1978).

More germane to the topic of this article is the potential usefulness of the nonverbal behavioral cues themselves and the ways in which they are interpreted, in revealing information about how they were produced. The relevant evidence is reviewed next.

Spontaneous communications

Evidence has been accumulating that at least for expressions of happiness, spontaneity and genuineness can indeed be discerned. Enjoyment smiles, indicative of truly experienced happiness, differ in a variety of ways from other smiles, such as those donned by people who are simply pretending to be happy. Enjoyment smiles are produced by two particular facial muscles working in concert: the zygomatic major, which pulls the corners of the lips up, and the outer strands of the orbicularis oculi, which surrounds the eye. When enjoyment smiles occur, the orbicularis oculi "raises the cheek and gathers skin inward from around the eye socket" (Ekman & Friesen, 1982, p. 242). Although the zygomatic major can be moved voluntarily, it is rare for people to move that muscle and the outer strands of the orbicularis oculi when genuine enjoyment is not being experienced (Ekman et al., 1990; see also Ekman, Friesen, & Ancoli, 1980).

Enjoyment smiles may also differ from other smiles in symmetry, location, duration, onset time, and offset time (Ekman, 1985; Ekman & Friesen, 1982). Spontaneous facial expressions are likely to be symmetrical, whereas deliberately produced expressions are relatively more likely to be asymmetrical and (if produced by a person who is right-handed) stronger on the left side of the face (Hager, 1982; Rinn, 1984). Enjoyment smiles, Ekman and Friesen (1982) suggest (though more data are needed), rarely last less than 2/3 s or more than 4 s. Other smiles, in contrast, might last either for a longer or a shorter time than that. Smiles that are not spontaneously expressive of genuine enjoyment sometimes appear on the face or leave the face too abruptly or irregularly. They may also appear too quickly or too slowly in relation to the experience that should have engendered the enjoyment (e.g., the punch line of a joke).

Ekman and his colleagues have also documented specific facial actions that characterize spontaneous expressions of certain negative emotions, such as disgust (Ekman et al., 1980), but in general there has been little research on the detectability of spontaneity for expressions other than those of enjoyment. However, the same types of variables that have proved useful in the study of enjoyment might also prove useful in future investigations of other emotions and states.

Clarifying, dampening, exaggerating, and posing

When people are trying deliberately to communicate accurate, exaggerated, or deintensified expressions of the internal state that they really are experiencing, their expression can be, in part, a reflection of that experienced state. Particularly with regard to accurate and exaggerated communications, people are working with, rather than against, their internal state. Still, once they have superimposed willful movements on those that may have appeared naturally, the new expressions will probably differ in discernible ways from the completely spontaneous versions of those same expressions. The dimensions of difference are likely to include those already described above, such as the particular muscles involved, the symmetry of the expression, and its timing, location, and duration.

Deintensified versions of expressions may be easier to detect than exaggerated or purposefully accurate versions, because it is necessary, to some extent, to work against the experienced state. With regard to enjoyment, Ekman (1985) has described a "dampened smile," which may be characterized by lips that are pressed together, lip corners that are tightened or pulled down, or a lower lip that is pushed down. Any of these movements would result in a smile that is potentially distinguishable from a genuine enjoyment smile.

When people are trying to deintensify the expression of an internal state, discrepancies may develop between different nonverbal cues or between nonverbal cues and verbal cues. This might happen because it is difficult for people to dampen all behaviors to the same degree. Alternatively, people who are trying to convey a deintensified version of their experience may choose deliberately to do so by using some cues, but not others, to convey that experience. For instance, a tennis player who has just scored a stunning victory over a much loathed opponent may allow himself a smug smile while purposefully suppressing his inclination to leap high in the air and emit a jubilant yelp. A discrepancy has developed, but it was intended.

Posed smiles, produced by people who are experiencing neutral affect, are unlikely to be accompanied by the movement of the muscles around the eyes, and they may differ in timing, duration, and location from enjoyment smiles. People's subjective impressions of whether an expression was posed versus produced spontaneously may be more accurate than would be expected by chance. Still, perceivers might tend to see most expressions as spontaneous, just as they tend to see most communications as truthful (even in paradigms in which half of the communications they observe are actually lies). The relevant data have not yet been collected but could be quite readily. Data relevant to a related question have been reported, and they show that naive observers can discern at least some difference between expressive performances that vary in the degree to which they were deliberately regulated (B. M. DePaulo, Lanier, & Davis, 1983). Participants were videotaped while answering questions that were or were not revealed to them in advance. When judges observed the participants, either on a videotape without sound or in other kinds of presentations that included words, they were more accurate than chance at distinguishing the planned responses from the unplanned ones. They thought that the planned responses seemed more rehearsed and less spontaneous than the unplanned responses.

Posed and exaggerated expressions may also be more intense than are spontaneous expressions of the same states. In addition, when people are deliberately posing or exaggerating an internal state, the expression of that state may be conveyed more consistently across various nonverbal and verbal channels than would the unregulated spontaneous expressions of those states.

Deceiving

When smiles are used falsely to mask a negative affective state such as fear, anger, or distress, they will have many of the characteristics of posed smiles, such as asymmetry, irregularities in timing, duration, and location, and lack of involvement of the muscles around the eyes. In addition, there may be leakage of facial movements indicative of the negative affect. This leakage may be especially likely to occur in the forehead region but may also blend in with the smile that appears in the lower part of the face (Ekman, 1985).

Dozens of studies have been conducted in which specific nonverbal behaviors were measured while participants were lying and telling the truth. Meta-analyses of these findings (B. M. DePaulo et al., 1985a; Zuckerman, DePaulo, & Rosenthal, 1981) have pointed to a variety of behaviors that distinguish lies from truths. Probably because it is often more arousing to lie than to tell the truth, liars blink more, hesitate more, and make more errors when they are speaking. They also speak in higher pitched voices and have more dilated pupils. The speech hesitations and the pupil dilations are also consistent with the fact that lying is usually a cognitively more demanding task than is telling the truth. So is the finding that people about to tell a lie take longer to plan their communication than do people who are about to tell the truth.

Liars often feel guilty or anxious; these states may be partly responsible for the findings that liars fidget more, speak more hesitantly and less fluently, and make more negative and more nonimmediate (distancing) statements than do truth tellers. The tone of liars' voices sometimes sounds more negative, too. Liars may be reluctant to commit themselves to their untruths, and this is reflected in the fact that liars sometimes have less to say than truth tellers and that what they do say is distancing and overly generalized.

193

The meta-analyses of cues to deception are summaries of lies that differ in many theoretically relevant ways. For example, lies that masked positive affects were not distinguished from lies that masked negative affects, and lies that people may have felt very badly about telling were not differentiated from lies that they did not feel as badly about telling. In the face of this diversity, it is impressive that any reliable cues to deception emerged. Summaries that are more sensitive to such moderator variables might uncover even stronger relationships.

An exception to the tendency to summarize across all types of lies is a summary that classified lies according to the liar's motivation to succeed at the lie (Zuckerman, DePaulo, & Rosenthal, 1981). According to this summary, liars who are especially concerned with telling an effective lie try too hard to control their expressive behavior. Their communications appear rigid and inhibited. For example, compared with those who are less highly motivated to lie successfully, more highly motivated communicators give deceptive responses that are shorter than truthful ones and spoken more slowly and in a higher pitch. Motivated communicators, when lying, also gaze less, move their heads less, shift around in their seats less, fidget less, and even blink less. Perhaps they believe that this suppression of behavior makes it harder for others to know that they are lying. In fact, though, it probably makes it easier (e.g., B. M. DePaulo & Kirkendol, 1989; B. M. DePaulo et al., 1988).

Another feature that distinguishes lies from truths is the occurrence of interchannel discrepancies (e.g., B. M. DePaulo et al., 1985a). Such inconsistencies may develop because liars are not able successfully to control all of their verbal and nonverbal behaviors simultaneously, and because certain behaviors are less amenable to deliberate control than are others (e.g., Ekman & Friesen, 1969; Rosenthal & DePaulo, 1979a, 1979b). When verbal and nonverbal behaviors conflict, it will often be the nonverbal behaviors that are more revealing of the liars' true feelings or attitudes and the verbal behaviors that are more reflective of the affects that they are trying to feign. For example, in their study of communications in the courtroom, Blanck et al. (1985) found that judges who expected the defendant to be found guilty appeared wiser and fairer to people who could hear the words they used when delivering their instructions to the jurors, but they appeared less wise and less fair to those who could see only their visual behaviors or hear the tone of their voice. Nonverbal revealingness has also been documented in research on marital interactions. When distressed and nondistressed couples were instructed to try to act happy, the distressed couples could not be distinguished from the nondistressed by their verbal behavior, but they could be distinguished by their nonverbal behavior (Vincent, Friedman, Nugent, & Messerly, 1979; see also Gottman, Markman, & Notarius, 1977). Suggestive evidence of nonverbal revealingness has also been reported in studies of cross-racial interactions (e.g., Weitz, 1972; Word, Zanna, & Cooper, 1974).

Finally, another source of evidence relevant to the question of whether deliberately false self-presentations can be detected is observers' judgments. Although untrained laypersons are far from perfect in their attempts to discern when lying is occurring, their intuitions do tell them that deceptive communications are indeed more deceptive than are truthful ones. Observers' impressions of dimensions that are related to deceptiveness also discriminate lies from truths. For example, when watching or listening to people who are telling lies, observers think that those people seem more ambivalent and indifferent than they do when they are telling the truth (B. M. DePaulo, Rosenthal, et al., 1982).

Conveying mistaken impressions

Although there has been some discussion of the mistakes people make when lying (e.g., Ekman, 1981, 1985), much less has been said about the kinds of mistakes people make in their nonverbal communications when they are not trying to lie. It is probably rare, for example, for people intending to convey disliking to produce a whole constellation of nonverbal behaviors all of which ordinarily suggest liking. Instead, what might happen is that they convey a variety of cues that together add up to a confusing and ambiguous message.

Emotional and Social, Expressive and Regulatory Bases of Nonverbal Behaviors

Recently, theorists such as Fridlund (1991a; see also Smith, 1977, 1985) have begun to argue that there is no necessary emotional basis for nonverbal behaviors (which they prefer to call "displays" or "signals"). Fridlund (1991a) suggests, for example, that hard-wired affect programs may not exist and that displays may be based primarily, or perhaps even solely, on social/communicative motives. An example of research cited as consistent with this point of view was described earlier, that is, Kraut and Johnston's (1979) studies showing stronger and more reliable covariations of smiling with social factors (such as facing or talking with other people) than with emotional factors (such as bowling a strike or experiencing pleasant weather).

It is beyond the scope of this article to address in detail each of the arguments for the social motive point of view. However, the most central lines of evidence are discussed. To discredit the emotional perspective, one of the most compelling lines of evidence that must be reinterpreted is the corpus of studies (reviewed above) showing that people produce recognizable facial expressions of emotions when viewing emotion-laden stimulus materials while totally alone. Fridlund's (1991a) explanation of these findings is that people's displays can be implicitly social even when they are alone. For example, people may grimace to others who are present only in their imaginations, and they may even treat themselves as social interactants, as when they talk to themselves. In his empirical research, Fridlund (1991b; Fridlund et al., 1990) has shown that people's facial actions can in fact be responsive to implicit audiences. However, showing that this can occur is not sufficient evidence that it always does occur. That is, he has not shown (and probably cannot show) that every time people smile while alone, they are smiling to implicit audiences. For example, in instances of sudden intense stimuli (such as noticing that a huge tree is about to come crashing through the window where one is sitting in solitude), an emotional expression is very likely to occur, and it is very unlikely to be produced for the benefit of an imaginary audience.

Even in the studies that Fridlund cites as especially supportive of the social motive perspective (e.g., Fridlund, 1991b; S. S. Jones & Raag, 1989; Kraut & Johnston, 1979), there is clear evidence for emotional as well as social bases for nonverbal behaviors. Furthermore, his arguments do not convincingly dismiss the growing body of physiological data that are consistent with the emotional perspective (e.g., Davidson, Ekman, Saron, Senulis, & Friesen, 1990; Ekman et al., 1990; Levenson, Ekman, & Friesen, 1990).

The Fridlund point of view is most inconsistent with the spirit of the present article when it attempts to pit the social motive perspective against the emotional perspective. Instead, the argument here is that both are necessary and important. This article is about nonverbal behaviors as they are regulated deliberately in the service of a particular class of social motives: self-presentational ones. It posits that one of the most interesting and perhaps one of the most powerful sets of constraints on the fulfillment of self-presentational motives through nonverbal means are those imposed by the emotion system. The important questions may be how the social and emotional systems work with and against each other in the drama of social interaction and psychic life (perhaps even becoming conceptually inseparable at times) and not which of the two is more deserving of the best actor award.

Another related challenge to the emotional perspective has been issued by those who view emotions in terms of regulation. For example, Campos, Campos, and Barrett (1989) define emotions as "processes of establishing, maintaining, or disrupting the relations between the person and the internal or external environment, when such relations are significant to the individual" (p. 395). They decry the emphasis in classic theories on emotions as intrapsychic feeling states and the insufficient attention in such theories to processes such as people's evaluation of the significance of events for their own goals and strivings. The present article, though it draws in ways from traditional emotion perspectives, is hardly incompatible with the regulatory perspective. According to the present argument, people are quite frequently (though not always consciously) evaluating the significance of events for a particular class of goals: self-presentational ones. They then regulate their nonverbal (and other) behaviors in ways that they believe will facilitate such goals. The contribution of the traditional emotional perspective to this argument is its delineation of the ways in which the emotion system can enable and constrain the attainment of self-presentational goals.

Summary and Conclusions

Whenever people are motivated to convey a particular impression of themselves to others in social interactions, they are highly likely to try to do so in part by managing their nonverbal behaviors. Attempts to regulate nonverbal behaviors for self-presentational purposes occur in interactions with intimates, as well as with strangers, acquaintances, and friends. Although the deliberate control of nonverbal behaviors can be undertaken with the goal of trying to deceive others, more often it is used to edit the images of oneself that are conveyed to others, in such a way that they are at least partially veridical. Deliberate regulation is also used in the service of accuracy and honesty, as when people use their nonverbal behaviors to try to make their true feelings about themselves perfectly clear. There are situations in which people are unlikely to be attempting to control their nonverbal behaviors for self-presentational purposes, for example, when they are totally absorbed in a task. Even then, however, their nonverbal behavior might bear the stamp of attempts at regulation that were undertaken deliberately in the past but have long since become habitual.

Nonverbal behavior is of special significance to the dynamics of self-presentation for a variety of reasons. First, it is impossible to regulate nonverbal behavior in such a way that no impression at all is conveyed. Thus, with regard to its attributional implications, nonverbal behavior is irrepressible. Nonverbal expressions of the basic emotions may be especially difficult to suppress because there may be hard-wired links between the elicitation of those emotions and their expressions. People's feelings, then, tend to appear on their face, and perhaps in other expressive behaviors as well, unless they try deliberately to mask or mute the expressions of those feelings. Nonverbal behaviors are also of special self-presentational significance because they are more accessible to the people who are observing them than to the people who are producing them; thus, with regard to their nonverbal self-presentations, people cannot know themselves as well as others can. Nonverbal behaviors are elusive and off-the-record in that they are difficult to describe or to repeat, and it is impossible to look up their meanings in a dictionary. Nonverbal behaviors can occur very quickly, and it is possible that they convey certain meanings that cannot be communicated in any other way.

One of the most important implications of the special characteristics of nonverbal behaviors is that those behaviors cannot always be regulated successfully. There are important constraints on people's success at translating their self-presentational intentions into the actual production of the relevant nonverbal behaviors. The hard-wired substrate of the emotion system may be one of those constraints. In addition, there are constraints imposed by people's demeanors (which can make it difficult for them to convey particular impressions), by their characteristic level of expressiveness, by their personal style, by the range of expressive cues that they can command, by the amount of practice and experience they have or have not had at regulating their nonverbal behaviors, and by their (lack of) confidence. Also, certain nonverbal behaviors are difficult for most everyone to control, and others that can be controlled under optimal conditions can become less tractable under suboptimal conditions, as when the level of motivation to succeed in conveying a particular impression becomes debilitatingly high.

There are also constraints on the kinds of self-presentational intentions that people will form. These are imposed by knowledge of cultural, situational, and other norms regulating nonverbal expressive behaviors. Finally, there are also constraints on the accuracy with which people can assess the effectiveness of their own nonverbal performances and modify those performances accordingly.

Can people overcome the many factors that can undermine the regulation of nonverbal behaviors for self-presentational purposes? Much of the relevant data come from studies of people's nonverbal "posing" abilities. These are studies in which people are asked to try to use their nonverbal behaviors to try to convey particular affects or emotions or states that they are not necessarily experiencing at the time. People are reasonably skilled posers when using their face and voice; they also seem to be able effectively to regulate their body movements and postures and even their styles of walking, although the database for these conclusions is less substantial. People can also on occasion use their nonverbal behaviors with some measure of success to convey the impression that they are experiencing something very different from what they really are experiencing. That is, they can use their nonverbal behaviors to lie. They can do so not only for affects and emotions but also for dispositions. Extraverts, for example, can convincingly come across as introverts and vice versa, at least in short-term interactions.

Can perceivers tell when other people are deliberately regulating their nonverbal behaviors for self-presentational ends? This is, in a way, the flip side of the question of whether people can control their nonverbal behaviors for self-presentational purposes, especially when deception is involved. When one person succeeds at using nonverbal behaviors to lie, another is taken in by the lie. What results for both the self-presenters and the perceivers is an ample degree of success, particularly for the self-presenters, as well as a generous sprinkling of failures. This is perhaps as it should be. It would be neither desirable nor useful to have a social system in which anyone could successfully claim any image at any time. Nor would it do to have a system in which no one could ever succeed at conveying anything other than their genuine feelings. As it is, it appears that people can succeed in claiming nonverbally many, though not all, images and that they are best at claiming those identities that are closer to their "true selves," as they perceive them. There is much potential, throughout the life-span, for all interactants to develop and refine their abilities to regulate their own nonverbal behaviors and to discern others' attempts to do the same. This is part of the richness, flexibility, and intrigue of social life.

References

1. Abbott, A. R. & Sebastian, R. J. (1981). *Personality & Social Psychology Bulletin, 7*, 481-486.
2. Abrami, P. C., Leventhal, L. & Perry, R. P. (1982). *Review of Educational Research, 52*, 446-464.
3. Allen, V. L. & Atkinson, M. L. (1978). *Journal of Educational Psychology, 70*, 298-305.
4. Allport, G. W. (1937). Personality. New York: Holt.
5. Allport, G. W., & Vernon, P. E. (1933). Studies in expressive movement. New York: Hafner.
6. Apple, W. & Hecht, K. (1982). *Journal of Personality & Social Psychology, 42*, 864-875.
7. Argyle, M. & Dean, J. (1965). *Sociometry, 28*, 289-304.

8. Arkin, R. M., Lake, E. A., & Baumgardner, A. H. (1986). Shyness and self-presentation. In W. H. Jones, J. M. Cheek, & S. R. Briggs (Eds.), Shyness: Perspectives on research and treatment (pp. 189-204). New York: Plenum Press.

9. Baldwin, M. W. & Holmes, J. G. (1987). *Journal of Personality & Social Psychology, 52,* 1087-1098.

10. Basow, S. A. & Distenfeld, M. S. (1985). *Journal of Educational Psychology, 77,* 45-52.

11. Baumeister, R. F. (1982). *Psychological Bulletin, 91,* 3-26.

12. Baumeister, R. F. (1984). *Journal of Personality & Social Psychology, 46,* 610-620.

13. Baumeister, R. F. & Scher, S. J. (1988). *Psychological Bulletin, 104,* 3-22.

14. Baumeister, R. F. & Showers, C. J. (1986). *European Journal of Social Psychology, 16,* 361-383.

15. Baumeister, R. F., Hutton, D. G. & Tice, D. M. (1989). *Journal of Experimental Social Psychology, 25,* 59-78.

16. Bavelas, J. B., Black, A., Lemery, C. R. & Mullett, J. (1986). *Journal of Personality & Social Psychology, 50,* 322-329.

17. Berglas, S. & Jones, E. E. (1978). *Journal of Personality & Social Psychology, 36,* 405-41.7

18. Berry, D. S. & McArthur, L. Z. (1985). *Journal of Personality & Social Psychology, 48,* 312-323.

19. Berry, D. S. & McArthur, L. Z. (1986). *Psychological Bulletin, 100,* 3-18.

20. Berry, D. S. & Zebrowitz-McArthur, L. (1988). *Personality & Social Psychology Bulletin, 14,* 23-33.

21. Birdwhistell, R. L. (1970). Kinesics and context. Philadelphia: University of Pennsylvania Press.

22. Blanck, P. D., Rosenthal, R. & Cordell, L. H. (1985). *Stanford Law Review, 38,* 89-164.

23. Blanck, P. D., Rosenthal, R., Snodgrass, S. E., DePaulo, B. M. & Zuckerman, M. (1981). *Journal of Personality & Social Psychology, 41,* 391-396.

24. Block, J. H. (1978). Another look at sex differences in the socialization behaviors of mothers and fathers. In J. Sherman & F. L. Denmark (Eds.), The psychology of women. New York: Psychological Dimensions.

25. Blum, R. H. (1972). Deceivers and deceived. Springfield, IL: Charles C Thomas.

26. Blumberg, H. H. (1972). *Journal of Personality & Social Psychology, 23,* 157-162.

27. Blurton-Jones, N. (1967). An ethological study of some aspects of social behaviour of children in nursery school. In D. Morris (Ed.), Primate ethology (pp. 347-368). London: Weidenfeld & Nicholson.

28. Boice, R. & Monti, P. M. (1982). *Journal of Nonverbal Behavior, 7,* 79-94.

29. Bond Jr., C. F., Kahler, K. N. & Paolicelli, L. M. (1985). *Journal of Experimental Social Psychology, 21,* 331-345.

30. Braginsky, B. M., Braginsky, D. D., & Ring, K. (1969). Methods of madness. New York: Holt, Rinehart & Winston.

31. Brody, L. R. (1985). *Journal of Personality, 53,* 102-149.

32. Brownlow, S. & Zebrowitz, L. A. (1990). *Journal of Nonverbal Behavior, 14,* 51-60.

33. Buck, R. (1975). *Journal of Personality & Social Psychology, 31,* 644-653.

34. Buck, R. (1977). *Journal of Personality & Social Psychology, 33,* 225-236.

35. Buck, R. (1979). Individual differences in nonverbal sending accuracy and electrodermal responding: The externalizing -internalizing dimension. In R. Rosenthal (Ed.), Skill in nonverbal communication (pp. 140-170). Cambridge, MA: Oelgeschlager, Gunn, & Hain.

36. Buck, R. (1984). The communication of emotion. New York: Guilford Press.

37. Buck, R. (1985). *Psychological Review, 92,* 389-413.

38. Buck, R. (1988). Emotional education and mass media: A new view of the global village. In R. P. Hawkins, J. M. Weimann, & S. Pingree (Eds.), Advancing communication science: Merging mass and interpersonal perspectives (pp. 44-76). Newbury Park, CA: Sage.

39. Buck, R. (1989). Emotional communication in personal relationships: A developmental -interactionist view. In C. D. Hendrick (Ed.), Close relationships. Review of Personality and Social Psychology (Vol. 10, pp. 84-96). Newbury Park, CA: Sage.

40. Buck, R., Baron, R. & Barrette, D. (1982). *Journal of Personality & Social Psychology, 42,* 506-517.

41. Buck, R., Baron, R., Goodman, N. & Shapiro, B. (1980). *Journal of Personality & Social Psychology, 39,* 522-529.

42. Bugental, D. E. (1986). *Personality & Social Psychology Bulletin, 12,* 7-16.

43. Bugental, D. E., Kaswan, J. W. & Love, L. R. (1970). *Journal of Personality & Social Psychology, 16,* 647-655.

44. Bugental, D. E., Kaswan, J. W., Love, L. R. & Fox, M. N. (1970). *Developmental Psychology, 2,* 367-375.

45. Bugental, D. E., Love, L. R. & Gianetto, R. M. (1971). *Journal of Personality & Social Psychology, 17,* 314-318.

46. 46. Burgoon, J. K., Buller, D. B., & Woodall, W. G. (1989). Nonverbal communication. New York: Harper & Row.

47. Buss, A. H. & Briggs, S. R. (1984). *Journal of Personality & Social Psychology, 47,* 1310-1324.

48. Buss, A. H., & Plomin, R. (1975). A temperament theory of personality development. New York: Wiley.

49. Cacioppo, J. T., Martzke, J. S., Petty, R. E. & Tassinary, L. G. (1988). *Journal of Personality & Social Psychology, 54,* 592-604.

50. Cacioppo, J. T., Petty, R. E., Losch, M. E. & Kim, H. S. (1986). *Journal of Personality & Social Psychology, 50,* 260-268.

51. Campos, J. J., Campos, R. G. & Barrett, K. C. (1989). *Developmental Psychology, 25,* 394-402.

52. Camras, L. (1982). Ethological approaches to nonverbal communication. In R. S. Feldman (Ed.), Development of nonverbal behavior in children (pp. 3-28). New York: Springer-Verlag.

53. Cappella, J. N. (1981). *Psychological Bulletin, 89,* 101-132.

54. Cappella, J. N. (1983). Conversational involvement: Approaching and avoiding others. In J. M. Wiemann & R. P. Harrison (Eds.), Nonverbal interaction (pp. 113-148). Beverly Hills, CA: Sage.

55. Cappella, J. N. (1985). Controlling the floor in conversation. In A. W. Siegman & S. Feldstein (Eds.), Multichannel integrations of nonverbal behavior (pp. 69-103). Hillsdale, NJ: Erlbaum.

56. Cappella, J. N. (1988). Personal relationships, social relationships and patterns of interaction. In S. W. Duck (Ed.), Handbook of personal relationships (pp. 325-342). New York: Wiley.

57. Carnegie, D. (1936). How to win friends and influence people. New York: Simon & Schuster.

58. Carnevale, P. J. D., Pruitt, D. G. & Seilheimer, S. D. (1981). *Journal of Personality & Social Psychology, 40,* 111-120.

59. Carver, C. S., & Scheier, M. F. (1981). Attention and self-regulation: A control-theory approach to human behavior. New York: Springer-Verlag.

60. Cash, T. T. & Begley, P. J. (1976). *Psychological Reports, 38,* 1205-1206.

61. Chapman, A. J. & Wright, D. S. (1976). *Journal of Experimental Child Psychology, 21,* 201-218.

62. Cheek, J. M., & Hogan, R. (1983). Self-concepts, self-presentations, and moral judgments. In J. Suls & A. G. Greenwald (Eds.), Psychological perspectives on the self (Vol. 2, pp. 249-273). Hillsdale, NJ: Erlbaum.

63. Cheyne, J. A. (1976). *Child Development, 47,* 820-823.

64. Cialdini, R. B., Borden, R. J., Thorne, A., Walker, M. R., Freeman, S. & Sloan, L. R. (1976). *Journal of Personality & Social Psychology, 34,* 366-375.

65. Cohen, A. A. (1977). *The Journal of Communication, 27,* 54-63.

66. Cole, P. M. (1986). *Child Development, 57,* 1309-1321.

67. Cozby, P. C. (1973). *Psychological Bulletin, 79,* 73-91.

68. Craig, K. D. & Patrick, C. J. (1985). *Journal of Personality & Social Psychology, 48,* 1080-1091.

69. Crowne, D. P., & Marlowe, D. (1964). The approval motive. New York: Wiley.

70. Cummings, E. M. (1987). *Child Development, 58,* 976-984.

71. Cunningham, M. R. (1977). *Journal of Personality, 45,* 564-584.

72. Cunningham, M. R. (1986). *Journal of Personality & Social Psychology, 50,* 925-935.

73. Dabbs Jr., J. M., Evans, M. S., Hopper, C. H. & Purvis, J. A. (1980). *Journal of Personality & Social Psychology, 39,* 278-284.

74. Daly, J. A., Hogg, E., Sacks, D., Smith, M. & Zimring, L. (1983). *Journal of Nonverbal Behavior, 7,* 183-189.

75. Darwin, C. (1965). The expression of the emotions in man and animals. New York: Appleton. (Original work published 1872)

76. Davidson, R. J., Ekman, P., Saron, C. D., Senulis, J. A. & Friesen, W. V. (1990). *Journal of Personality & Social Psychology, 58,* 330-341.

77. Davis, M. (Ed.). (1982). Interaction rhythms: Periodicity in communicative behavior. New York: Human Sciences Press.

78. DePaulo, B. M. (1981). *Annals of the New York Academy of Sciences, 364,* 245-255.

79. DePaulo, B. M. & Coleman, L. M. (1986). *Journal of Personality & Social Psychology,* 51, 945-959.
80. DePaulo, B. M. & Coleman, L. M. (1987). *Journal of Nonverbal Behavior,* 11, 75-88.
81. DePaulo, B. M., & Kirkendol, S. E. (1989). The motivational impairment effect in the communication of deception. In J. Yuille (Ed.), Credibility assessment (pp. 51-70). Norwell, MA: Kluwer Academic.
82. DePaulo, B. M. & Pfeifer, R. L. (1986). *Journal of Applied Social Psychology,* 16, 249-267.
83. DePaulo, B. M. & Rosenthal, R. (1979). *Journal of Personality & Social Psychology,* 37, 1713-1722.
84. DePaulo, B. M., Blank, A. L., Swaim, G. W., & Hairfield, J. G. (in press). Expressiveness and expressive control. Personality & Social Psychology Bulletin.
85. DePaulo, B. M., Brittingham, G. L. & Kaiser, M. K. (1983). *Journal of Personality & Social Psychology,* 45, 1045-1060.
86. DePaulo, B. M., Epstein, J. A. & LeMay, C. S. (1990). *Journal of Personality,* 58, 623-640.
87. DePaulo, B. M., Jordan, A., Irvine, A. & Laser, P. S. (1982). *Child Development,* 53, 701-709.
88. DePaulo, B. M., Kenny, D. A., Hoover, C., Webb, W. & Oliver, P. (1987). *Journal of Personality & Social Psychology,* 52, 303-315.
89. DePaulo, B. M., Kirkendol, S. E., Tang, J. & O'Brien, T. (1988). *Journal of Nonverbal Behavior,* 12, 177-202.
90. DePaulo, B. M., Lanier, K. & Davis, T. (1983). *Journal of Personality & Social Psychology,* 45, 1096-1103.
91. DePaulo, B. M., Lassiter, G. D. & Stone, J. I. (1982). *Personality & Social Psychology Bulletin,* 8, 273-279.
92. DePaulo, B. M., LeMay, C. S. & Epstein, J. (1991). *Personality & Social Psychology Bulletin,* 17, 14-24.
93. DePaulo, B. M., Rosenthal, R., Green, C. R. & Rosenkrantz, J. (1982). *Journal of Experimental Social Psychology,* 18, 433-446.
94. DePaulo, B. M., Stone, J. I., & Lassiter, G. D. (1985a). Deceiving and detecting deceit. In B. R. Schlenker (Ed.), The self and social life (pp. 323-370). New York: McGraw-Hill.
95. DePaulo, B. M., Stone, J. I. & Lassiter, G. D. (1985). *Journal of Personality & Social Psychology,* 48, 1191-1203.
96. DePaulo, P. J. & DePaulo, B. M. (1989). *Journal of Applied Social Psychology,* 19, 1552-1557.
97. DePaulo, P. J., DePaulo, B. M., Tang, J., & Swaim, G. W. (1989). Lying and detecting lies in organizations. In R. A. Giacalone & P. Rosenfeld (Eds.), Impression management in the organization (pp. 377-393). Hillsdale, NJ: Erlbaum.
98. Diener, E., Sandvik, E. & Larsen, R. J. (1985). *Developmental Psychology,* 21, 542-546.
99. DiMatteo, M. R. (1979). Nonverbal skill and the physician-patient relationship. In R. Rosenthal (Ed.), Skill in nonverbal communication (pp. 104-134). Cambridge, MA: Oelgeschlager, Gunn, & Hain.
100. Dodge, K. A. (1989). *Developmental Psychology,* 25, 339-342.
101. Dovidio, J. F., Brown, C. E., Heltman, K., Ellyson, S. L. & Keating, C. F. (1988). *Journal of Personality & Social Psychology,* 55, 580-587.
102. Duncan, S., Jr. (1983). Speaking turns: Studies of structure and individual differences. In J. M. Wiemann & R. P. Harrison (Eds.), Nonverbal interaction (pp. 149-179). Beverly Hills, CA: Sage.
103. Duncan, S., Jr., & Fiske, D. W. (1977). Face-to-face interaction: Research, methods, and theory. Hillsdale, NJ: Erlbaum.
104. Duval, S., & Wicklund, R. A. (1972). A theory of objective self-awareness. San Diego, CA: Academic Press.
105. Edelmann, R. J. & Hampson, S. E. (1981). *Personality & Social Psychology Bulletin,* 7, 109-116.
106. Edinger, J. A. & Patterson, M. L. (1983). *Psychological Bulletin,* 93, 30-56.
107. Efron, D. (1941). Gesture and environment. Morningside Heights, NY: King's Crown Press.
108. Ekman, P. (1972). Universals and cultural differences in facial expressions of emotion. In J. K. Cole (Ed.), Nebraska symposium on motivation, 1971 (pp. 207-283). Lincoln: University of Nebraska Press.
109. Ekman, P. (1976). *The Journal of Communication,* 26, 14-26. 110. Ekman, P. (1977). Biological and cultural contributions to body and facial movement. In J. Blacking (Ed.), The anthropology of the body (pp. 39-84). San Diego, CA: Academic Press.
110. Ekman, P. (1977). Biological and cultural contributions to body and facial movement. In J. Blacking (Ed.), The anthropology of the body (pp. 39-84). San Diego, CA: Academic Press.

111. Ekman, P. (1981). *Annals of the New York Academy of Sciences,* 364, 269-278.

112. Ekman, P. (1985). Telling lies. New York: Norton.

113. Ekman, P., & Friesen, W. (1975). Unmasking the face. Englewood Cliffs, NJ: Prentice-Hall.

114. Ekman, P. & Friesen, W. V. (1969). *Semiotica,* 1, 49-98.

115. Ekman, P. & Friesen, W. V. (1974). *Journal of Personality & Social Psychology,* 29, 288-298.

116. Ekman, P. & Friesen, W. V. (1982). *Journal of Nonverbal Behavior,* 6, 238-252.

117. Ekman, P., Davidson, R. & Friesen, W. V. (1990). *Journal of Personality & Social Psychology,* 58, 342-353.

118. Ekman, P., Friesen, W. V. & Ancoli, S. (1980). *Journal of Personality & Social Psychology,* 39, 1125-1134.

119. Ekman, P., Friesen, W. V., & Ellsworth, P. (1972). Emotion in the human face. New York: Pergamon Press.

120. Ekman, P., Friesen, W. V., & Ellsworth, P. (1982). What are the similarities and differences in facial behavior across cultures? In P. Ekman (Ed.), Emotion in the human face (2nd ed., pp. 128-143). Cambridge, England: Cambridge University Press.

121. Ekman, P., Friesen, W. V. & O'Sullivan, M. (1988). *Journal of Personality & Social Psychology,* 54, 414-420

122. Ekman, P., Friesen, W. V., O'Sullivan, M., Chan, A., Diacoyanni -Tarlatzis, I., Heider, K., Krause, R., LeCompte, W. A., Pitcairn, T., Ricci-Bitti, P. E., Scherer, K. & Tomita, M. (1987). *Journal of Personality & Social Psychology,* 53, 712-717.

123. Ekman, P., Roper, G. & Hager, J. C. (1980). *Child Development,* 51, 886-891.

124. Ellgring, H. (1986). *European Archives of Psychiatry and Neurological Sciences,* 236, 31-34.

125. Elliott, G. C. (1979). *Journal of Personality & Social Psychology,* 37, 1282-1292.

126. Elman, D., Schulte, D. C. & Bukoff, A. (1977). *Environmental Psychology and Nonverbal Behavior,* 2, 93-99.

127. Exline, R. V. (1963). *Journal of Personality,* 31, 1-20.

128. Feldman, R. S. (1976). *Journal of Educational Psychology,* 68, 807-816.

129. Feldman, R. S. & White, J. B. (1980). *The Journal of Communication,* 30, 121-129.

130. Feldman, R. S., Devin-Sheehan, L. & Allen, V. L. (1978). *American Educational Research Journal,* 15, 217-231.

131. Feldman, R. S., Jenkins, L. & Popoola, O. (1979). *Child Development,* 50, 350-355.

132. Feldman, R. S., Philippot, P., & Custrini, R. (1991). Social skills, psychopathology, and nonverbal behavior. In R. S. Feldman & B. Rime (Eds.), Fundamentals of nonverbal behavior (pp. 329-350). Cambridge, England: Cambridge University Press.

133. Feldman, R. S., White, J. B., & Lobato, D. (1982). Social skills and nonverbal behavior. In R. S. Feldman (Ed.), Development of nonverbal behavior in children (pp. 259-278). New York: Springer-Verlag.

134. Feldstein, S. & Sloan, B. (1984). *Journal of Personality,* 52, 188-204.

135. Feldstein, S., Alberti, L., BenDebba, M., & Welkowitz, J. (1974, September). Personality and simultaneous speech. Paper presented at the 82nd Annual Convention of the American Psychological Association, New Orleans, LA.

136. Felson, R. B. (1980). *Social Psychology Quarterly,* 43, 223-233.

137. Fenigstein, A., Scheier, M. F. & Buss, A. (1975). *Journal of Consulting & Clinical Psychology,* 43, 522-527.

138. Field, T., & Walden, T. (1982). Production and perception of facial expressions in infancy and early childhood. In H. Reese & L. Lipsitt (Eds.), Advances in child development (Vol. 16 pp. 169-211). San Diego, CA: Academic Press.

139. Fine, G. A., Stitt, J. L. & Finch, M. (1984). *Social Psychology Quarterly,* 47, 282-287.

140. Flett, G. L., Boase, P., McAndrews, M. P., Pliner, P. & Blankstein, K. R. (1986). *Journal of Research in Personality,* 20, 447-459.

141. Foot, H. C., Chapman, A. J. & Smith, J. R. (1977). *Journal of Personality & Social Psychology,* 35, 401-411.

142. Forgas, J. P. (1987). *Personality & Social Psychology Bulletin,* 13, 478-489.

143. Forgas, J. P., O'Connor, K. V. & Morris, S. L. (1983). *Personality & Social Psychology Bulletin,* 9, 587-596.

144. Frable, D. E. S. (1987). *Journal of Personality & Social Psychology,* 53, 391-396.

145. Freedman, J. L. & Perlick, D. (1979). *Journal of Experimental Social Psychology,* 15, 295-303.

146. Fridlund, A. J. (1991). *Biological Psychology,* 32, 3-100.

147. Fridlund, A. J. (1991). *Journal of Personality & Social Psychology,* 60, 229-240.

148. Fridlund, A. J., Sabini, J. P., Hedlund, L. E., Schaut, J. A., Shenker, J. I. & Knauer, M. J. (1990). *Journal of Nonverbal Behavior,* 142, 113-137.

149. Friedman, H. S. & Miller-Herringer, T. (1991). *Journal of Personality & Social Psychology,* 61, 766-775.

150. Friedman, H. S. & Riggio, R. E. (1981). *Journal of Nonverbal Behavior,* 6, 96-104.

151. Friedman, H. S., DiMatteo, M. R. & Taranta, A. (1980). *Journal of Research in Personality,* 14, 351-364.

152. Friedman, H. S., Prince, L. M., Riggio, R. E. & DiMatteo, M. R. (1980). *Journal of Personality & Social Psychology,* 39, 333-35.

153. Friedman, H. S., Riggio, R. E. & Casella, D. F. (1988). *Personality & Social Psychology Bulletin,* 14, 203-211.

154. Friedman, H. S., Riggio, R. E. & Segall, D. O. (1980). *Journal of Nonverbal Behavior,* 5, 35-48.

155. Fugita, S. S., Hogrebe, M. C. & Wexley, K. N. (1980). *Personality & Social Psychology Bulletin,* 6, 637-643.

156. Fulcher, J. S. (1942). *Archives of Psychology,* 38, 1-49.

157. Gallois, C. & Callan, V. J. (1986). *Journal of Personality & Social Psychology,* 51, 755-762.

158. Gilbert, D. T. & Krull, D. S. (1988). *Journal of Personality & Social Psychology,* 54, 193-202.

159. Gilbert, D. T., Krull, D. S. & Pelham, B. W. (1988). *Journal of Personality & Social Psychology,* 55, 685-694.

160. Gnepp, J. & Hess, D. L. R. (1986). *Developmental Psychology,* 22, 103-108.

161. Godfrey, D. K., Jones, E. E. & Lord, C. G. (1986). *Journal of Personality & Social Psychology,* 50, 106-115.

162. Goffman, E. (1959). The presentation of self in everyday life. Garden City, NY: Doubleday/Anchor Books.

163. Goffman, E. (1963). Behavior in public places. New York: Free Press.

164. Goffman, E. (1971). Relations in public. New York: Basic Books.

165. Goffman, E. (1974). Frame analysis. New York: Harper Colophon Books.

166. Goffman, E. (1979). Gender advertisements. New York: Harper & Row.

167. Goldenthal, P., Johnston, R. E. & Kraut, R. E. (1981). *Ethology and Sociobiology,* 2, 127-133.

168. Goldsmith, H. H., Buss, A. H., Plomin, R., Rothbart, M. K., Thomas, A., Chess, S., Hinde, R. A. & McCall, R. B. (1987). *Child Development,* 58, 505-529.

169. Goldstein, A. G. (1983). *Journal of Nonverbal Behavior,* 7, 223-255.

170. Gottman, J., Markman, H. & Notarius, C. (1977). *Journal of Marriage & Family,* 49, 461-477.

171. Graham, J. W., Gentry, K. W. & Green, J. (1981). *Personality & Social Psychology Bulletin,* 7, 467-474.

172. Greenberg, J., Pyszczynski, T. & Stine, P. (1985). *Journal of Research in Personality,* 19, 1-11.

173. Greenwald, A. G., & Breckler, S. J. (1985). To whom is the self presented? In B. R. Schlenker (Ed.), The self and social life (pp. 126-145). New York: McGraw-Hill.

174. Hager, J. C. (1982). Assymetries in facial expression. In P. Ekman (Ed.), Emotion in the human face (2nd ed., pp. 318-352). Cambridge, England: Cambridge University Press.

175. Hager, J. C. & Ekman, P. (1979). *Ethology and Sociobiology,* 1, 77-82.

176. Halberstadt, A. G. (1983). *Journal of Nonverbal Behavior,* 8, 14-26.

177. Halberstadt, A. G. (1984). Family expression of emotion. In C. Z. Malatesta & C. E. Izard (Eds.), Emotion in adult development (pp. 235-252). Beverly Hills, CA: Sage.

178. Halberstadt, A. G. (1986). *Journal of Personality & Social Psychology,* 51, 827-836.

179. Halberstadt, A. G. (1991). Family patterns of nonverbal development. In R. S. Feldman & B. Rime (Eds.), Fundamentals of nonverbal behavior (pp. 106-160). Cambridge, England: Cambridge University Press.

180. Halberstadt, A. G. & Saitta, M. B. (1987). *Journal of Personality & Social Psychology,* 53, 257-272.

181. Halberstadt, A. G., Hayes, C. W. & Pike, K. M. (1988). *Sex Roles,* 19, 589-604.

182. Hall, E. T. (1959). The silent language. New York: Doubleday.

183. Hall, J. A. (1984). Nonverbal sex differences: Communication accuracy and expressive style. Baltimore: Johns Hopkins University Press.

184. Hall, J. A. & Braunwald, K. G. (1981). *Journal of Personality & Social Psychology, 40,* 99-110.

185. Hall, J. A. & Veccia, E. M. (1990). *Journal of Personality & Social Psychology, 59,* 1155-1162.

186. Hall, J. A., Roter, D. L. & Katz, N. R. (1987). *Medical Care, 25,* 399-412.

187. Harper, R. G., Wiens, A. N., & Matarazzo, J. D. (1978). Nonverbal communication. New York: Wiley.

188. Harris, P. L. (1989). Children and emotions. Oxford, England: Basil Blackwell.

189. Harris, P. L., Donnelly, K., Guz, G. R. & Pitt-Watson, R. (1986). *Child Development, 57,* 895-909.

190. Hatfield, E., & Sprecher, S. (1986). Mirror, mirror. Albany: State University of New York Press.

191. Hayano, D. M. (1980). *The Journal of Communication, 30,* 113-120.

192. Heckhausen, H. & Strang, H. (1988). *Journal of Personality & Social Psychology, 55,* 489-498.

193. Higgins, E. T. (1981). Role-taking and social judgment: Alternative developmental perspectives and processes. In J. H. Flavell & L. Ross (Eds.), Social cognitive development (pp. 119-153). Cambridge, England: Cambridge University Press.

194. Hochschild, A. R. (1979). *American Journal of Sociology, 85,* 552-575.

195. Hochschild, A. R. (1983). The managed heart. Berkeley: University of California Press.

196. Hogan, R. (1982). A socioanalytic theory of personality. In M. M. Page (Ed.), Nebraska symposium on motivation (Vol. 29, pp. 55-89). Lincoln: University of Nebraska Press.

197. Holtgraves, T. & Srull, T. K. (1989). *Personality & Social Psychology Bulletin, 15,* 452-462.

198. Huston, A. C. (1983). Sex typing. In P. H. Mussen (Series Ed.) & E. M. Hetherington (Vol. Ed.), Handbook of child psychology: Vol. 4. Socialization, personality, and social development (4th ed., pp. 387-468). New York: Wiley.

199. Ickes, W., Patterson, M. L., Rajecki, D. W. & Tanford, S. (1982). *Social Cognition, 1,* 160-190.

200. Izard, C. E. (1971). The face of emotion. New York: Appleton-Century -Crofts.

201. Izard, C. E. (1977). Human emotions. New York: Plenum Press.

202. Izard, C. E., Huebner, R. R., Risser, D., McGinnes, G. C. & Dougherty, L. M. (1980). *Developmental Psychology, 16,* 132-140.

203. Jaeger, J., Borod, J. C. & Peselow, E. (1986). *Journal of Affective Disorders, 11,* 43-50.

204. Jones, E. E. (1964). Ingratiation. New York: Appleton-Century -Crofts.

205. Jones, E. E. (1979). *American Psychologist, 34,* 104-117.

206. Jones, E. E. (1986). *Science, 234,* 41-46.

207. Jones, E. E. (1990). Interpersonal perception. New York: W. H. Freeman.

208. Jones, E. E. & Berglas, S. (1978). *Personality & Social Psychology Bulletin, 4,* 200-206.

209. Jones, E. E., & Davis, K. E. (1965). From acts to dispositions: The attribution process in person perception. In L. Berkowitz (Ed.), Advances in experimental social psychology (Vol. 2, pp. 219-266). San Diego, CA: Academic Press.

210. Jones, E. E., & Pittman, T. S. (1982). Toward a general theory of strategic self-presentation. In J. Suls (Ed.), Psychological perspectives on the self (Vol. 1, pp. 231-262). Hillsdale, NJ: Erlbaum.

211. Jones, E. E., & Wortman, C. (1973). Ingratiation: An attributional approach. Morristown, NJ: General Learning Press.

212. Jones, E. E., Davis, K. E. & Gergen, K. J. (1961). *Journal of Abnormal and Social Psychology, 63,* 302-310.

213. Jones, H. E. (1935). *American Journal of Psychology, 47,* 241-251.

214. Jones, S. S. & Raag, T. (1989). *Child Development, 60,* 811-818.

215. Jones, S. S., Collins, K. & Hong, H. (1991). *Psychological Science, 2,* 45-49.

216. Kagan, J., Reznick, J. S., Snidman, N., Gibbons, J. & Johnson, M. O. (1988). *Child Development, 59,* 1580-1589.

217. Kahneman, D. (1973). Attention and effort. Englewood Cliffs, NJ: Prentice-Hall.

218. Kaye, K. & Fogel, A. (1980). *Developmental Psychology, 16,* 454-464.

219. Keating, C. F. (1985). Human dominance signals: The primate in us. In S. L. Ellyson & J. F. Dovidio (Eds.), Power, dominance, and nonverbal behavior (pp. 89-108). New York: Springer-Verlag.

220. Keating, C. F., Mazur, A., Setgall, M. H., Cysneiros, P. G., Divale, W. T., Kilbride, J. E., Komin, S., Leahy, P., Thurman, B. & Wirsing, R. (1981). *Journal of Personality & Social Psychology, 40,* 615-626.

221. Kenner, A. N. (1984). *Journal of Nonverbal Behavior,* 8, 159-171.

222. Kenny, D. A., & DePaulo, B. M. (1991). Do we know how others view us? An empirical and theoretical account. Manuscript submitted for publication.

223. Kilbride, J. E. & Yarczower, M. (1980). *Journal of Cross-Cultural Psychology,* 11, 281-296.

224. King, L. A. & Emmons, R. A. (1990). *Journal of Personality & Social Psychology,* 58, 864-877.

225. Kleck, R. E. & Mendolia, M. (1990). *Journal of Nonverbal Behavior,* 14, 35-49.

226. Kleck, R. E. & Strenta, A. (1980). *Journal of Personality & Social Psychology,* 39, 861-873.

227. Kleck, R. E., Vaughan, R. C., Cartwright-Smith, J., Vaughan, K. B., Colby, C. Z. & Lanzetta, J. T. (1976). *Journal of Personality & Social Psychology,* 34, 1211-1218.

228. Knapp, M. L. (1978). Nonverbal communication in human interaction (2nd ed.). New York: Holt, Rinehart & Winston.

229. Krause, R., Steimer, E., Sanger-Alt, C. & Wagner, G. (1989). *Psychiatry: Interpersonal & Biological Processes,* 52, 1-12.

230. Krauss, R. M., Apple, W., Morency, N., Wenzel, C. & Winton, W. (1981). *Journal of Personality & Social Psychology,* 40, 312-320.

231. Kraut, R. E. (1978). *Journal of Personality & Social Psychology,* 36, 380-391.

232. Kraut, R. E. (1982). *Journal of Personality & Social Psychology,* 42, 853-863.

233. Kraut, R. E. & Johnston, R. E. (1979). *Journal of Personality & Social Psychology,* 37, 1539-1553.

234. Kwint, L. (1934). *Child Development,* 5, 1-12.

235. LaFrance, M. (1985). *Personality & Social Psychology Bulletin,* 11, 207-217.

236. LaFrance, M. & Carmen, B. (1980). *Journal of Personality & Social Psychology,* 38, 36-49.

237. Lanzetta, J. T. & Kleck, R. E. (1970). *Journal of Personality & Social Psychology,* 16, 12-19.

238. Larrance, D. T. & Zuckerman, M. (1981). *Journal of Personality,* 49, 349-362.

239. Larsen, R. J. & Diener, E. (1987). *Journal of Research in Personality,* 21, 1-39.

240. Leary, M. R. (1983). Understanding social anxiety. Beverly Hills, CA: Sage.

241. Leary, M. R. & Kowalski, R. M. (1990). *Psychological Bulletin,* 107, 34-47.

242. Leary, M. R. & Meadows, S. (1991). *Journal of Personality & Social Psychology,* 60, 254-262.

243. Lee, M. T. & Ofshe, R. (1981). *Social Psychology Quarterly,* 44, 73-82.

244. Lefebvre, L. M. (1975). *British Journal of Social & Clinical Psychology,* 14, 33-42.

245. Levenson, R. W., Ekman, P. & Friesen, W. V. (1990). *Psychophysiology,* 27, 363-384.

246. Lewis, H. (1971). Shame and guilt in neurosis. New York: International University Press.

247. Lewis, M., & Michalson, L. (1985). Faces as signs and symbols. In G. Zivin (Ed.), The development of expressive behavior (pp. 153-180). San Diego, CA: Academic Press.

248. Lewis, M., Stanger, C. & Sullivan, M. W. (1989). *Developmental Psychology,* 25, 439-443.

249. Lippa, R. (1976). *Journal of Personality,* 44, 541-559.

250. Lippa, R. (1978). *Journal of Personality,* 46, 438-461.

251. Lippa, R. (1978). *Journal of Research in Personality,* 12, 1-14.

252. Lippa, R. (1983). Expressive behavior. In L. Wheeler (Ed.), Review of personality and social psychology (Vol. 4, pp. 181-205). Beverly Hills, CA: Sage.

253. Mackey, W. C. (1976). *Journal of Genetic Psychology,* 129, 125-130.

254. Major, B., Schmidlin, A. M. & Williams, L. (1990). *Journal of Personality & Social Psychology,* 58, 634-643.

255. Malatesta, C. A., & Izard, C. E. (1984). The facial expression of emotion: Young, middle-aged, and other adult expressions. In C. Z. Malatesta & C. E. Izard (Eds.), Emotion in adult development (pp. 253-273). Beverly Hills, CA: Sage.

256. Malatesta, C. Z. & Haviland, J. M. (1982). *Child Development,* 53, 991-1003.

257. Manstead, A. (1991). Expressiveness as an individual difference. In R. S. Feldman & B. Rime (Eds.), Fundamentals of nonverbal behavior (pp. 285-328). Cambridge, England: Cambridge University Press.

258. Maslow, A. H. (1949). *Psychological Review,* 56, 261-272.

259. Maurer, D. W. (1940). The big con. New York: Bobbs-Merrill.

260. Mazur, A., Mazur, J. & Keating, C. (1984). *American Journal of Sociology,* 90, 125-150.

261. McAdams, D. P., Jackson, R. J. & Kirshnit, C. (1984). *Journal of Personality,* 52, 261-273.

262. McArthur, L. Z. & Baron, R. M. (1983). *Psychological Review,* 90, 215-238.

263. McCanne, T. R. & Anderson, J. A. (1987). *Journal of Personality & Social Psychology,* 52, 759-768.

264. McConnell-Ginet, S. (1978). *Signs: Journal of Women in Culture and Society,* 3, 541-559.

265. McCoy, C. L., & Masters, J. C. (1990). Children's strategies for the control of emotion in themselves and others. In A. Isen & B. Moore (Eds.), Affect and social behavior (pp. 231-268). Cambridge, England: Cambridge University Press.

266. McHugo, G. J., Lanzetta, J. T., Sullivan, D. G., Masters, R. D. & Englis, B. G. (1985). *Journal of Personality & Social Psychology,* 49, 1513-1529.

267. Mehrabian, A. (1972). Nonverbal communication. In J. K. Cole (Ed.), Nebraska symposium on motivation, 1971 (pp. 107-161). Lincoln: University of Nebraska Press.

268. Miller, L. C. & Cox, C. L. (1982). *Personality & Social Psychology Bulletin,* 8, 748-751.

269. Miller, P. & Sperry, L. L. (1987). *Merrill-Palmer Quarterly,* 33, 1-31.

270. Millham, J., & Jacobson, L. I. (1978). The need for approval. In H. London & J. E. Exner, Jr. (Eds.), Dimensions of personality (pp. 365-390). New York: Wiley.

271. Mitchell, R. W., & Thompson, N. S. (1986). Deception: Perspectives on human and nonhuman deceit. Albany: State University of New York Press.

272. Montepare, J. M. & Vega, C. (1988). *Personality & Social Psychology Bulletin,* 14, 103-113.

273. Montepare, J. M. & Zebrowitz-McArthur, L. (1987). *Journal of Experimental Social Psychology,* 23, 331-349.

274. Montepare, J. M., Goldstein, S. B. & Clausen, A. (1987). *Journal of Nonverbal Behavior,* 11, 33-42.

275. Moore, S. (1984). The Stanislavski system. New York: Penguin Books.

276. Morency, N. L., & Krauss, R. M. (1982). Children's nonverbal encoding and decoding of affect. In R. S. Feldman (Ed.), Development of nonverbal behavior in children (pp. 181-199). New York: Springer-Verlag.

277. Mullen, B., Futrell, D. E., Stairs, D., Tice, D. M., Baumeister, R. F., Dawson, K. E., Riordan, C. A., Radloff, C. E., Goethals, G. R., Kennedy, J. G. & Rosenfeld, P. (1986). *Journal of Personality & Social Psychology,* 51, 291-295.

278. Nasby, W., Hayden, B. & DePaulo, B. M. (1980). *Journal of Abnormal Psychology,* 89, 459-468.

279. Natale, M. (1975). *Journal of Personality & Social Psychology,* 32, 790-804.

280. Noller, P. (1980). *Journal of Nonverbal Behavior,* 5, 115-129.

281. Noller, P. (1982). *Journal of Personality & Social Psychology,* 43, 732-741.

282. Notarius, C. I. & Levenson, R. W. (1979). *Journal of Personality & Social Psychology,* 37, 1204-1210.

283. Ortony, A. & Turner, T. J. (1990). *Psychological Review,* 97, 315-331.

284. Pankratz, L. (1988). Malingering on intellectual and neuropsychological measures. In R. Rogers (Ed.), Clinical assessment of malingering and deception (pp. 169-192). New York: Guilford Press.

285. Parham, I. A., Feldman, R. S., Oster, G. D. & Popoola, O. (1981). *Journal of Social Psychology,* 113, 261-269.

286. Patterson, M. L. (1983). Nonverbal behavior: A functional perspective. New York: Springer-Verlag.

287. Patterson, M. L. (1987). *Journal of Nonverbal Behavior,* 11, 110-122.

288. Patterson, M. L. (1988). Functions of nonverbal behavior in close relationships. In S. W. Duck (Ed.), Handbook of personal relationships (pp. 41-56). New York: Wiley.

289. Patterson, M. L. (1991). Functions of nonverbal behavior in interpersonal interaction. In R. S. Feldman & B. Rime (Eds.), Fundamentals of nonverbal behavior (pp. 458-495). Cambridge, England: Cambridge University Press.

290. Paulhus, D. L., Graf, P. & van Selst, M. (1989). *Social Cognition,* 7, 389-401.

291. Pellegrini, R. J., Hicks, R. A. & Gordon, L. (1970). *British Journal of Social & Clinical Psychology,* 9, 373-374.

292. Pennebaker, J. W. (1980). *Basic & Applied Social Psychology,* 1, 83-91.

293. Pitman, R. K., Kolb, B., Orr, S. P. & Singh, M. M. (1987). *American Journal of Psychiatry,* 144, 99-101.

294. Pliner, P., Chaiken, S. & Flett, G. L. (1990). *Personality & Social Psychology Bulletin,* 16, 263-273.

295. Polanyi, M. (1962). Personal knowledge. Chicago: University of Chicago Press.

296. Prideaux, E. (1922). *British Journal of Medical Psychology,* 2.

297. Purvis, J. A., Dabbs Jr., J. M. & Hopper, C. H. (1984). *Personality & Social Psychology Bulletin,* 10, 61-66.

298. Rafaeli, A. (1989). *Journal of Applied Psychology,* 74, 385-393.

299. Rejeski, W. J. & Lowe, C. A. (1980). *Personality & Social Psychology Bulletin, 6,* 436-440.

300. Riess, M. & Rosenfeld, P. (1980). *Journal of Applied Communication Research, 8,* 22-30.

301. Riggio, R. E. (1986). *Journal of Personality & Social Psychology, 51,* 649-660.

302. Riggio, R. E. & Friedman, H. S. (1982). *Journal of Nonverbal Behavior, 7,* 33-45.

303. Riggio, R. E. & Friedman, H. S. (1986). *Journal of Personality & Social Psychology, 50,* 421-427.

304. Riggio, R. E., Tucker, J. & Throckmorton, B. (1987). *Personality & Social Psychology Bulletin, 13,* 568-577.

305. Riggio, R. E., Tucker, J. & Widaman, K. F. (1987). *Journal of Nonverbal Behavior, 11,* 126-145.

306. Rinn, W. E. (1984). *Psychological Bulletin, 95,* 52-77.

307. Rinn, W. E. (1991). Neuropsychology of facial expression. In R. S. Feldman & B. Rime (Eds.), Fundamentals of nonverbal behavior (pp. 3-30). Cambridge, England: Cambridge University Press.

308. Rosenfeld, H. M. (1965). *Psychological Reports, 17,* 120-122.

309. Rosenfeld, H. M. (1966). *Journal of Personality & Social Psychology, 4,* 597-605.

310. Rosenthal, R., & DePaulo, B. M. (1979a). Sex differences in accommodation in nonverbal communication. In R. Rosenthal (Ed.), Skill in nonverbal communication (pp. 68-103). Cambridge, MA: Oelgeschlager, Gunn, & Hain.

311. Rosenthal, R. & DePaulo, B. M. (1979). *Journal of Personality & Social Psychology, 37,* 273-285.

312. Ross, L. (1977). The intuitive psychologist and his shortcomings: Distortions in the attribution process. In L. Berkowitz (Ed.), Advances in experimental social psychology (Vol. 10, pp. 173-220). San Diego, CA: Academic Press.

313. Ruback, R. B. (1981). *Personality & Social Psychology Bulletin, 7,* 677-681.

314. Saarni, C. (1984). *Child Development, 55,* 1504-1513.

315. Saarni, C. (1988). *Journal of Nonverbal Behavior, 12,* 275-294.

316. Saarni, C. (1990). Emotional competence: How emotions and relationships become integrated. In R. Thompson (Ed.), Nebraska symposium on motivation: Vol. 36. Socioemotional development (pp. 115-182). Lincoln: University of Nebraska Press.

317. Sabatelli, R. M. & Rubin, M. (1986). *Journal of Nonverbal Behavior, 10,* 120-133.

318. Scheflen, A. E. (1974). How behavior means. Garden City, NY: Anchor Books.

319. Scheier, M. F., & Carver, C. S. (1981). Private and public aspects of self. In L. Wheeler (Ed.), Review of personality and social psychology (Vol. 2, pp. 189-216). Beverly Hills, CA: Sage.

320. Scherer, K. R. (1979). Nonlinguistic vocal indicators of emotion and psychopathology. In C. E. Izard (Ed.), Emotions in personality and psychopathology (pp. 493-529). New York: Plenum Press.

321. Scherer, K. R. (1986). *Psychological Bulletin, 99,* 143-165.

322. Schlenker, B. R. (1980). Impression management. Monterey, CA: Brooks/Cole.

323. Schlenker, B. R. (1984). Identities, identifications, and relationships. In V. Derlega (Ed.), Communication, intimacy, and close relationships (pp. 71-104). San Diego, CA: Academic Press.

324. Schlenker, B. R. (1987). Threats to identity: Self-identification and social stress. In C. R. Snyder & C. Ford (Eds.), Coping with negative life events: Clinical and social psychological perspectives (pp. 273-321). San Diego, CA: Academic Press.

325. Schlenker, B. R. & Leary, M. R. (1982). *Psychological Bulletin, 92,* 641-669.

326. Schlenker, B. R. & Leary, M. R. (1985). *Journal of Language & Social Psychology, 4,* 171-192.

327. Schlenker, B. R., & Weigold, M. F. (1989). Goals and the self-identification process: Constructing desired identities. In L. Pervin (Ed.), Goals concepts in personality and social psychology (pp. 243-290). Hillsdale, NJ: Erlbaum.

328. Schlenker, B. R. & Weigold, M. F. (1990). *Journal of Personality & Social Psychology, 59,* 820-828.

329. Schneider, D. J., Hastorf, A. H., & Ellsworth, P. C. (1979). Person perception. Reading, MA: Addison-Wesley.

330. Shennum, W. A., & Bugental, D. B. (1982). The development of control over affective expression in nonverbal behavior. In R. S. Feldman (Ed.), Development of nonverbal behavior in children (pp. 101-121). New York: Springer-Verlag.

331. Shrout, P. E. & Fiske, D. W. (1981). *Journal of Personality, 49,* 115-128.

332. Siegman, A. W. & Reynolds, M. A. (1983). *Journal of Personality & Social Psychology, 45,* 1325-1333 10.1037//0022-3514 .45.6.1325.

333. Simpson, W. E. & Crandall, S. J. (1972). *Psychonomic Science, 29,* 197-200.

334. Singer, J. L. & Spohn, H. E. (1956). *Journal of Abnormal and Social Psychology, 53,* 375-377.

335. Smith, W. J. (1977). The behavior of communicating. Cambridge, MA: Harvard University Press.

336. Smith, W. J. (1985). Consistency and change in communication. In G. Zivin (Ed.), The development of expressive behavior (pp. 51-76). San Diego, CA: Academic Press.

337. Snyder, C. R. & Higgins, R. L. (1988). *Journal of Nonverbal Behavior,* 12, 237-252.

338. Snyder, M. (1974). *Journal of Personality & Social Psychology,* 30, 526-537.

339. Snyder, M. (1979). Self-monitoring processes. In L. Berkowitz (Ed.), Advances in experimental social psychology (Vol. 7, pp. 85-128). San Diego, CA: Academic Press.

340. Snyder, M. (1987). Public appearances, private realities: The psychology of self-monitoring. New York: WH Freeman.

341. Solomon, M. R. & Schopler, J. (1982). *Personality & Social Psychology Bulletin,* 8, 508-514.

342. Sommers, S. (1981). *Journal of Personality & Social Psychology,* 41, 553-561.

343. Sommers, S. & Scioli, A. (1986). *Journal of Personality & Social Psychology,* 51, 417-422.

344. Stanislavski, C. (1965). An actor prepares (E. Reynolds Hapgood, Trans.). New York: Theatre Arts Books. (Original work published in 1948).

345. Steckler, N. A. & Rosenthal, R. (1985). *Journal of Applied Psychology,* 70, 157-163.

346. Stier, D. S. & Hall, J. A. (1984). *Journal of Personality & Social Psychology,* 47, 440-459.

347. Sullins, E. S. (1989). *Personality & Social Psychology Bulletin,* 15, 584-595.

348. Sullins, E. S. (1991). *Personality & Social Psychology Bulletin,* 17, 166-174.

349. Sullins, E. S., Friedman, H. S. & Harris, M. J. (1985). *Journal of Nonverbal Behavior,* 9, 229-238.

350. Sullivan, D. G. & Masters, R. D. (1988). *American Journal of Political Science,* 32, 345-368.

351. Tesser, A., & Rosen, S. (1975). The reluctance to transmit bad news. In L. Berkowitz (Ed.), Advances in experimental social psychology (Vol. 8, pp. 194-232). San Diego, CA: Academic Press.

352. Tetlock, P. E. & Manstead, A. S. R. (1985). *Psychological Review,* 92, 59-77.

353. Thomas, A., & Chess, S. (1985). The behavioral study of temperament. In J. Strelau, F. Farley, & A. Gale (Eds.), The biological bases of personality and behavior (Vol. 1, pp. 213-226). Washington, DC: Hemisphere.

354. Thomas, A., Chess, S., & Birch, H. G. (1968). Temperament and behavior disorders in children. New York: New York University Press.

355. Tomkins, S. S. (1962). Affect, imagery, and consciousness (Vol. 1). New York: Springer.

356. Toris, C. & DePaulo, B. M. (1984). *Journal of Personality & Social Psychology,* 47, 1063-1073.

357. Tucker, J. S. & Riggio, R. E. (1988). *Journal of Nonverbal Behavior,* 12, 87-97.

358. van Hooff, J. A. R. A. M. (1972). A comparative approach to the phylogeny of laughter and smiling. In R. A. Hinde (Ed.), Non-verbal communication (pp. 209-238). Cambridge, England: Cambridge University Press.

359. Vincent, J. P., Friedman, L. C., Nugent, J. & Messerly, L. (1979). *Journal of Consulting & Clinical Psychology,* 47, 557-566 10.1037//0022-006X .47.3.557.

360. von Baeyer, C. L., Sherk, D. L. & Zanna, M. P. (1981). *Personality & Social Psychology Bulletin,* 7, 45-51.

361. von Bertalanffy, L. (1968). General system theory (Rev. ed.). New York: Braziller.

362. Wagner, H. L., MacDonald, C. J. & Manstead, A. S. R. (1986). *Journal of Personality & Social Psychology,* 50, 737-743.

363. Wallbott, H. G. & Scherer, K. R. (1986). *Journal of Personality & Social Psychology,* 51, 690-699.

364. Warner, M. G. & Fineman, H. (1988). *News-week,* pp, 19-20.

365. Weitz, S. (1972). *Journal of Personality & Social Psychology,* 24, 14-21.

366. Williams, C. E. & Stevens, K. N. (1972). *Journal of the Acoustical Society of America,* 52, 1238-1250.

367. Word, C. O., Zanna, M. P. & Cooper, J. (1974). *Journal of Experimental Social Psychology,* 10, 109-120.

368. Yarczower, M. & Daruns, L. (1982). *Journal of Personality & Social Psychology,* 43, 831-837.

369. Yarczower, M., Kilbride, J. E. & Hill, L. A. (1979). *Developmental Psychology,* 15, 453-454.

370. Zaidel, S. F. & Mehrabian, A. (1969). *Journal of Experimental Research in Personality,* 3, 233-241.

371. Zivin, G. (1982). Watching the sands shift: Concetualizing development of nonverbal mastery. In R. S. Feldman (Ed.), Development of nonverbal behavior in children (pp. 63-98). New York: Springer-Verlag.

372. Zivin, G. (Ed.). (1985). The development of expressive behavior: Biology-environment interactions. San Diego, CA: Academic Press.

373. Zuckerman, M., & Larrance, D. T. (1979). Individual differences in perceived encoding and decoding abilities. In R. Rosenthal (Ed.), Skill in nonverbal communication (pp. 171-203). Cambridge, MA: Oelgeschlager, Gunn, & Hain.

374. Zuckerman, M. & Przewuzman, S. J. (1979). *Environmental Psychology and Nonverbal Psychology,* 3, 147-163.

375. Zuckerman, M., Amidon, M. D., Bishop, S. E. & Pomerantz, S. D. (1982). *Journal of Personality & Social Psychology,* 43, 347-357.

376. Zuckerman, M., DeFrank, R. S., Hall, J. A., Larrance, D. T. & Rosenthal, T. (1979). *Journal of Experimental Social Psychology,* 15, 378-396.

377. Zuckerman, M., DePaulo, B. M., & Rosenthal, R. (1981). Verbal and nonverbal communication of deception. In L. Berkowitz (Ed.), Advances in experimental social psychology (Vol. 14, pp. 1-59). San Diego, CA: Academic Press.

378. Zuckerman, M., Hall, J. A., DeFrank, R. S. & Rosenthal, R. (1976). *Journal of Personality & Social Psychology,* 34, 966-977.

379. Zuckerman, M., Koestner, R. & Driver, R. (1981). *Journal of Nonverbal Behavior,* 6, 105-114.

380. Zuckerman, M., Larrance, D. T., Hall, J. A., DeFrank, R. S. & Rosenthal, R. (1979). *Journal of Personality,* 47, 712-733.

381. Zuckerman, M., Larrance, D. T., Spiegel, N. H. & Klorman, R. (1981). *Journal of Experimental Social Psychology,* 17, 506-524.

382. Zuckerman, M., Lipets, M. S., Koivumaki, J. H. & Rosenthal, R. (1975). *Journal of Personality & Social Psychology,* 32, 1068-1076

Footnotes

1. This bias is usually not shared by those who view nonverbal behaviors from an ethological perspective (e.g., Mitchell & Thompson, 1986; Smith, 1985) or by those who have long maintained that nonverbal behaviors are learned and culturally patterned (e.g., Birdwhistell, 1970; Efron, 1941; E. T. Hall, 1959).

2. Ortony and Turner (1990) have argued that the criteria that have traditionally been used for defining basic emotions are ambiguous and unconvincing. They propose that a necessary component of any emotion is a valenced appraisal (such as an awareness of an inescapable threat) and that biologically basic emotions are "those for which the connection between the valenced appraisal and some other response is hardwired" (p. 324). They discourage the search for basic emotions, though, and instead urge an emphasis on the components of emotions. From their perspective, it might be better to state that there are hardwired links between components of emotions (such as particular appraisals) and components of expressions, rather than stating that the links are between an emotion (as a whole) and an expression (as a whole). Also, from their perspective, there are hard-wired links between internal states and components of expressions for certain internal states that are not emotions. The arguments presented here can be recast in the ways suggested by Ortony and Turner. The most important implication, however, remains the same: When there are hard-wired links between internal states (or components of them) and nonverbal expressions (or components of expressions), people's ability to convey nonverbally impressions that differ from those states will be constrained, and their ability to work with those states and convey clear or exaggerated expressions of them will be enhanced.

3. Patterson (1983, 1987, 1988, 1991) has developed a taxonomy of functions of nonverbal behaviors that anticipated several of the distinctions made here. The major functional categories in his system are providing information, regulating interaction, expressing intimacy, social control, affect management, the service–task function, and the presentation function. The presentation function is in a way more encompassing than the self-presentational function described here, in that it includes the management of impressions about people other than the self, as well as the management of impressions about the self. It is in another way less broad, in that it refers only to impressions conveyed to third parties and not to those conveyed to the target of the social interaction. In Patterson's taxonomy, deliberate attempts to convey impressions to the target person are included under the general category of social control (attempting to accomplish something non-verbally that

would not have been accomplished if no attempt had been made). In addition to impression management, the other subcategories of the social control function are "(1) exercising power and dominance over others, (2) initiating persuasive communications, (3) providing feedback and reinforcement, and (4) deceiving others" (Patterson, 1988, p. 52). As Patterson acknowledges (Edinger & Patterson, 1983), all of these subcategories can also involve the management of impressions. Self-presentation is also part of Patterson's (1988) informational function, which has been described as making available "information about the actor's states, traits, or specific isolated reactions to self, to other people, or to the environment" (p. 47). There are two subcategories: indicative, which is spontaneous or reactive nonverbal behavior, and communicative, which is purposeful or managed nonverbal behavior. It is the latter category, of course, that would overlap with the self-presentational function as described here.

4. The definition of expressiveness in this article differs from that of Buss and Briggs (1984), who see expressive behavior as spontaneous, unrehearsed, unshy, and informal. Expressiveness, in their conceptualization, is at the opposite end of the dimensions of pretense, shyness, and formality. The key difference from the present definition is the assumption that expressiveness and spontaneity co-occur. In the present conceptualization, in contrast, expressiveness is a continuum ranging from expressive (readable) to unexpressive (illegible), and it is measured in a context in which behavior is likely to be emitted spontaneously rather than deliberately regulated. (Typically, the context involves watching emotionally loaded slides when no one else is present.) Deliberate behavior can also range from expressive to unexpressive. As indicated in the section on posing, when people are instructed to try deliberately to convey certain emotions, the nonverbal behaviors of some people will seem expressive and legible, but the nonverbal behaviors of others will appear unexpressive and undecipherable. The present construal, then, is a two-by-two: Nonverbal behavior can be spontaneous or deliberate, and crossed with that, it can be expressive or unexpressive.

5. Bob Kleck suggested this interpretation of the literature on con men.

6. More generally, Cappella (1983) has argued that a whole range of cues often interpreted as cues to liking or positivity are more aptly characterized as involvement cues. In positively toned interactions, behaviors such as maintaining eye contact and leaning forward can indeed signal liking, but in negatively toned interactions, they are more likely to be expressions of hostility (cf. Carnevale, Pruitt, & Seilheimer, 1981; Noller, 1980).

7. This study also included a condition in which subjects were to convey deliberately impressions that were consistent and inconsistent with their experience. That is, they sometimes tried to appear as though they were sniffing an unpleasant odor and other times tried to make it clear that they were sniffing a pleasant odor, when in both cases they really were sniffing something pleasant. They did the same for the unpleasant odors. Because the consistent and inconsistent communications were analyzed together, however, the results cannot be interpreted unambiguously.

8. Tetlock and Manstead (1985) have reviewed findings from a variety of domains (such as dissonance, reactance, and group polarization) in which attempts have been made to distinguish impression-management interpretations from intrapsychic explanations. The paradigms used in such studies include several that were considered here (e.g., manipulations of the publicness of the interaction or of the characteristics of the audience). Their conclusion is that alternative explanations of the findings from these and other paradigms can always be generated and that ultimately, then, neither purely intrapsychic nor purely self-presentational explanations can ever be definitively established for any given phenomenon. As an alternative to conducting critical tests of intrapsychic versus impression-management explanations, they suggest that researchers focus on delineating processes common to both perspectives, with the goal of developing a unified framework. The Tetlock and Manstead position is, of course, open to debate. For example, it could be argued that the kinds of intrapsychic explanations posed as alternative interpretations of the impression-management studies are more diverse and therefore less parsimonious than are the impression-management accounts of the intrapsychic studies. It could also be maintained that competitive theory testing helps to delineate the range of easy application of each perspective and to uncover the themes that the major perspectives share. As applied to the present article, the implication of the Tetlock and Manstead position is that all of the findings that have been presented as evidence of the self-presentational use of nonverbal behaviors can be reinterpreted from an

intrapsychic perspective. For example, the motor mimicry finding that participants who face an injured experimenter show more expressions of pain on their own faces was interpreted by Bavelas et al. (1986) as a deliberate communicative act by which participants conveyed to the injured person that they are like him and feel the same way he does. Alternatively, however, participants who are directly facing an injured person, compared with those who have a less direct orientation, might experience more distress themselves. Their more negative facial expressions, then, would simply be a direct manifestation of the amount of distress they actually were experiencing. Although it may in fact be possible to concoct these kinds of alternative explanations for all of the relevant findings, at least some of them would probably be strained. Regardless of the ultimate utility or validity of the Tetlock and Manstead position, there are numerous questions addressed by this article that are not challenged by their position. For example, the questions of whether people can deliberately regulate their own nonverbal behavior so as to convey particular impressions, should they choose to do so, is orthogonal to the issue of whether they ever do choose to do so. Additionally, studies in which self-presentational motivation is manipulated by direct instructions (e.g., participants are told to seek or to avoid approval) are less convincingly interpretable from alternative perspectives.

Psychological Bulletin, January 2003, Vol. 129, No. 1, p 74-118

Cues to Deception

Bella M. DePaulo, James J. Lindsay, Brian E. Malone, Laura Muhlenbruck, Kelly Charlton, Harris Cooper

Abstract

Do people behave differently when they are lying compared with when they are telling the truth? The combined results of 1,338 estimates of 158 cues to deception are reported. Results show that in some ways, liars are less forthcoming than truth tellers, and they tell less compelling tales. They also make a more negative impression and are more tense. Their stories include fewer ordinary imperfections and unusual contents. However, many behaviors showed no discernible links, or only weak links, to deceit. Cues to deception were more pronounced when people were motivated to succeed, especially when the motivations were identity relevant rather than monetary or material. Cues to deception were also stronger when lies were about transgressions.

Do people behave in discernibly different ways when they are lying compared with when they are telling the truth? Practitioners and laypersons have been interested in this question for centuries (Trovillo, 1939). The scientific search for behavioral cues to deception is also longstanding and has become especially vigorous in the past few decades.

In 1981, Zuckerman, DePaulo, and Rosenthal, published the first comprehensive meta-analysis of cues to deception. Their search for all reports of the degree to which verbal and nonverbal cues occurred differentially during deceptive communications compared with truthful ones produced 159 estimates of 19 behavioral cues to deception. These estimates were from 36 independent samples. Several subsequent reviews updated the Zuckerman et al. (1981) meta-analysis (B. M. DePaulo, Stone, & Lassiter, 1985a; Zuckerman, DePaulo, & Rosenthal, 1986; Zuckerman & Driver, 1985), but the number of additional estimates was small. Other reviews have been more comprehensive but not quantitative (see Vrij, 2000, for the most recent of these). In the present review, we summarize quantitatively the results of more than 1,300 estimates of 158 cues to deception. These estimates are from 120 independent samples.

We define deception as a deliberate attempt to mislead others. Falsehoods communicated by people who are mistaken or self-deceived are not lies, but literal truths designed to mislead are lies. Although some scholars draw a distinction between deceiving and lying (e.g., Bok, 1978), we use the terms interchangeably. As Zuckerman et al. (1981) did in their review, we limit our analysis to behaviors that can be discerned by human perceivers without the aid of any special equipment. We also limit our review to studies of adults, as the dynamics of deceiving may be markedly different in children (e.g., Feldman, Devin-Sheehan, & Allen, 1978; Lewis, Stanger, & Sullivan, 1989; Shennum & Bugental, 1982).

Predicting Cues to Deception: Previous Approaches

Ekman and Friesen (1969)

In 1969, Ekman and Friesen, published the first influential theoretical statement about cues to deception. They described two broad categories of cues, leakage cues and deception cues. Leakage cues reveal what the liars are trying to hide—typically, how they really feel. Anticipating the self-presentational perspective that would become important later, Ekman and Friesen (1969) noted that the operation of display rules (i.e., culturally and socially determined norms for managing facial expressions of emotions) can result in leakage cues. For example, when deceivers try to squelch the facial expression of an emotion they are trying to conceal, the resulting expression—a micro affect display—may be briefer than it is ordinarily, but the nature of the affect may still be identifiable. If instead the facial expression is so brief that the emotion cannot be discerned, then the resulting micro affect display functions as a deception cue. Deception cues indicate that deception may be occurring, without indicating the nature of the information that is being concealed. Almost all of the cues that have been reported in the literature are deception cues.

Ekman and Friesen (1969) described various conditions under which liars would be especially likely to succeed in their deception attempts (e.g., perhaps by evidencing fewer or less obvious cues). Their formulation was based on the psychology of both the liars and the targets of lies as they relate to each other. For example, they predicted that success is more likely when the salience of deception is asymmetrical such that the liars are focused on getting away with their lies while the issue of deception is not salient to the targets or that the liars are focusing primarily on deceiving while the targets are simultaneously trying to deceive and detect deceit.

Zuckerman et al. (1981)

Zuckerman et al. (1981) began their formulation with the widely accepted premise that no one behavior or set of behaviors would ever be found that always occurs when people are lying and never occurs any other time. Instead, they argued, the search should be for the kinds of thoughts, feelings, or psychological processes that are likely to occur more or less often when people are lying compared with when they are telling the truth and for the behavioral cues that may be indicative of those states. They then delineated four factors that could be used to predict cues to deception: generalized arousal, the specific affects experienced during deception, cognitive aspects of deception, and attempts to control behavior so as to maintain the deception.

Arousal

Citing the research and theory available at the time on the psychophysiological detection of deception, Zuckerman et al. (1981) proposed that liars may experience greater undifferentiated arousal than truth tellers. That arousal could be evidenced by liars' greater pupil dilation, increased blinking, more frequent speech disturbances, and higher pitch. However, Zuckerman et al. (1981) also acknowledged that autonomic responses that seem characteristic of deception may be explained by the specific affects experienced while lying without invoking the notion of diffuse arousal.

Feelings While Lying

To the extent that liars experience guilt about lying or fear of getting caught lying, behaviors indicative of guilt and fear are shown more often by liars than truth tellers. Zuckerman et al. (1981) suggested that liars might fidget more than truth tellers, and they may also sound more unpleasant. They also suggested that guilt and anxiety could become apparent in liars' distancing of themselves from their deceptive communications. Drawing from Wiener and Mehrabian's (Wiener and Mehrabian's, 1968; see also Mehrabian, 1972) account of the verbal and nonverbal cues indicative of distancing (which they called nonimmediacy), Zuckerman et al. (1981) predicted that liars would communicate in more evasive and indirect ways than truth tellers and that they would maintain less eye contact with their interaction partners.

Cognitive Aspects of Deception

Zuckerman et al. (1981) conceptualized lying as a more cognitively complex task than telling the truth. Liars, they claimed, need to formulate communications that are internally consistent and consistent with what others already know. The greater cognitive challenges involved in lying (relative to truth telling) were predicted to result in longer response latencies, more speech hesitations, greater pupil dilation, and fewer illustrators (hand movements that accompany and illustrate speech).

Attempted Control of Verbal and Nonverbal Behaviors

Liars' attempts to control their behaviors so as to maintain their deception can paradoxically result in cues that instead betray it. For example, liars' behaviors may seem less spontaneous than truth tellers'. Also, liars' inability to control all aspects of their behavior equally effectively could result in verbal and nonverbal discrepancies.

Ekman (1985/ 1992)

Ekman (1985/ 1992) described two major categories of cues, thinking cues and feeling cues. Liars who prepare their deceptions inadequately or who cannot keep their stories straight produce inconsistencies that betray their deceits. Those who overprepare produce stories that seem rehearsed. If liars need to think carefully about their lies as they tell them, they may speak more slowly than truth tellers. These are all thinking cues.

Ekman's (1985/ 1992) more important contribution, however, was his conceptualization of the role of emotions in deceiving. By understanding the emotions that liars are experiencing, Ekman argued, it is possible to predict behaviors that distinguish liars from truth tellers. For example, the cues indicative of detection apprehension are fear cues. These include higher pitch, faster and louder speech, pauses, speech errors, and indirect speech. The greater the liars' detection apprehension, the more evident these fear cues should be. For example, liars should appear more fearful as the stakes become higher and the anticipated probability of success becomes lower.

Similarly, liars who feel guiltier about their lies, such as those who are lying to people who trust them, should show more behavioral indicators of guilt. Ekman (1985/ 1992) noted that guilt cues have not been clearly determined, but they could include cues to sadness such as lower pitch, softer and slower speech, and downward gazing.

Liars' feelings about lying are not necessarily negative ones. Ekman (1985/ 1992) suggested that liars sometimes experience "duping delight," which could include excitement about the challenge of lying or pride in succeeding at the lie. This delight could become evident in cues to excitement such as higher pitch, faster and louder speech, and more use of illustrators. The duping delight hypothesis has not yet been tested.

Ekman (1985/ 1992) pointed out that emotions become significant not only when liars feel apprehensive, guilty, or excited about their lies but also when liars are experiencing emotions that they are trying to hide or when they are faking emotions that they are not really experiencing. The particular cues that signal lying depend on the particular emotions that the liars are experiencing and simulating. For example, people who are only pretending to be enjoying a film would show fewer genuine enjoyment smiles and more feigned smiles than people who really are enjoying a film. These differences in smiling would not be predicted if the feelings that people really were experiencing or just pretending to experience were, for example, feelings of pain instead of enjoyment. From this perspective, cues to emotions that liars are trying to hide or to simulate cannot be combined across all studies in the literature. Instead, the relevant subset of studies must be selected (e.g., only those in which liars are hiding or simulating enjoyment). This is also a perspective that eschews the notion of undifferentiated arousal and instead argues for the study of specific emotions (Ekman, Levenson, & Friesen, 1983; Levenson, Ekman, & Friesen, 1990).

Buller and Burgoon (1996)

From a communications perspective, Buller and Burgoon (1996) argued that to predict the behavior of deceivers, it is important to consider not just individual psychological variables such as motivations and emotions but also interpersonal communicative processes. Reiterating Ekman and Friesen's (1969) point about the importance of multiple roles, Buller and Burgoon noted that when people are trying to deceive, they are engaged in several tasks simultaneously. They are attempting to convey their deceptive message, and at the same time, they are continually monitoring the target of their deception for signs of suspiciousness and then adapting their behavior accordingly. Although these multiple demands can prove challenging at first, compromising effectiveness at maintaining credibility, "these difficulties should typically dissipate over time as participants acquire more feedback, attempt further repairs, and gain greater control over their performance" (Buller & Burgoon, 1996, p. 220). They therefore predicted that "deceivers in interactive contexts should display increasing immediacy and involvement, pleasantness, composure, fluency, and smooth turn taking over the course of the interaction" (Buller & Burgoon, 1996, p. 220). They also noted that patterns of behavior vary with factors such as the deceivers' expectations, goals, motivations, and relationship with the targets and with the targets' degree of suspiciousness, so that there would be no one profile of deceptive behaviors.

One of the moderator variables for which Buller and Burgoon (1996) made predictions is deceivers' motivations. A number of taxonomies of motivations for deceiving have been proposed (e.g., Camden, Motley, & Wilson, 1984; B. M. DePaulo, Kashy, Kirkendol, Wyer, & Epstein, 1996; Hample, 1980; Lippard, 1988; Metts, 1989; Turner, Edgley, & Olmstead, 1975), and some are quite complex. For example, Metts (1989) described four categories of motives (partner focused, teller focused, relationship focused, and issue focused) and 15 subcategories. Buller and Burgoon considered three motivations: instrumental, relational (e.g., avoiding relationship problems), and identity (e.g., protecting the liar's image). They predicted that liars would experience more detection apprehension when motivated by self-interest than by relational or identity goals. As a result, instrumentally motivated liars exhibit more nonstrategic behaviors (unintentional behaviors that

Buller & Burgoon, 1996, have described as arousal cues). Those liars were also predicted by Buller and Burgoon to engage in more strategic behaviors, which are behaviors used in the pursuit of high level plans.

The Present Approach to Predicting Cues to Deception: A Self-Presentational Perspective

In 1992, B. M. DePaulo, 1992 described a self-presentational perspective for understanding nonverbal communication. Her formulation was not specific to the communication of deception. In this section, we further articulate her perspective, incorporating subsequent research and theory and specifying the implications of a self-presentational perspective for the prediction of cues to deception. We begin with a review of the incidence and nature of lying in everyday life and a comparison of the lies people typically tell in their lives with the lies studied in the research literature on deception.

Lies in Social Life

Lying is a fact of everyday life. Studies in which people kept daily diaries of all of their lies suggest that people tell an average of one or two lies a day (B. M. DePaulo & Kashy, 1998; B. M. DePaulo, Kashy, et al., 1996; Kashy & DePaulo, 1996; see also Camden et al., 1984; Feldman, Forrest, & Happ, 2002; Hample, 1980; Lippard, 1988; Metts, 1989; Turner et al., 1975). People lie most frequently about their feelings, their preferences, and their attitudes and opinions. Less often, they lie about their actions, plans, and whereabouts. Lies about achievements and failures are also commonplace.

Occasionally, people tell lies in pursuit of material gain, personal convenience, or escape from punishment. Much more commonly, however, the rewards that liars seek are psychological ones. They lie to make themselves appear more sophisticated or more virtuous than they think their true characteristics warrant. They lie to protect themselves, and sometimes others, from disapproval and disagreements and from getting their feelings hurt. The realm of lying, then, is one in which identities are claimed and impressions are managed. It is not a world apart from nondeceptive discourse. Truth tellers edit their self-presentations, too, often in pursuit of the same kinds of goals, but in ways that stay within boundaries of honesty. The presentations of liars are designed to mislead.

There are only a few studies in which people have been asked how they feel about the lies they tell in their everyday lives (B. M. DePaulo & Kashy, 1998; B. M. DePaulo, Kashy, et al., 1996; Kashy & DePaulo, 1996). The results suggest that people regard their everyday lies as little lies of little consequence or regret. They do not spend much time planning them or worrying about the possibility of getting caught. Still, everyday lies do leave a smudge. Although people reported feeling only low levels of distress about their lies, they did feel a bit more uncomfortable while telling their lies, and directly afterwards, than they had felt just before lying. Also, people described the social interactions in which lies were told as more superficial and less pleasant than the interactions in which no lies were told.

Interspersed among these unremarkable lies, in much smaller numbers, are lies that people regard as serious. Most of these lies are told to hide transgressions, which can range from misdeeds such as cheating on tests to deep betrayals of intimacy and trust, such as affairs (B. M. DePaulo, Ansfield, Kirkendol, & Boden, 2002; see also Jones & Burdette, 1993; McCornack & Levine, 1990; Metts,

1994). These lies, especially if discovered, can have serious implications for the liars' identities and reputations.

Lies in Studies of Cues to Deception

In the literature on cues to deception, as in everyday life, lies about personal feelings, facts, and attitudes are the most commonplace. Participants in studies of deception might lie about their opinions on social issues, for example, or about their academic interests or musical preferences. Sometimes emotions are elicited with video clips, and participants try to hide their feelings or simulate entirely different ones. The literature also includes lies about transgressions, as in studies in which participants are induced to cheat on a task and then lie about it. There are a few studies (Hall, 1986; Horvath, 1973; Horvath, Jayne, & Buckley, 1994) of lies about especially serious matters, such as those told by suspects in criminal investigations, and one study (Koper & Sahlman, 2001) of the truthful and deceptive communications of people whose lies were aired in the media (e.g., Richard Nixon, Pete Rose, Susan Smith).

Self-Presentation in Truthful and Deceptive Communications

The prevalence of self-presentational themes in the kinds of lies that people most often tell and in their reasons for telling them suggests the potential power of the self-presentational perspective for predicting cues to deception. Following Schlenker (Schlenker, 1982, Schlenker, 2002; Schlenker & Pontari, 2000), we take a broad view of self-presentation as people's attempts to control the impressions that are formed of them. In self-presenting, people are behaving "in ways that convey certain roles and personal qualities to others" (Pontari & Schlenker, 2000, p. 1092). From this perspective, all deceptive communications involve self-presentation—so do all truthful communications.

Fundamental to the self-presentational perspective is the assumption, based on our understanding of the nature of lying in everyday life, that cues to deception ordinarily are quite weak. There are, however, conditions under which cues are more apparent. As we explain, such moderators of the strength of deception cues can be predicted from the self-presentational processes involved in communicating truthfully and deceptively.

The Deception Discrepancy

Lies vary markedly in the goals they serve and in the kinds of self-presentations enacted to achieve those goals. Yet this vast diversity of lies is united by a single identity claim: the claim of honesty. From the friend who feigns amusement in response to the joke that actually caused hurt feelings to the suspect who claims to have been practicing putts on the night of the murder, liars succeed in their lies only if they seem to be sincere.1 However, this claim to honesty does not distinguish liars from truth tellers either. Truth tellers fail in their social interaction goals just as readily as liars if they seem dishonest. The important difference between the truth teller's claim to honesty and the liar's is that the liar's claim is illegitimate. From this discrepancy between what liars claim and what they believe to be true, we can predict likely cues to deceit.

216

Implications of the Deception Discrepancy

Two implications of the deception discrepancy are most important: First, deceptive self-presentations are often not as convincingly embraced as truthful ones. Second, social actors typically experience a greater sense of deliberateness when their performances are deceptive than when they are honest. These predictions are the starting point for our theoretical analyses. There are also qualifications to the predictions, and we describe those as well.

Deceptive Self-Presentations Are Not as Fully Embraced as Truthful Ones

The most significant implication of the deception discrepancy is that social actors typically are unwilling, or unable, to embrace their false claims as convincingly as they embrace their truthful ones (cf. Mehrabian, 1972; Weiner & Mehrabian, 1968). Several factors undermine the conviction with which liars make their own cases. First, liars, in knowingly making false claims, may suffer moral qualms that do not plague truth tellers. These qualms may account for the faint feelings of discomfort described by the tellers of everyday lies (B. M. DePaulo, Kashy, et al., 1996). Second, even in the absence of any moral misgivings, liars may not have the same personal investment in their claims as do truth tellers. When social actors truthfully describe important aspects of themselves, their emotional investment in their claims may be readily apparent (B. M. DePaulo, Epstein, & LeMay, 1990). Furthermore, those self-relevant claims are backed by an accumulation of knowledge, experience, and wisdom that most liars can only imagine (Markus, 1977). Liars may offer fewer details, not only because they have less familiarity with the domain they are describing, but also to allow for fewer opportunities to be disproved (Vrij, 2000).

In sum, compared with truth tellers, many liars do not have the moral high ground, the emotional investment, or the evidentiary basis for staking their claims. As a result, liars relate their tales in a less compelling manner, and they appear less forthcoming, less pleasant, and more tense.

Deceptive Self-Presenters Are Likely to Experience a Greater Sense of Deliberateness Than Truthful Ones

Cues to deliberateness. When attempting to convey impressions they know to be false, social actors are likely to experience a sense of deliberateness. When instead people are behaving in ways they see as consistent with their attitudes, beliefs, emotions, and self-images, they typically have the sense of "just acting naturally." They are presenting certain roles and personal qualities to others, and they expect to be seen as truthful, but they do not ordinarily experience this as requiring any special effort or attention. Our claim is not that people acting honestly never experience a sense of deliberateness. Sometimes they do, as for example, when the thoughts or feelings they are trying to communicate are difficult to express or when the stakes for a compelling performance are high; however, the focus of their deliberateness is typically limited to the content of their performance and not its credibility. Liars usually make an effort to seem credible; truth tellers more often take their credibility for granted (B. M. DePaulo, LeMay, & Epstein, 1991).[2]

Deliberate attempts to manage impressions, including impressions of credibility, are attempts at self-regulation, and self-regulation consumes mental resources (Baumeister, 1998). Social actors who are performing deceptively may experience greater self-regulatory busyness than those who are performing honestly. Even when the attempted performance is the same (e.g., conveying enthusiasm), the self-regulatory demands may be greater for the liar. Enthusiasm flows effortlessly from those who truly are experiencing enthusiasm, but fakers have to marshal theirs. Liars can be

217

preoccupied with the task of reminding themselves to act the part that truth tellers are not just role-playing but living.

Other thoughts and feelings could also burden liars more than truth tellers (Ekman, 1985/ 1992). These include thoughts about whether the performance is succeeding, feelings about this (e.g., anxiety), and feelings about the fabricated performance (e.g., guilt) or about discreditable past acts that the liar is trying to hide.

To the extent that liars are more preoccupied with these intrusive mental contents than are truth tellers, their performance could suffer. For example, they could seem less involved and engaged in the interaction, and any attempts at cordiality could seem strained. People busy with self-regulatory tasks, compared with those who are not so busy, sometimes process concurrent information less deeply (Gilbert & Krull, 1988; Gilbert, Krull, & Pelham, 1988; Richards & Gross, 1999) and perform less well at subsequent self-regulatory tasks (Baumeister, Bratslavsky, Muraven, & Tice, 1998; Muraven, Tice, & Baumeister, 1998). One potential implication of this regulatory depletion may be that liars fail to notice some of the ways in which the targets of their lies are reacting (cf. Butterworth, 1978). (This is contrary to Buller & Burgoon's, 1996, assumption that liars monitor targets closely for feedback.) Another implication is that liars' busyness could compromise their attempts to generate detailed responses of their own.

One likely response to the offending thoughts and feelings liars experience is to try to control them. For example, liars can try not to think about their blemished past or the insincerity of their ongoing performance. However, attempts at thought suppression can backfire, resulting in even greater preoccupation with those thoughts (Wegner, 1994). Attempts to regulate emotional experiences can also augment rather than dissipate the targeted feelings (e.g., Wegner, Erber, & Zanakos, 1993) and increase physiological activation (Gross, 1998; Gross & Levenson, 1993; Richards & Gross, 1999).

The primary target of liars' efforts at self-regulation, though, is probably not their thoughts and feelings but their overt behaviors. In theory, liars could adopt the goal of trying to appear honest and sincere, which in some instances could involve trying to behave in the generally positive and friendly way that they believe to be more characteristic of truth tellers than of liars (Malone, DePaulo, Adams, & Cooper, 2002). Especially confident and skilled liars may do just that, and succeed (cf. Roney, Higgins, & Shah, 1995). However, it may be more commonplace for people who are misleading others to adopt the defensive goal of trying not to get caught (e.g., Bell & DePaulo, 1996; B. M. DePaulo & Bell, 1996). Liars pursuing this strategy may try to avoid behaving in the ways that they think liars behave. One risk to this strategy is that some of their beliefs about how liars behave may be wrong. For example, social perceivers typically believe that liars cannot stay still; they expect them to fidget, shift their posture, and shake their legs (Malone et al., 2002; Vrij, 2000). In trying to avoid these movements (either directly or as a result of the higher level goal of trying not to give anything away), liars may appear to be holding back. A sense of involvement and positive engagement would be lacking.

Deliberate attempts by liars at controlling expressive behaviors, such as attempts to control thoughts and feelings, can be the seeds of their own destruction (e.g., B. M. DePaulo, 1992; B. M. DePaulo & Friedman, 1998). One route to failure is to try to regulate expressive behaviors, such as tone of voice, that may not be so amenable to willful control (e.g., Scherer, 1986). It is possible, for example, that people's attempts not to sound anxious would result in an even higher pitched and anxious sounding tone of voice than would have resulted if they had not deliberately tried to quiet the sounds of their insecurity. Another path to self-betrayal is to direct efforts at expressive control at the wrong level

(Vallacher & Wegner, 1987; Vallacher, Wegner, McMahan, Cotter, & Larsen, 1992). For example, social actors who ordinarily convey convincing impressions of sincerity and friendliness may instead seem phony if they deliberately try to smile and nod. In focusing on specific behaviors, they may be unwittingly breaking apart the components of the well-practiced and established routine of acting friendly (e.g., Kimble & Perlmuter, 1970). The process may be akin to what happens to experienced typists who try to focus on the location of each of the characters on the keyboard instead of typing in their usual un-self-conscious way. Finally, if some behaviors are more controllable than others, or if liars only try to control some behaviors and not others, discrepancies could develop.

In sum, we predicted that to the extent that liars (more than truth tellers), deliberately try to control their expressive behaviors, thoughts, and feelings, their performances would be compromised. They would seem less forthcoming, less convincing, less pleasant, and more tense.

Moderators of the strength of cues to deliberateness. As the motivation to tell a successful lie increases, liars may redouble their deliberate efforts at self-regulation, resulting in an even more debilitated performance (B. M. DePaulo & Kirkendol, 1989; B. M. DePaulo, Kirkendol, Tang, & O'Brien, 1988; B. M. DePaulo, Stone, & Lassiter, 1985b; see also Ben-Shakhar & Elaad, in press). We tested this proposed moderator of cues to deception by comparing the results of studies in which inducements were offered for success at deceit with studies in which no special attempts were made to motivate the participants.

As we have noted all along, identity-relevant concerns are fundamental to deceptive and nondeceptive communications. They appear even in the absence of any special motivational induction. Such concerns can, however, be exacerbated by incentives that are linked specifically to people's identities and images. In the literature we are reviewing, identity-relevant motivators include ones in which skill at deception was described as indicative of people's competence or of their prospects for success at their chosen careers. Other identity-relevant motivators raised the self-presentational stakes by informing participants that their performances would be evaluated or scrutinized. Compared with other kinds of incentives such as money or material rewards, identity-relevant incentives are more likely to exacerbate public self-awareness, increase rumination, and undermine self-confidence. All of these factors can further disrupt performance (e.g., Baumeister, 1998; Carver & Scheier, 1981; B. M. DePaulo et al., 1991; Wicklund, 1982; Wine, 1971; see also Gibbons, 1990). Consequently, tellers of identity-relevant lies seem especially less forthcoming, less pleasant, and more tense. They also tell tales that seem less compelling.

In sum, our predictions were that cues to deception would be stronger and more numerous among people who have been motivated to succeed in their self-presentations than for those who have not been given any special incentive. This predicted impairment would be even more evident when incentives are identity relevant than when they are not.

Qualifications. There are two important qualifications to our discussion of the effects of deliberate attempts at self-regulation. One is that an increase in self-regulatory demands does not always result in a decrement in performance. When attempts at self-regulation shift the focus of attention away from negative self-relevant thoughts (Pontari & Schlenker, 2000) or from the individual components of the task (Lewis & Linder, 1997), performance can improve.

The second is that the self-regulatory demands of lying do not always exceed those of telling the truth. For example, honest but insecure actors may be more preoccupied with thoughts of failure than deceptive but cocky ones. In addition, for most any social actor, the telling of truths that impugn the truth teller's character or cause pain or harm to others may pose far greater self-regulatory challenges than the telling of lies about the same topics.

Finally, it is important, as always, to bear in mind the nature of the lies that people tell in their everyday lives. Most are little lies that are so often practiced and told with such equanimity that the self-regulatory demands may be nearly indistinguishable from the demands of telling the truth. Therefore, we expected the consequences of deliberate self-regulation that we have described to be generally weak and that stronger effects of attempted control would be evident in studies in which participants were motivated to get away with their lies, particularly if the motivations were identity relevant.

The Formulation of Deceptive and Nondeceptive Presentations

The self-regulatory demands we have just described are those involved in executing the deceptive and nondeceptive performances. Earlier descriptions of deceptive communications focused primarily on the processes involved in formulating lies. We consider those next. As we elaborate below, we reject the argument that lies are necessarily more difficult to construct than truths. Still, we predicted that lies would generally be shorter and less detailed than truths. In doing so, we drew from the literatures on the use of scripts as guides to storytelling, the differences between accounts of events that have or have not been personally experienced, and lay misconceptions about the nature of truthful communications.

Cues to the Formulation of Lies

Previous formulations have typically maintained that it is more difficult to lie than to tell the truth because telling lies involves the construction of new and never-experienced tales whereas telling the truth is a simple matter of telling it like it is (e.g., Buller & Burgoon, 1996; Miller & Stiff, 1993; Zuckerman et al., 1981; but see McCornack, 1997, for an important exception). We disagree with both assumptions—that lies always need to be assembled and that truths can simply be removed from the box. When the truth is hard to tell (e.g., when it would hurt the other person's feelings), then a careful piecing together of just the right parts in just the right way would be in order. But even totally mundane and nonthreatening truths can be conveyed in a nearly infinite variety of shapes and sizes. For example, in response to the question "How was your day?" on a day when nothing special happened, the answer could be "Fine," a listing of the main events (but, what counts as a main event?), or a description of a part of the day. Even in the latter instance, there is no one self-evident truth. As much work on impression management has indicated (e.g., Schlenker, 1980, Schlenker, 1985), presentations are edited differently depending on identity-relevant cues, such as the teller's relationship with the other person and the interaction goals. Yet all of this editing can occur within the bounds of truthfulness.

Truths, then, are not often prepackaged. But lies can be. A teenage girl who had permission to spend the night at a girlfriend's home but instead went camping with a boyfriend may have no difficulty spinning a tale to tell to her parents the next morning. For example, she can easily access a script for what spending the night at a girlfriend's home typically involves. Or, she could relate her best friend's favorite story about an evening at the home of a girlfriend. Lies based on scripts or familiar stories are unlikely to be marked by the signs of mental effort (described below) that may characterize lies that are fabricated. The teller of scripts and of familiar stories may also be less likely to get tangled in contradictions than the liar who makes up a new story.

220

Even prepackaged lies, however, may be shorter and less detailed than truthful answers. Liars working from scripts may have only the basics of the scripted event in mind (e.g., Smith, 1998), and liars who have borrowed their stories have at hand only those details they were told (and of those, only the ones they remember).

All lies, whether scripted, borrowed, or assembled anew, could be shorter and less detailed than truthful accounts for another reason: The truthful accounts are based on events that were actually experienced, whereas the lies are not. The literature on reality monitoring (e.g., Johnson & Raye, 1981) suggests ways in which memories of past experiences or perceptions (i.e., memories based on external sources) differ from memories of experiences that were imagined (i.e., memories based on internal sources). This perspective can be applied to the prediction of cues to deception only by extrapolation, because reality monitoring describes processes of remembering whereas deception describes processes of relating (Vrij, 2000). In relating a story, even a truthful one, people often fill in gaps and in other ways create a more coherent tale than their memories actually support. Nonetheless, deceptive accounts may differ from truthful ones in ways that weakly parallel the ways in which memories of imagined experiences differ from memories of externally based experiences. If so, then truthful accounts would be clearer, more vivid, and more realistic than deceptive ones, and they would include more sensory information and contextual cues. Deceptive accounts, in contrast, should be more likely to include references to cognitive processes such as thoughts and inferences made at the time of the event.

The conventional wisdom that lies are more difficult to formulate than truths is most likely to be supported when liars make up new stories. Lies that are fabricated mostly from scratch are likely to be shorter and more internally inconsistent than truths and to be preceded by longer latencies. Signs of mental effort may also be evident. These could include increases in pauses and speech disturbances (Berger, Karol, & Jordan, 1989; Butterworth & Goldman-Eisler, 1979; Christenfeld, 1994; Goldman-Eisler, 1968; Mahl, 1987; Schachter, Christenfeld, Ravina, & Bilous, 1991; Siegman, 1987), more pupil dilation (E. H. Hess & Polt, 1963; Kahneman, 1973; Kahneman & Beatty, 1967; Kahneman, Tursky, Shapiro, & Crider, 1969; Stanners, Coulter, Sweet, & Murphy, 1979; Stern & Dunham, 1990), decreased blinking (Bagley & Manelis, 1979; Holland & Tarlow, 1972, Holland & Tarlow, 1975; Wallbott & Scherer, 1991), and decreased eye contact (Fehr & Exline, 1987). People who are preoccupied with the formulation of a complex lie may appear to be less involved and expressive, as well as less forthcoming.

Unfortunately, in the literature we are reviewing, liars were almost never asked how they came up with their lies, and truth tellers were not asked how they decided which version of the truth to relate (e.g., a short version or a long one). In the only study we know of in which liars were asked about the origins of their lies (Malone, Adams, Anderson, Ansfield, & DePaulo, 1997), the most common answer was not any we have considered so far. More than half the time, liars said that they based their lies on experiences from their own lives, altering critical details. With this strategy, liars may be just as adept as truth tellers at accessing a wealth of details, including clear and vivid sensory details.

Still, even the most informed and advantaged liars may make mistakes if they share common misconceptions of what truthful accounts really are like (Vrij, Edward, & Bull, 2001). For example, if liars believe that credible accounts are highly structured and coherent, with few digressions or inessential details, their accounts may be smoother and more pat than those of truth tellers. The embedding of a story in its spatial and temporal context and the relating of the specifics of the conversation may provide a richness to the accounts of truth tellers that liars do not even think to simulate. Liars may also fail to appreciate that memory is fallible and reporting skills are imperfect even when people are telling the truth and that truth tellers who are not concerned about their credibility may not be defensive about admitting their uncertainties. Consequently, truth tellers may express self-doubts, claim they do not remember things, or spontaneously correct something they already said, whereas liars would scrupulously avoid such admissions of imperfection. The stories told by liars, then, would be too good to be true.

Liars can also fail if they know less than their targets do about the topic of the deceit. The babysitter who claims to have taken the kids to the zoo and relates how excited they were to see the lion, would be undone by the parent who knows that there are no lions at that zoo. The man suspected of being a pedophile who points to his service as leader of his church's youth group may believe he is painting a picture of a pillar of the community, whereas instead he has unwittingly described just the sort of volunteer work that is a favorite of known pedophiles (Steller & Kohnken, 1989; Undeutsch, 1989; Yuille & Cutshall, 1989).3

Moderators of Cues to the Formulation of Lies

Factors that alter the cognitive load for liars are candidates for moderators of cognitive cues to deception. We consider two such moderators in this review: the opportunity to plan a presentation and the duration of that presentation.

Liars who have an opportunity to plan their difficult lies, relative to those who must formulate their lies on the spot, may be able to generate more compelling presentations (e.g., H. D. O'Hair, Cody, & McLaughlin, 1981; Vrij, 2000). Because they can do some of their thinking in advance, their response latencies could be shorter and their answers longer. However, mistakes that follow from misconceptions about the nature of truthful responses would not be averted by planning and may even be exacerbated.

We think that, in theory, cues to deception could occur even for the simplest lies. For example, when just a "yes" or "no" answer is required, a lie could be betrayed by a longer response latency in instances in which the truth comes to mind more readily and must be set aside and replaced by the lie (Walczyk, Roper, & Seeman, in press). However, we believe that the cognitive burdens generally would be greater when a short answer would not suffice and that cues to deception would therefore become clearer and more numerous as the duration of the response increases. For example, lies may be especially briefer than truths when people are expected to tell a story rather than to respond with just a few words. Also, liars who are experiencing affects and emotions that they are trying to hide may be more likely to show those feelings when they need to sustain their lies longer (cf. Ekman, 1985/ 1992).

The Role of Identity-Relevant Emotions in Deceptive and Nondeceptive Presentations

People experience the unpleasant emotional state of guilt when they have done something wrong or believe that others may think that they have (Baumeister, Stillwell, & Heatherton, 1994). Even more aversive is the feeling of shame that occurs when people fail to meet their own personal moral standards (Keltner & Buswell, 1996; Tangney, Miller, Flicker, & Barlow, 1996; see also Scheff, 2001). Some lies, especially serious ones, are motivated by a desire to cover up a personal failing or a discreditable thought, feeling, or deed (e.g., B. M. DePaulo, Ansfield, et al., 2002). Yet those who tell the truth about their transgressions or failings may feel even greater guilt and shame than those whose shortcomings remain hidden by their lies. If the behavior of truthful transgressors was compared with that of deceptive transgressors, cues to these self-conscious emotions would be more in evidence for the truth tellers, if they distinguished them from the liars at all. In most studies, however (including all of the studies of transgressions included in this review), liars who had transgressed were compared with truth tellers who had not. For those comparisons, then, we expected to find that liars, compared with truth tellers, showed more shame and guilt cues.

There is no documented facial expression that is specific to guilt; therefore, we expected to find only more general cues to negativity and distress (Keltner & Buswell, 1996; Keltner & Harker, 1998). Shame, however, does seem to have a characteristic demeanor that includes gaze aversion, a closed posture, and a tendency to withdraw (Keltner & Harker, 1998).

Lies about transgressions, though, are the exceptions, both in everyday life and in the studies in this review. The more commonplace lies cover truths that are not especially discrediting. For example, people may not feel that it is wrong to have an opinion that differs from someone else's or to hide their envy of a coworker's success. In most instances, then, we did not, on the basis of the hidden information alone, expect to find more guilt cues in liars than in truth tellers.

By definition, though, there is a sense in which all liars are candidates for experiencing guilt and shame, as they all have done something that could be considered wrong: They have intentionally misled someone. Truth tellers have not. It is important to note, however, that liars do not always feel badly about their lies, and truth tellers do not always feel good about their honesty. In fact, liars often claim that in telling their lies, they have spared their targets from the greater distress that would have resulted had they told the truth (B. M. DePaulo, Kashy, et al., 1996).

Guilt and shame are not the only emotions that have been hypothesized to betray liars. Fear of being detected has also been described as responsible for cues to deception (e.g., Ekman, 1985/ 1992). We believed fear of detection would also vary importantly with factors such as the nature of the behavior that is covered by the lie. Liars would fear detection when hiding behaviors such as transgressions, which often elicit punishment or disapproval. But the more typical liars, those who claim that their movie preferences match those of their dates or who conceal their pride in their own work, would have little to fear from the discovery of that hidden information.

People may fear detection not only because of the nature of the behavior they are hiding but also because of the implications of being perceived as dishonest (Schlenker, Pontari, & Christopher, 2001). The blemishes in perceived and self-perceived integrity that could result from a discovered deception depend on factors such as the justifiability of the deceit and are often quite minimal. But even utterly trivial lies told in the spirit of kindness, such as false reassurances about new and unbecoming hairstyles, have identity implications if discovered. For instance, the purveyors of such kind lies may be less often trusted when honest feedback really is desired.

Across all of the lies in our data set, we expected to find weak cues to anxiety and negativity. For example, liars may look and sound more anxious than truth tellers (Slivken & Buss, 1984) and speak less fluently (Kasl & Mahl, 1965; Mahl, 1987) and in a higher pitch (Kappas, Hess, & Scherer, 1991; Scherer, 1986). They may also blink more (Harrigan & O'Connell, 1996), and their pupils may be more dilated (Scott, Wells, Wood, & Morgan, 1967; Simpson & Molloy, 1971; Stanners et al., 1979). Relative to truth tellers, liars may also make more negative statements and complaints, sound less pleasant, and look less friendly and less attractive. In a moderator analysis comparing lies about transgressions with other kinds of lies, we expected to find more pronounced distress cues in the lies about transgressions.

Convergent Perspectives on the Strength of Cues to Deceit

Our self-presentational perspective has led us to reject the view that lie telling is typically a complicated, stressful, guilt-inducing process that produces clear and strong cues. Instead, we believe that most deceptive presentations are so routinely and competently executed that they leave only faint behavioral residues. Fiedler and Walka (1993) offered a similar point of view. They argued that ordinary people are so practiced, so proficient, and so emotionally unfazed by the telling of untruths that they can be regarded as professional liars. Therefore, they also expected to find mostly only weak links between verbal and nonverbal behaviors and the telling of lies. Bond, Kahler, and Paolicelli (1985), arguing from an evolutionary perspective, drew a similar conclusion. Any blatantly obvious cues to deceit, they contended, would have been recognized by human perceivers long ago; evolution favors more flexible deceivers.

Methodological Implications of the Self-Presentational Perspective

Our self-presentational perspective suggests that social actors try to convey particular impressions of themselves, both when lying and when telling the truth, and that social perceivers routinely form impressions of others. We have conceptualized the ways in which lies could differ from truths in terms of the different impressions that deceptive self-presentations could convey. For example, we hypothesized that liars would seem more distant than truth tellers. One way to assess differences in distancing is to code the many behaviors believed to be indicative of nonimmediacy, such as the use of the passive rather than the active voice, the use of negations rather than assertions, and looking away rather than maintaining eye contact. This approach, which is the usual one, has the advantage that the behaviors of interest are clearly defined and objectively measured. However, for many of the kinds of impressions that social actors attempt to convey, the full range of behaviors that contribute to the impression may be unknown. For example, Wiener and Mehrabian (Wiener and Mehrabian, 1968; Mehrabian, 1972) have described a precise set of behaviors that they believed to be indicative of verbal and nonverbal immediacy and have reported some supportive data. However, others who have discussed immediacy and related constructs have included other cues (e.g., Brown & Levinson, 1987; Fleming, 1994; Fleming & Rudman, 1993; Holtgraves, 1986; Searle, 1975). This raises the possibility that social perceivers, who can often form valid impressions even from rather thin slices of social behavior (e.g., Ambady & Rosenthal, 1992), can discriminate truths from lies by their subjective impressions of the constructs of interest (e.g., distancing) just as well, if not better, than can objective coding systems (cf. B. M. DePaulo, 1994; Malone & DePaulo, 2001). To test this possibility, we used objective and subjective measurement as levels of a moderator variable in analyses of cues for which multiple independent estimates of both levels were available.

Summary of Predictions

Predicted Cues

The self-presentational perspective predicts five categories of cues to deception. First, liars are predicted to be less forthcoming than truth tellers. The model predicts they will respond less, and in less detail, and they will seem to be holding back. For example, liars' response latencies would be longer (an indication of cognitive complexity in the Zuckerman et al., 1981, model) and their speech would be slower (a thinking cue in Ekman's, 1985/ 1992, formulation). Second, the tales told by liars are predicted to be less compelling than those told by truth tellers. Specifically, liars would seem to make less sense than truth tellers (e.g., there would be more discrepancies in their accounts), and they would seem less engaging, less immediate, more uncertain, less fluent, and less active than truth tellers. Zuckerman et al. (1981) predicted that discrepancies would occur as a result of attempted control, and Ekman (1985/ 1992) regarded them as a thinking cue. Less immediacy (more distancing) was described as a possible cue to detection apprehension and guilt by Ekman (1985/ 1992) and Zuckerman et al. (1981), and it was regarded as a strategic behavior by Buller and Burgoon (1996).

The self-presentational perspective also predicts that liars will be less positive and pleasant than truth tellers, as is also suggested by the description of cues to guilt and apprehensiveness put forth by Ekman (1985/ 1992) and Zuckerman et al. (1981). The fourth prediction of the self-presentational perspective is that liars will be more tense than truth tellers. Some cues to tension, such as higher pitch, have sometimes been conceptualized as indicative of undifferentiated arousal (e.g., Zuckerman et al., 1981). Finally, the self-presentational perspective alone predicts that liars will include fewer ordinary imperfections and unusual contents in their stories than will truth tellers.

Predicted Moderators

A number of perspectives, including the self-presentational one, maintain that cues to deception, when combined across all lies, will be weak. However, several factors are predicted to moderate the strength of the cues. From a self-presentational point of view, cues to negativity and tension should be stronger when lies are about transgressions than when they are not. The self-presentation formulation also maintains that cues will be clearer and more numerous when told under conditions of high motivation to succeed, especially when the motivation is identity relevant. Buller and Burgoon (1996), in contrast, predicted stronger cues when the liars' motives are instrumental. They also predicted more pleasantness, immediacy, composure, and fluency with increasing interactivity.

The self-presentation model predicts that for social actors who have an opportunity to plan their performances, compared with those who do not, response latency will be a less telling cue to deception. Also, as the duration of a response increases, cues to deception will be more in evidence. Finally, the model predicts that cues assessed by subjective impressions will more powerfully discriminate truths from lies than the same cues assessed objectively.

A predicted moderator of cues to deception can be tested only if the moderator variable can be reliably coded from the information that is reported and if multiple estimates of the relevant cues are available for each of the levels of the moderator. Some of the predictions generated by the perspectives we have reviewed could not be tested, and that obstacle limited our ability to evaluate each of the perspectives comprehensively. The self-presentational perspective, for example, points to the potential importance of a number of moderators we could not test, such as the communicator's confidence and focus of attention and the emotional implications of the truths or lies for the targets of those messages. The self-presentational perspective, as well as the formulations of Ekman (1985/ 1992) and Buller and Burgoon (1996), all suggest that the liar's relationship with the target may be another important moderator of cues to deception (see also Anderson, DePaulo, & Ansfield, 2002; Levine & McCornack, 1992; Stiff, Kim, & Ramesh, 1992). However, the number of studies in which the liars and targets were not strangers was too small to test this moderator.

Method

Literature Search Procedures

We used literature search procedures recommended by Cooper (1998) to retrieve relevant studies. First, we conducted computer-based searches of Psychological Abstracts (PsycLIT) and Dissertation Abstracts International through September of 1995 using the key words deception, deceit, lie, and detection and combinations of those words. Second, we examined the reference lists from previous reviews (B. M. DePaulo et al., 1985a; Zuckerman et al., 1981; Zuckerman & Driver, 1985). Third, we reviewed the reference lists from more than 300 articles on the communication of deception from Bella M. DePaulo's personal files and the references lists from any new articles added as a result of the computer search. Fourth, we sent letters requesting relevant papers to 62 scholars who had published on the communication of deception. We also asked those scholars to continue to send us their papers in the coming years. We repeated our computer search in October of 1999. No other reports were added after that date.

Criteria for Inclusion and Exclusion of Studies

We included reports in which behavior while lying was compared with behavior while telling the truth. Behaviors that were measured objectively, as well as those based on others' impressions (e.g., impressions that the social actors seemed nervous or evasive), were all included. Physiological indices with no discernible behavioral manifestation (e.g., galvanic skin response, heart rate) were not included, nor were senders' (i.e., social actors') reports of their own behaviors. We excluded reports that were not in English and reports in which the senders were not adults (i.e., under 17 years old). We included data from adult senders in reports of children and adults if we could compute effect sizes separately for the subset of the data in which both the senders and the judges were adults. We excluded reports in which senders role-played an imagined person in an imagined situation because we were concerned that the imaginary aspects of these paradigms could sever the connection between social actors and their self-presentations that is important to our theoretical analysis.

There were several reports from which we could not extract useful data. For example, Yerkes and Berry (1909) reported one experiment based on just one sender and another based on two. Studies comparing different kinds of lies without also comparing them with truths (e.g., di Battista & Abrahams, 1995) were not included. Studies describing individual differences in cues to deception that did not also report overall differences between truths and lies (e.g., Siegman & Reynolds, 1983) were also excluded. A series of reports based on the same independent sample (e.g., Buller, Burgoon, Buslig, & Roiger, 1996, Study 2) were excluded as well. (For a detailed explanation, see B. M. DePaulo, Ansfield, & Bell, 1996).

Determining Independent Samples

Our final data set consisted of 120 independent samples from 116 reports (see Table 1). Of those 120 samples in our review, only 32 were included in the Zuckerman et al. (1981) review.4

[**Table 1** is available from Bella DePaulo: BellaDePaulo [at] gmail.com.]

Most often, the behaviors of a particular sample of senders were described in just one report. For example, Bond et al. (1985) coded 11 different cues from 34 different senders. The behaviors of those 34 senders were not described in any other report. Therefore, we considered the sample of senders from that study to be an independent sample. Sometimes senders were divided into different subgroups (e.g., men and women, Jordanians and Americans, senders who planned their messages and different senders who did not), and cues to deception were reported separately for each of those subgroups. In those instances, we considered each of the subgroups to be an independent sample. For example, Bond, Omar, Mahmoud, and Bonser (1990) coded 10 different cues separately for the 60 Jordanian senders and the 60 American senders. Therefore, the Jordanian senders were one independent sample and the Americans were another. In 11 instances, data from the same senders were published in different reports. For example, Hadjistavropoulos and Craig (1994) coded 11 cues from 90 senders, and Hadjistavropoulos, Craig, Hadjistavropoulos, and Poole (1996) coded two cues from the same 90 senders. Therefore, the samples described in those two reports were not independent. In Table 1, they have the same letter code in the column labeled "Ind. sample code." Most samples listed in Table 1 have no letter code in that column; all of those samples are independent samples.

All estimates of a particular cue were included in the analyses of that cue. We used independent sample codes, not to exclude data, but to estimate degrees of freedom properly and to weight estimates appropriately. As we explain in more detail below, multiple estimates of the same cue that came from the same independent sample were averaged before being entered into the analyses.

Cue Definitions

Within the sample of studies, 158 different behaviors or impressions, which we call cues to deception, were reported. These are defined in Appendix A. We categorized most of the 158 cues into the five categories that followed from our theoretical analysis. To determine whether liars are less forthcoming than truth tellers, we looked at cues indicative of the amount of their responding (e.g., response length), the level of detail and complexity of their responses, and the degree to which they seemed to be holding back (e.g., pressing lips; Keltner, Young, Heerey, Oemig, & Monarch, 1998). To explore whether liars tell less compelling tales than truth tellers, we examined cues indicating whether the presentations seemed to make sense (e.g., plausibility), whether they were engaging (e.g., involving), and whether they were immediate (e.g., eye contact) instead of distancing. Self-presentations that fell short on characteristics such as certainty, fluency, or animation may also seem less compelling, so we included those cues, too. In the third category, we included cues indicating whether liars are less positive and pleasant than truth tellers, and in the fourth, we collected behaviors indicating whether liars are more tense than truth tellers. Finally, in the last category, we determined whether deceptive self-presentations included fewer ordinary imperfections and unusual contents than truthful ones by examining cues such as spontaneous corrections and descriptions of superfluous details.

For clarity, we assigned a number, from 1 to 158, to each cue. Cue numbers are shown along with the cue names and definitions in Appendix A. The last column of Table 1 lists all of the cues reported in each study and the number of estimates of each.

[Appendix A is available from Bella DePaulo: BellaDePaulo [at] gmail.com.]

Variables Coded From Each Report

From each report, we coded characteristics of the senders, characteristics of the truths and lies, publication statistics, and methodological aspects of the studies (see Table 2). In the category of sender characteristics we coded the population sampled (e.g., students, suspects in crimes, patients in pain clinics, people from the community), the senders' country, and the relationship between the sender and the interviewer or target of the communications (e.g., strangers, acquaintances, friends). We also coded senders' race or ethnicity and their precise ages, but this information was rarely reported and therefore could not be analyzed.

Table 2

Summary of Study Characteristics

Characteristic	k	Characteristic	k
Senders		**Truths and Lies**	
Population sampled		**Length of messages**	
Students	101	Under 20 sec	14
Suspects	3	20-60 sec	14
Community members and students	3	More than 60 sec	8
Patients in a pain clinic	2	Unable to determine from report	84
Community members	2	**Message preparation**	
Immigrants to United States	2	No preparation	44
Salespersons and customers	1	Messages were prepared	43
Travelers in an airport	1	Some prepared, some unprepared	18
Shoppers in a shopping center	1	Messages were scripted	7
Heroin addicts (and nonaddicts)	1	Unable to determine from report	8
Publicly exposed liars	1	**Paradigm**	
Unable to determine from report	2	Described attitudes or facts	44
Country		Described films, slides, or pictures	16
United States	88	Cheating	8
Canada	9	Mock crime	8
Germany	7	Card test or guilty knowledge test	8
England	4	Person descriptions	7
Spain	3	Simulated job interview	6
Japan	2	Described personal experiences	5
Immigrants to United States	2	Naturalistic	4
Jordan	1	Responded to personality items	3
Italy	1	Reactions to pain	3
Romania	1	Other paradigms	7
The Netherlands and England	1	Unable to determine from report	1
The Netherlands and Surinam	1	**Lies were about transgressions**	
Relation betw sender & interviewer or target		No	99
Strangers	103	Yes	21
Acquaintances	2	**Publication Statistics**	
Acquaintances or friends and strangers	2	**Year of report**	
Friends	1	Before 1970	3
Intimates, friends, and strangers	1	1970-1979	34
No interviewer	9	1980-1989	46
Unable to determine from report	2	1990-2000	37
Motivation for telling successful lies		**Source of Study**	
None	68	Journal article	96
Identity relevant	13	Dissertation, thesis	10
Instrumental	31	Book chapter	4
Identity and instrumental	8	Unpublished paper	3
		Multiple sources	7

(continued on next page)

(Table 2 *continued*)

Characteristic	k
Methodological aspects	
Sample size (no. of senders)	
5-20	41
21-59	43
60-192	36
Experimental design	
Within-sender (senders told truths and lies)	78
Between-senders (senders told truths or lies)	42
In between-sender designs, number of liars	
Fewer than 20	15
20-32	16
More than 32	11
In between-sender designs, number of truth tellers	
Fewer than 20	15
20-32	13
More than 32	14
Number of messages communicated by each sender	
1	21
2-4	59
More than 4	40
Degree of interaction between sender and interviewer or target	
No interaction	12
Partial interaction	83
Fully interactive	8
No one else present	12
Unable to determine from report	4
Reliability of measurement of cues [a, b]	
Under .70	36
.70-.79	43
.80-.89	251
.90-1.00	239
Unable to determine from report	769

[a] Includes correlational measures as well as percentage of agreement (divided by 100).

[b] k refers to number of estimates (not number of independent estimates).

To test our predictions about the links between senders' motivations and cues to deception, we determined whether senders had identity-relevant incentives, instrumental incentives, both kinds of incentives, or no special incentives. Coded as identity-relevant were studies in which senders' success was described as indicative of their competence at their chosen profession or reflective of their intelligence or other valued characteristics. Also included were studies in which senders expected to be evaluated or scrutinized. Studies in which senders were motivated by money or material rewards were coded as primarily instrumental. Studies in which both incentives were offered to senders were classified separately.

The characteristics of the messages that we coded included their duration and whether senders had an opportunity to prepare. If senders had an opportunity to prepare some but not all of their messages, but behavioral differences were not reported separately, we classified the study as having some prepared and some unprepared messages. In other studies, the messages were scripted. For example, senders may have been instructed to give a particular response in order to hold verbal cues constant so that investigators could assess nonverbal characteristics of truths and lies more precisely.

We also coded the experimental paradigm used to elicit the truths and lies or the context in which they occurred. In some studies, senders lied or told the truth about their beliefs or opinions or about personal facts. In others, senders looked at videotapes, films, slides, or pictures and described (text continues on page 89) what they were seeing truthfully or deceptively. In cheating paradigms, senders were or were not induced to cheat and then lie about it. Mock crime paradigms included ones in which some of the senders were instructed to "steal" money or to hide supposed contraband on their persons and to then lie to interviewers about their crime. Some paradigms involved card tests (in which the senders chose a particular card and answered "no" when asked if they had that card) and guilty knowledge tests (in which senders who did or did not know critical information, such as information about a crime, were asked about that information); most of these were modeled after tests often used in polygraph testing. In person-description paradigms, senders described other people (e.g., people they liked and people they disliked) honestly and dishonestly. Some paradigms were simulations of job interviews; typically in those paradigms, senders who were or were not qualified for a job tried to convince an interviewer that they were qualified. In other paradigms, participants described personal experiences (e.g., times during which they acted especially independently or dependently; traumatic experiences that did or did not actually happen to them). Naturalistic paradigms were defined as ones in which the senders were not instructed to tell truths or lies but instead did so of their own accord. These included interrogations of suspects later determined to have been lying or telling the truth (Hall, 1986; Horvath, 1973; Horvath, Jayne, & Buckley, 1994) and a study (Koper & Sahlman, 2001) of people who made public statements later exposed as lies. In another paradigm, senders indicated their responses to a series of items on a personality scale, then later lied or told the truth about their answers to those items. In a final category, senders who really were or were not experiencing pain sometimes expressed their pain freely and other times masked their pain or feigned pain that they were not experiencing. A few other paradigms used in fewer than three independent samples were assigned to a miscellaneous category.

We recoded the paradigms into two categories to test our prediction that lies about transgressions would produce clearer cues than lies that were not about transgressions. The lies about mock crimes or real crimes, cheating, and other misdeeds were categorized as lies about transgressions, the others as lies that were not about transgressions.

The two publication statistics that we coded were the year of the report and the source of the report (e.g., journal article, dissertation, thesis). In some instances, the same data were reported in two places (typically a dissertation and a journal article); in those cases, we coded the more accessible report (i.e., the journal article).

The methodological aspects of the studies that we coded included the sample size and the design of the study. The design was coded as within senders if each sender told both truths and lies or between senders if each sender told either truths or lies. This determination was based on the messages that were included in the analyses of the behavioral cues. For example, if senders told both truths and lies, but the cues to deception were assessed from just one truth or one lie told by each sender, the design was coded as between senders. For each between-senders study, we coded the number of liars and the number of truth tellers. For all studies, we coded the total number of messages communicated by each sender.

We also coded the degree of interaction between the sender and the interviewer or target person. Fully interactive paradigms were ones in which the senders and interviewers interacted freely, with no scripts. In partially interactive paradigms, the senders and interviewers interacted, but the interviewers' behavior was typically constrained, usually by a predetermined set of questions they were instructed to ask. In noninteractive paradigms, an interviewer or target person was present in the room but did not interact with the sender. In still other paradigms, the senders told truths and lies (usually into a tape recorder) with no one else present.

We categorized each cue as having been either objectively or subjectively assessed. Behaviors that could be precisely defined and measured (often in units such as counts and durations) were coded as objectively assessed. Cues were coded as subjectively assessed when they were based on observers' impressions.

Behavioral cues were usually coded from videotapes, audiotapes, or transcripts of the truths and lies. If reliabilities of the measures of the cues were reported (percentages or correlations), we recorded them.

We attempted to compute the effect size for each cue in each study. To this end, we indicated whether the effect sizes were (a) ones that could be precisely calculated (which we call known effects), (b) ones for which only the direction of the effect was known, or (c) effects that were simply reported as not significant (and for which we were unable to discern the direction).

Coding decisions were initially made by James J. Lindsay, Laura Muhlenbruck, and Kelly Charlton, who had participated in standard training procedures (discussion of definitions, practice coding, discussion of disagreements) before beginning their task. Each person coded two thirds of the studies. Therefore, each study was coded by two people and discrepancies were resolved in conference. For objective variables such as the year and the source of the report, the percentage of disagreements was close to zero. The percentage ranged as high as 12 for more subjective decisions, such as the initial categorization of paradigms into more than 12 different categories. However, agreement on the two levels of the paradigm variable that were used in the moderator analysis (transgressions vs. no transgressions) was again nearly perfect. Bella M. DePaulo also independently coded all study characteristics, and any remaining discrepancies were resolved in consultation with Brian E. Malone, who was not involved in any of the previous coding. A meta-analysis of accuracy at detecting deception (Bond & DePaulo, 2002) included some of the same studies that are in this review. Some of the same study characteristics were coded for that review in the same manner as for this one. Final decisions about each characteristic were compared across reviews. There were no discrepancies.

Meta-Analytic Techniques

Effect Size Estimate

The effect size computed for each behavioral difference was d, defined as the mean for the deceptive condition (i.e., the lies) minus the mean for the truthful condition (i.e., the truths), divided by the mean of the standard deviations for the truths and the lies (Cohen, 1988). Positive ds therefore indicate that the behavior occurred more often during lies than truths, whereas negative ds indicate that the behavior occurred less often during lies than truths. In cases in which means and standard deviations were not provided but other relevant statistics were (e.g., rs, χ^2s, ts, or Fs with 1 df) or in which corrections were necessary because of the use of within-sender designs (i.e., the same senders told both truths and lies), we used other methods to compute ds (e.g., Hedges & Becker, 1986; Rosenthal, 1991).

With just a few exceptions, we computed effect sizes for every comparison of truths and lies reported in every study. For example, if the length of deceptive messages relative to truthful ones was measured in terms of number of words and number of seconds, we computed both ds. If the same senders conveyed different kinds of messages (e.g., ones in which they tried to simulate different emotions and ones in which they tried to mask the emotions they were feeling) and separate ds were reported for each, we computed both sets of ds. We excluded a few comparisons in cases in which the behavior described was uninterpretable outside of the context of the specific study and in which an effect size could be computed but the direction of the effect was impossible to determine. Also, if preliminary data for a particular cue were reported in one source and more complete data on the same cue were reported subsequently, we included only the more complete data.

If the difference between truths and lies was described as not significant, but no further information was reported, the d for that effect was set to zero. If the direction of the effect could be determined, but not the precise magnitude, we used a conservative strategy of assigning the value +0.01 when the behavior occurred more often during lies than truths and −0.01 when it occurred less often during lies than truths. This procedure resulted in a total of 1,338 effect sizes. Of these, 787 could be estimated precisely, 396 were set to zero, and 155 were assigned the values of ±0.01. Twenty-seven (2%) of the effect sizes (ds) were greater than ±1.50 and were windsorized to ±1.50.

Estimates of Central Tendency

The most fundamental issue addressed by this review is the extent to which each cue is associated with deceit. To estimate the magnitude of the effect size for each cue, we averaged within cues and within independent samples. For example, within a particular independent sample, all estimates of response length were averaged. As a result, each independent sample could contribute to the analyses no more than one estimate of any given cue. Table 1 shows the number of effect sizes computed for each report and the number of cues assessed in each report. If the number of effect sizes is greater than the number of cues, then there was more than one estimate of at least one of the cues.

The mean d for each cue within each independent sample was weighted to take into account the number of senders in the sample.5 Sample sizes ranged from 5 to 192 (M = 41.73, SD = 31.93) and are shown in the second column of Table 1. Because larger samples provide more reliable estimates of effect sizes than do smaller ones, larger studies were weighted more heavily in the analyses. For within-sender designs, we weighted each effect size by the reciprocal of its variance. For between-senders designs, we computed the weight from the formula: $[2(n_1 + n_2)n_1n_2]/[2(n_1 + n_2)2 + (n_1n_2d_2)]$. A mean d is significant if the confidence interval does not include zero.

To determine whether the variation in effect sizes for each cue was greater than that expected by chance across independent samples, we computed the homogeneity statistic Q, which is distributed as chi-square with degrees of freedom equal to the number of independent samples (k) minus 1. The p level associated with the Q statistic describes the likelihood that the observed variance in effect sizes was generated by sampling error alone (Hedges & Olkin, 1985).

Moderator Analyses

We have described several factors that have been predicted to moderate the size of the cues to deception: whether an incentive was provided for success, the type of incentive that was provided (identity relevant or instrumental), whether the messages were planned or unplanned, the duration of the messages, whether the lies were about transgressions, and whether the context was interactive. All of the moderator variables except planning were ones that could be examined only on a between-studies basis. For example, it was usually the case that in any given study, all of the senders who lied were lying about a transgression or they were all lying about something other than a transgression. Conclusions based on those analyses (e.g., that the senders' apparent tension is a stronger cue to lies about transgressions than to lies that are not about transgressions) are open to alternative interpretations. Any way that the studies differed (other than the presence or absence of a transgression) could explain the transgression differences.

Stronger inferences can be drawn when the levels of the moderator variable occur within the same study. Seven independent samples (indicated in Table 1) included a manipulation of whether senders' messages were planned or unplanned.6 For each cue reported in each of these studies, we computed a d for the difference in effect sizes between the unplanned and planned messages. We then combined these ds in the same manner as we had in our previous analyses.

Of the remaining moderator variables, all except one (the duration of the message) were categorical variables. For the categorical moderator variables, we calculated fixed-effect models using the general linear model (regression) program of the Statistical Analysis System (SAS Institute, 1985). The model provides a between-levels sum of squares, Q_B, that can be interpreted as a chi-square, testing whether the moderator variable is a significant predictor of differences in effect sizes. A test of the homogeneity of effect sizes within each level, Q_W, is also provided. For the continuous moderator variable (the duration of the messages), we also used the general linear model (leaving duration in its continuous form) and tested for homogeneity (Hedges & Olkin, 1985). A significant Q_B indicates that duration did moderate the size of the effect, and the direction of the unstandardized beta (b) weight indicates the direction of the moderation.

Results

Description of the Literature

Characteristics of the Senders

As indicated in Table 2, the senders in most of the studies were students from the United States who were strangers to the interviewer or target of their communications. In 52 of the 120 independent samples, incentives for success were provided to the senders.

Characteristics of the Truths and Lies

The duration of the messages was 1 min or less for 28 of the 36 samples for which that information was reported. The number of samples in which senders were given time to prepare their communications was about the same as the number in which they were not given any preparation time.

In 44 of the 120 samples, senders told truths and lies about their attitudes or personal facts. In 16 others, they looked at films, slides, or pictures and described them honestly or dishonestly. All other paradigms were used in fewer than 9 samples. In 21 of the samples, senders told lies about transgressions.

Publication Statistics and Methodological Aspects

Table 2 also shows that only 3 of the 120 independent samples were published before 1970. Most reports were journal articles.

In 84 of the samples, there were fewer than 60 senders. The samples included a mean of 22.4 male senders (SD = 24.6) and a mean of 19.2 female senders (SD = 19.2). In 25 samples, all of the senders were men, and in 15 samples, all were women. In 16 samples, the sex of the senders was not reported.

Within-sender designs (in which senders told truths and lies) were nearly twice as common as between-senders designs (in which senders told truths or lies). In the between-senders designs, the number of liars was typically the same as the number of truth tellers. Senders usually communicated between one and four messages.

In most studies, there was some interaction between the sender and the interviewer or target. In 24 of the 120 samples, there was no interaction or there was no one else present when the senders were telling their truths or lies.

When the reliability of the measurement was reported, the reliability was usually high (see Table 2). Of the 1,338 estimates of the 158 cues to deception, 273 (20%) were based on the subjective impressions of untrained raters.

Meta-Analysis of the Literature

Overview

We first present the combined effect sizes for each individual cue to deception. The individual cues to deception are grouped by our five sets of predictions. Cues suggesting that liars may be less forthcoming than truth tellers are shown in Table 3; cues suggesting that liars may tell less compelling tales than truth tellers are shown in Table 4; cues suggesting that liars communicate in a less positive and more tense way are shown in Tables 5 and 6, respectively; and cues suggesting that liars tell tales that are too good to be true are shown in Table 7. Any given cue is included in Tables 3–7 only if there are at least three independent estimates of it, at least two of which could be calculated precisely (as opposed to estimates of just the direction of the effect or reports that the effect was not significant). All other cues are reported in Appendix B. Five of the 88 cues that met the criteria for inclusion in the tables but did not fit convincingly into any particular table are also included in Appendix B (brow raise, lip stretch, eyes closed, lips apart, and jaw drop).

[**Appendix B** is available from Bella DePaulo: BellaDePaulo [at] gmail.com.]

Table 3

Are Liars Less Forthcoming Than Truth Tellers?

Cue	N	k_1	k_2	d	CI		Q
Amount of responding							
001 Response length	1,812	49	26	-0.03	-0.09,	0.03	92.1*
002 Talking time	207	4	3	-0.35*	-0.54,	-0.16	8.1
003 Length of interaction	134	3	2	-0.20	-0.41,	0.02	0.7
Detailed, complex responses							
004 Details	883	24	16	-0.30*	-0.38,	-0.21	76.2*
005 Sensory information (RM)	135	4	3	-0.17	-0.39,	0.06	13.2*
006 Cognitive complexity	294	6	3	-0.07	-0.23,	0.10	0.9
007 Unique words	229	6	3	-0.10	-0.26,	0.06	6.2
Holding back							
008 Blocks access to information	218	5	4	0.10	-0.13,	0.33	19.8*
009 Response latency	1,330	32	20	0.02	-0.06,	0.10	112.4*
010 Rate of speaking	806	23	14	0.07	-0.03,	0.16	21.7
011 Presses lips	199	4	3	0.16*	0.01,	0.30	30.9*

Note. Cue numbers are of the cues described in the current article as indexed in Appendix A. N = total number of participants in the studies; k_1 = total number of independent effect sizes (ds); k_2 = number of ds that could be estimated precisely; CI = 95% confidence interval; Q = homogeneity statistic (significance indicates rejection of the null hypothesis of homogeneity of ds); RM = reality monitoring.

   * $p < .05$.

Table 4
Do Liars Tell Less Compelling Tales Than Truth Tellers?

Cue	N	k_1	k_2	d	CI		Q
Makes Sense							
012 Plausibility	395	9	6	-0.23*	-0.36,	-0.11	13.1
013 Logical structure	223	6	6	-0.25*	-0.46,	-0.04	21.5*
014 Discrepant, ambivalent	243	7	3	0.34*	0.20,	0.48	14.3*
Engaging							
015 Involved, expressive (overall)	214	6	4	0.08	-0.06,	0.22	23.3*
016 Verbal and vocal involvement	384	7	3	-0.21*	-0.34,	-0.08	5.8
017 Facial expressiveness	251	3	2	0.12	-0.05,	0.29	9.6*
018 Illustrators	839	16	10	-0.14*	-0.24,	-0.04	23.9
Immediate							
019 Verbal immediacy (all categories)	117	3	2	-0.31*	-0.50,	-0.13	2.4
020 Verbal immediacy, temporary	109	4	3	0.15	-0.04,	0.34	2.3
021 Generalizing terms	275	5	3	0.10	-0.08,	0.28	1.7
022 Self-references	595	12	9	-0.03	-0.15,	0.09	30.1*
023 Mutual and group references	275	5	4	-0.14	-0.31,	0.02	4.4
024 Other references	264	6	5	0.16	-0.01,	0.33	5.6
025 Verbal and vocal immediacy (impressions)	373	7	4	-0.55*	-0.70,	-0.41	26.3*
026 Nonverbal immediacy	414	11	3	-0.07	-0.21,	0.07	6.9
027 Eye contact	1,491	32	17	0.01	-0.06,	0.08	41.1
028 Gaze aversion	411	6	4	0.03	-0.11,	0.16	7.4
029 Eye shifts	218	7	3	0.11	-0.03,	0.25	43.8*
Uncertain							
030 Tentative constructions	138	3	3	-0.16	-0.37,	0.05	12.5*
031 Verbal and vocal uncertainty (impressions)	329	10	4	0.30*	0.17,	0.46	11.0
032 Amplitude, loudness	177	5	3	-0.05	-0.26,	0.15	2.2
033 Chin raise	286	4	4	0.25*	0.12,	0.37	31.9*
034 Shrugs	321	6	3	0.04	-0.13,	0.21	3.3
Fluent							
035 Non-ah speech disturbances	750	17	12	0.00	-0.09,	0.09	60.5*
036 Word and phrase repetitions	100	4	4	0.21*	0.02,	0.41	0.5
037 Silent pauses	655	15	11	0.01	-0.09,	0.11	18.5
038 Filled pauses	805	16	14	0.00	-0.08,	0.08	22.2
039 Mixed pauses	280	7	3	0.03	-0.11,	0.17	3.6
040 Mixed disturbances (ah plus non-ah)	283	7	5	0.04	-0.14,	0.23	7.0
041 Ritualized speech	181	4	3	0.20	-0.06,	0.47	2.3
042 Miscellaneous dysfluencies	144	8	5	0.17	-0.04,	0.38	13.9

(*continued on next page*)

(Table 4 *continued*)

Cue	N	k_1	k_2	d	CI		Q
Active							
043 Body animation, activity	214	4	4	0.11	-0.03,	0.25	11.7*
044 Posture shifts	1,214	29	16	0.05	-0.03,	0.12	14.1
045 Head movements (undifferentiated)	536	14	8	-0.02	-0.12,	0.08	9.4
046 Hand movements	951	29	11	0.00	-0.08,	0.08	28.0
047 Arm movements	52	3	3	-0.17	-0.54,	0.20	3.5
048 Foot or leg movements	857	28	21	-0.09	-0.18,	0.00	20.5

Note. Cue numbers are of the cues described in the current article as indexed in Appendix A. N = total number of participants in the studies; k_1 = total number of independent effect sizes (ds); k_2 = number of ds that could be estimated precisely; CI = 95% confidence interval; Q = homogeneity statistic (significance indicates rejection of the null hypothesis of homogeneity of ds).
* $p < .05$.

Table 5

Are Liars Less Positive and Pleasant Than Truth Tellers?

Cue	N	k_1	k_2	d	CI		Q
049 Friendly, pleasant (overall)	216	6	3	-0.16	-0.36,	0.05	11.3
050 Cooperative (overall)	222	3	3	-0.66*	-0.93,	-0.38	11.2*
051 Attractive (overall)	84	6	3	-0.06	-0.27,	0.16	3.1
052 Negative statements and complaints	397	9	6	0.21*	0.09,	0.32	21.5*
053 Vocal pleasantness	325	4	2	-0.11	-0.28,	0.05	1.4
054 Facial pleasantness	635	13	6	-0.12*	-0.22,	-0.02	25.1*
055 Head nods	752	16	3	0.01	-0.09,	0.11	1.5
056 Brow lowering	303	5	4	0.04	-0.08,	0.16	9.0
057 Sneers	259	4	3	0.02	-0.11,	0.15	38.1*
058 Smiling (undifferentiated)	1,313	27	16	0.00	-0.07,	0.07	18.3
059 Lip corner pull (AU 12)	284	4	3	0.00	-0.12,	0.12	1.9
060 Eye muscles (AU 6), not during positive emotions	284	4	4	-0.01	-0.13,	0.11	3.6

Note. Cue numbers are of the cues described in the current article as indexed in Appendix A. N = total number of participants in the studies; k_1 = total number of independent effect sizes (ds); k_2 = number of ds that could be estimated precisely; CI = 95% confidence interval; Q = homogeneity statistic (significance indicates rejection of the null hypothesis of homogeneity of ds).

   * $p < .05$.

Table 6

Are Liars More Tense Than Truth Tellers?

Cue	N	k_1	k_2	d	CI		Q
061 Nervous, tense (overall)	571	16	12	0.27*	0.16,	0.38	37.3*
062 Vocal tension	328	10	8	0.26*	0.13,	0.39	25.4*
063 Frequency, pitch	294	12	11	0.21*	0.08,	0.34	31.2*
064 Relaxed posture	488	13	3	-0.02	-0.14,	0.10	19.6
065 Pupil dilation	328	4	4	0.39*	0.21,	0.56	1.1
066 Blinking	850	17	13	0.07	-0.01,	0.14	54.4*
067 Object fidgeting	420	5	2	-0.12	-0.26,	0.03	4.0
068 Self-fidgeting	991	18	10	-0.01	-0.09,	0.08	19.5
069 Facial fidgeting	444	7	4	0.08	-0.09,	0.25	7.7
070 Fidgeting (undifferentiated)	495	14	10	0.16*	0.03,	0.28	28.2*

Note. Cue numbers are of the cues described in the current article as indexed in Appendix A. N = total number of participants in the studies; k_1 = total number of independent effect sizes (ds); k_2 = number of ds that could be estimated precisely; CI = 95% confidence interval; Q = homogeneity statistic (significance indicates rejection of the null hypothesis of homogeneity of ds).

* $p < .05$.

Table 7

Do Lies Include Fewer Ordinary Imperfections and Unusual Contents Than Truths?

Cue	N	k_1	k_2	d	CI		Q
071 Unstructured productions	211	5	4	-0.06	-0.27,	0.15	24.8*
072 Spontaneous corrections	183	5	5	-0.29*	-0.56,	-0.02	3.8
073 Admitted lack of memory	183	5	5	-0.42*	-0.70,	-0.15	18.7*
074 Self-doubt	123	4	3	-0.10	-0.42,	0.21	5.1
075 Self-deprecation	64	3	3	0.21	-0.19,	0.61	0.9
076 Contextual embedding	159	6	6	-0.21	-0.41,	0.00	21.5*
077 Verbal and nonverbal interactions	163	5	4	-0.03	-0.25,	0.19	8.6
078 Unexpected complications	223	6	5	0.04	-0.16,	0.24	2.2
079 Unusual details	223	6	5	-0.16	-0.36,	0.05	9.5
080 Superfluous details	223	6	5	-0.01	-0.21,	0.19	11.0
081 Related external associations	112	3	3	0.35*	0.02,	0.67	2.1
082 Another's mental state	151	4	4	0.22	-0.02,	0.46	7.2
083 Subjective mental state	237	6	6	0.02	-0.18,	0.22	8.1

Note. Cue numbers are of the cues described in the current article as indexed in Appendix A. N = total number of participants in the studies; k_1 = total number of independent effect sizes (ds); k_2 = number of ds that could be estimated precisely; CI = 95% confidence interval; Q = homogeneity statistic (significance indicates rejection of the null hypothesis of homogeneity of ds).

$* p < .05$.

The placement of cues into the five different categories was to some extent arbitrary. For example, because blinking may be indicative of anxiety or arousal, we included it in the "tense" category (see Appendix A). However, decreased blinking can also be suggestive of greater cognitive effort; therefore, we could have placed it elsewhere. Rate of speaking is another example. We included that cue under "forthcoming" because people who are speaking slowly may seem to be holding back. However, faster speech can also be indicative of confidence (C. E. Kimble & Seidel, 1991); thus, we could have included it under "compelling" (certainty) instead.

In Table 8, we have arranged the 88 cues (the ones based on at least three estimates) into four sections by the crossing of the size of the combined effect (larger or smaller) and the number of independent estimates contributing to that effect (more or fewer). We also present a stem and leaf display of the 88 combined effect sizes in Table 9. The results of our analyses of the factors that might moderate the magnitude of the differences between liars and truth tellers are presented in subsequent tables.

Table 8

Cues With Larger and Smaller Effect Sizes Based on Larger and Smaller Numbers of Estimates

Larger Number of Estimates (k > 5)					
Larger effect size (d > |0.20|)	d	k	Smaller effect size (d < or = |0.20|)	d	k
025 Verbal and vocal immediacy (impressions)	-.55*	7	042 Miscellaneous dysfluencies	.17	8
014 Discrepant, ambivalent	.34*	7	070 Fidgeting (undifferentiated)	.16*	14
004 Details	-.30*	24	049 Friendly, pleasant	-.16	6
031 Verbal and vocal uncertainty (impressions)	.30*	10	024 Other references	.16	6
061 Nervous, tense (overall)	.27*	16	079 Unusual details	-.16	6
062 Vocal tension	.26*	10	018 Illustrators	-.14*	16
013 Logical structure	-.25*	6	054 Facial pleasantness	-.12*	13
012 Plausibility	-.23*	9	029 Eye shifts	.11	7
063 Frequency, pitch	.21*	12	007 Unique words	-.10	6
052 Negative statements and complaints	.21*	9	048 Foot or leg movements	-.09	28
016 Verbal and vocal involvement	-.21*	7	069 Facial fidgeting	.08	7
076 Contextual embedding	-.21	6	015 Involved, expressive (overall)	.08	6
			010 Rate of speaking	.07	23
			066 Blinking	.07	17
			026 Nonverbal immediacy	-.07	11
			006 Cognitive complexity	-.07	6
			051 Attractive	-.06	6
			044 Posture shifts	.05	29
			040 Mixed disturbances (ah + non-ah)	.04	7
			034 Shrugs	.04	6
			078 Unexpected complications	.04	6
			001 Response length	-.03	49
			022 Self-references	-.03	12
			039 Mixed pauses	.03	7
			028 Gaze aversion	.03	6
			009 Response latency	.02	32
			045 Head movements (undiff)	-.02	14
			064 Relaxed posture	-.02	13
			083 Subjective mental state	.02	6
			027 Eye contact	.01	32
			068 Self-fidgeting	-.01	18
			055 Head nods	.01	16
			037 Silent pauses	.01	15
			080 Superfluous details	-.01	6
			046 Hand movements	.00	29
			058 Smiling (undifferentiated)	.00	27
			035 Non-ah speech disturbances	.00	17
			038 Filled pauses	.00	16

(continued on next page)

(Table 8 *continued*)

Smaller Number of Estimates (k < or = 5)					
Larger effect size (d > |0.20|)	d	k	**Smaller effect size (d < or = |0.20|)**	d	k
050 Cooperative	-.66*	3	041 Ritualized speech	.20	4
073 Admitted lack of memory	-.42*	5	003 Length of interaction	-.20	3
065 Pupil dilation	.39*	4	005 Sensory information	-.17	4
002 Talking time	-.35*	4	047 Arm movements	-.17	3
081 Related external associations	.35*	3	011 Presses lips	.16*	4
019 Verbal immediacy (all categories)	-.31*	3	030 Tentative constructions	-.16	3
072 Spontaneous corrections	-.29*	5	020 Verbal immediacy, temporal	.15	4
033 Chin raise	.25*	4	023 Mutual and group references	-.14	5
082 Another's mental state	.22	4	067 Object fidgeting	-.12	5
036 Word and phrase repetitions	.21*	4	017 Facial expressiveness	.12	3
075 Self-deprecation	.21	3	043 Body animation, activity	.11	4
			053 Vocal pleasantness	-.11	4
			008 Blocks access to information	.10	5
			021 Generalizing terms	.10	5
			074 Self-doubt	-.10	4
			132 Lips apart (AU 25)	-.08	5
			071 Unstructured productions	-.06	5
			131 Eyes closed	-.06	3
			032 Amplitude, loudness	-.05	5
			056 Brow lowering	.04	5
			130 Lip stretch (AU 20)	-.04	4
			077 Descriptions of verbal and nonverbal interactions	-.03	5
			057 Sneers	.02	4
			129 Brow raise (AU 1)	.01	5
			060 Eye muscles (AU 6), not during positive emotions	-.01	4
			133 Jaw drop (AU 26)	.00	5
			059 Lip corner pull (AU 12)	.00	4

Note. AU = facial action unit (as categorized by Ekman & Friesen, 1978).
* $p < .05$.

Table 9

Stem and Leaf Plot of Combined Effect Sizes (ds) for Individual Cues to Deception

Stem	Leaf
0.6	6
0.6	
0.5	5
0.5	
0.4	
0.4	2
0.3	559
0.3	0014
0.2	55679
0.2	0011111123
0.1	5666666777
0.1	000011122244
0.0	5566677778889
0.0	00000011111112222233333344444

Note. Included are the 88 cases for which at least three independent effect size estimates were available (at least two of which could be computed precisely).

Individual Cues to Deception

Are liars less forthcoming than truth tellers? Table 3 shows the results of the cues indicating whether liars were less forthcoming than truth tellers. We examined whether liars had less to say, whether what they did say was less detailed and less complex, and whether they seemed to be holding back.

We had more independent estimates of the length of the responses (k = 49) than of any other cue, but we found just a tiny and nonsignificant effect in the predicted direction (d = −0.03). When amount of responding was operationalized in terms of the percentage of the talking time taken up by the social actor compared with the actor's partner, then liars did take up less of that time than did truth tellers (d = −0.35). The entire interaction tended to terminate nonsignificantly sooner when 1 person was lying than when both were telling the truth (d = −0.20).

Our prediction that liars would provide fewer details than would truth tellers was clearly supported (d = −0.30). Extrapolating from reality monitoring theory, we also predicted that there would be less sensory information in deceptive accounts than in truthful ones. There was a nonsignificant trend in that direction (d = −0.17). The finding that liars pressed their lips more than truth tellers did (d = 0.16) was the only cue in the "holding back" subcategory that was statistically reliable.

In sum, the most reliable indicator (in terms of the size of the effect and the number of independent estimates) that liars may have been less forthcoming than truth tellers was the relatively smaller number of details they provided in their accounts. The directions of the cues in Table 3 tell a consistent story: All except 1 of the 11 cues (rate of speaking) was in the predicted direction, indicating that liars are less forthcoming than truth tellers, though usually nonsignificantly so.

Are deceptive accounts less compelling than truthful ones? To determine whether deceptive accounts were less compelling than truthful ones, we asked whether the lies seemed to make less sense than the truths and whether they were told in a less engaging and less immediate manner. We also asked whether liars seemed more uncertain or less fluent than truth tellers and whether they seemed less active or animated. The results are shown in Table 4.

By all three of the indicators, the lies made less sense than the truths. They were less plausible (d = −0.23); less likely to be structured in a logical, sensible way (d = −0.25); and more likely to be internally discrepant or to convey ambivalence (d = 0.34).

For the four cues to the engagingness of the message, the results of two were as predicted. Liars seemed less involved verbally and vocally in their self-presentations than did truth tellers (d = −0.21). They also displayed fewer of the gestures used to illustrate speech (d = −0.14).

The set of immediacy cues includes three composite measures and a number of individual immediacy measures. The individual cues were the ones described by Mehrabian (1972) that were reported separately in several studies or other cues that seemed to capture the immediacy construct (e.g., Fleming, 1994). The composite measures were verbal immediacy (all categories), verbal and vocal immediacy, and nonverbal immediacy. The verbal immediacy composite is an index consisting of all of the linguistic categories described by Wiener and Mehrabian (1968). They are all verbal constructions (e.g., active vs. passive voice, affirmatives vs. negations) that are typically coded from transcripts. The verbal and vocal immediacy measure is based on raters' overall impressions of the degree to which the social actors seemed direct, relevant, clear, and personal. The nonverbal immediacy measure includes the set of nonverbal cues described by Mehrabian (1972) as indices of immediacy (e.g., interpersonal proximity, leaning and facing toward the other person).

The verbal composite and the verbal and nonverbal composite both indicated that liars were less immediate than truth tellers (d = −0.31 and −0.55, respectively). Liars used more linguistic constructions that seemed to distance themselves from their listeners or from the contents of their presentations, and they sounded more evasive, unclear, and impersonal. The nonverbal composite was only weakly (nonsignificantly) suggestive of the same conclusion (d = −0.07).

The results of other individual indices of immediacy were inconsistent and unimpressive. It is notable that none of the measures of looking behavior supported the widespread belief that liars do not look their targets in the eye. The 32 independent estimates of eye contact produced a combined effect that was almost exactly zero (d = 0.01), and the Q statistic indicated that the 32 estimates were homogeneous in size. The estimates of gaze aversion were equally unimpressive (d = 0.03). Estimates of eye shifts produced just a nonsignificant trend (d = 0.11).

The one cue that was consistent with our prediction that liars would seem less certain than truth tellers was verbal and vocal uncertainty (as measured by subjective impressions); liars did sound more uncertain than truth tellers (d = 0.30). One other behavior unexpectedly produced results in the opposite direction. More often than truth tellers, liars raised their chins (d = 0.25). In studies of facial expressions in conflict situations, a particular facial constellation, called a plus face, has been identified (Zivin, 1982). It consists of a raised chin, direct eye contact, and medially raised brows. People who show this plus face during conflict situations are more likely to prevail than those who do not show it or who show a minus face, consisting of a lowered chin, averted eyes, and pinched brows (Zivin, 1982). That research suggests that raising the chin could be a sign of certainty.

Mahl and his colleagues (e.g., Kasl & Mahl, 1965; Mahl, 1987) have suggested that the large variety of disturbances that occur in spontaneous speech can be classified into two functionally distinct categories: non-ah disturbances, which indicate state anxiety (Mahl, 1987), and the commonplace filled pauses such as "ah," "um," and "er," which occur especially often when the available options for what to say or how to say it are many and complex (Berger, Karol, & Jordan, 1989; Christenfeld, 1994; Schachter et al., 1991). Of the non-ah disturbances, the most frequently occurring are sentence changes, in which the speaker interrupts the flow of a sentence to change its form or content, and superfluous repetitions of words or phrases. The other non-ah disturbances are stutters, omissions of words or parts of words, sentences that are not completed, slips of the tongue, and intruding incoherent sounds.

Most studies reported a composite that included all non-ah disturbances, or one that included non-ahs as well as ahs. When individual disturbances were reported separately, we preserved the distinctions. In the fluency subcategory, we also included silent pauses, mixed pauses (silent plus filled, for studies in which the two were not reported separately), ritualized speech (e.g., "you know," "well," "I mean"), and miscellaneous dysfluencies, which were sets of dysfluencies that were not based on particular systems such as Mahl's (1987).

Results of the fluency indices suggest that speech disturbances have little predictive power as cues to deceit. The categories of disturbances reported most often, non-ah disturbances, filled pauses, and silent pauses, produced combined effect sizes of 0.00, 0.00, and 0.01, respectively. Only one type of speech disturbance, the repetition of words and phrases, produced a statistically reliable effect (d = 0.21).

Under the subcategory of "active," we included all movements except those defined as expressive (i.e., illustrators were included in the subcategory of "engaging" cues) and those believed to be indicative of nervousness (i.e., forms of fidgeting, included in the tense category). There were nearly 30 independent estimates of posture shifts (d = 0.05), hand movements (d = 0.00), and foot or leg movements (d = −0.09), but we found little relationship with deceit for these or any of the other movements.

In sum, there were three ways in which liars told less compelling tales than did truth tellers. Their stories made less sense, and they told those stories in less engaging and less immediate ways. Cues based on subjective impressions of verbal and vocal cues (typically rated from audiotapes) were most often consistent with predictions. Specifically, liars sounded less involved, less immediate, and more uncertain than did truth tellers.

Are liars less positive and pleasant than truth tellers? All of the cues that assessed pleasantness in a global way produced results in the predicted direction, although some of the effects were small and nonsignificant (see Table 5). A small number of estimates (k = 3) indicated that liars were less cooperative than truth tellers (d = −0.66). Liars also made more negative statements and complaints (d = 0.21), and their faces were less pleasant (d = −0.12).

Each of the more specific cues to positivity or negativity (e.g., head nods, brow lowering, sneers) produced combined effects very close to zero. The most notable finding was that the 27 estimates of smiling produced a combined effect size of exactly zero. The measures of smiling in those studies did not distinguish among different types of smiles. Ekman (1985/ 1992) argued that for smiling to predict deceptiveness, smiles expressing genuinely positive affect (distinguished by the cheek raise, facial action unit 6 [AU; as categorized by Ekman & Friesen, 1978], produced by movements of the muscles around the outside corner of the eye) must be coded separately from feigned smiles. Because our review contained only two estimates of genuine smiling and two of feigned smiling, the results are reported in Appendix B with the other cues for which the number of estimates was limited. The combined effects tend to support Ekman's position. When only pretending to be experiencing genuinely positive affect, people were less likely to show genuine smiles (d = −0.70) and more likely to show feigned ones (d = 0.31). There were no differences in the occurrence of the cheek raise for liars versus truth tellers in studies in which the participants were not experiencing or faking positive emotions (d = −0.01; e.g., studies of the expression and concealment of pain). Also as predicted by Ekman, the easily produced lip corner pull (AU 12) did not distinguish truths from lies either, again producing a combined effect size of exactly zero.

Are liars more tense than truth tellers? Except for two types of fidgeting, the results of every cue to tension were in the predicted direction, though again some were quite small and nonsignificant (see Table 6). Liars were more nervous and tense overall than truth tellers (d = 0.27). They were more vocally tense (d = 0.26) and spoke in a higher pitch (d = 0.21). Liars also had more dilated pupils (d = 0.39).

In studies in which different kinds of fidgeting were not differentiated, liars fidgeted more than truth tellers (d = 0.16). However, the effect was smaller for facial fidgeting (e.g., rubbing one's face, playing with one's hair; d = 0.08), and the results were in the opposite direction for object fidgeting (e.g., tapping a pencil, twisting a paper clip; d = −0.12) and self-fidgeting (e.g., scratching; d =

−0.01). The best summary of these data is that there is no clear relationship between fidgeting and lying.

Do lies include fewer ordinary imperfections and unusual contents than do truths? The people who made spontaneous corrections while telling their stories were more likely to be telling truths than lies (d = −0.29). This is consistent with our prediction that liars would avoid behaviors they mistakenly construe as undermining the convincingness of their lies (see Table 7). Liars also seemed to avoid another admission of imperfection that truth tellers acknowledge: an inability to remember something (d = −0.42). There were also indications that liars stuck too closely to the key elements of the story they were fabricating. For example, like good novelists, truth tellers sometimes describe the settings of their stories; liars were somewhat less likely to do this (d = −0.21 for contextual embedding), and they provided nonsignificantly fewer unusual details (d = −0.16). However, liars did mention events or relationships peripheral to the key event (d = 0.35 for related external associations) more often than truth tellers did.

Summary of individual cues to deception. The most compelling results in this review are the ones based on relatively large numbers of estimates that produced the biggest combined effects. In Table 8, the 88 cues are arranged into four sections according to the number of independent estimates and the size of the combined effects. On the top half of the table are the cues for which six or more independent estimates were available. These were the 50 cues that were above the median in the number of estimates on which they were based (see also Field, 2001). On the bottom half are the 38 cues for which just three, four, or five estimates were available. In the first column are the 23 cues with combined effect sizes larger than |0.20|. In the second column are the 65 effect sizes equal to |0.20| or smaller. The value of |0.20| was selected based on Cohen's (1988) heuristic that effect sizes (d) of |0.20| are small effects. Within each section, cues with the biggest effect sizes are listed first; within cues with the same effect sizes, those based on a larger number of estimates (k) are listed first.

Twelve cues are in the larger d and k section. These cues were based on at least six independent estimates and produced combined effects greater than |0.20|. Half of these cues were from the compelling category, including all three of the cues in the subcategory "makes sense." The effects for those three cues indicate that self-presentations that seem discrepant, illogically structured, or implausible are more likely to be deceptive than truthful. Verbal and vocal immediacy, from the "immediacy" subcategory, tops the list. Verbal and vocal uncertainty, from the subcategory "uncertain," is in this section, as is verbal and vocal involvement, a cue in the subcategory "engaging."

The larger d and k section also includes one of the cues in the forthcoming category (details) and one from the "positive, pleasant" category (negative statements and complaints). There are also three cues from the tense category (overall tension, vocal tension, and pitch) and one from the category of "ordinary imperfections and unusual details" (contextual embedding).

In the larger d and smaller k section of Table 8 are cues that produced relatively bigger effects but were based on smaller numbers of estimates. For example, a handful of estimates suggest that liars were less cooperative than truth tellers, were less likely to admit that they did not remember something, and had more dilated pupils.

Some of the cues in the smaller d and larger k section of Table 8 are noteworthy because the very tiny cumulative ds were based on large numbers of estimates. For example, response length, response latency, and eye contact were all based on more than 30 independent estimates, but they produced cumulative effect sizes of just −0.03, 0.02, and 0.01, respectively.

Table 9 is a stem and leaf display of the absolute values of the 88 effect sizes. The median effect size is just |0.10|. Only two of the effect sizes meet Cohen's (1988) criterion of |0.50| for large effects.

Moderators of Cues to Deception

In Tables 3–7, in which we present the combined results of the estimates of individual cues to deception, we included cues only if they were based on at least three effect sizes, at least two of which were precise estimates. In our moderator analyses, we needed to use a more stringent criterion to have a sufficient number of estimates at each level of the moderator variables. We began by considering all cues for which we had at least 10 precise estimates. Eighteen cues met that criterion: response length, details, response latency, rate of speaking, illustrators, eye contact, non-ah speech disturbances, silent pauses, filled pauses, posture shifts, hand movements, foot or leg movements, smiling (undifferentiated), nervous, pitch, blinking, self-fidgeting, and fidgeting (undifferentiated). Our initial analyses that combined across all estimates (as reported in Tables 3–7) indicated that for some of these cues, the estimates were homogeneous. Because our predictions were theoretically driven, we proceeded to test the moderator variables for all 18 of the cues. Four of the cues for which the estimates were homogeneous—illustrators, posture shifts, smiling (undifferentiated), and hand movements—produced no significant effects in any of our moderator analyses, indicating that the size of the effects was also homogeneous across levels of the moderators.

For the moderator analyses, we report three homogeneity statistics for each moderator. The Q T statistic indicates the variability among all of the estimates of the cue included in the analysis. The Q B statistic indicates between-groups variation. Significant between-groups effects indicate that the size of the effects differed across the levels of the moderator. The Q W statistic indicates variability within each level of the moderator variable; a significant value indicates additional variability that has not been explained.

Motivation to succeed at lying

We predicted that cues to deception would be stronger in studies in which the social actors were motivated to get away with their lies than in studies in which no special incentives were provided. Table 10 shows the effect sizes for each cue for those two kinds of studies. Patterns of eye contact differed significantly between the motivated senders and the senders with no special motivation. When social actors were motivated to succeed, they made significantly less eye contact when lying than when telling the truth (d = −0.15). When no special incentive was provided to social actors, they made nonsignificantly more eye contact when lying (d = 0.09).

Table 10

Cues to Deception When Incentives for Success Were or Were Not Provided

Cue		No motivation	Motivation	Q_T (df)	Q_B (1)
		Condition			
001 Response length					
	d)	-0.03	-0.03	92.1* (48)	0.0
	Qw (k)	59.6* (21)	32.5 (28)		
009 Response latency					
	d	0.04	0.00	112.4*	0.3
	Qw (k)	50.1* (18)	62.0* (15)		
010 Rate of speaking					
	d	0.10	0.04	21.7 (22)	0.5
	Qw (k)	8.7 (8)	12.5 (15)		
027 Eye contact					
	d	0.09	-0.15*	41.1 (31)	9.0*
	Qw (k)	13.3 (20)	18.8 (12)		
035 Non-ah disturbances					
	d	0.13	-0.10	60.5* (16)	6.3*
	Qw (k)	24.6* (7)	29.7* (10)		
037 Silent pauses					
	d	-0.02	0.06	18.5 (14)	0.5
	Qw (k)	7.1 (8)	10.8 (7)		
038 Filled pauses					
	d	0.09	-0.13	22.2 (15)	6.5*
	Qw (k)	8.3 (8)	7.4 (8)		
048 Foot or leg movements					
	d	-0.02	-0.13*	20.4 (27)	1.4
	Qw (k)	5.0 (9)	14.0 (19)		
061 Nervous, tense					
	d	0.15	0.35*	37.3* (15)	3.0
	Qw (k)	10.8 (8)	23.4* (8)		
063 Frequency, pitch					
	d	-.02	0.59*	31.2* (11)	18.6*
	Qw (k)	2.9 (6)	9.7 (6)		
066 Blinking					
	d	0.05	0.09	54.4* (16)	0.5
	Qw (k)	23.9* (9)	30.3* (8)		
068 Self-fidgeting					
	d	0.08	-0.12	19.5 (17)	5.5*
	Qw (k)	10.1 (11)	3.9 (7)		
070 Fidgeting (undifferentiated)					
	d	0.09	0.18	28.2* (13)	0.3
	Qw (k)	11.3* (3)	16.6* (11)		

Note. Cue numbers are of the cues described in the current article as indexed in Appendix A. The Q statistics are homogeneity statistics; significance indicates rejection of the hypothesis of homogeneity of effect sizes (ds). Therefore, bigger Qs indicate less homogeneity. Q_T = homogeneity among all estimates for a particular cue; Q_B = homogeneity between the levels of the moderator being compared; Q_W = homogeneity of ds within the level of the moderator; k = number of independent estimates.

    * $p < .05$.

Two of the fluency cues, non-ah disturbances and filled pauses, varied with the motivation moderator. In studies in which no special incentive was provided, there was a small positive effect for both cues; deceptive self-presentations were nonsignificantly more likely to include non-ah disturbances (d = 0.13) and filled pauses (d = 0.09) than truthful ones. However, when incentives were provided, this effect reversed, and deceptive self-presentations included nonsignificantly fewer non-ah speech disturbances (d = −0.10) and filled pauses (d = −0.13) than truthful ones.

Several cues to tension also discriminated cues to deception under the two motivational conditions. Social actors were more tense overall when lying compared with when telling the truth, and this effect was significant only when they were motivated to succeed (d = 0.35 vs. 0.15). Also, it was only in the incentive condition that lies were communicated in more highly pitched voices than were truths (d = 0.59 vs. −0.02).

Differences in the magnitude of the effects (absolute values) for studies in which social actors were or were not motivated to succeed are also telling. For studies in which there was no special incentive for succeeding, cues to deception were generally weak. Overall, the size of the effects increased somewhat when some incentive was provided.

Identity-relevant motivations to succeed

We had predicted that across all of the estimates in our data set, we would find that liars' responses would be shorter than those of truth tellers', would be preceded by a longer response latency, and would include more silent pauses. None of these predictions was supported in the overall analyses. However, all of these predictions were significantly more strongly supported under conditions of identity-relevant motivation than under no-motivation conditions (see Table 11). Within the identity-relevant condition, the effect sizes were nearly significant for response length (d = −0.23) and silent pauses (d = 0.38) but not significant for response latency (d = 0.36).

Table 11

Cues to Deception Under Conditions of No Motivation, Identity-Relevant Motivation, and Instrumental Motivation

Cue	d			Q_B (1)		
	No Motivation (NM)	Identity-Relevant (IR)	Instru-mental (IN)	NM vs. IR	NM vs. IN	IR vs. IN
001 Response length	-0.03	-0.23	-0.05	4.9*	0.1	3.6
009 Response latency	0.04	0.36	-0.01	4.6*	0.2	4.2*
010 Rate of speaking	0.10	0.06	-0.03	0.1	1.3	0.2
027 Eye contact	0.09*	-0.19	-0.08	2.3	3.2	0.3
035 Non-ah disturbances	0.13		-0.17		8.0*	
037 Silent pauses	-0.02	0.38	-0.03	4.6*	0.0	3.5
038 Filled pauses	0.09		-0.14		6.4*	
048 Foot or leg movements	-0.02	-0.28*	-0.09	3.2	0.6	1.7
061 Nervous, tense	0.15	-0.02		1.2		
063 Frequency, pitch	-0.02	0.67*		14.1*		
066 Blinking	0.05	0.05			0.0	
068 Self-fidgeting	0.08	-0.09			2.4	
070 Fidgeting (undifferentiated)	0.09	0.11	0.33	0.0	1.9	1.6

Note. Cue numbers are of the cues described in the current article as indexed in Appendix A. The Q statistics are homogeneity statistics; significance indicates rejection of the hypothesis of homogeneity of effect sizes (ds). Therefore, bigger Qs indicate less homogeneity. Q_B = homogeneity between the levels of the moderator being compared. k = number of independent estimates.

  * $p < .05$.

In the identity-relevant condition, the voice pitch of liars was significantly higher than that of truth tellers; the effect size was significant (d = 0.67), and it differed significantly from the effect size in the no-motivation condition (d = −0.02). Liars in the identity-relevant condition also made significantly fewer foot or leg movements than truth tellers (d = −0.28); however, the size of the effect was not significantly different when compared with the no-motivation condition (d = −0.02).

Instrumental motivations

Table 11 also shows cues to deception for studies in which the incentives were primarily instrumental (e.g., financial). Only two cues differed significantly in size between the studies that provided no incentives to the social actors and those that provided instrumental incentives. Non-ah disturbances (d = −0.17) and filled pauses (d = −0.14) occurred nonsignificantly less often in the speech of the liars than of the truth tellers in the studies that provided instrumental incentives. In the studies in which no incentives were provided, the speech of liars included somewhat more non-ah disturbances (d = 0.13) and filled pauses (d = 0.09) than the speech of truth tellers. Within the instrumental-motivation condition, there were no effect sizes that differed significantly from chance.

Identity-relevant versus instrumental motivations

The self-presentational perspective predicts stronger effects when incentives are identity relevant than when they are instrumental. Results (also shown in Table 11) indicate that the responses of liars tended to be even shorter than those of truth tellers when the social actors were motivated by identity-relevant incentives than when they were instrumentally motivated (d = −0.23 vs. −0.05; for the difference between conditions, p =.06). Response latencies were significantly longer (d = 0.36 vs. −0.01), and there were somewhat more silent pauses (d = 0.38 vs. −0.03; for the difference between conditions, p =.07). There were no cues that were significantly or nearly significantly stronger in the instrumental-motivation condition.

Unplanned and planned presentations

Seven independent samples (described in eight reports) included a manipulation of whether the senders' messages were unplanned or planned. Results for 33 specific cues were reported by the authors. However, there were only two cues (response length and response latency) that met our criterion of being based on at least three independent estimates (at least two of which were estimated precisely). Table 12 shows the results for those cues as well as several others that met a less stringent criterion: At least two independent estimates were available, and at least one was estimated precisely. Those results should be interpreted with caution.

255

Table 12

Cues to Deception: Differences Between Unplanned and Planned Communications

Cue	k_1	k_2	d	CI		Q
001 Response length	6	3	0.07	-0.06,	0.20	6.3
009 Response latency	4	1	0.20*	0.07,	0.34	8.7
018 Illustrators	3	1	0.03	-0.18,	0.11	0.4
027 Eye contact	3	1	-0.09	-0.23,	0.06	0.8
037 Silent pauses	2	2	0.57	0.00,	1.14	10.1*
055 Head nods	3	1	-0.11	-0.25,	0.04	3.1
058 Smiling	3	1	0.07	-0.08,	0.22	1.2
070 Fidgeting (undifferentiated)	3	2	-0.03	0.19,	0.14	1.6

Note. Cue numbers are of the cues described in the current article as indexed in Appendix A. N = total number of participants in the studies; k_1 = total number of independent effect sizes (ds); k_2 = number of ds that could be estimated precisely; CI = 95% confidence interval; Q = homogeneity statistic (significance indicates rejection of the null hypothesis of homogeneity of ds).

    * $p < .05$.

We computed the effect sizes in Table 12 by subtracting the effect size for the planned messages from the effect size from the unplanned messages. Therefore, more positive effect sizes indicate that the relationship of the cue to deception was more positive for the unplanned messages than for the planned messages.

As predicted, the combined effect for response latency was statistically reliable (d = 0.20). When social actors did not plan their messages, there was a longer latency between the end of the question and the beginning of their answer when they were lying than when they were telling the truth, but when the senders planned their messages, they began responding relatively more quickly when lying than when telling the truth. There were also somewhat more silent pauses in the deceptive presentations than the truthful ones when those presentations were not planned than when they were planned (d = 0.57, p =.05).

Duration of the presentations

We predicted that if social actors needed to sustain their presentations for greater lengths of time, cues to deception would be clearer and more numerous. We used the mean duration of the messages in each study as an approximation of the degree to which social actors needed to sustain their presentations over time. Because duration is a continuous variable, there are no separate groups. Instead, a significant Q B statistic indicates that the effect sizes were not homogeneous (i.e., the moderator was significant), and the unstandardized beta indicates the direction of the effect.

There were three cues for which at least eight independent estimates were available: response length (Q B = 5.4, k = 13); response latency (Q B = 6.1, k = 8); and pitch (Q B = 6.6, k = 8), and for all three, Q B indicated that the effect sizes were not homogeneous across message lengths. This means that all three cues varied significantly with the duration of the presentations. When presentations were sustained for greater amounts of time, deceptive responses were especially shorter than truthful ones (b = −0.008), and they were preceded by a longer latency (b = 0.034). Lies, relative to truths, were also spoken in an especially higher pitched voice when the presentations lasted longer (b = 0.002).

Communications that were or were not about transgressions

We expected to find stronger cues to negativity and tension in studies in which social actors lied about transgressions than in those in which the lies were not about transgressions. As shown in Table 13, this was an important moderator of cues to deception.

257

Table 13

Cues to Deception When Senders Did and Did Not Commit a Transgression

Cue		No transgression	Transgression	Q_T (df)	Q_B (1)
		Condition			
001 Response length					
	d)	-0.02	-0.08	92.1* (48)	0.7
	Qw (k)	74.6*	16.7 (11)		
009 Response latency					
	d	-0.07	0.27	112.4* (31)	13.7*
	Qw (k)	67.4* (24)	31.3* (8)		
010 Rate of speaking					
	d	0.01	0.32*	21.7 (22)	6.6*
	Qw (k)	8.7 (18)	6.4 (5)		
027 Eye contact					
	d	0.04	-0.13	41.1 (31)	3.3
	Qw (k)	24.4 (26)	13.3* (6)		
035 Non-ah disturbances					
	d	0.17	-0.24	60.5* (16)	19.7*
	Qw (k)	6.5 (11)	34.3* (6)		
037 Silent pauses					
	d	-0.01	0.10	18.5 (14)	0.5
	Qw (k)	11.8 (10)	6.2 (5)		
038 Filled pauses					
	d	0.01	-0.03	22.2 (15)	0.1
	Qw (k)	9.5 (11)	12.6* (5)		
048 Foot or leg movements					
	d	-0.04	-0.24*	20.4 (27)	3.8*
	Qw (k)	11.4 (21)	5.2 (7)		
061 Nervous, tense					
	d	0.09	0.51*	37.3* (15)	13.9*
	Qw (k)	15.2 (12)	8.2 (4)		
066 Blinking					
	d	0.01	0.38*	54.4* (16)	12.2*
	Qw (k)	40.5* (13)	1.7 (4)		
068 Self-fidgeting					
	d	0.07	-0.14	19.5 (17)	5.7*
	Qw (k)	8.2 (12)	5.5 (6)		
070 Fidgeting (undifferentiated)					
	d	0.24*	-0.16	28.2*	6.1*
	Qw (k)	18.1 (10)	4.1 (4)		

Note. Cue numbers are of the cues described in the current article as indexed in Appendix A. The Q statistics are homogeneity statistics; significance indicates rejection of the hypothesis of homogeneity of effect sizes (ds). Therefore, bigger Qs indicate less homogeneity. Q_T = homogeneity among all estimates for a particular cue; Q_B = homogeneity between the levels of the moderator being compared; Q_W = homogeneity of ds within the level of the moderator; k = number of independent estimates.

   * $p < .05$.

When the lie was about a transgression, compared with when it was not, liars took longer to begin responding than did truth tellers (d = 0.27 vs. −0.01). Once they started talking, they talked significantly faster than truth tellers (d = 0.32 vs. 0.01). They also seemed more tense overall (d = 0.51 vs. 0.09), and they blinked more (d = 0.38 vs. 0.01). A trend suggested that they tended to avoid eye contact more (d = −0.13 vs. 0.04, p =.07). There were also some cues suggestive of inhibition: People lying about transgressions made fewer foot or leg movements (d = −0.24 vs. −0.04), and they fidgeted less (d = −0.14 vs. 0.07 for self-fidgeting, d = −0.16 vs. 0.24 for undifferentiated fidgeting). Once again, the effect for non-ah disturbances was contrary to expectations: Lies about transgressions included fewer such disturbances than truths; the lies that were not about transgressions included relatively more of them (d = −0.24 vs. 0.17). Within the transgression condition, the effect sizes for response latency, rate of speaking, non-ah disturbances, foot or leg movements, tension, blinking, and self-fidgeting all differed significantly, or nearly so, from zero. Within the no-transgression condition, only the effect for undifferentiated fidgeting differed from zero.

Overall differences in the magnitude of the cues to deception for lies about transgressions compared with lies about other topics are also noteworthy. For 11 of the 12 cues, the absolute value of the effect was bigger for the lies about transgressions than for the other lies. In some instances, however, the direction of the effect was contrary to predictions (e.g., non-ah disturbances, fidgeting).

Interactivity

Buller and Burgoon's (1996) formulation predicts greater pleasantness, fluency, composure, involvement, and immediacy with increasingly interactive contexts. Effect sizes differed significantly for interactive paradigms relative to noninteractive ones for three cues: details (Q B = 4.41), pitch (Q B = 8.21), and blinking (Q B = 13.15). Liars offered significantly fewer details than truth tellers in interactive contexts (d = −0.33; 95% confidence interval [CI] = −0.51, −0.15; k = 20); for noninteractive contexts, the effect was negligible (d = −0.06; CI = −0.51, 0.39; k = 4). This result does not seem consistent with Buller and Burgoon's predictions. Liars in interactive contexts spoke in a significantly higher pitched voice than did truth tellers (d = 0.35; CI = 0.07, 0.64; k = 9); for noninteractive contexts, there was a very small effect in the opposite direction (d = −0.06; CI = −0.45, 0.33; k = 3). In that pitch typically rises with stress, this result is inconsistent with the prediction that liars would show more composure with increasing interactivity. Finally, liars in noninteractive contexts blinked significantly more than truth tellers (d = 0.29; CI = 0.03, 0.56; k = 4); in interactive contexts, there was little difference (d = −0.06; CI = −0.21, 0.80; k = 12). In that blinking can be a sign of tension, this result is consistent with predictions.

Cues measured objectively and subjectively

To test our prediction that cues based on subjective impressions would more powerfully discriminate truths from lies than cues measured objectively, we searched the data set for cues that were assessed subjectively and objectively and that had at least three estimates per assessment type. Five cues that met the criterion are shown in Table 14. In addition, we compared the verbal immediacy composite (Cue 019), which is based on the objective scoring of linguistic forms, with the verbal and vocal immediacy cue (Cue 025), which is based on subjective impressions.

259

Table 14

Cues to Deception Based on Objective and Subjective Measures

Cue		Objective	Subjective	Q_T (df)	Q_B (1)
		Measurement			
004 Details					
	d)	-0.27*	-0.32*	76.2*	0.3
	Qw (k)	34.9* (14)	41.0 (10)		
019 Verbal immediacy with 025 Verbal, vocal immediacy					
	d	-0.31	-0.55*	28.7* (8)	3.9*
	Qw (k)	2.4 (3)	26.3* (7)		
026 Nonverbal immediacy					
	d	-0.08	-0.07	6.9 (10)	0.0
	Qw (k)	2.2 (7)	4.6 (4)		
027 Eye contact					
	d	0.04	-0.28	41.1 (31)	5.1*
	Qw (k)	30.0 (27)	5.9 (5)		
054 Facial pleasantness					
	d	0.07	-0.20*	25.1 (12)	6.7*
	Qw (k)	2.3 (8)	16.1* (5)		
064 Relaxed posture					
	d	-0.00	-0.05	19.6 (12)	0.2
	Qw (k)	0.0 (9)	19.5* (4)		

Note. Cue numbers are of the cues described in the current article as indexed in Appendix A. The Q statistics are homogeneity statistics; significance indicates rejection of the hypothesis of homogeneity of effect sizes (ds). Therefore, bigger Qs indicate less homogeneity. Q_T = homogeneity among all estimates for a particular cue; Q_B = homogeneity between the levels of the moderator being compared; Q_W = homogeneity of ds within the level of the moderator; k = number of independent estimates.

    * $p < .05$.

Three of the six comparisons were significant, and all of them showed that the effect sizes were stronger when the cues were assessed subjectively than when they were measured objectively. Impressions of immediacy separated truths from lies more powerfully than did objective measures of immediacy (d = −0.55 vs. −0.31; only the d for subjective impressions was significant). When eye contact was based on subjective impressions, liars showed somewhat less eye contact than truth tellers (d = −0.28); there was virtually no difference when eye contact was measured objectively (d = 0.04). Similarly, subjective impressions of facial pleasantness indicated that liars were significantly less facially pleasant than truth tellers (d = −0.20), but this did not occur when facial pleasantness was measured objectively (d = 0.07).

Discussion

Previous perspectives on cues to deception have pointed to the predictive value of factors such as the feelings of guilt or apprehensiveness that people may have about lying, the cognitive challenges involved in lying, and the attempts people make to control their verbal and nonverbal behaviors (e.g., Ekman, 1985/ 1992; Ekman & Friesen, 1969; Zuckerman et al., 1981). Unlike past formulations, our self-presentational perspective is grounded in psychology's growing understanding of the nature of lying in everyday life. Lying, we now know, is a fact of daily life, and not an extraordinary event. Lies, like truths, are often told in the pursuit of identity-relevant goals. People frequently lie to make themselves (or sometimes others) look better or feel better; they try to appear to be the kind of person they only wish they could truthfully claim to be (B. M. DePaulo, Kashy, et al., 1996). Now that we have recognized the pedestrian nature of most lie telling in people's lives, the factors underscored by others assume their rightful place.

Previous Perspectives on Cues to Deception

Feelings While Lying

In that the behaviors or feelings that people try to hide with their lies are usually only mildly discrediting, feelings of guilt should be mild as well. Similarly, for most lies, the sanctions attendant on getting caught are minimal; thus, liars should ordinarily seem only slightly more apprehensive than truth tellers. Perhaps these faint feelings of guilt and apprehensiveness account for the twinge of discomfort reported by the tellers of everyday lies. We believe that the discomfort is also born of the one identity-relevant implication that is common to all liars: They are willing to make claims they believe to be untrue.

Two predictions follow from this analysis. First, cues to negativity and tension will generally be weak. However, when liars have reason to feel especially guilty about their lies or apprehensive about the consequences of them, as when they are lying about transgressions, then those cues should be stronger. Consistent with predictions, we did find some of the expected cues in our analyses that combined across all studies. For example, liars made more negative statements than did truth tellers, and they appeared more tense. When we looked separately at the lies that were and were not about transgressions, we found that the cues to lies about transgressions were more plentiful and more robust than the cues to deception for any level of any of the other moderators we examined. In contrast, lies that were not about transgressions were barely discriminable from the truths.

261

The self-presentational perspective accords importance, not only to the feelings that liars experience more routinely than do truth tellers, but also to the feelings that truth tellers genuinely experience and that liars can only try to fake. When social actors are truthfully presenting aspects of themselves that are especially important to them, they have an emotional investment that is not easily simulated by those who only pretend to have such personal qualities. They also have the support of a lifetime of experiences at living the part. Liars' performances, then, would pale in comparison. Consistent with this formulation is our finding that liars were generally less forthcoming than truth tellers, and their tales were less compelling. For example, liars provided fewer details than did truth tellers. In contrast, truth tellers sounded more involved, more certain, more direct, and more personal.

Arousal

Pupil dilation and pitch did function as cues to deception and could be regarded as supportive of the hypothesized importance of generalized arousal. However, we believe that it is theoretically and empirically more precise and defensible to interpret these cues as indicative of particular attentional or information-processing activities or of specific affective experiences (e.g., Cacioppo, Petty, & Tassinary, 1989; Ekman et al., 1983; Neiss, 1988; Sparks & Greene, 1992).

Cognitive Complexities

Several theoretical statements share the assumption that lie telling is more cognitively challenging than telling the truth (e.g., Buller & Burgoon, 1996; Zuckerman et al., 1981). From our self-presentational perspective, we instead agree with McCornack (1997) in questioning that assumption. Because lie telling is so routinely practiced, it may generally be only slightly more challenging than telling the truth.

In the overall analyses combining all estimates of a given cue, we found some indications that liars may have been more preoccupied and more cognitively taxed than truth tellers. The level of involvement in their words and in their voices, which does not quite measure up to that of truth tellers, is one such possibility. So, too, is the impression of uncertainty that they convey. The discrepancies in their self-presentations may also be telling. Some of the expected cues, such as the longer response latencies, the shorter responses, and the more hesitant responses, did not emerge in the analyses that combined results across all studies. However, moderator analyses show that, as we had predicted, these cues were more revealing when the self-presentations may have been more challenging to generate. When social actors could not plan their presentations, compared with when they could, the response latencies of deceivers were greater than those of truth tellers, and their presentations tended to include more silent pauses. When presentations were sustained for greater lengths of time, liars' latencies to respond were again greater than those of truth tellers, and their responses were briefer and spoken in a higher pitch.

Attempted Control

From our self-presentational perspective, liars are attempting to control not just their behaviors (e.g., Zuckerman et al., 1981) but also their thoughts and feelings. Truth tellers attempt these forms of self-regulation as well, but liars' efforts are experienced as more deliberate. Deliberate self-regulatory efforts may be especially likely to usurp mental resources, leaving liars more preoccupied than truth tellers. Liars' tales therefore seem less compelling and less forthcoming. Because so many of the little lies that people tell require scant self-regulatory effort, the resulting cues generally are weak.

However, when self-regulatory efforts intensify, as when social actors are highly motivated (especially by identity-relevant goals) to get away with their lies, then cues intensify, too.

Consistent with our formulation is our finding that motivated liars (compared with less motivated ones) had even higher pitched voices than truth tellers, and they seemed even more tense and inhibited. When the motivation was one that linked success at deceit to identity and self-presentational concerns, cues became clearer still. When social actors saw their success as reflective of important aspects of themselves, compared with when there were no particular incentives, their lies were betrayed by the time it took them to begin their deceptive responses (relative to their truthful ones), the relative brevity of those responses, the silent hesitations within them, and the higher pitch in which they were spoken. Incentives that were not self-relevant resulted in cues to deception that differed less markedly from the cues that occurred when no special incentive was in place.

Interactivity

In Buller and Burgoon's (1996) interpersonal model of deception, the central theoretical construct is the degree of interaction between the liar and the target of the lies. The model predicts greater involvement and immediacy with greater interactivity, but our review found that liars in interactive contexts, relative to noninteractive ones, provided fewer details than did truth tellers. Eye contact, a nonverbal immediacy cue, did not differentially predict deception in interactive versus noninteractive contexts. Buller and Burgoon's model predicts greater composure with greater interaction, but we found that higher pitch—an indicator of lack of composure—was a cue to deception in interactive contexts only. Blinking was a more powerful cue to deception in noninteractive contexts. Other cues to composure, such as nervousness and fidgeting, did not vary with the interactivity of the context. Their model predicts greater fluency with increasing interaction, but our analysis indicates interactivity was not a significant moderator of any of the cues to fluency (non-ah speech disturbances, silent pauses, filled pauses).

We think Buller and Burgoon's (1996) interactivity predictions failed because their construct is theoretically imprecise (B. M. DePaulo, Ansfield, & Bell, 1996). Totally noninteractive contexts (e.g., leaving a lie on a target person's voicemail) differ from totally interactive ones (e.g., unscripted face-to-face interactions) in many important ways. One is the mere presence of the other person, even apart from any interaction with that person. That presence has the potential to affect self-awareness, awareness of the potential impact of the lie on that person, the salience of self-presentational goals, and feelings of accountability (e.g., Schlenker, 2002; Schlenker, Britt, Pennington, Murphy, & Doherty, 1994; Wicklund, 1982). Interactive exchanges entangle participants in multiple roles and tasks (Buller & Burgoon, 1996; Ekman & Friesen, 1969), which can be cognitively challenging. However, to the extent that interactive exchanges are the more familiar mode of communication, participants may find them less challenging than noninteractive communications. From a conversational analysis perspective, the significance of interactive processes may lie in the interpretive frame they provide (e.g., Brown & Levinson, 1987; Grice, 1989; Jacobs, Brashers, & Dawson, 1996; McCornack, 1992). For example, whether a person has provided too little, too much, unclear, or irrelevant information in response to an inquiry is more readily assessed within the context of the conversation than apart from it. To Buller and Burgoon, what was especially important about interaction is the opportunity it affords the participants to evaluate the effectiveness of their attempts (e.g., the liars can determine whether their targets seem suspicious) and adjust their behavior accordingly.

Some of the ways in which interactive contexts differ from noninteractive ones may be inconsistent with each other in their implications for cues to deception. Clarity should follow, not from Buller and Burgoon's (1996) approach of enumerating variables that moderate the effects of interactivity, but from looking separately at the important component processes. An example of this approach is (Levine and McCornack's, 1996, 2002) analysis of the "probing effect," which is the counterintuitive finding that communicators who are probed by their targets are perceived as more honest than those who are not probed. The initial explanation for this effect was behavioral adaptation: Probed communicators recognized the skepticism of their targets, and adapted their behavior to appear more truthful (e.g., Buller & Burgoon, 1996; Stiff & Miller, 1986). However, when Levine and McCornack (2002) manipulated the presence of probes in videotaped interviews in which the communicators' behavior was held constant (ruling out the behavioral adaptation explanation) the probing effect still occurred.

The Self-Presentational Perspective on Cues to Deception

Ordinary Imperfections and Unusual Contents

Only the self-presentational perspective predicts that lies are characterized by fewer ordinary imperfections and unusual contents than truths. Drawing from research and theory on credibility assessment (e.g., Yuille, 1989), we suggested that liars try to anticipate the kinds of communications that targets would find credible and that in doing so, fall prey to their own misconceptions about the nature of truth telling. Some of our results were consistent with that prediction. People who spontaneously corrected themselves and who admitted that they could not remember everything about the story they were relating, were more likely to be telling the truth than to be lying. It was also truth tellers who were somewhat more likely to tell stories richer in contextual embedding and unusual details.

The Looks and Sounds of Deceit Are Faint

We found evidence for all five of the categories of cues we predicted: Deceptive presentations (relative to truthful ones) were in some ways less forthcoming, less compelling, more negative, more tense, and suspiciously bereft of ordinary imperfections and unusual details. Fundamental to the self-presentational perspective is the prediction that these cues would be weak. In fact, they were. The median effect size of the 88 cues was just |0.10|. Only 3 of these cues had effect sizes greater than |0.40|.

Results of the moderator analyses suggest that pronouncements about the faintness of the signs of deceit are both understated and exaggerated. Lies told by social actors who have no special motivation to succeed in their presentations and lies that are not about transgressions leave almost no discernible cues. Even some of the cues that did seem promising in the results combined across all estimates—for example, cues to tension and to pitch—lost a bit of their luster for self-presentations that were not about transgressions and that were not driven by any particular incentives. These nearly cueless lies most closely resemble the deceptive presentations of self in everyday life. However, when social actors were using their lies to hide matters that could spoil their identities (such as when they were lying about transgressions), and when their success at lying was linked to important aspects of their self-concepts, then cues to deception were no longer quite so faint.

Using our self-presentational perspective, we were able to predict some important moderators of the strength of cues to deception. In this section, we consider five other ways in which the results of our overall analyses may have underestimated the potential for verbal and nonverbal cues to separate truths from lies.

First, perhaps effect sizes for cues to deception would be more impressive if they were computed separately for the different emotions that senders may be trying to conceal or to convey (Ekman, 1985/ 1992). There were not enough relevant studies available to test this possibility adequately in the present review. Second, in this review, as in most of the studies in the literature, we tested the predictive power of each behavioral cue individually. However, the degree to which lies can be discriminated from truths could potentially be improved if combinations of cues were considered (e.g., Ekman, O'Sullivan, Friesen, & Scherer, 1991; Vrij, Edward, Roberts, & Bull, 2000). Third, if the replicability of a set of cues within a particular context can be established, the implications could be important even if the particular cues could not be generalized to different contexts. For example, behavioral cues believed to be indicative of deceit in the context of polygraph testing (e.g., Reid & Arthur, 1953) or criminal interrogations (e.g., Macdonald & Michaud, 1987) are worth establishing even if some of them occur infrequently outside of those contexts. Fourth, it is possible that particular individuals telegraph their lies in idiosyncratic yet highly reliable ways (Vrij & Mann, 2001) that are not captured by our meta-analytic approach. Finally, our results suggest that truths and lies may be discriminated more powerfully by using subjective measures rather than objective ones. However, detailed coding systems that are carefully validated and used to test theoretically based predictions may enable more precise discriminations than untrained observers could achieve with their subjective impressions (e.g., Ekman & Friesen, 1978; Scherer, 1982).

When Truths and Lies Switch Sides

It is important to emphasize that there are exceptions to the predictions we derived from the self-presentational perspective. There are times when people more readily embrace their deceptive presentations than their truthful ones. For example, a man who has long fantasized about being a war hero and has claimed repeatedly to have been one may eventually make that false claim more convincingly than he can describe his actual war-year experiences teaching in his homeland, which was at peace. There are also times when truthful presentations are enacted with a greater sense of deliberateness than are deceptive ones. Self-incriminating truths are examples of this (cf. Kraut, 1978). When the tables are turned, the cues are too; it is the truth tellers who seem less forthcoming, more tense, and more negative, and it is they who tell stories that sound less compelling.

The behaviors we have described as cues to deception, then, may be more accurately described as cues to the hypothesized processes (e.g., attempts to regulate thoughts, feelings, and behaviors) and to psychological states (e.g., investment in, and familiarity with, the attempted performance). Experimental research that directly tests the role of these processes in producing the predicted cues remains to be done.

Cues to Truths, to Personalities, and to Situations

Our use of the term cues to deception could suggest that we are describing the ways that liars behave, but in fact we are describing the ways in which liars act differently than truth tellers. Experimental manipulations and individual differences can be linked to cues to deception by their implications for the behavior of liars or truth tellers, or both. For example, in a study in which participants were selected because they saw themselves as very independent (B. M. DePaulo et al., 1991), the truthful life stories they told that showcased their independence were more responsive to the experimental manipulations than were the life stories that were fabricated.

Caution is also in order in interpreting the moderators of cues to deception. For example, when we say that eye contact is a cue to deception when senders are motivated to get away with their lies but not when they are not motivated, we are not necessarily claiming that liars more often avoid eye contact when they have an incentive to succeed than when they do not (though they may). Instead, we are saying that the degree to which liars avoid eye contact more than truth tellers do is greater when they are motivated to succeed than when they are not. The cues we describe in our analyses of motivation as a moderator are not cues to motivation (that is a different question), they are cues to deception under different levels of motivation.

For example, people telling lies in high stakes circumstances (e.g., while on trial for murder) may be expected to seem more nervous than people telling comparable lies when the stakes are lower (e.g., in traffic court). But truth tellers may also seem more nervous in the high stakes setting. Nervousness would only be a cue to deception in the murder trial if liars feel even more nervous than truth tellers. It would be a stronger cue to deception in the murder trial than in traffic court only if the degree to which liars are more nervous than truth tellers is greater in the murder trial than in traffic court.

To make these important distinctions clearer in future research, we suggest investigators adopt a reporting style that has rarely been used in the deception literature: Mean levels of the cues should be reported separately for truths and lies at each level of the experimental manipulations and for each of the individual difference categories. Results could then be analyzed in the familiar factorial. That would clearly indicate, for example, whether people seem more nervous when the stakes are high than when they are low, regardless of whether they are lying or telling the truth; whether they are more nervous when lying than when telling the truth, regardless of the stakes; and whether the degree to which they are more nervous when lying than when telling the truth is greater when the stakes are high than when they are low.

The implications for our understanding of individual differences are also important. For example, we claimed above that liars make an effort to seem credible whereas truth tellers take their credibility for granted. This may seem readily countered by the familiar finding from the social anxiety literature indicating that socially anxious people rarely take anything positive about themselves for granted (e.g., B. M. DePaulo, Kenny, Hoover, Web, & Oliver, 1987; Leary & Kowalski, 1995; Schlenker & Leary, 1982), but that is a main-effect finding about the ways in which socially anxious people differ from socially secure people. If socially anxious people do indeed feel insecure about the credibility of their truths, but they feel even more insecure about the credibility of their lies, then the predictions we outlined should apply to them as well as to others.

When Confounded Designs Are of Practical Significance

All of the studies of transgressions were marred by a confound: The people who lied were only those who committed a transgression, and the people who told truths were only those who did not. It is not clear, then, whether any of the resulting cues were cues to deception at all. They may have been cues to the transgression. From a scientific stance, we have no unambiguous data from these studies about the ways that lies differ from truths. However, when considered from an applied perspective, these studies may tell practitioners exactly what they want to know. We do not wish to minimize the frequency or significance of false confessions (Kassin, 1997), but ordinarily, credibility is not much at issue when people admit to discrediting acts. Of greater interest are the ways in which truthful denials can be distinguished from deceptive ones.

Blurring the Line Between Truths and Lies

In the studies we reviewed, the line between truths and lies was drawn clearly. There were good methodological reasons for this. To distinguish the characteristics of lies from those of truths, it is of course necessary to first distinguish lies from truths. However, outside of the lab, the line between them is often blurred.

The self-presentational perspective underscores the similarities between truths and lies. Telling the whole truth and nothing but the truth is rarely possible or desirable. All self-presentations are edited. The question is one of whether the editing crosses the line from the honest highlighting of aspects of identity that are most relevant in the ongoing situation to a dishonest attempt to mislead. This suggests that truthful and deceptive self-presentations may be construed more aptly as aligned along a continuum rather than sorted into clear and distinct categories. But there may be categorical aspects as well. For example, B. R. Schlenker (1982) distinguished among self-presentations that fit within people's private latitudes of acceptance, neutrality, or rejection (cf. Sherif & Hovland, 1961). Self-presentations that are well within the boundaries of the latitude of acceptance are clearly truths. These presentations capture attitudes, feelings, and personal qualities that people unambiguously accept as their own. Self-presentations that are at the cusp of the latitude of acceptance just barely pass as truths. Self-presentations that are well within people's private latitudes of rejection are clearly lies. The most elusive statements are those falling in the latitude of neutrality; the editing of these self-statements slips beyond the bounds of honesty but stops just short of the brink of deceit. One implication of this conceptualization is that the effect sizes we reported for cues to deception, though generally small, may actually be overestimates of the true differences between truths and lies in everyday life (McCornack, 1997). In the studies we reviewed, the truths and lies were typically well within the bounds of acceptance and rejection. In many naturalistic situations, they are not.

Definitional dilemmas also arise in situations in which neither truths nor lies are entirely satisfying to people trying to decide what to say. (Bavelas, Black, Chovil, and Mullett, 1990a, 1990b) have described many of these intriguing predicaments in which people may prefer not to lie but dislike the alternative of telling a hurtful or costly truth. For example, what do people say when an acquaintance asks their opinion of a class presentation that was poorly organized and badly delivered? (Bavelas et al.'s, 1990a, 1990b) answer was that they equivocate: They make themselves unclear; they refrain from answering the question directly and avoid stating their true opinions. Yet, (Bavelas et al., 1990a, 1990b) argued that equivocal answers are truthful. When participants in those studies read the responses to the classmate, they rated the responses as closer to the truthful end of the scale (labeled as presentation was poorly organized and badly delivered) than closer to the deceptive end (labeled as well organized and well delivered). This criterion of truthfulness bypasses the question of intentionality. The perceivers of self-presentations have the full authority to make the judgments that determine what counts as deceptive.

We are not yet ready to hand over that authority to the perceivers. Definitional issues aside, though, we think that studies of social actors' responses to communicative dilemmas such as the ones described by (Bavelas et al., 1990a, 1990b) are important for another reason. They point to some of the ways in which people's self-presentational strategies can be more imaginative and their goals more complex than much of the current literature on cues to deception might suggest.

In a pair of studies, B. M. DePaulo and Bell (1996) created the kind of dilemma that (Bavelas et al., 1990a, 1990b) described. Students chose their favorite and least favorite paintings from the ones on display in the room, and then each interacted with an artist who claimed that the student's least favorite painting was one of her own. When students were asked what they thought of that painting, they amassed misleading evidence (i.e., they mentioned aspects of the painting they really did like while neglecting to note all of the aspects they disliked), and they implied that they liked the painting by emphasizing how much they disliked other paintings in the room that were painted by other artists (without stating directly that they liked the painting in question). B. M. DePaulo and Bell (1996) posited a "defensibility postulate" to account for these ploys. The students were trying to communicate in ways that could be defended as truthful (e.g., they really did like the aspects of the paintings they mentioned, and they really did dislike the other artists' work) but that would also mislead the artist about their true opinions. These strategies are not captured by any of the objectively measured cues we reviewed. Yet, they provide hints about what people are trying to accomplish in these challenging situations that are perhaps more telling than what can be learned by counting behaviors such as foot movements and speech disturbances.

Laboratory Lies

The studies we reviewed included lies told by criminal suspects and people in the news, but in most of the studies, college students told truths and lies in laboratory experiments. One common critique of such studies (e.g., Miller & Stiff, 1993) is that the participants typically are not highly motivated to get away with their lies. In many of these studies, there were neither rewards for successful lies nor sanctions for unsuccessful ones. Moreover, the participants often told their truths and lies because they were instructed to do so as part of the experimental procedures; they did not freely choose to lie or to tell the truth. A related critique (Miller & Stiff, 1993) is that in many studies, the degree of interaction between the social actor and another person was minimal; sometimes participants told their truths and lies with little or no feedback or skepticism from any other person.

Although these critiques are often cast as attacks on the ecological validity of studies of deception, as such they may be largely wrong. The critiqued characteristics of studies of deception may in fact aptly capture the nature of the vast majority of lies (B. M. DePaulo, Ansfield, & Bell, 1996; B. M. DePaulo, Kashy, et al., 1996). The everyday lies that people tell are rarely consequential. In many instances, they are essentially obligatory. The guest who is treated to an extensively prepared but unpalatable dinner rarely feels free to say truthfully that the food was disgusting. The students whose late-night partying has interfered with the timely completion of their take-home exams tell lies to the course instructor just as readily as if they had been explicitly instructed to do so. Furthermore, the little lies of everyday life rarely trigger an extended discourse. The host or hostess nods in appreciation, and the course instructor waits for the students to depart before rolling his or her eyes.

One way that truths and lies told in the laboratory really may fail to reflect the dynamics of self-presentation outside of the lab is that people may be more self-conscious about their truthful presentations than they are ordinarily. If this is so, then the feeling of deliberateness that we have underscored in our analysis may separate truths from lies less definitively in the lab. In this respect, the effect sizes of the cues to deception we have reported may underestimate the true magnitude of the effects.

Discriminating Cues to Deception From Cues to Other Processes and States

We have combined the results of more than 1,300 estimates of the relationship between behaviors and deceit; therefore, we can name with some confidence some of the cues to deceit. But the behaviors that are indicative of deception can be indicative of other states and processes as well. In fact, we used a consideration of such states and processes to generate predictions about the kinds of behaviors we might expect to be indicative of deceit. However, the issue of discriminant validity still looms large. For example, is it possible to distinguish the anxiety that is sometimes associated with lying from the fear of being unfairly accused of lying (e.g., Bond & Fahey, 1987) or even from anxiety that has no necessary connection to deceit (e.g., nervousness about public speaking, shyness, distress about a personal problem)? Lying sometimes results in verbal and nonverbal inconsistencies, but so does genuine ambivalence (B. M. DePaulo & Rosenthal, 1979a, 1979b). Can the two be differentiated? Some attempts have been made to begin to address these kinds of issues (e.g., deTurck & Miller, 1985), and we expect to see some progress in the future. However, we also expect most future reports to end with the same cautionary note we issue here: Behavioral cues that are discernible by human perceivers are associated with deceit only probabilistically. To establish definitively that someone is lying, further evidence is needed.

References

1. Alonso-Quecuty, M. (1992). Deception detection and reality monitoring: A new answer to an old question? In F. Losel, D. Bender, & T. Bliesener (Eds.), Psychology and law: International perspectives (pp. 328-332). New York: de Gruyter.

2. Ambady, N. & Rosenthal, R. (1992). *Psychological Bulletin,* 111, 256-274 10.1037//0033-2909 .111.2.256.

3. Anderson, D. E., DePaulo, B. M. & Ansfield, M. E. (2002). *Personality & Social Psychology Bulletin,* 28, 536-545.

4. Anolli, L. & Ciceri, R. (1997). *Journal of Nonverbal Behavior,* 21, 259-284.

5. Bagley, J. & Manelis, L. (1979). *Perceptual & Motor Skills,* 49, 591-594.

6. Bargh, J. A. (1989). Conditional automaticity: Varieties of automatic influence in social perception and cognition. In J. Uleman & J. A. Bargh (Eds.), Unintended thought (pp. 3-51). New York: Guilford Press.

7. Baumeister, R. F. (1998). The self. In D. T. Gilbert, S. T. Fiske, & G. Lindzey (Eds.), Handbook of social psychology (4th ed., Vol. 1, pp. 680-740). Boston: McGraw-Hill.

8. Baumeister, R. F., Bratslavsky, E., Muraven, M. & Tice, D. M. (1998). *Journal of Personality & Social Psychology,* 74, 1252-1265.

9. Baumeister, R. F., Stillwell, A. M. & Heatherton, T. F. (1994). *Psychological Bulletin,* 115, 243-267.

10. Bavelas, J. B., Black, A., Chovil, N., & Mullett, J. (1990a). Equivocal communication. Newbury Park, CA: Sage.

11. Bavelas, J. B., Black, A., Chovil, N. & Mullett, J. (1990). *Journal of Language & Social Psychology,* 9, 135-161.

12. Bell, K. L. & DePaulo, B. M. (1996). *Basic & Applied Social Psychology,* 18, 243-266.

13. Ben-Shakhar, G. & Elaad, E. *Journal of Applied Psychology.*

14. Berger, C. R., Karol, S. H. & Jordan, J. M. (1989). *Human Communication Research,* 16, 91-119.

15. Berrien, F. K. & Huntington, G. H. (1943). *Journal of Experimental Psychology,* 32, 443-449.

16. Bok, S. (1978). Lying: Moral choice in public and private life. New York: Pantheon.

17. Bond, C. F., Jr., & DePaulo, B. M. (2002). Accuracy and truth bias in the detection of deception: A meta-analytic review. Manuscript in preparation.

18. Bond Jr., C. F. & Fahey, W. E. (1987). *British Journal of Social Psychology,* 26, 41-46.

19. Bond Jr., C. F., Kahler, K. N. & Paolicelli, L. M. (1985). *Journal of Experimental Social Psychology,* 21, 331-345.

20. Bond Jr., C. F., Omar, A., Mahmoud, A. & Bonser, R. N. (1990). *Journal of Nonverbal Behavior,* 14, 189-204.

21. Bradley, M. T. & Janisse, M. P. (1979). *Psychology: A Quarterly Journal of Human Behavior,* 16, 33-39.

22. Bradley, M. T. & Janisse, M. P. (1981). *Psychophysiology,* 18, 307-315.

23. Brown, P., & Levinson, S. (1987). Politeness: Some universals in language usage. New York: Cambridge University Press.

24. Buller, D. B. & Aune, R. K. (1987). *Journal of Nonverbal Behavior,* 11, 269-290.

25. Buller, D. B. & Burgoon, J. K. (1996). *Communication Theory,* 3, 203-242.

26. Buller, D. B., Burgoon, J. K., Buslig, A. & Roiger, J. (1996). *Communication Theory,* 6, 268-289.

27. Buller, D. B., Comstock, J., Aune, R. K. & Strzyzewski, K. D. (1989). *Journal of Nonverbal Behavior,* 13, 155-170.

28. Burgoon, J. K. & Buller, D. B. (1994). *Journal of Nonverbal Behavior,* 18, 155-184.

29. Burgoon, J. K., Buller, D. B., Afifi, W., White, C., & Buslig, A. (1996, May). The role of immediacy in deceptive interpersonal interactions. Paper presented at the annual meeting of the International Communication Association, Chicago, IL.

30. Burgoon, J. K., Buller, D. B., Floyd, K. & Grandpre, J. (1996). *Communication Research,* 23, 724-748.

31. Burgoon, J. K., Buller, D. B., Guerrero, L. K., Afifi, W. A. & Feldman, C. M. (1996). *Communication Monographs,* 63, 50-69.

32. Burns, J. A. & Kintz, B. L. (1976). *Bulletin of the Psychonomic Society,* 7, 87-89.

33. Butterworth, B. (1978). *Semiotica,* 24, 317-339.

34. Butterworth, B., & Goldman-Eisler, F. (1979). Recent studies on cognitive rhythm. In A. W. Siegman & S. Feldstein (Eds.), Of speech and time: Temporal patterns in interpersonal contexts (pp. 211-224). Hillsdale, NJ: Erlbaum.

35. Cacioppo, J. T., Petty, R. E., & Tassinary, L. G. (1989). Social psychophysiology: A new look. In L. Berkowitz (Ed.), Advances in experimental social psychology (Vol. 22, pp. 39-91). San Diego, CA: Academic Press.

36. Camden, C., Motley, M. T. & Wilson, A. (1984). *Western Journal of Speech Communication,* 48, 309-325.

37. Carver, C. S., & Scheier, M. F. (1981). Attention and self-regulation: A control-theory approach to human behavior. New York: Springer-Verlag.

38. Chiba, H. (1985). *Journal of Human Development,* 21, 22-29.

39. Christenfeld, N. J. (1994). *Journal of Language & Social Psychology,* 13, 192-199.

40. Christensen, D. (1980). Decoding of intended versus unintended nonverbal messages as a function of social skill and anxiety. Unpublished doctoral dissertation, University of Connecticut, Storrs.

41. Ciofu, I. (1974). *Archiv fuer Psychologie,* 126, 170-180.

42. Cody, M. J. & O'Hair, H. D. (1983). *Communication Monographs,* 50, 175-192.

43. Cody, M. J., Lee, W. S., & Chao, E. Y. (1989). Telling lies: Correlates of deception among Chinese. In J. P. Forgas & J. M. Innes (Eds.), Recent advances in social psychology: An international perspective (pp. 359-368). Amsterdam: North-Holland.

44. Cody, M. J., Marston, P. J., & Foster, M. (1984). Deception: Paralinguistic and verbal leakage. In R. N. Bostrom & B. H. Westley (Eds.), Communication yearbook 8 (pp. 464-490). Beverly Hills, CA: Sage.

45. Cohen, J. (1988). Statistical power analysis for the behavioral sciences (Rev. ed.). Hillsdale, NJ: Erlbaum.

46. Cooper, H. (1998). Synthesizing research: A guide for literature reviews (3rd ed.). Beverly Hills, CA: Sage.

47. Craig, K. D., Hyde, S. A. & Patrick, C. J. (1991). *Pain,* 46, 161-172.

48. Cutrow, R. J., Parks, A., Lucas, N. & Thomas, K. (1972). *Psychophysiology,* 9, 578-588.

49. DePaulo, B. M. (1992). *Psychological Bulletin,* 111, 203-243.

50. DePaulo, B. M. (1994). *Current Directions in Psychological Science,* 3, 83-86.

51. DePaulo, B. M. & Bell, K. L. (1996). *Journal of Personality & Social Psychology,* 71, 703-716.

52. DePaulo, B. M., & Friedman, H. S. (1998). Nonverbal communication. In D. Gilbert, S. T. Fiske, & G. Lindzey (Eds.), Handbook of social psychology (4th ed., Vol. 2, pp. 3-40). New York: Random House.

53. DePaulo, B. M. & Kashy, D. A. (1998). *Journal of Personality & Social Psychology, 74*, 63-79.

54. DePaulo, B. M., & Kirkendol, S. E. (1989). The motivational impairment effect in the communication of deception. In J. C. Yuille (Ed.), Credibility assessment (pp. 51-70). Dordrecht, the Netherlands: Kluwer Academic.

55. B. M., & Rosenthal, R. (1979a). Ambivalence, discrepancy, and deception in nonverbal communication. In R. Rosenthal (Ed.), Skill in nonverbal communication (pp. 204-248). Cambridge, MA: Oelgeschlager, Gunn, & Hain.

56. DePaulo, B. M. & Rosenthal, R. (1979). *Journal of Personality & Social Psychology, 37*, 1713-1722.

57. DePaulo, B. M., Ansfield, M. E. & Bell, K. L. (1996). *Communication Theory, 3*, 297-310.

58. DePaulo, B. M., Ansfield, M. E., Kirkendol, S. E., & Boden, J. M. (2002). Serious lies. Manuscript submitted for publication.

59. DePaulo, B. M., Blank, A. L., Swain, G. W. & Hairfield, J. G. (1992). *Personality & Social Psychology Bulletin, 18*, 276-285.

60. DePaulo, B. M., Epstein, J. A. & LeMay, C. S. (1990). *Journal of Personality, 58*, 623-640.

61. DePaulo, B. M., Jordan, A., Irvine, A. & Laser, P. S. (1982). *Child Development, 53*, 701-709.

62. DePaulo, B. M., Kashy, D. A., Kirkendol, S. E., Wyer, M. M. & Epstein, J. A. (1996). *Journal of Personality & Social Psychology, 70*, 979-995.

63. DePaulo, B. M., Kenny, D. A., Hoover, C., Webb, W. & Oliver, P. (1987). *Journal of Personality & Social Psychology, 52*, 303-315.

64. DePaulo, B. M., Kirkendol, S. E., Tang, J. & O'Brien, T. P. (1988). *Journal of Nonverbal Behavior, 12*, 177-202.

65. DePaulo, B. M., Lanier, K. & Davis, T. (1983). *Journal of Personality & Social Psychology, 45*, 1096-1103.

66. DePaulo, B. M., LeMay, C. S. & Epstein, J. A. (1991). *Personality & Social Psychology Bulletin, 17*, 14-24.

67. DePaulo, B. M., Rosenthal, R., Green, C. R. & Rosenkrantz, J. (1982). *Journal of Experimental Social Psychology, 18*, 433-446.

68. DePaulo, B. M., Rosenthal, R., Rosenkrantz, J. & Green, C. R. (1982). *Basic & Applied Social Psychology, 3*, 291-312.

69. DePaulo, B. M., Stone, J. I., & Lassiter, G. D. (1985a). Deceiving and detecting deceit. In B. R. Schlenker (Ed.), The self and social life (pp. 323-370). New York: McGraw-Hill.

70. DePaulo, B. M., Stone, J. I. & Lassiter, G. D. (1985). *Journal of Personality & Social Psychology, 48*, 1191-1203.

71. DePaulo, P. J. & DePaulo, B. M. (1989). *Journal of Applied Social Psychology, 19*, 1552-1577.

72. deTurck, M. A. & Miller, G. R. (1985). *Human Communication Research, 12*, 181-201.

73. di Battista, P. & Abrahams, M. (1995). *Communication Reports, 8*, 120-127.

74. Dulaney Jr., E. F. (1982). *Human Communication Research, 9*, 75-82.

75. Ekman, P. (1992). Telling lies. New York: Norton. (Original work published 1985)

76. Ekman, P. & Friesen, W. V. (1969). *Psychiatry: Interpersonal & Biological Processes, 32*, 88-106.

77. Ekman, P. & Friesen, W. V. (1972). *The Journal of Communication, 22*, 353-374.

78. Ekman, P., & Friesen, W. V. (1978). The facial action coding system. Palo Alto, CA: Consulting Psychologists Press.

79. Ekman, P., Friesen, W. V. & O'Sullivan, M. (1988). *Journal of Personality & Social Psychology, 54*, 414-420.

80. Ekman, P., Friesen, W. V. & Scherer, K. R. (1976). *Semiotica, 16*, 23-27.

81. Ekman, P., Friesen, W. V. & Simons, R. C. (1985). *Journal of Personality & Social Psychology, 49*, 1416-1426.

82. Ekman, P., Levenson, R. W. & Friesen, W. V. (1983). *Science, 221*, 1208-1210.

83. Ekman, P., O'Sullivan, M., Friesen, W. V. & Scherer, K. R. (1991). *Journal of Nonverbal Behavior, 15*, 125-135.

84. Elliott, G. L. (1979). *Journal of Personality & Social Psychology, 37*, 1282-1292.

85. Exline, R. V., Thibaut, J., Hickey, C. B., & Gumpert, P. (1970). Visual interaction in relation to Machiavellianism and an unethical act. In R. Christie & F. Geis (Eds.), Studies in Machiavellianism (pp. 53-75). New York: Academic Press.

86. Feeley, T. H. & deTurck, M. A. (1998). *Journal of Nonverbal Behavior, 22,* 189-204.

87. Fehr, B. J., & Exline, R. V. (1987). Social visual interaction: Conceptual and literature review. In A. W. Siegman & S. Feldstein (Eds.), Nonverbal behavior and communication (2nd ed., pp. 225-326). Hillsdale, NJ: Erlbaum.

88. Feldman, R. S., Devin-Sheehan, L. & Allen, V. L. (1978). *American Educational Research Journal, 15,* 217-231.

89. Feldman, R. S., Forrest, J. A. & Happ, B. R. (2002). *Basic & Applied Social Psychology, 24,* 163-170.

90. Fiedler, K. (1989). Suggestion and credibility: Lie detection based on content-related cues. In V. A. Gheorghiu, P. Netter, H. J. Eysenck, & R. Rosenthal (Eds.), Suggestion and suggestibility (pp. 323-335). New York: Springer-Verlag.

91. Fiedler, K. & Walka, I. (1993). *Human Communication Research, 20,* 199-223.

92. Fiedler, K., Schmid, J., Kurzenhauser, S., & Schroter, V. (1997). Lie detection as an attribution process: The anchoring effect revisited. Unpublished manuscript.

93. Field, A. P. (2001). *Psychological Methods, 6,* 161-180.

94. Finkelstein, S. (1978). The relationship between physical attractiveness and nonverbal behaviors. Unpublished honors thesis, Hampshire College, Amherst, MA.

95. Fleming, J. H. (1994). *Advances in Experimental Social Psychology, 26,* 215-292.

96. Fleming, J. H. & Rudman, L. A. (1993). *Journal of Personality & Social Psychology, 64,* 44-59.

97. Frank, M. G. (1989). Human lie detection ability as a function of the liar's motivation. Unpublished doctoral dissertation, Cornell University, Ithaca, NY.

98. Gagnon, L. R. (1975). The encoding and decoding of cues to deception. Unpublished doctoral dissertation, Arizona State University, Tempe.

99. Galin, K. E. & Thorn, B. E. (1993). *Journal of Social & Clinical Psychology, 12,* 182-197.

100. Gibbons, F. X. (1990). *Advances in experimental social psychology, 23,* 249-303.

101. Gilbert, D. T. & Krull, D. S. (1988). *Journal of Personality & Social Psychology, 54,* 193-202.

102. Gilbert, D. T., Krull, D. S. & Pelham, B. W. (1988). *Journal of Personality & Social Psychology, 55,* 685-694.

103. Goldman-Eisler, F. (1968). Psycholinguistics: Experiments in spontaneous speech. New York: Academic Press.

104. Goldstein, E. R. (1923). *American Journal of Psychology, 34,* 562-581.

105. Greene, J. O., O'Hair, H. D., Cody, M. J. & Yen, C. (1985). *Human Communication Research, 11,* 335-364.

106. Grice, P. (1989). Studies in the way of words. Cambridge, MA: Harvard University Press.

107. Gross, J. J. (1998). *Journal of Personality & Social Psychology, 74,* 224-237.

108. Gross, J. J. & Levenson, R. W. (1993). *Journal of Personality & Social Psychology, 64,* 970-986.

109. Hadjistavropoulos, H. D. & Craig, K. D. (1994). *Journal of Consulting & Clinical Psychology, 62,* 341-349.

110. Hadjistavropoulos, H. D., Craig, K. D., Hadjistavropoulos, T. & Poole, G. D. (1996). *Pain, 65,* 251-258.

111. Hall, M. E. (1986). Detecting deception in the voice: An analysis of fundamental frequency, syllabic duration, and amplitude of the human voice. Unpublished doctoral dissertation, Michigan State University, East Lansing.

112. Hample, D. (1980). *Southern Speech Communication Journal, 46,* 33-47.

113. Harrigan, J. A. & O'Connell, D. M. (1996). *Personality & Individual Differences, 21,* 205-212.

114. Harrison, A. A., Hwalek, M., Raney, D. & Fritz, J. G. (1978). *Social Psychology, 41,* 156-161.

115. Hedges, L. V., & Becker, B. J. (1986). Statistical methods in the meta-analysis of research on gender differences. In J. S. Hyde & M. C. Linn (Eds.), The psychology of gender: Advances through meta-analysis (pp. 14-50). Baltimore: Johns Hopkins University Press.

116. Hedges, L. V., & Olkin, I. (1985). Statistical methods for meta-analysis. Orlando, FL: Academic Press.

117. Heilveil, I. (1976). *Journal of Clinical Psychology, 32,* 675-676.

118. Heilveil, I. & Muehleman, J. T. (1981). *Psychotherapy: Theory, Research, and Practice, 18,* 329-335.

119. Heinrich, C. U. & Borkenau, P. (1998). *Journal of Personality,* 66, 687-712.

120. Hemsley, G. D. (1977). Experimental studies in the behavioral indicants of deception. Unpublished doctoral dissertation, University of Toronto, Toronto, Ontario, Canada.

121. Hernandez-Fernaud, E. & Alonso-Quecuty, M. (1997). *Applied Cognitive Psychology,* 11, 55-68.

122. Hess, E. H. & Polt, J. M. (1963). *Science,* 140, 1190-1192.

123. Hess, U. (1989). On the dynamics of emotional facial expression. Unpublished doctoral dissertation. Dartmouth College, Hanover, NH.

124. Hess, U. & Kleck, R. E. (1990). *European Journal of Social Psychology,* 20, 369-385.

125. Hess, U. & Kleck, R. E. (1994). *European Journal of Social Psychology,* 24, 367-381.

126. Hocking, J. E. & Leathers, D. G. (1980). *Communication Monographs,* 47, 119-131.

127. Holland, M. K. & Tarlow, G. (1972). *Psychological Reports,* 31, 119-127.

128. Holland, M. K. & Tarlow, G. (1975). *Psychological Reports,* 41, 403-406.

129. Holtgraves, T. (1986). *Journal of Personality & Social Psychology,* 51, 305-314.

130. Horvath, F. (1978). *Journal of Applied Psychology,* 63, 338-344.

131. Horvath, F. (1979). *Journal of Applied Psychology,* 64, 323-330.

132. Horvath, F. S. (1973). *Journal of Police Science and Administration,* 1, 138-152.

133. Horvath, F., Jayne, B. & Buckley, J. (1994). *Journal of Forensic Sciences,* 39, 793-807.

134. Jacobs, S., Brashers, D. & Dawson, E. J. (1996). *Communication Monographs,* 63, 98-103.

135. Janisse, M. P. & Bradley, M. T. (1980). *Perceptual & Motor Skills,* 50, 748-750.

136. Johnson, M. K. & Raye, C. L. (1981). *Psychological Bulletin,* 88, 67-85.

137. Jones, W. H., & Burdette, M. P. (1993). Betrayal in close relationships. In A. L. Weber & J. Harvey (Eds.), Perspectives on close relationships (pp. 1-14). New York: Allyn & Bacon.

138. Kahneman, D. (1973). Attention and effort. Englewood Cliffs, NJ: Prentice-Hall.

139. Kahneman, D. & Beatty, J. (1967). *Perception & Psychophysics,* 2, 101-105.

140. Kahneman, D., Tursky, B., Shapiro, D. & Crider, A. (1969). *Journal of Experimental Psychology,* 79, 164-167.

141. Kappas, A., Hess, U., & Scherer, K. R. (1991). Voice and emotion. In R. S. Feldman & B. Rime (Eds.), Fundamentals of nonverbal behavior (pp. 200-238). Cambridge, England: Cambridge University Press.

142. Kashy, D. A. & DePaulo, B. M. (1996). *Journal of Personality & Social Psychology,* 70, 1037-1051.

143. Kasl, S. V. & Mahl, G. F. (1965). *Journal of Personality & Social Psychology,* 1, 425-433.

144. Kassin, S. M. (1997). *American Psychologist,* 52, 221-233.

145. Keltner, D. & Buswell, B. N. (1996). *Cognition & Emotion,* 10, 155-171.

146. Keltner, D., & Harker, L. A. (1998). Forms and functions of the nonverbal signal of shame. In P. Gilbert & B. Andrews (Eds.), Interpersonal approaches to shame (pp. 78-98). Oxford, England: Oxford University Press.

147. Keltner, D., Young, R. C., Heerey, E. A., Oemig, C. & Monarch, N. D. (1998). *Journal of Personality & Social Psychology,* 75, 1231-1247.

148. Kennedy, J. & Coe, W. C. (1994). *International Journal of Clinical & Experimental Hypnosis,* 42, 13-19.

149. Kimble, C. E. & Seidel, S. D. (1991). *Journal of Nonverbal Behavior,* 15, 99-105.

150. Kimble, G. A. & Perimuter, L. C. (1970). *Psychological Review,* 77, 361-384.

151. Knapp, M. L., Hart, R. P. & Dennis, H. S. (1974). *Human Communication Research,* 1, 15-29.

152. Kohnken, G., Schimossek, E., Aschermann, E. & Hofer, E. (1995). *Journal of Applied Psychology,* 80, 671-684.

153. Koper, R. J., & Sahlman, J. M. (2001). The behavioral correlates of naturally occurring, high motivation deceptive communication. Manuscript submitted for publication.

154. Krauss, R. M. (1981). Impression formation, impression management, and nonverbal behaviors. In E. T. Higgins, C. P. Herman, & M. P. Zanna (Eds.), Social cognition: Vol. 1. The Ontario Symposium (pp. 323-341). Hillsdale, NJ: Erlbaum.

155. Kraut, R. E. (1978). *Journal of Personality & Social Psychology,* 36, 380-391.

156. Kraut, R. E. & Poe, D. (1980). *Journal of Personality & Social Psychology,* 39, 784-798.

157. Kuiken, D. (1981). *Journal of Experimental Social Psychology,* 17, 183-196.

158. Kurasawa, T. (1988). *Japanese Psychological Research,* 30, 114-121.

159. Landry, K. L. & Brigham, J. C. (1992). *Law & Human Behavior,* 16, 663-676.

160. Leary, M. R., & Kowalski, R. (1995). Social anxiety. New York: Guilford Press.

161. Levenson, R. W., Ekman, P. & Friesen, W. V. (1990). *Psychophysiology, 27,* 363-384.

162. Levine, T. R. & McCornack, S. A. (1992). *Journal of Social & Personal Relationships, 9,* 143-154.

163. Levine, T. R. & McCornack, S. A. (1996). *Human Communication Research, 22,* 575-588.

164. Levine, T. R. & McCornack, S. A. (2002). *Human Communication Research, 27,* 471-502.

165. Lewis, B. P. & Linder, D. E. (1997). *Personality & Social Psychology Bulletin, 23,* 937-944.

166. Lewis, M., Stanger, C. & Sullivan, M. W. (1989). *Developmental Psychology, 25,* 439-443.

167. Lippard, P. V. (1988). *Western Journal of Speech Communication, 52,* 91-103.

168. Macdonald, J., & Michaud, D. (1987). The confession: Interrogation and criminal profiles for police officers. Denver: Apache Press.

169. Mahl, G. F. (1987). Explorations in nonverbal and vocal behavior. Hillsdale, NJ: Erlbaum.

170. Malone, B. E., & DePaulo, B. M. (2001). Measuring sensitivity to deception. In J. A. Hall & F. Bernieri (Eds.), Interpersonal sensitivity: Theory, measurement, and application (pp. 103-124). Mahwah, NJ: Erlbaum.

171. Malone, B. E., Adams, R. B., Anderson, D. E., Ansfield, M. E., & DePaulo, B. M. (1997, May). Strategies of deception and their correlates over the course of friendship. Poster presented at the annual meeting of the American Psychological Society, Washington, DC.

172. Malone, B. E., DePaulo, B. M., Adams, R. B., & Cooper, H. (2002). Perceived cues to deception: A meta-analytic review. Unpublished manuscript, University of Virginia, Charlottesville.

173. Manaugh, T. S., Wiens, A. N. & Matarazzo, J. D. (1970). *Journal of Clinical Psychology, 26,* 17-24.

174. Markus, H. (1977). *Journal of Personality & Social Psychology, 35,* 63-78.

175. Marston, W. M. (1920). *Journal of Experimental Psychology, 3,* 72-87.

176. Matarazzo, J. D., Wiens, A. N., Jackson, R. H. & Manaugh, T. S. (1970). *Journal of Clinical Psychology, 26,* 141-148.

177. McClintock, C. C. & Hunt, R. G. (1975). *Journal of Applied Social Psychology, 5,* 54-67.

178. McCornack, S. A. (1992). *Communication Monographs, 59,* 1-16.

179. McCornack, S. A. (1997). The generation of deceptive messages. In J. O. Greene (Ed.), Message production (pp. 91-126). Mahwah, NJ: Erlbaum.

180. McCornack, S. A. & Levine, T. R. (1990). *Communication Monographs, 57,* 119-138.

181. Mehrabian, A. (1971). *Journal of Experimental Research in Personality, 5,* 64-73.

182. Mehrabian, A. (1972). Nonverbal communication. Chicago: Aldine Atherton.

183. Metts, S. (1989). *Journal of Social & Personal Relationships, 6,* 159-179.

184. Metts, S. (1994). Relational transgressions. In W. R. Cupach & B. H. Spitzberg (Eds.), The dark side of interpersonal communication (pp. 217-239). Hillsdale, NJ: Erlbaum.

185. Miller, G. R., & Stiff, J. B. (1993). Deceptive communication. Newbury Park, CA: Sage.

186. Miller, G. R., deTurck, M. A. & Kalbfleisch, P. J. (1983). *Human Communication Research, 10,* 97-117.

187. Motley, M. T. (1974). *Western Speech, 38,* 81-87.

188. Muraven, M., Tice, D. M. & Baumeister, R. F. (1998). *Journal of Personality & Social Psychology, 74,* 774-789.

189. Neiss, R. (1988). *Psychological Bulletin, 103,* 345-366.

190. O'Hair, D. & Cody, M. J. (1987). *Human Relations, 40,* 1-13.

191. O'Hair, D., Cody, M. J., Wang, X. & Chen, E. (1990). *Communication Quarterly, 38,* 158-169.

192. O'Hair, H. D., Cody, M. J. & McLaughlin, M. L. (1981). *Human Communication Research, 7,* 325-339.

193. Pennebaker, J. W. & Chew, C. H. (1985). *Journal of Personality & Social Psychology, 49,* 1427-1433.

194. Pontari, B. A. & Schlenker, B. R. (2000). *Journal of Personality & Social Psychology, 78,* 1092-1108.

195. Porter, S. & Yuille, J. C. (1996). *Law & Human Behavior, 20,* 443-458.

196. Potamkin, G. G. (1982). Heroin addicts and nonaddicts: The use and detection of nonverbal deception cues. Unpublished doctoral dissertation, California School of Professional Psychology, Los Angeles.

197. Reid, J. E. & Arthur, R. O. (1953). *Journal of Criminal Law, Criminology, and Police Science, 44,* 104-108.

198. Richards, K. M. & Gross, J. J. (1999). *Personality & Social Psychology Bulletin, 25,* 1033-1044.

199. Riggio, R. E. & Friedman, H. S. (1983). *Journal of Personality & Social Psychology, 45,* 899-915.

200. Roney, C. J., Higgins, E. T. & Shah, J. (1995). *Personality & Social Psychology Bulletin,* 21, 1151-1160.

201. Rosenthal, R. (1991). Meta-analytic procedures for social research (Rev. ed.). Newbury Park, CA: Sage.

202. Ruby, C. L. & Brigham, J. C. (1998). *Law & Human Behavior,* 22, 369-388.

203. Rybold, V. S. (1994). Paralinguistic cue leakage during deception: A comparison between Asians and Euroamericans. Unpublished master's thesis, California State University, Fullerton.

204. SAS Institute. (1985). SAS user's guide: Statistics (Version 5). Cary, NC: Author.

205. Sayenga, E. R. (1983). Linguistic and paralinguistic indices of deception. Unpublished doctoral dissertation, University of Michigan, Ann Arbor.

206. Schachter, S., Christenfeld, N. J., Ravina, B. & Bilous, F. (1991). *Journal of Personality & Social Psychology,* 20, 362-367.

207. Scheff, T. J. (2001). Emotions, the social bond and human reality: Part/whole analysis. Cambridge, England: Cambridge University Press.

208. Scherer, K. R. (1982). Methods of research on vocal communication: Paradigms and parameters. In K. R. Scherer & P. Ekman (Eds.), Handbook of methods in nonverbal behavior research (pp. 136-198). Cambridge, England: Cambridge University Press.

209. Scherer, K. R. (1986). *Psychological Bulletin,* 99, 143-165.

210. Scherer, K. R., Feldstein, S., Bond, R. N. & Rosenthal, R. (1985). *Journal of Psycholinguistic Research,* 14, 409-425.

211. Schlenker, B. R. (1980). Impression management: The self-concept, social identity, and interpersonal relations. Monterey, CA: Brooks/Cole.

212. Schlenker, B. R. (1982). *Advances in Experimental Social Psychology,* 15, 193-247.

213. Schlenker, B. R. (1985). Identity and self-identification. In B. R. Schlenker (Ed.), The self and social life (pp. 65-99). New York: McGraw-Hill.

214. Schlenker, B. R. (2002). Self-presentation. In M. R. Leary & J. P. Tangney (Eds.), Handbook of self and identity (pp. 492-518). New York: Guilford Press.

215. Schlenker, B. R. & Leary, M. R. (1982). *Psychological Bulletin,* 92, 641-669.

216. Schlenker, B. R., & Pontari, B. A. (2000). The strategic control of information: Impression management and self-presentation in daily life. In A. Tesser, R. Felson, & J. Suls (Eds.), Perspectives on self and identity (pp. 199-232). Washington, DC: American Psychological Association.

217. Schlenker, B. R., Britt, T. W., Pennington, J., Murphy, R. & Doherty, K. (1994). *Psychological Review,* 101, 632-652.

218. Schlenker, B. R., Pontari, B. A. & Christopher, A. N. (2001). *Personality & Social Psychology Review,* 5, 15-32.

219. Schneider, S. M. & Kintz, B. L. (1977). *Bulletin of the Psychonomic Society,* 10, 451-453.

220. Scott, T. R., Wells, W. H., Wood, D. Z. & Morgan, D. I. (1967). *Journal of Clinical Psychology,* 23, 433-438.

221. Searle, J. R. (1975). Indirect speech acts. In P. Cole & J. L. Morgan (Eds.), Syntax and semantics: Vol. 3. Speech acts (pp. 59-82). New York: Academic Press.

222. Shennum, W. A., & Bugental, D. B. (1982). The development of control over affective expression in nonverbal behavior. In R. S. Feldman (Ed.), Development of nonverbal behavior in children (pp. 101-121). New York: Springer-Verlag.

223. Sherif, M., & Hovland, C. I. (1961). Social judgment. New Haven, CT: Yale University Press.

224. Siegman, A. W. (1987). The telltale voice: Nonverbal messages of verbal communication. In A. W. Siegman & S. Feldstein (Eds.), Nonverbal behavior and communication (2nd ed., pp. 351-434). Hillsdale, NJ: Erlbaum.

225. Siegman, A. W. & Reynolds, M. A. (1983). *Journal of Personality & Social Psychology,* 45, 1325-1333.

226. Simpson, H. M. & Molloy, F. M. (1971). *Psychophysiology,* 8, 491-496.

227. Sitton, S. C. & Griffin, S. T. (1981). *Journal of Counseling Psychology,* 28, 269-271.

228. Slivken, K. E. & Buss, A. H. (1984). *Journal of Personality & Social Psychology,* 47, 396-402.

229. Smith, E. R. (1998). Mental representation and memory. In D. T. Gilbert, S. T. Fiske, & G. Lindzey (Eds.), Handbook of social psychology (4th ed., Vol. 1, pp. 391-445). Boston: McGraw-Hill.

230. Sparks, G. G. & Greene, J. O. (1992). *Human Communication Research,* 18, 445-471.

231.Sporer, S. L. (1997). *Applied Cognitive Psychology,* 11, 373-397.

232.Stanners, R. F., Coutler, M., Sweet, A. W. & Murphy, P. (1979). *Motivation & Emotion,* 3, 319-340.

233.Steller, M., & Kohnken, G. (1989). Criteria-Based Content Analysis. In D. C. Raskin (Ed.), Psychological methods in criminal investigation and evidence (pp. 217-245). New York: Springer-Verlag.

234.Stern, J. A., & Dunham, D. N. (1990). The ocular system. In J. T. Cacioppo & L. G. Tassinary (Eds.), Principles of psychophysiology: Physical, social, and inferential elements (pp. 513-553). Cambridge, England: Cambridge University Press.

235.Stiff, J. B. & Miller, G. R. (1986). *Human Communication Research,* 12, 339-357.

236.Stiff, J. B., Kim, H. J. & Ramesh, C. N. (1992). *Communication Research,* 19, 326-345.

237.Streeter, L. A., Krauss, R. M., Geller, V., Olsen, C. & Apple, W. (1977). *Journal of Personality & Social Psychology,* 35, 345-350.

238.Tangney, J. P., Miller, R. S., Flicker, L. & Barlow, D. H. (1996). *Journal of Personality & Social Psychology,* 70, 1256-1269.

239.Todd-Mancillas, W. R. & Kibler, R. J. (1979). *Western Journal of Speech Communication,* 43, 108-122.

240.Trovillo, P. V. (1939). *Journal of Criminal Law and Criminology,* 29, 848-881.

241.Turner, R. E., Edgley, C. & Olmstead, G. (1975). *Kansas Journal of Sociology,* 11, 69-89.

242.Undeutsch, U. (1989). The development of Statement Reality Analysis. In J. C. Yuille (Ed.), Credibility assessment (pp. 101-119). Dordrecht, the Netherlands: Kluwer Academic.

243.Vallacher, R. R. & Wegner, D. M. (1987). *Psychological Review,* 94, 3-15.

244.Vallacher, R. R., Wegner, D. M., McMahan, S. C., Cotter, J. & Larsen, K. A. (1992). *Social Cognition,* 10, 335-355.

245.Vrij, A. (1993). *Journal of Social Psychology,* 133, 601-610.

246.Vrij, A. (1995). *Journal of Psychology,* 129, 15-28.

247.Vrij, A. (2000). Detecting lies and deceit. Chichester, England: Wiley.

248.Vrij, A. & Heaven, S. (1999). *Psychology, Crime, & Law,* 5, 203-215.

249.Vrij, A. & Mann, S. (2001). *Applied Cognitive Psychology,* 15, 187-203.

250.Vrij, A., & Winkel, F. W. (1990/1991). The frequency and scope of differences in nonverbal behavioral patterns: An observational study of Dutch and Surinamese. In N. Bleichrodt & P. J. D. Drenth (Eds.), Contemporary issues in cross-cultural psychology (pp. 120-136). Amsterdam: Swets & Zeitlinger.

251.Vrij, A. & Winkel, F. W. (1993). *Children, evidence and procedure: Issues in criminological and legal psychology,* 20, 51-57.

252.Vrij, A., Akehurst, L. & Morris, P. (1997). *Journal of Nonverbal Behavior,* 21, 87-101.

253.Vrij, A., Edward, K. & Bull, R. (2001). *Personality & Social Psychology Bulletin,* 27, 899-909.

254.Vrij, A., Edward, K., Roberts, K. P. & Bull, R. (2000). *Journal of Nonverbal Behavior,* 24, 239-264.

255.Vrij, A., Semin, G. R. & Bull, R. (1996). *Human Communication Research,* 22, 544-562.

256.Wagner, H. & Pease, K. (1976). *Journal of Personality,* 44, 1-15.

257.Walczyk, J. J., Roper, K., Seeman, E., & Humphrey, A. M. Cognitive mechanisms underlying lying. Criminal Justice & Behavior.

258.Wallbott, H. G. & Scherer, K. R. (1991). *Journal of Personality & Social Psychology,* 61, 147-156.

259.Wegner, D. M. (1994). *Psychological Review,* 101, 34-52.

260.Wegner, D. M., Erber, R. & Zanakos, S. (1993). *Journal of Personality & Social Psychology,* 65, 1093-1104.

261.Weiler, J. & Weinstein, E. (1972). *Sociometry,* 35, 316-331.

262.Wicklund, R. A. (1982). How society uses self-awareness. In J. Suls (Ed.), Psychological perspectives on the self (Vol. 1, pp. 209-230). Hillsdale, NJ: Erlbaum.

263.Wiener, M., & Mehrabian, A. (1968). Language within language: Immediacy, a channel in verbal communication. New York: Appleton-Century -Crofts.

264.Wine, J. D. (1971). *Psychological Bulletin,* 76, 92-104.

265.Yerkes, R. M. & Berry, C. S. (1909). *American Journal of Psychology,* 20, 22-37.

266.Yuille, J. C. (Ed.). (1989). Credibility assessment. Dordrecht, the Netherlands: Kluwer Academic.

267.Yuille, J. C., & Cutshall, J. (1989). Analysis of statements of victims, witnesses, and suspects. In J. C. Yuille (Ed.), Credibility assessment (pp. 175-191). Dordrecht, the Netherlands: Kluwer Academic.

268. Zaparniuk, J., Yuille, J. C. & Taylor, S. (1995). *International Journal of Law & Psychiatry,* 18, 343-352.

269. Zivin, G. (1982). Watching the sands shift: Conceptualizing the development of nonverbal mastery. In R. S. Feldman (Ed.), Development of nonverbal behavior in children (pp. 63-98). New York: Springer-Verlag.

270. Zuckerman, M., & Driver, R. E. (1985). Telling lies: Verbal and nonverbal correlates of deception. In A. W. Siegman & S. Feldstein (Eds.), Multichannel integrations of nonverbal behavior (pp. 129-147). Hillsdale, NJ: Erlbaum.

271. Zuckerman, M., DeFrank, R. S., Hall, J. A., Larrance, D. T. & Rosenthal, R. (1979). *Journal of Experimental Social Psychology,* 15, 378-396. 272. Zuckerman, M., DePaulo, B. M., & Rosenthal, R. (1981). Verbal and nonverbal communication of deception. In L. Berkowitz (Ed.), Advances in experimental social psychology (Vol. 14, pp. 1-59). New York: Academic Press.

272. Zuckerman, M., DePaulo, B. M., & Rosenthal, R. (1986). Humans as deceivers and lie detectors. In P. D. Blanck, R. Buck, & R. Rosenthal (Eds.), Nonverbal communication in the clinical-context (pp. 13-35). University Park: Pennsylvania State University Press.

273. Zuckerman, M., Driver, R. & Koestner, R. (1982). *Journal of Nonverbal Behavior,* 7, 95-100.

274. Zuckerman, M., Kernis, M. R., Driver, R. & Koestner, R. (1984). *Journal of Personality & Social Psychology,* 46, 1173-1182.

•

Footnotes

1. We could have described our theoretical formulation as impression management rather than self-presentation. Impression management includes attempts to control the impressions that are formed of others, as well as impressions formed of oneself (e.g., Schlenker, 2002). We chose self-presentation because of the central role in our formulation of the impression of sincerity conveyed by the actor. Even when people are lying about the characteristics of another person, the effectiveness of those lies depends on their own success at appearing sincere.

2. Certain deceptive exchanges are so often practiced that they, too, unfold in a way that feels effortless (e.g., looking at the baby picture proffered by the proud parents and exclaiming that the bald wrinkled blob is just adorable). Lies told in these instances may be guided by what Bargh (1989) described as goal-dependent automaticity. Although they may not feel like deliberate lies, the critical intent to mislead is clearly present. The flatterer would feel mortified if the parents realized he or she thought the baby was hideous. It is in part because the sense of deliberateness is critical to people's sense of having lied that these exchanges are so often unrecognized as lies.

3. Statement Validity (or Reality) Analysis was developed initially by Undeutsch (1989) to assess the credibility of child witnesses in cases of alleged sexual abuse. The overall assessment includes an evaluation of the characteristics and possible motives of the child witness. It also includes a set of 19 criteria to be applied to transcripts of statements made by the witness (Steller & Kohnken, 1989). This analysis of witness statements, called Criteria-Based Content Analysis (CBCA), was subsequently applied to the analysis of statements made by adults in other kinds of criminal proceedings and in experimental research (e.g., Yuille & Cutshall, 1989). All of the characteristics discussed in this section of our review, from the excessive structure and coherence of accounts to the typical characteristics of criminals or crimes related by people who do not realize their significance, are drawn from CBCA, though some of the interpretations are our own. The use of CBCA to analyze statements made by adults is controversial (e.g., Vrij, 2000).

4. There were three unpublished reports (describing results from four independent samples) in the Zuckerman et al. (1981) review that we were unable to retrieve for this review.

5. Only weighted mean ds are reported, and all estimates of a given cue are included in each mean. A table of all 1,338 individual effect sizes is available from Bella M. DePaulo. The table includes the weights for each effect size and information about the independence of each estimate. The table also indicates whether each estimate was a known effect (i.e., the magnitude could be determined precisely) or if only the direction of the effect or its nonsignificance was reported. Therefore, the information in that table can be used to calculate weighted effect sizes for each cue that include only the known estimates or to compute unweighted means that include all effect sizes or only the precisely estimated ones.

6. We did not include studies in which planning was confounded with another variable (e.g., Anolli & Ciceri, 1997).

www.ingramcontent.com/pod-product-compliance
Lightning Source LLC
Chambersburg PA
CBHW051955280526
45793CB00005B/722